THE APPRAISAL OF TEACHING:

CONCEPTS AND PROCESS

THE APPRAISAL OF TEACHING: CONCEPTS AND PROCESS

GARY D. BORICH
The University of Texas at Austin

with the assistance of
KATHLEEN S. FENTON
The Research and Development Center
for Teacher Education

ADDISON-WESLEY PUBLISHING COMPANY

Reading, Massachusetts
Menlo Park, California • London • Amsterdam • Don Mills, Ontario • Sydney

 Printed in the United States of America. Published simultaneously in Canada. Library of Congress Catalog Card No. 76-6007.

ISBN 0-201-00841-6
CDEFGHIJKL-MA-89876543210

PREFACE

One of the forces providing impetus for this book is the growing demand for accountability, a demand many school districts in this nation are now facing. The general term "accountability," however, does not adequately convey the day-to-day struggle schools undergo in their attempt to become answerable to their various constituencies: the community, professional groups, legislators, teachers, administrative staff, and pupils. Schools are subject to many different types of accountability, and each places on them distinct and unrelenting demands. This book is devoted to an examination of one of these demands—the demand to evaluate the performance of teachers.

THE ACCOUNTABILITY MOVEMENT

The concept of accountability, in its most general sense, emerged from congressional legislation passed in the 1960s. It did not, however, end there. Federal agencies responsible for funding innovative social and educational programs and documenting their effectiveness were only the first to feel the pressures for accountability. Because many of these national programs dealt directly with the schools, the accountability demanded of them automatically raised questions about the teachers who played a prominent role in their implementation. Consequently, teaching effectiveness and the administrative accountability of schools often became the focus of attempts to monitor and evaluate federally funded programs.

The "accountability," "cost-benefit," and "quality assurance" concepts, which in the last decade have been promoted by a succession of political administrations, very often filtered down in spirit, if not in substance, to the local school and teacher. Accountability movements, which began in Washington, D.C. during the 1960s, frequently wound up on the doorsteps of the cities in the 1970s as community groups pressed for concrete evidence of the effectiveness of their local schools, just as they had earlier demanded an accounting of federally funded programs.

As the accountability concept moved from the federal to the local level, it acquired a more dramatic and serious tone. Communities, now realizing that accountability was a legitimate *local* issue, began to exercise their right to scrutinize their schools. At stake now were the offspring and pocketbooks of local citizens, issues far more pressing than the seemingly remote concerns of federal bureaucracies.

With this shift in emphasis from federal to local accountability came a rapid, if not meteoric, increase in the cost of local education. While higher teacher salaries were responsible for a good portion of this cost, they unfortunately did not always translate into *measurable* gains in the classroom performance of pupils. The schools looked the same, and the pupils behaved the same. Thus, many questioned the value of these increased expenditures.

By 1970 community pressures began to slowly but methodically bear down on the local school, often demanding accountability in terms of pupil outcome per tax dollar spent. In some cases school administrators responded to these pressures by concentrating on the more obvious indicators of effectiveness, such as pupil performance on national achievement tests, number of college admissions, and National Merit scholarships. Others began exploring ways in which to make cost-effective decisions about the operation and management of their individual schools in order to prove that increased revenues actually produced more effective teaching. School administrators embraced accountability procedures to answer community pressures for more objectively determined and effective ways to spend school revenue and to make internal decisions that could be defended to school boards, PTAs, and professional groups.

Influenced by both federal accountability and widespread community concern about higher, but apparently unproductive, school expenditures, another force—state government—began to enact legislation requiring the appraisal of school-district personnel. As might be expected, these state-generated movements for accountability were, in general, warmly welcomed by the citizenry, cautiously accepted by the school personnel responsible for implementing them, and skeptically viewed by the teachers who were to be appraised. As will become clear from the readings in this volume, all three viewpoints are well founded.

A prime example of state-enacted accountability legislation is California's Stull Act. This Act, named after its author, Assemblyman John Stull, requires that school boards in that state evaluate their educators yearly and provide recommendations for improvement. The Stull Act gives local communities a mandate to develop procedures for appraising school-district personnel, thereby raising the anxiety (if not blood pressure) of the teachers who must be appraised.

Specifically, the Stull Act prescribes the legal grounds on which a certified public-school employee in California may be dismissed from his or her job and establishes procedures for determining the existence of such grounds. It has been described as both a certified employee "evaluation law" and as a certified employee "tenure law." Shannon explains the Act in the following manner.*

Teacher tenure	=	Specific, known reasons which are the exclusive grounds on which a teacher's employment may be terminated	+	Specific, known procedures for holding a hearing to determine whether there are valid reasons to terminate a teacher's employment

Thus, the Stull Act is divided into two parts, one providing for the professional evaluation of certified employees and the other specifying legal grounds for dismissal of these employees. It applies to *all* certified employees, from district superintendents to credentialed teacher aides in public elementary and secondary schools. Its greatest immediate impact, however, has been on classroom teachers, who in California have been the most ostensible target of public demands for accountability.

Though the evaluation procedures required by the Stull Act can vary from district to district, common sense tells us that any appraisal system implemented must be comprehensive enough to evaluate *multiple criteria* (i.e., the teacher's content knowledge *and* teaching skills) using *multiple methods* (i.e., systematic classroom observation, peer, supervisor, and self-appraisals, and indices of pupil achievement). Also, such plans must incorporate regular procedures for periodically reporting appraisal data to the teacher for diagnostic purposes—to assist the teacher in upgrading his or her performance through a continuing professional development program.

These are the *minimum* requirements of an appraisal system, but even they are often difficult to meet. The California experience and accountability efforts elsewhere† have shown that teacher appraisal is fraught with problems as well as potential. Among these problems are the resistance of teachers, the difficulty in obtaining reliable and valid measurements of teacher performance, and the identification of appropriate training resources. Consequently, this volume has been prepared to assist school and state administrators, evaluators, and teacher

---

* T. A. Shannon, "Legal Problems in Implementing the Stull Act," in *Mandated Evaluation of Educators,* ed. N. L. Gage (Washington, D.C.: Educational Resources Division, Capitol Publications, 1973), p. 5.

† The American Association of Colleges for Teacher Education, in a document dated February 1973, lists twenty-seven states having policies, resolutions, or guidelines similar to the Stull Act. (AACTE, Competency-Based Education: The State of the Scene, 1973, ERIC Document Reproduction Service No. SP 005 983.)

trainers in learning about the concepts that underpin the process of teacher appraisal and in acquiring the knowledge and fundamental understandings that can lead to a realistic evaluation of the problems inherent in that process.

INTENT OF THIS VOLUME

This volume is a sourcebook of conceptual frameworks and selected readings, the content of which, in the opinion of the author, is prerequisite to conducting appraisals of teaching. The text is intended to serve primarily as a graduate-level reader to be used in college classrooms, seminars, and workshops, or wherever opportunities exist to discuss and explore the issues and concepts introduced. Accordingly, readings that cover specific techniques as well as readings that attempt to place these techniques within an overarching framework for designing teacher-appraisal systems are included. The first quarter of the volume introduces fundamental concepts and organizational frameworks which the reader may then use to view and evaluate the readings that follow.

ORGANIZATION

This volume is divided into two parts: five introductory chapters (Part I) describing conceptual frameworks and fundamental concepts; and selected readings (Part II) chosen to illustrate or expand the frameworks and concepts introduced in Part I. These initial chapters together with the readings provide a reasonably representative sample of the teacher-appraisal concepts that have been discussed to date at national conferences and symposia and in the popular and professional literature.

The five topics covered in this volume are: defining teacher competencies; measuring teacher performance; applications of performance appraisal systems; using teacher appraisal techniques and procedures; and developing a valid appraisal system. The following provides an overview of the readings chosen for each of these areas.

"Toward Defining Teacher Competencies" contains six selections that discuss the identification of teacher behaviors, the translation of these behaviors into variables, and, finally, the definition and validation of teacher competencies for use in the appraisal process. These articles represent major empirical studies (some ongoing) which identify the teacher behaviors that at this time are our most promising prospects for use in appraising teaching performance.

"Measuring Teacher Performance" includes five selections describing general approaches to and problems in the measurement of teacher performance. These selections emphasize the various methods of assessing teacher performance and the measurement and instrumentation problems that must be resolved in order to obtain valid appraisal data.

"Applications of Performance Appraisal Systems" presents five selections describing specific appraisal models, both theoretical and applied. Each of these models demonstrates the step-by-step construction of an appraisal system and illustrates one or more of the various purposes of appraisal at the school and school-district levels.

"Using Appraisal Techniques and Procedures" contains six selections that identify specific assessment techniques used to appraise teacher performance. These range from general procedures, such as contract plans and performance tests of teaching proficiency, to specific techniques, such as domain-referenced testing and multiple matrix sampling.

"Developing a Valid Appraisal System" includes three selections that examine the validity of various procedures for assessing teacher performance. These readings report critical research on the stability and generalizability of teacher behaviors and pupil achievement, two concepts that are prerequisite to measuring teacher effectiveness.

In addition to the five introductory chapters, descriptive and explanatory remarks precede each group of readings, and an index of terms and concepts is provided at the conclusion of the volume.

Throughout this book the generic term, "teacher," is used to represent both inservice *and* preservice teachers. Thus, this volume is directed at training *and* appraisal within *both* inservice and preservice contexts.

ACKNOWLEDGMENTS

Many of the ideas in this book and in two related volumes, *Evaluating Classroom Instruction: A Sourcebook of Instruments* (Reading, Mass.: Addison-Wesley, 1977) and *Teacher Behavior and Pupil Self-Concept* (Reading, Mass.: Addison-Wesley, 1978), stem from a study funded by the National Institute of Education, titled *Evaluation of Teaching*. The primary purpose of this project was the investigation of methodological issues related to the appraisal of teaching and the development and testing of various instruments and analysis strategies for research on teacher effectiveness. Several members of the Evaluation of Teaching staff at the Research and Development Center for Teacher Education, The University of Texas at Austin, have contributed indirectly to the development of this volume, particularly Dr. Robert Godbout, who guided the collection and analysis of teacher performance data while I was serving as Scholar-in-Residence at the United States Office of Education during a portion of the project. I am grateful to Dr. Edwin Martin, Associate Commissioner of Education, and to Dr. Martin Kaufman, Director of the Intramural Research Program, Bureau of Education for the Handicapped, for enabling me to pursue this work in addition to my Washington duties.

I would also like to thank the individuals whose articles appear in this volume, particularly those who, at my request, prepared or revised material specifically for inclusion here. In planning this book, it became apparent that several areas related to teacher appraisal were either untreated or inadequately treated in the literature. To cover these areas I asked several researchers to prepare special articles. Richard Shavelson and Nancy Atwood of the University of California at Los Angeles contributed an important article on the generalizability of teacher behavior, which appears in Chapter 10; Jere Brophy and Carolyn Evertson of The University of Texas at Austin prepared an article summarizing the relationships between teacher behavior and student learning in the Texas Teacher Effectiveness Study, which appears in Chapter 6; and David Shoemaker of the Office of Planning, Budgeting, and Evaluation, U.S. Office of Education, contributed an article on his procedures for multiple matrix sampling, which appears in Chapter 9.

In addition, I would like to thank Barak Rosenshine of the University of Illinois and Nate Gage of Stanford University who scribbled their suggestions about the organization and content of this volume on several draft outlines. My thanks are also extended to J. T. Sandefur, Dean of Education at Western Kentucky University, and Beatrice A. Ward, Far West Laboratory for Educational Research and Development, who contributed useful suggestions during the planning and preparation of the volume. Last but not least, I would like to thank Susan Madden, who capably edited my chapters.

Austin, Texas
September 1976

G.D.B.

CONTENTS

PART I

The Appraisal of Teaching: Conceptual Frameworks and Fundamental Concepts

Chapter 1

Toward Defining Teacher Competencies*

The terms *teacher behavior, teacher variable,* and *teacher competence* appear frequently in the selections throughout this volume. Because these phrases describe increasingly complex steps in the assessment of teachers, defining and differentiating them will facilitate our study of the teacher appraisal process.

BEHAVIORS, VARIABLES, AND COMPETENCIES

Behavioral terms have long been an important part of the psychologist's vocabulary. Most problems, in fact, require that different psychological and physiological phenomena be described in behavioral terms. Thus, these phenomena are often designated *behaviors, variables,* and *competencies.* These terms represent complementary and progressively more specific ways of describing teacher performance.

The term *behavior,* for example, involves the most general level of description. At this level, an educational psychologist might define the concept of, say, a teacher's "warmth" toward children by describing the teacher's classroom behavior as friendly, intimate, or affectionate. He or she thus conveys the idea

---

* Readings for this topic appear in Chapter 6. For each of the five topics to be discussed in this portion of the volume an attendant selection of readings can be found in Chapters 6–10, respectively. My appreciation is extended to Dr. Martin Kaufman, Director, Intramural Research Program, Bureau of Education for the Handicapped, U.S.O.E., for providing me the opportunity to prepare the following five chapters while serving as Scholar-in-Residence.

of a behavior by using synonyms. This method defines the behavior by relating it to other constructs with which we are already familiar. At this level, the behavior may be described without being observed or measured, and, as we have seen, it may be described simply in terms of related or associated concepts. A teacher's clarity of presentation, variety of style, enthusiasm of manner, and organization of content are typical of behaviors described at this most general level. Because behaviors like these are described in such general terms, they must be tied to specific variables and competencies in order to be useful in the appraisal process. From behaviors, then, are variables and competencies derived.

The word *variable* refers to the terms in which a particular teacher behavior is to be observed and recorded. A variable specifies a behavior by stating explicitly the way in which the behavior is to be measured.

For example, the behavior "clarity" can be translated into a variable by further defining the concept as the number of minutes the teacher spends answering student questions that require elaboration of the teacher's presentation. Or, the behavior "variety" can be specified as the number of different activities and materials used during a thirty-minute social-studies lesson. Similarly, we can observe and measure the teacher's "enthusiasm" by constructing observer ratings on paired adjectives, such as stimulating versus dull, original versus ordinary, or alert versus apathetic. We can also derive a variable from the behavior "organization" by constructing a scale that requires an observer to rate the teacher's lesson as "very structured," "fairly structured," "average," "fairly unstructured," or "very unstructured."

Variables redefine behaviors in terms of the operations that are necessary to observe and to measure them. These operations must express the behavioral concept in the form of a scale, which represents the level of differentiation at which the particular behavior can be reliably observed and distinguished from other behaviors. In other words, a specific measurement scale is constructed in order to translate the behavioral concept into a continuum of gradations or levels. This scale may be relatively unrefined, merely requiring the observer to record the presence or absence of a particular teacher behavior, or it may be more sophisticated and multileveled, asking the observer to record fine gradations of a behavior—to rate, for example, the presence of a particular behavior on a ten-point scale, from "not present at all" (1) to "present all the time" (10).

It should be noted that behaviors can be translated into variables using any number of different operations. In the absence of any persuasive theory or research evidence specifying exactly how the behavior should be measured, these operations are usually chosen at the discretion of the researcher. Therefore, it is not uncommon for the same behavioral concept to be defined differently by different investigators in different studies. For this reason, once a variable has been derived from a more general behavioral concept, the variable itself, *not* the behavioral concept, is the most accurate description of the teaching performance being measured.

The next step in defining teacher performance involves the identification of teacher *competence*. While much of the literature, particularly in the area of competency-based training, has dealt with the nature of teacher competencies, rarely has discussion focused on the procedures needed to translate behavioral concepts and variables into competencies. Just as general behavioral concepts are used to derive variables, variables are used to determine the next level of behavioral description.

Competencies, like variables, are characterized by a metric or scale. However, unlike variables, competencies include the specification of a desired quantity of behavior, which is referenced in the metric. Competencies identify a single level of proficiency, or range of levels, determined through theoretical or empirical processes, at which a teacher should perform. Unlike variables, competencies are either attained or not attained. It is the *level* of proficiency which is critical, not, as in the case of variables, simply the separation and differentiation of various degrees of behavior.

To illustrate the process of translating variables into competencies, let us return to our four teacher behaviors: clarity, variety, enthusiasm, and organization. Suppose for the moment we wish to translate the variables associated with these behaviors into competencies. To do so, we must determine proficiency levels. For example, we might specify that proficiency is reached for the behavior *clarity* when all of the students understand 80 percent of what the teacher presents. Or, competency might be attained for the behavior *variety* when, on the average, at least three different activities or materials are used during each thirty-minute social-studies lesson. Similarly, proficiency for the behavior *enthusiasm* might require an average rating (on a seven-point scale) of 6 or above on a stimulating versus dull scale, 4 or above on original versus ordinary and 5 or above on alert versus apathetic. And, proficiency for the behavior *organization* might be defined as a rating of "very structured" on a scale ranging from "very structured" to "very unstructured."

Though the preceding examples illustrate the nature of teacher competencies, they were not constructed on the basis of any compelling theory or research evidence. Hopefully, educators will be cautious in accepting competencies derived without the benefit of theory or empirical evidence indicating that *a teacher who has achieved the stated proficiency level is more likely to engender desirable pupil outcomes than a teacher who has not.* Without empirical data to validate the relationship between attainment of a competency and meaningful pupil change, proficiency levels can become arbitrary, subjective, and functionally useless to the appraisal process. Needless to say, research must play a critical role in the identification and validation of appropriate levels of proficiency before competencies can be used for appraisal purposes. This is especially true when decisions concerning a teacher's employment, professional development program, or promotion are to be made on the basis of his or her attainment of given competencies. Since there are currently few theoretical frameworks and even fewer research investigations from which to derive valid proficiency levels, much of the work in identifying teacher competencies remains to be done.

Building an appraisal system based on teacher competencies is a lengthy developmental task. Behaviors must be translated into variables, and variables must be researched in order to identify and validate proficiency levels. This process is both multifaceted and longitudinal in nature. Since different teacher behaviors may, at any given time, be at different stages in the process of translation into competencies, a school district or preservice teacher training program might find it necessary to mount several development efforts simultaneously. One of these might be a literature search to identify teacher behaviors relevant to local or institutional goals and objectives; another might involve conversion of previously identified behaviors into variables by constructing various forms of instrumentation; and a third effort might entail research on previously defined variables in order to select and validate levels of proficiency, i.e., to determine whether or not attainment of a certain proficiency level does, indeed, lead to improved pupil performance. Teacher appraisal must be based on validated proficiency levels. Since research has to date produced very few of these, efforts at this point must focus on the identification and validation of teacher competencies, rather than their immediate application to the appraisal process. The most critical and tedious task in developing an appraisal system is that of identifying and validating proficiency levels for the teacher behaviors selected for assessment.

To summarize our discussion thus far, the developmental process of formulating teacher competencies is presented in Fig. 1.1.

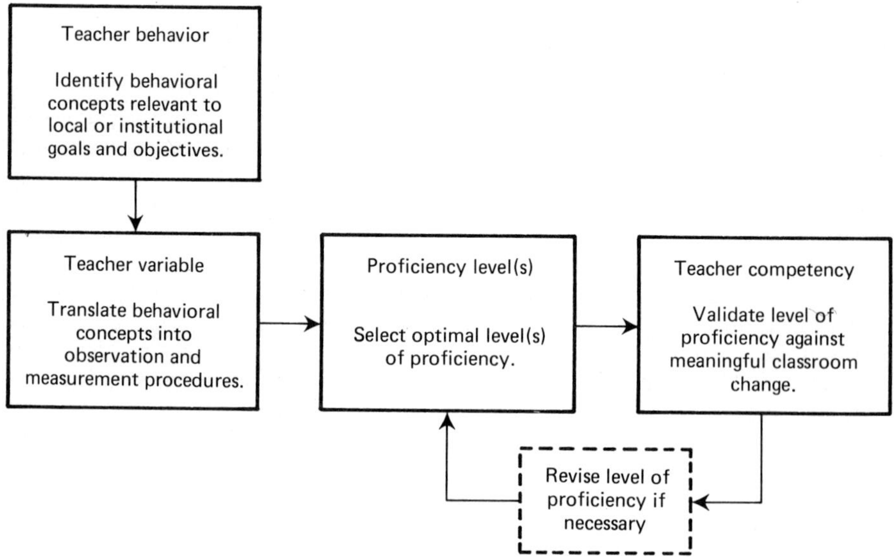

Fig. 1.1. The developmental task of deriving teacher competencies.

Teacher Competencies: Form and Structure

A more detailed discussion of competencies will provide background for the readings that appear in this volume. A competency can be described in terms of its form, which places it in a particular category of behavior, and its structure, which places it in a sequence with other competencies.

There are three forms of teacher competencies: (a) knowledge competencies, specifying cognitive understandings the teacher is expected to demonstrate; (b) performance competencies, specifying teaching processes the teacher is expected to demonstrate; and (c) consequence competencies, specifying pupil behaviors that are viewed as evidence of teaching effectiveness.

While the objectives of most preservice and inservice teacher training programs involve the attainment of teacher competencies, few of these programs provide related training experiences that acknowledge the interdependence of knowledge, performance, and consequence competencies. If any one form of competency is considered independent of its preceding, enabling competencies, it probably will not be attained by the teacher, since knowledge competencies are needed in order to attain performance competencies, and performance competencies are in turn needed to attain consequence competencies. Knowledge, performance, and consequence competencies are best viewed as a sequence of interrelated behaviors that work in partnership to build a comprehensive array of both teacher and pupil outcomes in the classroom. This view implies, of course, that an appraisal effort must not only formulate teacher competencies, but must also identify the learning sequence required for the attainment of competencies. That is, each form of competency must be considered a building block within a broader sequence of learnings. This complex process of creating a hierarchical training structure for teachers, composed of knowledge, performance, and consequence competencies, will be discussed in Chapter 5.

Knowledge Competencies. Since knowledge competencies can be derived from either teaching processes or subject-matter content, they are divided into two types: process and content. Knowledge competencies that involve the *process* of teaching might include, for example, a teacher's ability to describe ways of effectively managing the classroom, or to identify specific teacher behaviors associated with, say, the "inquiry approach to teaching." On the other hand, knowledge competencies related to *content* might include a teacher's knowledge of set theory, of the metric system, or of laws governing liquids and gases. Both process- and content-knowledge competencies can be measured directly by paper-and-pencil methods, or sometimes indirectly through the observation of teaching performance.

When knowledge competencies are measured indirectly through observation methods, a teacher's knowledge of the behavior is inferred from his or her ability to perform it. Failure to observe the teacher performing the behavior, however, might be due to *either* insufficient opportunity to practice the behavior or insufficient knowledge of the behavior. If the former were the case, continued practice and experience in using the behavior might be recommended to the teacher, while if the latter were the case, an instructional module or review exercise might be a more suitable recommendation. Therefore, when competencies are not observed at the performance level, it is sometimes necessary to measure the teacher's prerequisite knowledge competencies directly with paper-and-pencil methods in order to recommend the most appropriate source of training.

Performance Competencies. Performance competencies refer to ongoing teaching behaviors as they are performed in the classroom. Like knowledge competencies, they require appropriate assessment methods. Since performance competencies deal with classroom processes, the appropriate mode of measurement is classroom observation.

Since there is no consensus regarding the best observation tools to employ in the classroom, available instruments represent different philosophies of teacher training and appraisal. Typically, a combination of instruments is used to measure such behaviors as the teacher's ability to ask higher-order cognitive questions, to demonstrate enthusiasm, to use direct and indirect questioning techniques, to probe for pupil responses, to accept pupil feelings, to give directions, and to use pupil ideas. While knowledge of each of these behaviors is prerequisite to their execution, assessment of this knowledge alone is insufficient evidence of the teacher's competence in actually *performing* these behaviors. Thus, to measure *performance* competencies systematic observations of classroom behavior are most appropriate.

Consequence Competencies. The ultimate level of competence, and the form which has perhaps received most attention, is that of consequence competencies. Consequence competencies refer to pupil outcomes produced by the teacher's proper use of an array of knowledge and performance competencies. Like knowledge competencies, they can specify both content and process behaviors. Those that are content-related involve the pupil's mastery of subject matter. They are usually measured by standardized achievement tests or criterion-referenced tests, the latter recording the level of pupil performance vis-à-vis particular content objectives of the teacher. Those that involve process, on the other hand, refer to emotions and attitudes of pupils which are affected by the classroom teacher. Consequence competencies of the process type can be measured by observing classroom behavior of pupils, such as group problem solving and class discussion, or more directly, by administering classroom-climate scales, which attempt to assess the interaction pattern, mood, or atmosphere of the classroom.

In measuring consequence competencies, the presence of certain *pupil* behaviors is regarded as evidence that specified *teacher* behaviors have occurred. This measurement procedure clearly entails greater inference than those used to assess knowledge and performance competencies. Using pupil outcomes as an index of teacher competency involves a relatively high risk of error since variables unrelated to the teacher's performance may intervene to account for pupil behavior. For example, measurement of consequence competencies may be obscured by classroom conditions, the school's organization, administrative policies, socioeconomic status of the children, availability of curriculum materials, and prior learning for which the appraised teacher was not responsible. In spite of these problems, however, appraisal systems are increasingly adopting the practice of using pupil outcomes as a measure of teacher effectiveness. Research findings that can be used to support this procedure are presented in Chapter 6.

Some Methods of Deriving Teacher Competencies

The single greatest obstacle to the use of consequence competencies in teacher appraisal is the paucity of research evidence linking specific knowledge and performance competencies to pupil outcomes (consequence competencies). In the absence of such evidence, appraisers have, during the last two decades, relied primarily on four methods to derive knowledge and performance competencies: (a) professional judgment; (b) *in situ* observation of classrooms; (c) theoretical frameworks of teacher behavior; and (d) experimental studies.

Judgment. Throughout much of its history, the field of teacher education has lacked adequate research methods and appraisal techniques to link specific teacher behaviors with specific pupil outcomes. Yet the performance of teachers has been appraised nevertheless, though often with nonempirical methods and criteria. Typically, the appraiser has used his or her own personal judgment to determine which teachers are "effective" and which are not. As might be expected, this practice is considered the least valid of the four approaches presented here.

The judgmental approach is characterized by qualitative ratings of the teacher, customarily completed by the principal or supervisor. These ratings may represent the perceived similarity between the teacher's performance and the rater's past performance as a teacher; or, they may be based on a prototype of good teaching derived from the personal experiences of the appraiser. The good teacher might be identified as such because he or she is a "good" person: friendly to others, warm to children, hardworking, and punctual. Similarly, a teacher might be rated "good" if his or her general behavior and life-style are compatible with the values and expectations of the school and community. When these values and expectations are applied in the absence of other criteria, there is always the danger that school and community standards unrelated or even antithetical to improved pupil performance will be promoted. It should be clear that effective teaching cannot be reliably distinguished from ineffective teaching on the basis of behaviors that are unrelated to either the teachers' or their pupils' *classroom performance.* Hopefully, teacher appraisal methods that utilize systematic observations of teaching behaviors will replace the judgmental approach.

Observation. Among the alternatives to deriving teacher competencies from personal judgments is *in situ*—or in classroom—observation. *In situ* observation involves systematically recording a variety of specific, discrete teacher behaviors that are assumed, according to a theoretical framework, to be related to pupil growth. After these behaviors are observed and recorded, they are correlated with indices of pupil change to validate their importance.

In situ observation has several important advantages over the judgmental approach. For example, the behaviors observed *in situ* are both *prespecified* and *classroom-based.* The teacher is thus evaluated according to his or her performance in the classroom, not in the community, or in teachers' meetings, or elsewhere. Furthermore, though an observation instrument may to some extent reflect the professional and personal judgments of its creator, the behavioral categories to be observed are spelled out for both the teacher and the observer. The teacher knows which characteristics of his or her performance are being studied and thus has an opportunity to react to the appropriateness of the selected behaviors. Moreover, the use of a specific set of predefined behaviors benefits the observer by sharpening his or her observational skills. Prespecified observation categories permit comparison among various observers, which can provide an estimate of the interobserver reliability of the instrument, or the consistency with which different raters observing the same teacher record the same behavior.

Observation tools vary in length and specificity. Some measure what might be considered very minor interactions between teacher and pupil; others concentrate on more general forms of behavior. Categories of behavior commonly measured include: the type of questions the teacher asks (lower cognitive or higher cognitive); the teacher's use of reinforcement (preceding or following a correct pupil response); the teacher's use of criticism (toward the class or toward a child); and the amount of time devoted to various classroom activities (lecture, discussion, small groups). Some observation measures include the actual sequence in which these behaviors occur. These sequences are recorded in order to trace the teacher's interaction with pupils over an extended period of time, thereby producing a pattern of the teacher's "pedagogical moves" (sequential reactions to different kinds of pupil responses).

As mentioned previously, teacher competencies are derived from *in situ* observation by correlating observed teacher behaviors with pupil outcomes. Behaviors which relate positively to desirable pupil outcomes are selected as potential teacher competencies and are subjected to validation studies. In a second-stage process, the correlational data are used to identify "more effective" and "less effective" teachers according to, for example, achievement gains made by their pupils over a semester or school year. These groups of teachers are then systematically observed to determine which strategies, procedures, and pedagogical moves they employ. Use of classroom observation to identify effective teaching behaviors has proved to be a promising technique, at least in situations where the same content is taught to different pupils and where classroom observations focus upon teacher presentation, positive and neutral feedback, probing and classroom management variables (Shavelson and Atwood, Chapter 10).

Theory. A third procedure for deriving teacher competencies uses existing theory regarding the teaching-learning process to predict effective teacher behaviors. Since the researcher uses theory to plan his or her study, the development of a logical theory should precede the actual research. In the field of teacher behavior, however, persuasive theories providing a logical and coherent rationale for encouraging certain teacher behaviors have not been forthcoming. This has been perhaps the greatest weakness of the voluminous research, produced during the last decade, which empirically examines relationships between teacher and pupil behaviors in both classroom and laboratory settings. The dearth of theory in the field of teacher behavior is particularly disappointing considering the value a good theory can have in identifying and validating teacher competencies. Mandler and Kessen illustrate the potential power of theory by relating its use to that of a road map:

> The road map is an artificial, symbolic and reduced representation (or theory) of the terrain and the schooled reader of the map may act in a rea-

sonable way (behave functionally, behave factually) over that terrain with the help of the map. The rules for interpretation of the map correspond in a rough way to definition and theory construction.*

In simplest terms, a theory is a set of variables and a schema for interrelating these variables. It is a symbolic construction designed to bring behavioral concepts and variables into systematic relationship. These behavioral concepts and variables are used to make predictions about behavioral events. Theories can be used to guide the researcher by identifying the most promising behaviors for observation and measurement. Therefore, theory exercises selective power, allowing the researcher to measure a relatively few, theoretically promising variables and to eliminate a large number of behaviors which there is no reason to believe cause the desired pupil outcome. The relationship between theory, which identifies teacher competencies, and research, which validates these competencies, is crucial to the appraisal process. The actual use of theory in the design and validation of an appraisal system will be illustrated in Chapter 5.

Experimental Studies. Experimental research is the most sophisticated method of deriving teacher competencies. While the correlational research associated with *in situ* observation typically relates teacher behaviors to pupil outcomes, experimental research assigns teachers with observably different styles to separate categories for observation and analysis. This approach, usually referred to as "true" experimental research, recognizes that pupils are randomly assigned to teachers of differing types, and provides a basis for comparing two or more potentially competing varieties of teacher behavior.

The most valuable characteristic of the experimental approach in deriving teacher competencies is its capacity to give the investigator the opportunity to make cause-and-effect inferences. Using the experimental approach, the investigator may safely conclude that the teacher competencies being studied actually *cause* the pupil outcomes measured. A correlational or *in situ* study, on the other hand, allows the researcher to conclude only that teacher behaviors are *associated* with pupil outcomes. This is an important distinction since certification of a teacher based on attainment of a specific competency clearly implies that the competency will cause desirable pupil outcomes. For this reason, teacher competencies must ultimately be derived from experimental rather than correlational studies, so that causation can be inferred.

Perhaps the distinction between causative and correlational statements can best be illustrated with the following example. Suppose that a researcher correlated the number of births in the United States with the number of new highway miles being built, on a month-by-month basis, and found the relationship between them to be very high. It would be foolish for our researcher to infer from this relationship that one occurrence had caused the other. This relationship tells us *only* that both the number of births and the number of new highway miles constructed were increasing at the same time. While the relationship may not have been entirely coincidental (both could have been

* G. Mandler, and W. Kessen, *The Language of Psychology* (New York: John Wiley, 1959), p. 133.

caused by the same social and political events), one occurrence cannot be said to have been caused by the other. Similarly, in correlational studies, pupil outcomes cannot be attributed to those teacher behaviors with which they are associated. A research paradigm that separates observably different teachers into different experimental groups, and then randomly assigns pupils to these teachers, is the only research procedure that allows causal inferences and, thus, the eventual validation of teacher competencies.

We now turn to a discussion of the actual process of measuring teacher behavior and some of the problems inherent in this process.

Chapter 2

Measuring Teacher Performance

This chapter and its corresponding readings (Chapter 7) are designed to introduce the reader to some of the many measurement problems implicit in the appraisal process. These problems range from the identification of appropriate criteria against which to evaluate teachers to the selection and use of methodologies for validly and reliably measuring teacher performance. There are four basic measurement stages in which these problems commonly occur.

STAGES OF MEASUREMENT IN THE APPRAISAL PROCESS

If an appraisal system is to be used in making training and personnel decisions, it must measure a comprehensive set of teacher performance variables. Information must be gathered from multiple sources to assure the accuracy and usefulness of the instructional, administrative, and planning decisions which are to be based on the appraisal data. If the appraisal of teaching is viewed as a longitudinal process, with data collected at various points in time, four distinct and consecutive measurement stages are apparent. These are: (a) the preoperational stage, in which information about the teacher's attitudes, personality, aptitude, and experience is collected; (b) the immediate process stage, in which data about the teacher's ongoing classroom strategies, procedures, and techniques are gathered; (c) the intermediate process stage, in which information about the teacher's summative classroom performance is collected; and (d) the product stage, in which information about the teacher's pupils is obtained.

The Preoperational Stage of Appraisal

During the first stage of assessment, personality, attitude, experience, achievement, and aptitude variables are measured to provide a composite picture of the teacher at the beginning of the appraisal period. Though preoperational measurements do not involve the assessment of actual teaching behavior, the information they provide—when valid—aids in understanding and interpreting performance data collected at subsequent stages of the appraisal process.

Table 2.1 lists some of the most commonly researched variables in the preoperational stage of appraisal. Since little research evidence has to date linked these variables to meaningful pupil change, their usefulness is limited by certain problems, the most ostensible of which are summarized below.

Personality Variables. Unfortunately, only a few personality constructs have been developed to describe characteristics specifically related to teaching. Consequently, the usefulness of most personality measures for a particular teaching task must be inferred from their more general purpose. Since personality measures are often designed for and validated in clinical settings, some of the constructs they measure may be irrelevant to the classroom. The more useful "personality" variables may actually represent teachers' concerns about, or preferences for, specific teaching tasks, rather than true personality characteristics.

Attitude Variables. Attitude assessments may be global (e.g., attitude toward the school and the educational system), or specific (e.g., attitude toward a particular task, text, or curriculum). In either case, attitude instruments often suffer from inadequate predictive validity (i.e., the capacity to identify constructs that can predict subsequent teaching performance). Relationships between attitude and teacher performance in the classroom are commonly low and nonsignificant. Therefore, in the absence of clear-cut validity data, attitude measurement in the preoperational stage usually rests on the assumption that the attitudes assessed are intervening or enabling constructs, i.e., prerequisite to various affective and cognitive behaviors. Thus, as causative agents, responsible for engendering pupil change, these constructs are more remote and less credible than performance variables, which offer more immediate links to pupil achievement. Motivation to teach and attitude toward children are perhaps the most important attitude variables measured in the preoperational stage.

Experience Variables. Although two decades of research have shown experience variables to be almost worthless in predicting teacher performance, it is possible that these variables have in the past been measured too grossly to yield significant findings. The standard biographical data form, on which years of teaching and extent and type of training are recorded, defines the teacher's experience so broadly that it cannot be used to identify teachers who will be more or less effective in relation to specific performance criteria. For example, a teacher's experience with the type of curriculum or the kind of pupils he or she will be expected to teach may be far more relevant to that teacher's performance than number of years of teaching experience or graduate credits

Table 2.1. Summary of variables commonly researched in the preoperational stage.

Personality	*Attitude*	*Experience*	*Aptitude/Achievement*
Permissiveness	Motivation to teach	Years of teaching experience	National Teachers Exam
Dogmatism	Attitude toward children	Experience in subject taught	Graduate Record Exam
Authoritarianism	Attitude toward teaching	Experience in grade level taught	Scholastic Aptitude Test
Achievement-motivation	Attitude toward authority	Workshops attended	1. verbal
Introversion-extroversion	Vocational interest	Graduate courses taken	2. quantitative
Abstractness-concreteness	Attitude toward self (self-concept)	Degrees held	Special ability tests, e.g., reasoning ability, logical ability, verbal fluency
Directness-indirectness	Attitude toward subject taught	Professional papers written	Grade-point average
Locus of control			1. overall
Anxiety			2. in major subject
1. general			Professional recommendations
2. teaching			Student evaluations of teaching effectiveness
			Student teaching evaluations

earned. Yet, the latter rather than the former typically appear on the standard biographical form, leaving specific data related to the teaching context untapped.

Achievement and Aptitude Variables. Like experience variables, most achievement and aptitude data have been of little value in predicting teacher performance. The prior achievement of the teacher as measured by, say, college grades, rarely has a direct relationship to classroom performance. This may be accounted for by the relatively low variability which characterizes the prior achievement (e.g., course grades, GPA) of teachers. Standards set by training institutions generally insure that all teachers meet a minimum level of knowledge-related achievement, which is usually high enough to skew the distribution of this variable. Considerably greater success has been found in relating specific aptitude variables (e.g., verbal fluency, reasoning and logic) to teaching effectiveness.

The Immediate Process Stage of Appraisal

The second phase of the appraisal process is the immediate, or observation stage. In this stage, the teacher's actual classroom behavior is recorded. He or she is observed applying procedures, strategies, and techniques in the course of teaching, and these observations are recorded on presumably reliable instruments with explicitly stated behavioral categories. These categories focus the observer's attention on either low-inference (i.e., discrete and specific) or high-inference (i.e., general and cumulative) behaviors. Three characteristics distinguish the various observation instruments: (a) the recording procedure; (b) the item content; and (c) the coding format. Each of these is discussed briefly below.

Tools for observing continuing classroom events may employ either of two recording procedures—sign or category. A *sign* system records an event only once regardless of how often it occurs within a specified time period. The behavior is given a code which indicates merely its presence or absence within a particular block of time. A *category* system, on the other hand, records a given teacher behavior each time it appears and hence provides a frequency count for the occurrence of specific behaviors, rather than a mere indication of their presence or absence. A frequency count may also be obtained using a modified sign system, called a *rating* instrument, which estimates the degree to which a particular behavior occurs. For example, instead of simply noting the presence or absence of a behavior, a rating instrument may suggest the frequency at which the behavior occurs on, say, a 1–to–5 scale, with "5" indicating a high frequency of occurrence and "1" a low frequency of occurrence.

Observation systems can be further differentiated on the basis of item content. Generally, observation instruments, whether of the category, sign, or rating variety, focus on either high- or low-inference behaviors. Those which ask an observer to judge, for example, the presence, absence, or degree of a teacher's *warmth, effectiveness, clarity,* or *enthusiasm* require high inference, because the item content does not specify discrete behaviors that must occur in order for a teacher to be considered warm, effective, clear, or enthusiastic. Item content that is cumulative in nature, like that on many rating scales, forces the observer to make high-inference judgments about the behavior being observed. Observation instruments that name specific behaviors to be recorded, such as "teacher asks question" or "teacher uses example," require little inference on the observer's part. Low-inference item content generally reflects separate and distinct units of behavior which are easy to observe. It should be noted that not all observation systems are either high- or low-inference. Some combine the two types of item content, while others require an intermediate level of inference from the observer.

A third distinction among observation instruments concerns differences in coding format. Two coding formats are available: single and multiple. A single coding format records a behavior on one dimension. Multiple coding, on the other hand, divides a general behavior into two or more discrete subcategories that further define it. Each subcode deals with a different aspect of the initial behavior observed. For example, a single comment might be coded in three ways, according to (a) the identity of the speaker (i.e., teacher or pupil); (b) whether the speaker is on or off task; and (c) whether the speaker is making a statement or asking a question. Other multiple coding formats might include observation and recording of the teacher's pedagogical behaviors and the pupils' responses, as they occur sequentially. These sequential records show promise for studying patterns of classroom interaction, which on a single coding format would appear as a number of separate, unrelated behaviors. Figures 2.1 through 2.4 illustrate differences in recording procedures, item content, and coding format among the various observation systems.

Periods						Teacher practices
I	II	III	IV	V	VI	
✓			✓			1. T occupies center of attention.
		✓				2. T makes p center of attention.
						3. T makes some thing as a thing center of p's attention.
						4. T makes doing something center of p's attention.
	✓					5. T has p spend time waiting, watching, listening.
						6. T has p participate actively.
					✓	7. T remains aloof or detached from p's activities.
						8. T joins or participates in p's activities.
						9. T discourages or prevents p from expressing self freely.
				✓		10. T encourages p to express self freely.

Fig. 2.1. Sign system. (From "Teacher Practices Observation Record," in B. B. Brown, *The Experimental Mind in Education,* New York: Harper & Row, 1968.)

Observation coding systems are commonly used to record two general classes of teacher variables: those considered desirable as an end in themselves and those considered desirable *because* they promote pupil growth. The former are generally high-inference behaviors, and their inclusion in an observation system is easily justified since they reflect inherently "good" practices, such as "teacher shows warmth toward children," or "teacher uses student ideas." Because these behaviors are clearly desirable, they need not relate to pupil achievement to be employed on an observation instrument. The case for including low-inference item content on an observation instrument, however, is less obvious. Since it is not immediately apparent that low-inference items such as "teacher uses blackboard" or "teacher probes pupil for correct response" represent desirable behaviors, these items must be empirically linked to subsequent pupil performance.

			Teacher							Pupil			
	Category		1	2	3	4	5	6	7	8	9	10	Total
Teacher	Accepts feelings	1											0
	Praises	2											0
	Accepts ideas	3			1		1						2
	Asks questions	4				2	1			12		1	16
	Lectures	5				5	22	3					30
	Gives directions	6					1	5		3		4	13
	Criticizes	7											0
Pupil	Responds	8			1	7	4	4		14		1	31
	Initiates	9											0
	Silence	10				2	1	1		2		3	9
		Total	0	0	2	16	30	13	0	31	0	9	101

Fig. 2.2. Category system for recording sequential pairs of events. (From Flanders' "Interaction Analysis System," in N. A. Flanders, *Teacher Influence, Pupil Attitudes, and Achievement,* Final Report of Cooperative Research Project, No. 397, U.S. Office of Education, University of Minnesota, 1960.)

The justification of item content is only one of several methodological problems involved in the use of observation coding systems. Others concern the reliability and validity of these instruments.

Reliability refers to the consistency or agreement between two independently derived observations, recorded on the same coding instrument. It can be measured in several ways. For example, the reliability of a coding system can be determined by correlating observations recorded by different raters using the same instrument and observing a teacher for the same period of time. This procedure yields an estimate of interrater reliability, which is an index of consistency among raters. The interrater reliability of most observation systems is adequate, given sufficient resources and time in which to train observers in using the instrument.

1. *Amount of Criticism: High-Low*

High		Moderate		Low
1	2	3	4	5

2. *Criticism: Personal-General*

Personal		Mixed		General
1	2	3	4	5

3. *Criticism: Kind-Harsh*

Kind		Neutral		Harsh
1	2	3	4	5

4. *Warmth: Warm-Cold*

Warm		Neutral		Cold
1	2	3	4	5

5. *Enthusiasm: Enthusiastic-Apathetic*

Enthusiastic		Neutral		Apathetic
1	2	3	4	5

6. *Classroom Environment: Supportive-Nonsupportive*

High		Moderate		Low
1	2	3	4	5

7. *Task Orientation: Focused-Unfocused*

Focused		Moderate		Unfocused
1	2	3	4	5

8. *Clarity: High-Low*

High		Moderate		Low
1	2	3	4	5

9. *Structuring: High-Low*

High		Moderate		Low
1	2	3	4	5

10. *Variety of Methods: High-Low*

High		Moderate		Low
1	2	3	4	5

11. *Cognitive Variety: High-Low*

High		Moderate		Low
1	2	3	4	5

Fig. 2.3. Rating system. (From the Evaluation of Teaching Project, Research and Development Center for Teacher Education, The University of Texas at Austin, 1974.)

Of greater concern, however, is test-retest reliability, a measure of the stability of teacher behavior as recorded by a given observation instrument across changes in time, content, or pupils. This type of reliability is determined by correlating the results of two observations of the same teacher, recorded at different times by the same observer. Reliability across time refers to the stability of teacher behavior or the capacity of an observation instrument to record the stable components of teacher behavior at different times, whether these times are separated by a week, a month, or a year. Similarly, reliability across content concerns the stability of teacher behavior or the capacity of an observation instrument to record this stability, regardless of the subject matter being taught to a particular group of pupils. And, reliability across pupils refers to the stability of teacher behavior from one class of pupils to another, with content held constant. Observation coding systems have been relatively unsuccessful in establishing the stability of teacher behaviors measured over long periods of time and across different content, though they have achieved some consistency over brief instructional units and across different pupils. Research suggests that teacher behavior may be unstable across different content or over long periods of time, *or* that our observation coding systems fail to record the kind of teacher behavior which remains constant across these dimensions.

Categories	Makes statement		Asks question	
	On task	Off task	On task	Off task
Teacher	/// 3	/ 1	~~////~~ 5	// 2
Pupil	//// 4	~~////~~/ 6	~~////~~ 5	// 2

Fig. 2.4. Multiple coding system (simulated example).

Another problem that has recently emerged concerns the construct validity of observation coding systems. Specifically, this particular problem reflects the apparent inability of at least some coding systems to demonstrate convergent and discriminant validity. These concepts refer to the capacity of a given behavior on one observation instrument (e.g., "teacher lectures") to correlate significantly with the same or a similar behavior (e.g., "teacher lectures" or "teacher presents") on a second instrument. Logically we would expect this correlation to be higher than either that between dissimilar behaviors (e.g., "teacher lectures" and "student asks question") on the *same* instrument or that between dissimilar behaviors measured by *different* observation coding instruments. Initial research on the convergent and discriminant validation of classroom observation systems suggests that different coding systems, with the same item content, do not necessarily measure the same teaching behaviors.*

* G. Borich and D. Malitz, "Convergent and Discriminant Validation of Three Classroom Observation Systems: A Proposed Model," *Journal of Educational Psychology* **67,** no. 3 (1975): 426–431.

Finally, it is important to note that observation coding systems can require a considerable investment in cost and time if one is to insure the reliability and validity of the data derived from them. Appraisers who use observation systems must be carefully trained in order to assure that the instruments are being used and scored correctly. And, in the case of more complex observation instruments, coders must be trained to observe and distinguish fine gradations of behavior. The process of training coders, and the time involved in that process, should be considered in determining the type and number of observation systems to be employed in appraisal. When observation systems require that the teacher's performance be videotaped and played back several times in order to reliably record fine gradations of behavior, coding can consume a significant amount of time and money.

The Intermediate Process Stage of Appraisal

The next phase of the appraisal process is the intermediate stage, in which the teacher's cumulative behavior is rated on predetermined scales. These ratings differ in two ways from the coding of classroom behavior which occurs during the immediate stage. First, intermediate appraisals are made *after,* not in conjunction with, classroom observation. Second, these ratings are cumulative in nature, summarizing the frequency and quality of many behaviors in a single judgment. At the intermediate stage, for example, the appraiser may rate a teacher's attitude toward teaching, knowledge of unit or grade-level content, attitude toward particular tasks and lessons, or use of classroom management techniques. Such ratings are used primarily to fill the gap between observations of specific classroom events and various indices of pupil growth recorded on norm-referenced or criterion-referenced tests. Intermediate measures are thus, on the one hand, an attempt to summarize numerous, discrete classroom events and, on the other hand, an attempt to provide a global description of the teacher behaviors responsible for pupil growth. These summative ratings can be recorded on a variety of scales, using a number of techniques. Though all of these scales cannot be mentioned here, several of the more popular varieties and the problems they pose are noted below.

Summated Ratings (Likert Scales). The Likert scaling technique requires a large number of items that describe teacher behaviors, each yielding a high score for a favorable rating on a behavior and a lower score for a less favorable rating. The rater reacts to items on a five-point response continuum, which reflects either the quality of a behavior or the frequency at which it was perceived to occur. The Likert procedure customarily yields scales with moderate to high reliability. Validity, however, can vary, due to the following considerations. No attempt is made in the construction of a Likert scale to insure equal distances between units (e.g., between "very often" and "fairly often," or between "always relevant" and "mostly relevant"). Therefore, increments of change may have different meaning on different parts of the scale. Furthermore, the unidimensionality of the scale, i.e., the extent to which it measures a single, distinct behavior, must be inferred from high correlations between item and total scores. If item/total correlations are low, the construct is probably too multifaceted and factorially complex to allow simple and direct interpretation of the behavior. Finally, Likert scores are interpreted according to a distribution of sample scores, and *an individual teacher's score has meaning only in relation to the scores of other teachers.* A typical Likert scale appears below.

Teacher elicits pupils' ideas:
_______ very often
_______ fairly often
_______ sometimes
_______ fairly rarely
_______ very rarely

Semantic Differential Scales. The semantic differential is another method used to cumulatively record the quality or frequency of teacher behaviors. It requires the rater to judge the teacher's performance on a series of seven-point bipolar scales. The rater checks the appropriate space, indicating both the direction and intensity of his or her judgment. Scores are derived by assigning numbers (i.e., 1, 2, 3, 4, 5, 6, and 7) to each position on the rating scale. Since the semantic differential and Likert scales are similar, the cautions noted above also apply here: the semantic differential does not necessarily exhibit equal intervals between scale points; the unidimensionality of the concept being measured may vary from one scale to another (particularly when bipolar responses are not exact opposites); and scores are interpreted relative to the rated performance of others. In practice, differences between Likert and semantic differential scales are minor and are generally related to the use of five- or seven-point response formats. The similarity of these procedures is often reflected by high or moderate correlations between the two when they are used to measure the same behavior. A typical semantic differential scale appears below.

Today's Lesson

Relevant ____ ____ ____ ____ ____ ____ ____ Irrelevant

Unclear ____ ____ ____ ____ ____ ____ ____ Clear

Focused ____ ____ ____ ____ ____ ____ ____ Unfocused

Scalogram Analysis (the Guttman Scale). Another method of recording summative judgments of teacher performance is the Guttman scale. This method is based upon the idea that behaviors can be arranged hierarchically so that a teacher who manifests a particular behavior may be assumed to possess all other behaviors having a lower rank. When such an arrangement is found to be valid, the behaviors are said to be scalable.

In developing a Guttman scale, items are formulated and arranged in a hierarchical order. These items are then administered to a group of teachers, whose response patterns are analyzed to determine whether or not the items are scalable. If items require only agreement or disagreement, i.e., an indication of the presence or absence of a behavior, there are 2^n response patterns that might occur. If items are scalable, however, only $n + 1$ of these patterns can be obtained. The relatively low frequency of deviant patterns allows the computation of what is called a coefficient of reproducibility (R). R is equal to the proportion of responses that can be correctly reproduced from the knowledge of a teacher's score. The extent to which such inferences can be made depends upon the level of the coefficient of reproducibility. This value represents a measure of the unidimensionality of the scale and is an index of the scale's validity.

Like the Likert and semantic differential scales, the Guttman scale makes no attempt to insure equal units between items. However, unlike the Likert and semantic differential, *the Guttman scale need not be interpreted relative to the ratings of other teachers, since its items represent specific behaviors, the presence or absence of which can form the basis of an absolute as well as a relative judgment.* This is a desirable characteristic for any instrument used to evaluate the performance of individual teachers. A typical Guttman scale appears below.

☐ Teacher can elicit pupil achievement with technique.
☐ Teacher can correctly use technique in the classroom.
☐ Teacher can correctly apply technique in a controlled or simulated environment.
☐ Teacher knows mechanics of technique.

Expected pattern	Deviant pattern
☐	☐
X	X
X	☐
X	X

Checklists. When a behavior cannot be easily rated on a continuum of values, a simple indication of its presence or absence is used. If the appraiser is unable to make fine gradations in judging the quality or frequency of behavior, a simple yes-no, observed-unobserved, or present-absent format is used. Since checklists record only the presence or absence of behaviors they assume that the rater has had ample opportunity to observe these behaviors. However, this assumption may at times be unwarranted. When checklist data indicate the absence of a particular behavior, it should be determined whether this reflects a true absence or simply a lack of opportunity to observe the behavior. The latter situation may occur when the teacher's objectives are unrelated to or incompatible with the particular behavior in question, or when the rater has visited the classroom too infrequently to have had an opportunity to observe the behavior. In order for the rater to distinguish the absence of an event from inadequate opportunity to observe the event, checklists should provide three alternatives: (a) no opportunity to observe the event; (b) presence of the event; and (c) absence of the event. The rater would choose the first alternative whenever a behavior on the checklist was both unobserved and unlikely to have been been observed, given existing classroom conditions. The "true" presence or absence of a behavior would then be recorded using the second or third alternative.

The reliability of a checklist is usually determined by correlating the responses of two or more raters, while validity is primarily established according to the logic and intuitive value reflected in its items. Like all behaviors in the immediate and intermediate stages of appraisal, the variables recorded on checklists must be justified on the basis that they predict pupil growth, which is measured in the final, product, stage of appraisal. A typical checklist appears below.

No opportunity	Present	Absent	
☐	☐	☐	Teacher tolerates deviant behavior.
☐	☐	☐	Teacher follows curriculum guide.
☐	☐	☐	Teacher supervises pupils closely.

Cautions involved in using all of the above forms of measurement are summarized below.

1. Rating scales may lack unidimensionality, in which case judgments become so multifaceted and general that the behaviors identified are not sufficiently specific to be useful in diagnosing and improving teacher performance. Assessment of any type must be specific enough to suggest instructional resources and training to the teacher being appraised.

2. The distances between response alternatives on rating scales and Guttman scales are often unequal. This arrangement encourages raters to make judgments more frequently at one end of the scale than the other. For example, raters often view judgments recorded on the bottom half of a scale as so detrimental to the teacher that they are reluctant to use that end of the scale, regardless of their observations.

3. Rating scales and checklists may be difficult to interpret since the scores of other teachers must be used as an anchoring point. Ultimately, teachers should be judged according to their achievement of specific, well-defined competencies, and not on the basis of their standing relative to others who also may have failed to achieve the desired competency.

4. Finally, the rating scales and checklists used in the intermediate process stage of appraisal rely considerably on the rater's memory and perceptiveness, which may distort an otherwise objective assessment. The personalities, experiences, and training of raters can, if uncontrolled, produce idiosyncratic records of teacher performance. Though extensive efforts are usually made to control these biases, every teacher rating is susceptible to them.

The Product Stage of Appraisal

Although each stage of the teacher appraisal process involves specific measurement problems, a system that assesses behavior at each stage—preoperational, immediate, intermediate, and product—provides a composite picture of teacher performance in which errors of measurement are counterbalanced and limited. The product stage, considered by some the most important stage of appraisal, is therefore best viewed as a single component within a larger network of evaluative criteria. Product-stage assessments confirm observations and ratings made at earlier stages and at the same time contribute new data to the appraisal process.

Since the business of teachers is the promotion of pupil growth, the product stage of appraisal assesses teacher effectiveness by measuring changes in pupil achievement, both affective and cognitive, over a prespecified period of instruction. This period may be as brief as the span of a single lesson or as long as a semester or a school year. The teacher's pupils are assessed at Time 1, the beginning of a unit of instruction, and at Time 2, the end of the unit. The difference between pre- and posttest pupil achievement is attributed to the performance of the teacher. The method by which to assess this pupil growth, however, is an unsettled issue, addressed in more detail in Chapter 4 of this volume. Generally, either standardized (i.e., norm-referenced) or criterion-referenced tests are used.

Norm-referenced tests employed in the product stage of appraisal are designed to assess a pupil's status in relation to the status of other pupils measured with the same tests. Standardized achievement and aptitude tests, given yearly to students, are examples of norm-referenced measures, since they indicate a pupil's score in comparison to that of others who, for assessment purposes, are considered the normative group.

Criterion-referenced tests, on the other hand, are designed to assess pupils' status in relation to some predetermined criterion or standard of performance. They are closely linked to the instructional objectives of a particular teacher, unlike norm-referenced tests, which reflect national objectives for a given grade level. While both norm-referenced and criterion-referenced tests have a role in the assessment of educational performance, the latter are usually more appropriate when pupil performance is used as an index of teacher effectiveness. The pupils' success or failure in meeting the educational objectives of their own teachers should be more important to the appraiser than their relative status on a measure of more remote, national objectives.

The distinction between norm-referenced and criterion-referenced tests is reflected in the scores they produce. Criterion-referenced tests typically yield scores that are binary in nature. That is, a given score indicates one of two things—that the pupil has mastered the criterion or that he hasn't. For example, if the teacher's objective is that the pupil should demonstrate ability to solve quadratic equations, an end-of-unit test would amount to performance of the desired criterion behavior. Allowing for possible computation errors, the minimum proficiency level required for attaining the criterion might be, say, 90 percent. Pupils attaining 90 percent proficiency would achieve the criterion, while those failing to meet this level would be given additional instruction until they too reached the criterion.

In contrast, scores from norm-referenced tests are reported on a continuum, usually in the form of percentile ranks. A pupil who has taken a norm-referenced test might receive a score ranked at the 75th percentile, indicating that he or she scored better than 75 percent of the students in the norm group. Interpretation of the norm-referenced test focuses on a pupil's achievement relative to others who have taken the test, rather than on the pupil's attainment of a specified standard of performance. While norm-referenced and criterion-referenced test items may appear similar, the scores they yield are considerably different, as shown in Figs. 2.5 and 2.6.

MATHEMATICS Grade Two Skill	Date skill was achieved
Concepts	
Understands commutative property of addition (e.g., $4+3=3+4$)	9/27
Understands place value (e.g., $27=2$ tens $+7$ ones)	10/3
Addition	
Supplies missing addend under 10 (e.g., $3+?=5$)	10/8
Adds three single-digit numbers	____
Knows combinations 10 through 19	____
Adds two 2-digit numbers without carrying	____
Adds two 2-digit numbers with carrying	____
Subtraction	
Knows combinations through 9	10/4
Supplies missing subtrahend—under 10 (e.g., $6-?=1$)	____
Supplies missing minuend—under 10 (e.g., $?-3=4$)	____
Knows combinations 10 through 19	____
Subtracts two 2-digit numbers without borrowing	____
Measurement	
Reads and draws clocks (up to quarter hour)	____
Understands dollar value of money (coins up to $1.00 total)	____
Geometry	
Understands symmetry	____
Recognizes congruent plane figures—that is, figures which are identical except for orientation	____
Graph reading	
Knows how to construct simple graphs	____
Knows how to read simple graphs	____

Fig. 2.5. Individual pupil report based on a system of criterion-referenced measurement. From J. Millman, *Phi Delta Kappan* **52** (1970): 226–230.

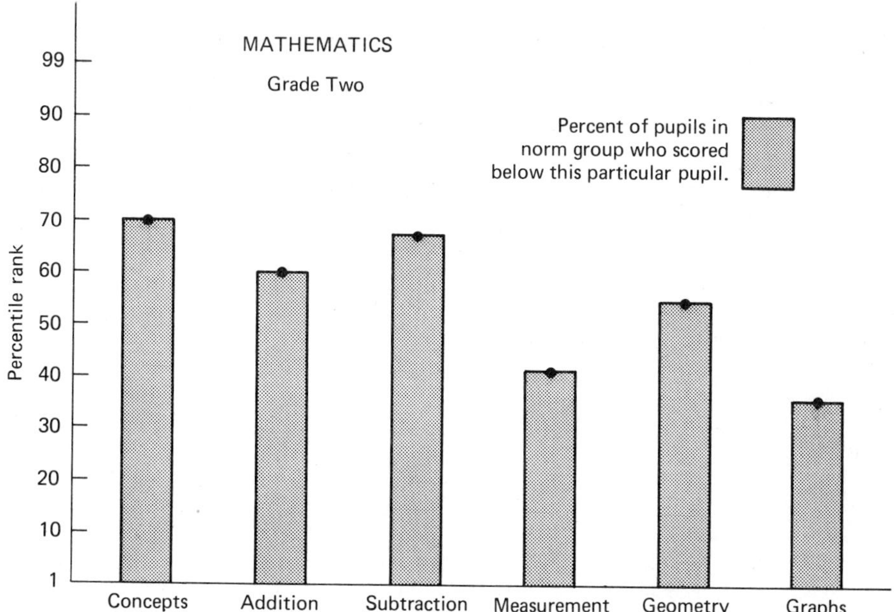

Fig. 2.6. Individual pupil report based on a system of norm-referenced measurement.

While other issues related to the measurement of pupil growth are treated in considerable technical detail in Chapter 4, the major cautions in this stage of appraisal involve:

1. *Determining and controlling the extent to which pupil performance is affected by influences other than the teacher.* Some studies have indicated that parental expectations, the pupil's prior achievement, the socioeconomic status of the family, and the general intellectual quality of the pupil's home life may have greater influence on the pupil's measured achievement than does the teacher. If this is true, to what extent can we infer teacher effectiveness from pupil performance?

2. *The unreliability of the difference between the pupils' pre- and posttest achievement.* This difference is relatively unreliable for two reasons. First, in calculating the difference score, the unreliability inherent in the pretest is added to that in the posttest, making the resulting score less reliable than either the pre- or posttest score alone. Second, research has indicated that teacher effects on pupil achievement may be unstable over long periods of time and across content. Thus, if a teacher's influence on pupil performance is inconsistent from one subject, or one time, to another, one can legitimately question the use of pupil gain as a measure of teacher effectiveness.

STAGE	*Preoperational measures*		*Immediate process measures*		*Intermediate process measures*		*Product measures*	
DOMAIN	*Affective*	*Cognitive*	*Affective*	*Cognitive*	*Affective*	*Cognitive*	*Affective*	*Cognitive*
HIGH INFERENCE	Personality, attitude	Achievement, experience, and aptitude	Observations of general affective characteristics, e.g., teacher's warmth	Observations of general content-related characteristics, e.g., teacher's business-like or systematic behavior	Ratings of attitudes toward teaching and learning	Ratings of teacher's knowledge of unit or grade level content	Pupil attitudes toward learning, the school, and teachers	Pupil achievement of unit or grade level content
LOW INFERENCE	Attitudes related to teaching and learning	Knowledge of teaching methods and content	Observations of specific affective characteristics, e.g., times teacher praises student	Observations of specific content-related characteristics, e.g., teacher's lecture to discussion ratio	Ratings of attitudes toward classroom tasks and lessons	Ratings of knowledge of classroom tasks and lessons	Pupil attitudes toward lesson content	Pupil achievement of lesson content

Fig. 2.7. A measurement framework for evaluating classroom instruction.

3. *The teacher's understandable desire to teach to the test when he or she knows that pupil growth is to be an index of teacher effectiveness.* Teachers may consciously or subconsciously plan classroom instruction that focuses on content they suspect will be measured by specific test items. For example, teachers may guess that pupil achievement tests will contain material that can be easily measured, rather than higher-order learning which requires more complex pupil knowledge and performance. Hence, they may proceed to teach the more straightforward, easily measured content. This is unfortunate since higher-order learning, reflecting more complex instructional objectives, may be a more important criterion than any other for distinguishing more effective and less effective teachers. Pupil growth in this area, however, may be imperceptible during any given appraisal period.

Figures 2.7 and 2.8 provide a measurement framework summarizing the four stages of appraisal discussed. Figure 2.7 gives general examples of affective and cognitive and high- and low-inference behaviors typically measured in the preoperational, immediate, intermediate, and product stages of appraisal. Figure 2.8 summarizes the various types of instrumentation typically used in each of these stages. Chapter 3 adds to this framework by indicating that there are not only different stages in the appraisal process but also different purposes to which appraisal data can be applied.

Stage	*Preoperational*	*Immediate process*	*Intermediate process*	*Product*
Major types of instrumentation	Archival records, interview data, baseline paper-and-pencil assessments, biographical questionnaire	Observational coding systems	Summative ratings: Likert scales, semantic differential scales, Guttman scales, checklists	Criterion-referenced tests
School personnel administering or using the instrumentation	Department chairperson, personnel officer, principals	Trained classroom coders, e.g., mature students, substitute teachers, clerical and administrative staff	Department chairperson principal, supervisors	Teacher

Fig. 2.8. Instrumentation and school personnel related to the measurement framework.

Chapter 3

Applications of Performance Appraisal Systems

The technical problems involved in measuring teacher performance often obscure the objectives of such measurement. Diligently collecting data, the appraiser may lose sight of one or more of the numerous purposes to which these data can be applied. Therefore, while the preceding chapter stressed the value of gathering different kinds of data at different stages using different instruments, this chapter discusses the application of these data to different purposes.

The objectives served by appraisal data fall into three broad categories—*diagnostic, formative,* and *summative*—roughly corresponding to the appraisal stages described in the previous chapter. Information collected at each stage is used by various school personnel to make diagnostic, formative, or summative decisions. The attitude, aptitude, and experience variables measured in the preoperational stage, for example, are generally applied by school administrators or teacher trainers to diagnostic decisions such as teacher selection, placement, and training needed *prior to* employment. Data from *in situ* observations made in the immediate stage are, on the other hand, used by inservice teachers to meet formative objectives related to the improvement of specific classroom skills and instructional strategies. Finally, cumulative ratings of teacher performance and indices of pupil gain collected during the intermediate and product stages of appraisal, respectively, are applied by administrators and evaluators to summative purposes, including teacher certification in broad areas of competence, determination of overall teaching effectiveness, and comparison of teachers across curricula or instructional programs.

The relationship between appraisal stages and purposes is depicted in Table 3.1. This graphic representation reveals the considerable overlap, from stage to stage, in diagnostic, formative, and summative objectives.

Table 3.1. The relationship between appraisal applications and measurement stages.

<table>
<tr><td>Measurement stages</td><td colspan="2">Preoperational</td><td colspan="2">Immediate</td><td colspan="2">Intermediate</td><td>Product</td></tr>
<tr><td>Applications</td><td colspan="3">Diagnostic</td><td colspan="2">Formative</td><td colspan="3">Summative</td></tr>
<tr><td>Objectives</td><td colspan="3">To diagnose weakness in or absence of behaviors and skills prerequisite to teaching</td><td colspan="2">To determine weakness in or absence of desirable behaviors and skills during teaching</td><td colspan="3">To support promotion, tenure and reemployment decisions</td></tr>
<tr><td></td><td colspan="3">To identify instructional resources and training for professional development</td><td colspan="2">To prescribe instructional resources and training</td><td colspan="3">To certify proficiency in the use of teaching strategies, procedures and techniques</td></tr>
<tr><td></td><td colspan="3">To determine extent of mastery of professional development objectives</td><td colspan="2">To control the implementation and quality of instructional programs and curricula</td><td colspan="3">To predict success in subsequent and alternative teaching assignments</td></tr>
<tr><td></td><td colspan="3">To match teaching assignment with teacher's characteristics and skills</td><td colspan="2">To forecast summative results</td><td colspan="3">To compare systematically different groups of teachers</td></tr>
<tr><td>Behavioral focus</td><td colspan="3">Prior experience and training
Personality traits
Attitudes
Preferences</td><td colspan="2">Observable and discrete behaviors and skills</td><td colspan="3">Comprehensive strategies, procedures, and techniques
Pupil change</td></tr>
</table>

Types of instrumentation	Biographical questionnaires Attitude and preference inventories Interviews Observation coding systems	Observation coding systems Low- to medium-inference rating scales	High-inference rating scales Criterion-referenced tests
Source of appraisal criteria	Characteristics of effective teachers Hypotheses about effective teaching Community and professional staff values	Conceptual model of effective teaching derived from: empirical research; professional experience; community values	Same as formative criteria
Interpretation of data	Mostly qualitative (presence/absence, strong points/weak points)	Mostly quantitative (means, frequencies, percentages)	Both quantitative and qualitative
Method of reporting	Individual plan for professional development indicating needed skills, behaviors, and training	Table of specifications: behaviors and skills by degree of proficiency	Table of certification: behaviors and skills by attainment (presence or absence)

The remainder of this chapter further explicates the diagnostic, formative, and summative applications of appraisal data shown in Table 3.1.

DIAGNOSTIC APPLICATIONS

Diagnostic applications of appraisal data involve the hiring, placement, and initial training of teachers. Specifically, preoperational data are used to determine the teacher's: (1) entry behaviors and skills; (2) need for inservice training; and (3) compatibility with various instructional strategies, pupil types, and curricula.

Though diagnosis is most commonly used to place teachers in appropriate positions *after* they have been hired, it can also be used profitably *prior* to employment. Diagnostic data collected from preservice teachers allow school administrators to consider the entry behaviors and skills of applicants in reference to specific teaching contexts, such as low SES areas, open classrooms, or schools implementing new curricula.

After employment decisions have been made, diagnostic data can be used to develop inservice training programs that build on the behaviors and skills already possessed by teachers. Such programs may require that teachers enroll in a specific graduate course, attend a series of workshops, or complete instructional materials related to the inservice training objectives of the school district. Clearly, if the school system fails to recommend the professional experiences needed by teachers, it is ignoring the means to improve teacher performance at later (e.g., intermediate and product) stages of appraisal. Preoperational measures, as well as observations recorded early in the immediate stage of appraisal, can provide a variety of diagnostic information. When related to the goals and objectives of a particular school district, these data can guide the selection of training experiences and the development of "in-house" instructional resources.

If the training indicated by diagnostic appraisal data is to be effective, it too must be evaluated. Training experiences conducted by the school district may be appraised by assessing the extent to which the "trained" teachers actually attain the behaviors and skills intended. When training fails to engender the desired behaviors in a sufficiently large number of participants, individual teachers cannot be held accountable—the training procedure itself obviously needs revision.

In addition to their use in hiring and training decisions, diagnostic data can also serve to estimate the compatibility between a teacher and his or her prospective teaching assignment. Although the degree of compatibility cannot be quantified with great accuracy, personality, experience, and attitudinal data can be used to reduce the likelihood of a mismatch between the teacher and the assigned instructional context. For example, school personnel officers, department chairpersons, and administrators might avoid potential mismatches prior to assignment by ranking teaching candidates on a scale similar to that shown in Fig. 3.1.

Such scales can incorporate a variety of data, including the number of years of prior teaching experience (or, in the case of a new teacher, a student teaching assignment) in a context similar to the employer's district. Enrollment in relevant workshops and familiarity with instructional programs and curricula used by the district can also serve as indices of compatibility between a given teacher and a specific teaching assignment.

Directions: Rate the teaching candidate on each of the following characteristics and sum the ratings to estimate the similarity of the instructional conditions experienced by the candidate during student teaching or prior assignment to those of the employing district. The more important characteristics may be weighted by multiplying their scores by 1.5, 2, . . . , etc.

Incompatibility		*Uncertain*	*Compatibility*	
high	low		low	high
(1)	(2)	(3)	(4)	(5)
______	______	______	______	______
Very dissimilar	Somewhat dissimilar	Uncertain or mixed	Somewhat similar	Very similar

Score	*Weight*	*Characteristic*
( )	( )	1. Horizontal organization: departmental or self-contained, team teaching or individual effort
( )	( )	2. Vertical organization: graded or ungraded, closed or open classroom
( )	( )	3. Pupils, e.g., SES, upper, upper-middle, middle, lower-middle, lower
( )	( )	4. Community, e.g., rural, urban, suburban
( )	( )	5. Texts and special materials, e.g., 16mm, film loops, filmstrips
( )	( )	6. Curriculum, special programs, e.g., BSCS, Harvard Physics, Distar, Individually Guided Education, Individually Prescribed Instruction
( )	( )	7. Ability groups, e.g., by curriculum, aptitude, etc.
( )	( )	8. Grading and testing, e.g., policies and expectations

Fig. 3.1. Hypothetical scale for estimating, prior to placement, the degree of similarity between experience of the teaching candidate and the instructional context to which he or she may be assigned.

To supplement this information, data describing the candidate's actual classroom behavior, collected by different observers over a number of *in situ* observations, can be used in making placement decisions. Diagnostic data of this type often counteract the fallacious assumption that all teachers possess comparable teaching skills and abilities and, therefore, are all equally adaptable to different teaching responsibilities. Descriptive studies have shown that the instructional strategies of teachers vary widely and that only a very few teaching behaviors and skills are effective for all teachers, in all circumstances. Thus, the demands of various grade levels, content areas, classroom contexts, curricula, and pupil types should be matched as closely as possible with the teachers' skills, abilities, and preferences.

Some teachers, for example, are more successful with certain types of pupils than with others. Diagnostic applications of appraisal data can take into account a teacher's preference for certain kinds of students by asking the teacher to list the "types" he or she considers most and least "teachable." The teacher can be directed to assign distinct characteristics to each category of pupil, thereby enabling the school district to compare these descriptions with the pupils in various instructional programs. A given teacher may, for instance, consider students of low and average ability most teachable, perhaps because of prior training or simply because of the challenge such pupils often present. Other teachers, particularly those well prepared and recently experienced in a specific content area, may view high-ability students as most teachable. While precise matching of teacher and pupil types is generally impractical, many school systems could be more flexible in tailoring teacher assignment to expressed interest in, and preference for, certain pupil types.

The curriculum to be implemented should also be considered in assigning teachers to various positions. Some curricula require specific process skills, possessed to different degrees by different teachers. Many of the newer curricula, for example, rely heavily on the teacher's effective use of group discussion skills, team teaching, or the inquiry approach. Teachers whose experience is concentrated in the lower grades, where programmed or semiprogrammed materials are frequently used, may be less effective in the higher grades where curricular materials often require skills unrelated to those used at elementary levels. Observational data recorded during the immediate stage of appraisal are helpful in determining whether or not a given teacher possesses the behaviors and skills required by a specific curriculum.

Knowledge and process skills related to a particular curriculum, however, do not insure proper implementation of that curriculum. If the former are absent, the latter will not occur. But, on the other hand, it must not be assumed that relevant knowledge and skills guarantee successful implementation. Indifference to or disagreement with the curriculum can hinder proper implementation. Therefore, in matching teacher and curriculum, interest and attitude as well as knowledge and ability should be considered.

FORMATIVE APPLICATIONS

Formative analyses, as the name implies, are conducted while the teacher is learning and practicing the behaviors and skills to be assessed in the final stages of the appraisal process. The objective of these analyses is the identification of absent or weak skills and the recommendation of instructional experiences designed to help the teacher attain or improve these skills.

Formative applications of appraisal data differ from summative applications, since the former focus on discrete, limited teacher behaviors and the latter focus on a comprehensive range of both teacher and pupil behaviors, usually summarized in an overall judgment. Though summative data are used to make cumulative ratings of teacher effectiveness, the credibility of such judgments depends to a large extent on the presence of formative data, collected earlier to identify specific behavioral strengths and weaknesses.

Characteristically, formative data provide specific information, collected in a manner that permits rapid feedback to the teacher, and reported in a way that reduces the negative implications of frequent and intense examination of the teacher's performance. Formative applications of appraisal data, therefore, are prescriptive rather than evaluative.

Formative, like diagnostic, objectives require that a behavioral record be kept for each teacher being appraised. Records used for formative purposes are dynamic, not static, in nature. They indicate not only the presence or absence of specific skills and behaviors, but also *improvement* in the teacher's use of these skills and behaviors over time.

Such records can be kept on a "table of specifications." The construction of a table of specifications begins with a list of the skills a school district or training institution believes its teachers should possess. These skills are then broken into a number of behavioral levels, each of which indicates a certain degree of proficiency. These levels may range, for example, from basic knowledge of a skill to repeated and effective use of that skill. An example of a table of specifications is given in Fig. 3.2.

A table of behavioral specifications is significant to teachers since it allows them to see the exact elements on which summative evaluations will be based. The behaviors listed in Fig. 3.2, for example, can be combined for summative purposes to form a single measure, perhaps referred to as the teacher's "adequacy of instructional style." Teachers and administrators should cooperate in developing a table of specifications to assure that those behaviors considered important to each will be included and given appropriate emphasis.

Once the table of specifications has been constructed and suitable assessment devices selected, the data obtained from these instruments can be used to (1) identify teacher difficulties, (2) prescribe resources, (3) control the quality of curricula and special programs, and (4) forecast summative results.

The primary application of formative data is to the identification and removal of specific performance deficiencies that can affect subsequent summative judgments. As noted earlier, formative data are most useful in providing feedback to the teacher about his or her classroom behavior. In performing this function, formative data should (1) identify behaviors and skills on the table of specifications which the teacher has not yet mastered, (2) suggest reasons for these deficiencies, and (3) indicate the relationship between measured deficiencies and available instructional resources or training. When data fail to supply all three kinds of information, they do not meet the objectives of formative appraisal and, therefore, do not provide a basis for interpreting later, summative judgments.

An equally important formative objective is the prescription of training experiences based on the initial assessment of behaviors contained in the table of specifications. Because training content and method are derived from the results of classroom observation, their effectiveness depends on the clarity and explicitness of the behaviors and skills listed in the table. Broad categories, encompassing many discrete behaviors and skills, are likely to produce equally

Behaviors and skills (selected for Phase 1, Oct. – Nov.)	Never observed when appropriate	Rarely observed when appropriate	Occasionally observed when appropriate	Often observed when appropriate	Always observed when appropriate
1. Reinforcement					
Waits (for child to respond)					
Prompts (with first word if child continues to have difficulty)				Area of minimum acceptable performance	
Immediately (lets child know right away that response is correct)					
Etc.					
2. Modeling					
Signal (precedes modeling with signal, waits for attention)					
Clearly (modeling loudly, close to children)					
Consistency (repeats the same model the same way each time)					
Etc.					
3. Correcting Errors					
Central (corrects errors central to lesson objective one at a time)					
Immediately (corrects errors immediately)					
Reinforces correct response (not the error)					
Etc.					

Behaviors and skills (selected for Phase 1, Oct. – Nov.)	Never observed when appropriate	Rarely observed when appropriate	Occasionally observed when appropriate	Often observed when appropriate	Always observed when appropriate
4. Inquiry and questioning					
Prompts (encourages pupil to respond even when knowledge is incomplete)					
Creates (asks pupil to go beyond original idea, to create new idea, show creativity)					
Delves (follows-up pupil response with higher-order, cognitive question)					
Etc.					
5. Discussion					
Evokes (stimulates group participation)					
Accepts (accepts divergent viewpoints)					
Involves (calls on lower ability pupils)					
Etc.					

Fig. 3.2. Example of a table of specifications for the formative use of appraisal data. Adapted from M. Luft, J. Lujan, and K. Bemis, "A Quality Assurance Model for Process Evaluation," in G. Borich, ed., *Evaluating Educational Programs and Products* (Englewood Cliffs, N.J.: Educational Technology Publications, 1974.)

broad training alternatives. Such general instructional experiences may provide the teacher with training in skills and behaviors only tangentially related to the specific proficiency desired. On the other hand, if behaviors in the table of specifications are explicit and clearly linked to classroom observation procedures, they are likely to yield relevant, unambiguous training recommendations that focus exclusively on the teacher's recorded behavior.

Formative application of appraisal data also insures that the behaviors taught are being practiced in the classroom. While diagnosis can determine the compatibility between a teacher and a given curriculum, formative analyses can reveal the extent to which a teacher who is comfortable with the curriculum actually implements the behaviors it requires. Subsequent measures of pupil growth in the product stage of appraisal will be appropriate indices of teacher performance only when the teacher has implemented the curriculum used during the appraisal period as its developers intended.

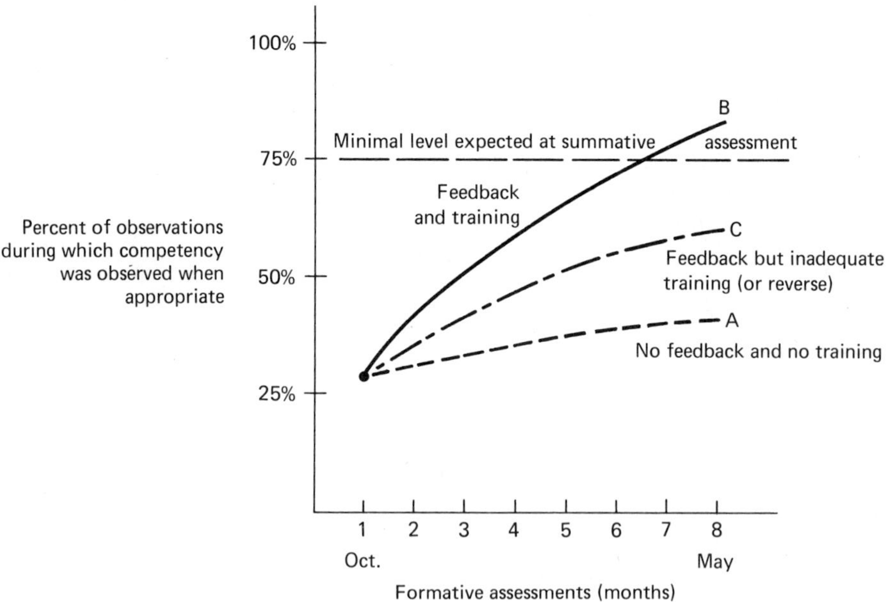

Fig. 3.3. The expected effects of withholding feedback and training on the attainment of teaching competencies.

Formative data give teachers and administrators an opportunity to periodically review implementation of new curricula or instructional materials. These performance reviews allow teachers to pinpoint behaviors that might affect the execution of the instructional program. If teachers are being appraised when a special curriculum or new materials are in use, opportunities should be provided to analyze classroom performance with videotape recordings or the results of *in situ* observations. Each teacher's implementation of the curriculum can be viewed in relation to that of other teachers or to a specified standard in order to identify behaviors that need improvement or redirection.

Such intensive analyses also serve to predict summative judgments. Ultimately, summative judgments function as an index of the teacher's overall effectiveness, while the measurements preceding them are used to revise and redirect behaviors to secure a favorable cumulative evaluation. Formative data collected periodically can indicate both the teacher's progress in correcting previously identified deficiencies and the effectiveness of recommended training experiences. Continuous collection of formative data can, early in the appraisal process, suggest whether or not needed skills will be attained prior to summative assessment. This forecast then permits appropriate alterations in the teacher's professional development program to improve the probability of receiving a favorable summative appraisal.

Figure 3.3 illustrates the expected outcome of three series of formative assessments. Curve *A* represents the effect of formative assessments that included neither feedback to the teacher nor appropriate training experiences. Curve *B*, on the other hand, indicates assessments that were followed by both feedback to the teacher and appropriate training experiences. Curve *C* illustrates a situation in which feedback was accompanied by insufficient or inadequate training experiences. In Curves *A* and *C*, the proficiency expected at the time of summative assessment is not attained. If formative data are not fed back to the teacher, and training is not provided (Curve *A*), it is likely that proficiency in a given area will change only slightly, if at all. Similarly, if training experiences are either inadequate or unrelated to a given proficiency (Curve *C*), improvement will most likely be insufficient to produce the level of performance expected at the time of summative assessment. Formative data, then, may be used not only for forecasting the outcome of summative assessment, but also for changing that forecast.

SUMMATIVE APPLICATIONS

While formative analyses are used to help the teacher focus on specific behaviors that can be improved through training, summative assessment yields a more comprehensive evaluation of the teacher's proficiency, concentrating on the attainment of a composite of related behaviors and skills. Whereas formative observations might record the amount of time the teacher spends giving verbal illustrations, providing instructions and directions, and answering student questions, summative assessments would subsume these behaviors under an overall judgment of, say, the teacher's clarity of presentation. If indices of pupil growth are used for summative purposes, the appraiser must infer the teacher's clarity, for example, from some aspect of pupil achievement.

Summative data are often too general to redirect the specific procedures, techniques, and strategies used by the teacher on a day-to-day basis. Instead they are used to form cumulative judgments about the teacher, incorporating a broad range of teacher performance variables, as opposed to the small, discrete, and individually observable bits of information required by formative objectives.

As indicated in the preceding section, formative data must be applied frequently in order to provide a constant flow of behavioral data to the teacher. Specific behaviors and skills are observed, these observations are fed back to the teacher, training activities are suggested, and a new assessment cycle begins. In contrast, summative assessments are conducted infrequently, since they must summarize all the behaviors and skills observed over repeated formative assessments. These behaviors and skills, in combination, define an area of proficiency which serves as the focus of summative assessment. Although summative assessments are most often made at the end of the appraisal period, they may also be taken at intervals coinciding with the completion of prespecified units of instruction or a block of training experiences.

The distinctions between formative and summative appraisal are summarized below.

Purpose	*Function*	*Time*	*Specificity*
Formative	To remove specific deficiencies and strengthen existing skills and behaviors	At end of small blocks of instruction: weekly, monthly	Individual skills and behaviors
Summative	To evaluate general performance	At end of large blocks of instruction: semester, yearly	Broad behavioral categories, i.e., competencies

Data obtained from summative assessments can be used for (1) establishing merit, (2) certifying additional skills and abilities, (3) predicting success in subsequent teaching assignments, and (4) comparing different groups of teachers who vary in systematic ways.

The inclusion of a large number of discrete skills and behaviors under a more comprehensive classification makes summative assessment particularly useful in reaching decisions involving the merit, tenure, and reemployment of teachers. If related to earlier formative assessments, summative data may be effectively used to document a teacher's proficiency in the behavioral categories represented in the table of specifications—a logical final objective of the appraisal process. If formative data have been diligently collected by the appraiser and used by the teacher, final, summative assessments should yield positive results. The summative use of data simply fulfills the generic function of appraisal—that of summarizing the teacher's proficiency in behaviors for which feedback and training have been provided—and thus serves as a means by which the teacher can certify the adequacy of his or her performance.

Summative assessments can also be used to predict the success a teacher is likely to have in a specific teaching assignment. Teachers who have been certified proficient in skills and behaviors required by a given curriculum should be chosen to teach that curriculum over teachers who have not been appraised or who have not achieved proficiency in the behaviors and skills required. It follows that a teacher who has been certified in all of the behaviors and skills deemed relevant to a particular instructional context should be able to choose from all assignments within that context, and a teacher who has not yet been certified in these areas should have a more limited number of assignments from which to choose. Thus, the summative function of appraisal should create a natural incentive for teachers to become proficient in many areas in order to qualify for the teaching contexts (e.g., open classroom, team teaching, etc.) they deem most desirable.

Given this incentive, teachers can refer to summative data to identify areas in which they should attain proficiency. Obviously, effective long-term teaching requires mastery of many more behaviors than can be acquired during a single appraisal period, regardless of its length. A teacher may use summative data to plan a course of professional growth, working cooperatively with the department chairperson, supervisor, or principal. Skills and behaviors can be selected for next semester's or next year's appraisal on the basis of current appraisal data. These newly identified behaviors and skills can be used to form the basis of a new table of specifications. The summative objective of, say, a three-year appraisal effort might be the attainment of proficiency in the behaviors and skills listed in several tables of specifications successively built upon the teacher's previously identified strengths and weaknesses.

Finally, summative data can be applied to the comparison of groups of teachers whose entering behaviors and skills are at different levels of proficiency. School systems or training institutions may wish to empirically determine whether teachers with different entering behaviors and skills are actually differentially effective. The use of summative information for such comparisons differs from other applications of summative data in that it involves the performance of selected *groups* of teachers rather than that of individuals. In making these comparisons, the school system, in effect, conducts applied research on the domain of behaviors and skills selected for the appraisal process. Certain experiences and behaviors assumed to be prerequisite to attainment of a particular proficiency might, in the face of these comparisons, prove irrelevant.

In concluding this chapter, it should be noted that appraisal data, whether applied to diagnostic, formative, or summative purposes, should serve not only to evaluate but also to improve teaching performance. Therefore, an appraisal system, regardless of its objectives, must incorporate training opportunities for inservice teachers, or alternative instructional resources for preservice teachers, if it is to have any lasting effect in the classroom.

We now turn to a discussion of the techniques and procedures used to meet the diagnostic, formative, and summative purposes of appraisal.

Chapter 4

Using Appraisal Techniques and Procedures

Two critical problems persistently impede the appraisal of teaching: (1) the collection of data that are valid and reliable, and (2) the presentation of these data to the teacher in an accurate and comprehensible form. Accurate and interpretable data are obtained when the appraisal system recognizes the many methodological problems that can render its efforts ineffective and its data invalid. Therefore, the first part of this chapter addresses the problem of collecting valid and reliable data. Because the most egregious methodological errors occur in the measurement of pupil growth, six guidelines are presented concerning procedures and techniques for collecting data in the product (pupil) stage of appraisal.

This chapter also focuses on the analysis and reporting of appraisal data. Throughout the previous chapters a case has been made for incorporating professional development programs for teachers into the appraisal system. The appraisal process should function as a cycle in which data are carefully planned, collected, analyzed, and finally *fed back* to the teacher as part of a development program aimed at improving existing skills or teaching new ones. Reporting data is an integral link in this cycle. Therefore, several popular techniques for analyzing and reporting appraisal data to the teacher are described in this chapter.

GUIDELINES FOR IMPROVING THE APPRAISAL PROCESS

The following guidelines were selected for presentation because they address particularly distressing problems. They apply primarily to appraisals that include the measurement of pupil change, an area plagued by the most troublesome stumbling blocks.

Guideline 1: Idiographic Rather Than Nomothetic Tests of Pupil Performance Should Be Used

An *idiographic* test produces a score that describes the individual's performance in relation to the *test,* while a nomothetic measure yields a score that describes the subject's performance in relation to that of *other examinees* who serve as a norm group. The former are more commonly referred to as "criterion-referenced" measures since they relate test performance to a predetermined standard or criterion rather than to the performance of others.

The suitability of criterion-referenced and norm-referenced measures for teacher appraisal becomes apparent when their objectives are compared. Idiographic, or criterion-referenced, tests attempt to determine whether or not the examinee has attained a particular skill, or mastered a given content area. The items on such tests determine mastery of situations, problems, or tasks essential to proficiency in the skill being measured. If the pupil can correctly answer a sufficient number of these items, he or she has achieved proficiency in the particular skill—regardless of how his or her classmates have performed on the test.

The purpose of norm-referenced tests, however, is to discriminate among pupils, to reveal differences in performance rather than mastery of a skill or subject area. This objective demands the inclusion of a variety of items, some necessarily more obscure or difficult, in order to differentiate among pupils. Accordingly, norm-referenced tests must contain items that cover not only the main ideas or skills taught, but also the finer points, knowledge of which may not be essential to proficiency in the subject area or skill under consideration. Table 4.1 illustrates a typical item-selection process for norm-referenced tests.

Table 4.1. Typical item-selection process for norm-referenced tests

Test item	*Percentage of pupils scoring in top 25% on total test getting item right*	*Percentage of pupils scoring in bottom 25% on total test getting item right*	*Comment*	*Decision*
1	70	30	Good discrimination in right direction	Accept item
2	30	70	Good discrimination in wrong direction	Reject item
3	30	30	No discrimination; item too difficult	Reject item
•				
•				
•				
n	70	70	No discrimination; item too easy	Reject item

In appraising teachers, pupil performance is often measured as an indication of the teacher's effectiveness in communicating specific content or skills. Therefore, tests used for this purpose must cover the content or skills the teacher has emphasized rather than more remote, highly discriminating content. The appraiser is not interested in differentiating among pupils but in determining the degree to which the teacher has achieved established objectives. This can best be accomplished using criterion-referenced tests, which are sensitive to content and skills stressed by the teacher over a particular period of instruction. Figure 4.1 illustrates the essential difference between the distribution of pupil scores on a criterion-referenced test, constructed to measure pupil performance over a specific lesson, and on a norm-referenced test, constructed to measure end-of-year pupil achievement.

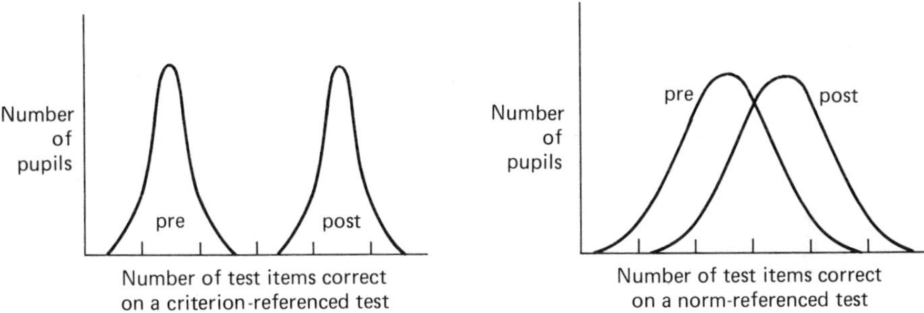

Fig. 4.1. Characteristic distributions of pupil scores for a criterion-referenced test (left) and a norm-referenced test (right).

Note that the criterion-referenced test produces less variability in pupil performance *within* each administration than *between* administrations. An ideal criterion-referenced measure would actually register zero variability among pupils on the pre- and posttests and maximum variability between the two administrations. In other words, all the pupils would answer all the items incorrectly on the pretest and correctly on the posttest. The truly effective teacher should be able to reduce variability in achievement among pupils by obtaining approximately 100-percent mastery of the specified objectives for each pupil taught. A criterion-referenced test shows the teacher's success in achieving this goal by indicating the number of pupils who have mastered the material taught. A norm-referenced test, on the other hand, by presenting content far more comprehensive than that taught during a brief period in the classroom, intentionally prevents all pupils from obtaining 100-percent mastery and thereby may show increased rather than reduced variability in pupil performance.

A criterion-referenced test, then, measures the outcomes of specific teaching processes better than a norm-referenced test. In fact, the latter may measure behaviors far beyond those taught by or even of interest to a particular teacher and, therefore, when used to appraise performance, may penalize the teacher for not teaching what was never intended to be taught.

Guideline 2: Both Process and Product Behaviors Should Be Measured

"Process" measures assess teacher performance, while "product" measures assess pupil change. Though pupil outcome can be unstable and difficult to measure, it nevertheless must stand as one index of teacher effectiveness.

Both process and product measures must be included in an appraisal system in order to validate the teacher behaviors and skills assumed to be associated with teaching effectiveness. These behaviors and skills are initially selected on a tentative basis. Thus, the appraiser has a commitment to examine their validity in predicting meaningful pupil change in the classroom. Relatively few of the many behaviors already studied demonstrate such validity. This situation often forces the appraiser to depend on guesses or hunches in selecting additional teaching behaviors for inclusion in the appraisal system. These intuitive choices, however, can be validated by determining the extent to which they actually cause or predict specific pupil outcomes.

The validation process incorporates at least three stages: (a) the development of procedures for describing teaching in a quantitative manner, i.e., the translation of behaviors into variables; (b) correlational studies relating these variables to measures of pupil growth; and (c) experimental studies testing the variables derived from correlational studies to determine if they are causative agents of pupil change, i.e., the translation of variables into competencies and the validation of levels of proficiency.

Translating Behaviors into Variables. As noted above, research has yielded relatively few variables on which to base a teacher appraisal system. The appraiser selects teacher behaviors intuitively and continually evaluates the efficacy of these selections by relating them to pupil outcomes. As indicated in Chapter 3, diagnostic and formative objectives of appraisal include the identification of behaviors and skills on which the appraisal system will focus. To meet these initial objectives, a table of specifications is constructed, listing behaviors that will serve as the target of formative assessments. The selection of these target behaviors and skills is guided by previous research, relevant professional experience, and community and professional values.

Correlational Studies. After the initial identification and description of the teaching behaviors to be evaluated, the appraisal system establishes relationships between these behaviors and a wide variety of pupil outcomes. This correlational stage constitutes the second evaluative function of appraisal. Here, however, the emphasis is on quantitative relationships between pupil outcome and those teacher behaviors identified from research, professional experience, and community values. While teacher behaviors can be selected and measured simply because they appear "valid," evidence of a relationship between these behaviors and desirable pupil change provides the only acceptable rationale for their permanent inclusion in the appraisal system.

Experimental Studies. The final validation of the appraisal system involves experimental procedures to test the causality of relationships identified by the correlational studies described above. Though a pupil outcome may be associated with a specific teacher behavior, it is not necessarily *caused* by that behavior. Only when a teacher behavior actually causes a desired pupil outcome should training experiences designed to promote that behavior be recommended to the teacher.

The appraisal system tests the causative power of immediate (Stage 2) and intermediate (Stage 3) process variables by conducting experimental studies that compare the pupil outcomes engendered by teachers who are proficient in a given behavior to those produced by teachers less proficient in that behavior. As noted in Chapter 1, experimental research assigns teachers with observably different behavior to separate categories for observation and analysis. This approach randomly assigns pupils to teachers of differing types and thereby provides a basis for comparing two or more competing styles of teaching behavior. When causal relationships are identified, significant effort can then be expended in developing training programs and materials to teach the more effective behaviors.

The identification of these causal relationships, however, requires the assessment of pupil outcome. Therefore, *both* process and product measures of teaching effectiveness are essential to each of these three stages of validation and should be made available to researchers who wish to do this analytic work.

Guideline 3: Performance Measured Should Match Objectives Planned

Teacher and pupil performance measures that are unrelated or only tangentially related to the teacher's instructional goals and objectives are virtually worthless for appraisal. Yet, it is not uncommon to find the behaviors and skills selected for appraisal incongruent with the objectives of the teacher.

To maximize the probability of congruence, a simple sequence of events can be followed. This sequence involves the following process: (a) determining the educational goals of teachers, administrators, and the community; (b) selecting teacher behaviors attainable through professional development programs related to these goals; and (c) logically relating these behaviors to affective and cognitive pupil outcomes. The instructional goals of teachers and others are used to select the teaching behaviors to be measured and, in turn, these teaching behaviors are used as a basis for extracting desired pupil outcomes. A comparison of pupil outcomes and instructional goals serves as a logical check on the appropriateness of the assessment tools and related outcome behaviors used in the teacher appraisal study. While pupil outcomes may sometimes be implied in the instructional goals, more often they must be extracted from the teacher behaviors and skills themselves. This process is illustrated in Fig. 4.2. If pupil outcomes are selected for appraisal in this manner, the performance measured should reflect the objectives planned.

Guideline 4: Objectives Planned Should Match Objectives Taught

Even when instructional objectives are congruent with appraisal criteria, factors outside the teacher's control can disrupt planned instruction. The appraisal system must take into account such factors as extreme ability differences among the pupils in a class, the teacher's unfamiliarity with new materials, unexpected curriculum changes requested by department heads, and interruptions for non-academic activities (sporting events, pep rallies, and classroom visitors), all of which may alter planned instruction and thereby deprive the teacher of opportunities to perform the behaviors to be observed.

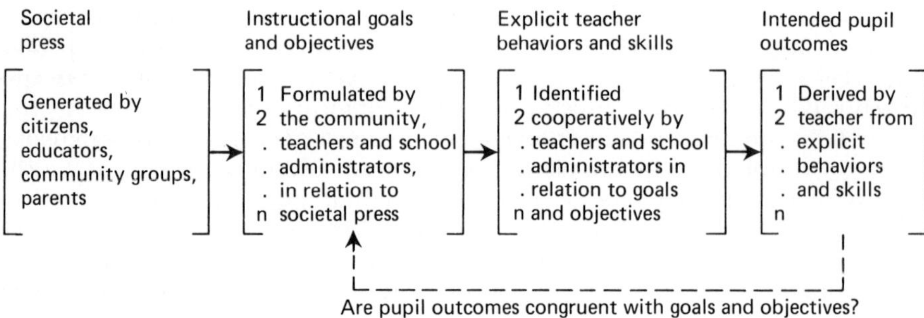

Fig. 4.2. A model for matching teaching behaviors and skills with selected pupil outcomes for the appraisal process.

To determine whether planned content was actually taught, the appraisal system must embody a method of monitoring the congruence between instructional activities and appraisal criteria during the assessment period. Throughout the immediate stage of appraisal in particular, data can be collected to determine if practical constraints have prevented adequate instruction in relation to predetermined objectives. This may be accomplished by: (1) giving a list of objectives organized by various content areas to *teachers,* who then check those they feel have been taught, and (2) giving a list of content areas arranged according to concepts and principles to *pupils,* who then check those areas they perceive have been taught. If both teacher and pupil checklists indicate that particular content was not covered, data collected relevant to that content should be eliminated from the appraisal or left uninterpreted. If a large proportion of students (but not the teacher) agree that certain material was not covered, that material should be ignored or interpreted cautiously, though the teacher should be notified of the discrepancy. In this case, pupils' perceptions may help identify content areas needing greater emphasis or clarification.

Guideline 5: Short Appraisal Periods Are Preferable to Long Appraisal Periods

Teacher-effectiveness research suggests that the length of an appraisal period may be as short as a single lesson or as long as a full year of instruction. While both extremes are possible, a short appraisal period incorporating a series of interrelated lessons, commonly referred to as a teaching unit, is preferable. Long appraisal periods may be appropriate when higher-order objectives (those, for example, requiring the pupil to analyze, synthesize, and evaluate content) are taught.

A factor favoring shorter appraisal periods is the tendency of events outside of the classroom to interfere with the teacher's instructional plans. When appraisal covers a relatively brief span of time, considerations such as the pupil's home life, the instructional experiences encountered outside of school (via the library, television, and peer-groups), and the effect of holidays and vacations are less likely to influence student performance. A relatively brief assessment period, linked to a specific area of instruction, reduces the chances that potent external forces will interact with the behaviors and skills being measured.

Shorter appraisal periods, though, require multiple assessments obtained at systematic intervals throughout the school year, for single assessments, while minimizing the influence of external factors on pupil performance, increase the chances of measuring *atypical* teacher behaviors. These assessments can be planned randomly to obtain a general "picture" of teacher behavior or systematically to capture behaviors or skills associated with particular content areas and teaching objectives.

Guideline 6: Adjusted Gain Rather Than Raw Gain Should Be Used for the Analysis of Pupil Growth

The term raw gain refers to the difference between a pupil's pre- and posttest score, while the term adjusted gain refers to a considerably more complex score derived from several intermediate calculations. Although raw-gain—or difference—scores are sometimes used to assess pupil change, adjusted gain is preferable. Raw-gain scores suffer from several critical deficiencies which render them virtually uninterpretable.

Two of these deficiencies are unreliability and susceptibility to distortion by the regression effect. The regression effect refers to the tendency of scores that deviate considerably from the mean to approximate, or lean toward, the mean on subsequent assessments. This phenomenon affects the measurement of pupil change when a student's pretest score is subtracted from the posttest score in order to obtain a "difference score." Those pupils scoring high on the pretest tend to score lower on the posttest, and vice versa, *regardless* of the average gain or loss registered for the entire class. This regression effect is particularly distressing since it operates unequally on pupils. That is, one pupil's posttest score may be affected by the pretest score to a greater degree than another pupil's posttest score. This differential effect of the pretest upon the posttest distorts any meaning the raw-gain score might have for determining pupil change.

To correct for this distortion, residual gain or a *conceptually* similar technique, analysis of covariance, is used. Residual gain is computed by correlating the pre- and posttest scores of all pupils, predicting a posttest score for each pupil on the basis of his or her pretest score, and subtracting this from the pupil's actual posttest score. This procedure creates a measure of gain which is independent of the pupil's initial standing and therefore more representative of the true change that has occurred during the appraisal period. Analysis of covariance, which statistically holds constant the effect of pretest scores, can be used to correct for this distortion in a somewhat more efficient manner.*

The raw-gain score, besides being subject to distortion caused by the regression effect, is also notoriously unreliable. The use of two scores (pre- and posttest) in calculating raw gain assumes that any difference between the two is due to the effect of intervening instruction. This procedure also assumes that any gain from pre- to posttest indicates pupil improvement. What the appraiser often overlooks is the fact that the new gain score is derived from two measures that are less than totally reliable. The raw-gain score inherits unreliability from both the pre- and the posttest and is therefore considerably *less* reliable than either of the sources from which it is derived. For example, if the correlation between pre- and posttest is .70 and the reliability of each is .80 (coefficients that in practice are fairly common), then the reliability of the gain score would be .33. Clearly, raw-gain scores are not sufficiently reliable to serve as indices of pupil change. Residual gain, in spite of its imprecision, and analysis of covariance are more appropriate procedures for this purpose.†

THE ANALYSIS AND REPORTING OF DATA

Data describing the teacher's progress in attaining the behaviors and skills identified in the table of specifications can be reported as: (a) raw and derived scores, i.e., frequencies, percentages, and measures of variation and central ten-

---

* Residual gain, unfortunately, is not an entirely satisfactory correction for the regression effect. It requires adjustment, depending on the extremeness of pretest scores. A gain score is increased if the pretest score is high and decreased if it is low. In other words, pupils who score high on the pretest have points added to their posttests (because the regression effect has artificially pushed their posttest scores down, toward the mean), and pupils who score low on the pretest have points subtracted from their posttest (because the regression effect has artificially pushed their posttest scores up, toward the mean). Since the amount of adjustment depends on the position of the pretest score in relation to the mean, it varies from pupil to pupil. Unfortunately, the adjustment also depends on the characteristics of the pupils being tested, and this information is generally unavailable.

While residual gain scores and analysis of covariance are repeatedly discussed in the literature as "parallel" techniques, they, in fact, are not. These different computational procedures are not mathematically equivalent and, therefore, can, in any given appraisal, lead to quite different results. Generally, analysis of covariance is the preferred technique since its power to detect a significant finding, when one is present, exceeds that of the residual gain procedure. Hence, I refer to these techniques as *conceptually* similar because they both offer methods of dealing with pretest performance.

† For a more thorough discussion of residual gain and covariance procedures, see A. Porter and T. Chibucos, "Selecting Analysis Strategies," in G. Borich (ed.), *Evaluating Educational Programs and Products* (Englewood Cliffs, N.J.: Educational Technology Publications, 1974) and G. Borich, "Sources of Invalidity in Measuring Classroom Behavior," *Instructional Science* 5 (1976).

dency; (b) computerized normative scales derived from a single appraisal; (c) continuous profiles derived from multiple appraisals; and (d) verbal feedback provided through interviews and conferences.

Reporting Data as Raw and Derived Scores

Reducing the data to their simplest form for direct interpretation by the teacher is the easiest, and often most useful, reporting technique. The appraiser may, for example, record the presence or absence, the frequency, the percentage of occurrence, the average occurrence, and the variability (both within and across appraisal periods) of specific behaviors and skills. Depending on the way in which they have been recorded, these raw data may be reported in one of two formats.

When the presence or absence of behaviors and skills has been recorded, the appraiser can use a timeline to report the level of attainment of each competency on the table of specifications. Recall that competencies can be attained at three levels: knowledge (cognitive understandings); performance (teacher behaviors); and consequence (pupil behaviors). Data collected in the immediate, intermediate, and product stages of appraisal on each behavior in the table of specifications can be compared to minimum levels of proficiency expected for *knowledge, performance,* and *consequence* competencies.

A record of this progress can take the form of that presented in Table 4.2. This timeline indicates a hypothetical rate of attainment for each of three types of competencies. Charts like this facilitate revision of the professional development program by revealing areas in which further training is needed. They also provide the teacher with a baseline to which he or she may compare subsequent performance assessments or standards established collectively by teachers and school district personnel.

Table 4.2. A cumulative chart showing date of attainment of knowledge, performance, and consequence competencies.

Competency areas	*Behaviors and skills*	*Showed knowledge of behavior or skill*	*Observed performing behavior or skill*	*Obtained desired (pupil) consequence as a result of using behavior or skill*
Questioning skills	1	• 9/7 ———	• 11/8	•
Modeling behavior	2	• 9/16 ———	• 10/21 ———	• 1/2
Reinforcement techniques	3	•	•	•
Individualization procedures	4	• 10/28 ———	• 10/14	•
	•			
	•			
	•			
	n	•	•	•

If frequency, percentage, and variability data have been collected, the occurrence of selected behaviors during the immediate stage of appraisal can be revealed in a more detailed manner. A two-part table can be used to report these data for a given appraisal period as well as previous appraisal periods. These data are divided into six categories, two pertaining to the most recent appraisal period and four pertaining to all previous appraisal periods. The categories, depicted in Table 4.3, are from left to right: (a) the frequency of a behavior observed during the most recent appraisal; (b) the percentage of time this behavior was observed during the most recent appraisal (relative to its possible occurrence or to the occurrence of some other behavior); (c) the frequency of the behavior observed during all previous appraisals; (d) the percentage of time this behavior was observed during all previous appraisals; (e) the average frequency of the behavior over all preceding appraisals; and (f) the variability in observed frequencies across all preceding appraisals, i.e., the standard deviation of the mean frequency. Used as a whole, this table allows the teacher to compare performance measured during the most recent appraisal period with past performance, with self-imposed standards, or with standards set collectively by teachers and school district personnel.

Table 4.3. Selected teacher data for the ___th appraisal period based on ___ minutes of observation

Behavior or skill observed	*Frequency observed during most recent appraisal*	*Percent observed out of total or a selected subset of behaviors during most recent appraisal*	*Cumulative frequency over all previous appraisal periods*	*Cumulative percent over all previous appraisal periods*	*Mean frequency*	*Variation in frequency (standard deviation)*
1						
2						
•						
•						
•						
n						

Reporting Data as Normative Scales

Data can also be reported as normative feedback, which allows the teacher to compare his or her performance with that of others who have been appraised. Normative scales apply primarily to summative data collected during the intermediate stage of appraisal. These data are recorded along a continuum of behavior, e.g., with a five-, seven-, or nine-point scale. The following scale, for example, might be completed over a series of observations for each teacher in a particular school district.

Number of times pupils are criticized exceeds number of times pupils are reinforced.	_ _ _ _ N _Y_ _	Number of times pupils are reinforced exceeds number of times pupils are criticized.

The "Y" above the line represents the teacher's rating, and the "N" below the line the mean for all teachers similarly appraised. Ideally, such a scale is based upon a number of observations relevant to the behavior in question, with the rating representing an average of these observations. When normative feedback is computerized, diagnostic statements can be provided, indicating the extent to which the individual teacher's score differs from the group mean. These differences can be reported as percentiles or standard deviations.

The normative approach requires considerable consensus about the desirability of the behaviors being measured and the standards by which they are scored. Accordingly, such scales are inappropriate for rating behaviors that are not clearly considered either desirable or undesirable. The scale above, for example, would be unsuitable if the ratio of criticism to reinforcement were not of interest to a particular teacher or if the instructional context from which the scale was derived were dissimilar to that of the teacher being appraised. The normative technique provides teachers with a picture of their status in reference to a specified group of peers. If the appraised teacher shares behavioral objectives and important contextual characteristics with this specified group of peers, the normative feedback is likely to become an important adjunct to other appraisal data.

Reporting Data as Continuous Profiles

By combining the intrapersonal data on the table of frequencies and percentages and the interpersonal comparisons supplied by normative feedback, the appraisal system can provide a continuous profile of teaching behaviors and skills. The continuous profile allows the appraiser to summarize teacher performance in a number of areas and to illustrate the teacher's precise rate of improvement across appraisal periods for each behavior or skill. It provides a graphic indication of the proficiency level attained by a particular teacher as well as a basis for comparing this level with the performance of various subgroups of teachers. For example, profiles can be constructed which compare a teacher's performance on selected behaviors and skills with: (a) that of other teachers in the school district who are at a similar stage in their professional development program; (b) the average performance of teachers who are at a more advanced stage in their professional development program; (c) the average performance of all teachers who have been appraised; and (d) an ideal performance profile representing standards of proficiency suggested by the school district or training institution. A continuous profile of this type is pictured in Fig. 4.3.

Continuous profiles can also be used to conduct applied research on the effectiveness of recommended instructional resources and training experiences by illustrating the relationship between the resource or training and the teacher behavior being measured. Unless a similar relationship emerges for each teacher receiving training, the appraisal system is compelled to identify those specific variables that distinguish the teachers who have benefited from training from those who have not. If a training exercise can successfully strengthen a particular behavior in nine teachers but not in a tenth, the appraisal system should attempt to identify the behavioral characteristics that distinguish the tenth teacher from the other nine. When these characteristics are identified, the appraisal system can systematically alter the training experience until the effect is established for the tenth teacher or assign alternative training resources more suited to the characteristics and needs of the tenth teacher.

Continuous-profile data permit several kinds of analyses: (a) the magnitude of any teacher's score in relation to the magnitude of a previous score can be determined; (b) data describing the teacher's performance under different training conditions or during different appraisal periods can be recorded; (c) a trend line or slope indicating the rate at which a teacher is reaching proficiency can be drawn; (d) the trend lines of teachers known to have different background variables and characteristics can be compared; and (e) changes in each teacher's trend line from one appraisal period to the next can be observed and attributed to the presence or absence of specific training experiences.

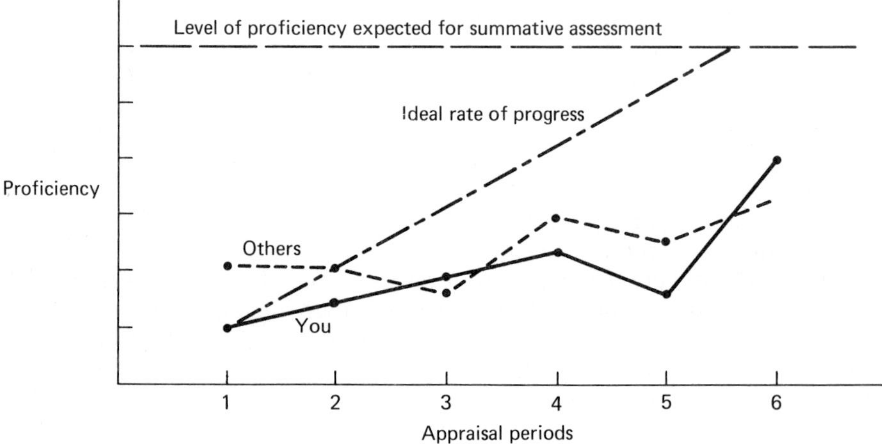

Fig. 4.3. A continuous profile based on a teacher's performance, the performance of other teachers, and an ideal rate of progress for the same behavior or skill measured across appraisal periods.

The value of this approach in studying the effect of professional development programs is its focus on individual rather than group performance. Differences among teachers are clearly described. Once a significant difference appears among teacher profiles, the appraiser can seek out the particular background variables or characteristics which caused the difference. An evaluation based on a detailed analysis of every case, with each teacher serving as his or her own control, allows the appraiser to relate significant findings to the individuals rather than the group, for whom homogeneity is only assumed. At the same time, such an evaluation allows the teacher to continuously compare present with past performance and rate of attainment with that of selected subgroups of teachers. These subgroups can be selected according to training, experience, or subject-matter and grade-level specialization. The individual teacher can often best judge which groups are most appropriate for comparison.

Reporting Data through Interviews and Conferences

Appraisal data can also be reported to the teacher through interviews and conferences. This approach is best used after descriptive reports have already been given to the teacher, since the interview or conference can then be devoted to interpreting or applying the data provided in these reports. Interviews are used to identify particular background variables and characteristics which might, in part, account for a teacher's performance—e.g., to explain sharp increases or decreases in proficiency from one stage of appraisal to another. Conferences, on the other hand, are used to clarify and interpret graphic or computerized feedback or to redesign or refocus the teacher's professional development program. Computer printouts and graphic profiles often fail to convey the primary objective of the appraisal system, i.e., the formulation and continual evaluation of a professional development program for the teacher. Consequently, interviews and conferences are helpful in discussing and interpreting the often sterile statistics characterizing other reporting methods. Both can reduce the threat that even the best appraisal system may unintentionally represent to the teacher. Therefore, they should be conducted in a cooperative manner that encourages the teacher to actively participate in interpreting and evaluating the appraisal data. A careful analysis of these data can help to formulate a professional development program specifying the instructional resources and training experiences appropriate for the next appraisal period.

We now turn to one final topic: the development of a valid appraisal system.

Chapter 5

Developing a Valid Appraisal System

The development of a valid appraisal system should comprise four stages: (a) the identification of an underlying philosophy, or *metatheory,* to guide the development process; (b) the selection or construction of *theories* based on this philosophy, which describe relationships between teacher behaviors and pupil outcomes; (c) the design of a prototypic *model,* which incorporates selected theories to form a sequential picture of the attainment of specific behaviors; and (d) the trial and revision of one or more portions, or *examples,* of the appraisal model to test its validity. This chapter describes the overall development and validation of an appraisal system in terms of these four stages.

USING METATHEORIES, THEORIES, MODELS, AND EXAMPLES IN THE DESIGN AND VALIDATION OF AN APPRAISAL SYSTEM

The four stages identified above describe the general sequence of events which should precede the implementation of an appraisal system. Since the outcome of each stage depends on that of preceding stages, decisions made at one point in the developmental sequence are validated before the next stage is reached. Intensive validation of each developmental component is approached through a series of research procedures that examine: (a) the validity and objectivity of the metatheory; (b) the validity of the system's theoretical predictions; (c) the validity of the sequence of teacher competencies implied by these predictions; and (d) the validity of examples or portions of the appraisal system as they are used in practice.

Examining the Validity of the Metatheory

Steps:

1. Identify internal, external, and contextual sources of influence.
2. Determine representativeness of each source of influence.
3. Weigh each source according to importance.
4. Construct an underlying philosophy of effective teaching, i.e., the metatheory.

A *metatheory* is a broad, overarching framework that specifies the rules by which a theory is formulated. In the appraisal of teaching, a metatheory provides the philosophical undergirding from which relevant behaviors, variables, and competencies are generated.

A metatheory, intentionally or unintentionally, reflects the values of the educational system. Appraisal systems may differentially value behavioral domains according to the metatheories that guide their development. The metatheory underlying an appraisal system represents the values and beliefs of parents, teachers, and educators and, therefore, determines the pattern of teacher behaviors and pupil outcomes to be evaluated.

Attempts to develop an appraisal system begin with the identification of cultural, social, and professional values that can be used to construct a philosophy of effective teaching for a given community or training institution. In any instructional environment, legitimate as well as illegitimate influences may affect the development of the appraisal system. Among the former are values of teachers, school administrators, and the community at large. Less-legitimate influences are pressures exerted by a minority of parents who believe teacher reemployment should be based solely on the cognitive achievement of their pupils, or by a small group of teacher trainers who emphasize a narrowly defined set of teacher behaviors. Minority opinions should be heard and considered, but their influence should not outweigh that of more representative community and institutional values.

The factors influencing the development of a metatheory may be described as *internal* (within the school and school system), *external* (within professional institutions, the state, and the nation), and *contextual* (within the immediate educational environment in which the appraisal system operates). These sources of influence are depicted in Fig. 5.1.

Internal Influences. Internal influences on the design of an appraisal system include the values and opinions expressed by teachers and administrators. Because these influences are most likely to produce explicit recommendations about the breadth of teacher behaviors to be measured, they are a valuable contribution to the development of the table of specifications. Questionnaires, interviews, and other polling devices can be used to determine which behaviors the instructional and administrative staff feel the appraisal system should measure and the purposes such measurement should serve.

External Influences. Sources outside of the school, such as state organizations, professional groups, curriculum specialists, teacher-effectiveness studies, and even congressional appropriations, national trends in teacher training, and the nationwide implementation of a particular curriculum, can also influence the philosophy of the appraisal system. Experience has shown that these external influences often promote recommendations that differ from those suggested by internal sources. Professional groups, for example, may feel that schools should perform functions which, though not contradictory to those espoused by local teachers and administrators, are nevertheless more expansive. These controversial functions often involve both curricular and extracurricular activities intended to produce both affective and cognitive pupil outcomes. The appraisal system's selection of teacher behaviors and pupil outcomes must, therefore, represent broad community concerns as well as more specific objectives tied directly to classroom instruction.

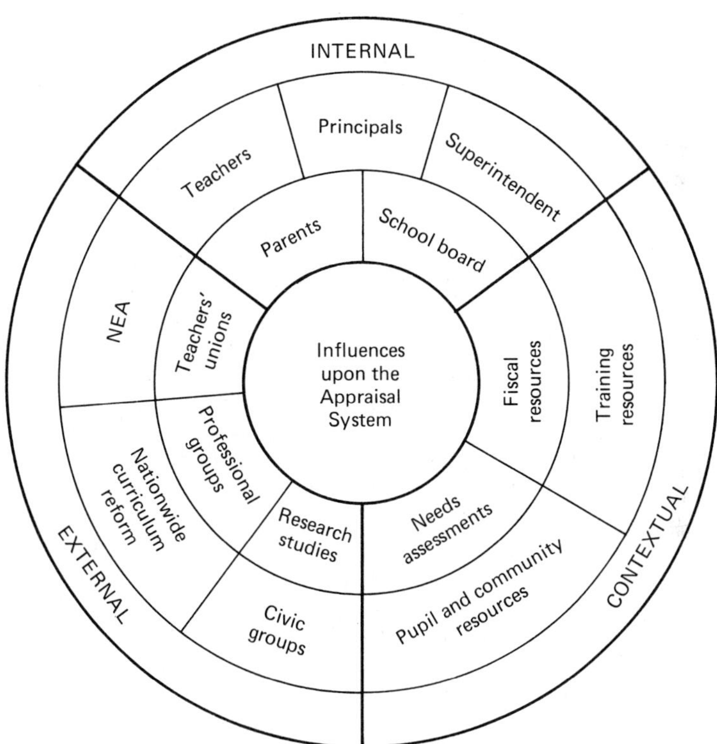

Fig. 5.1. Descriptive model of sources influencing the design of an appraisal system.

Contextual Influences. The appraisal system can also be affected by *contextual* influences. These include local needs assessments, pupil characteristics, and available training resources, all of which may demand the inclusion (or exclusion) of specific teacher behaviors in the appraisal system. Contextual influences generally serve to make the appraisal system congruent with local conditions and needs by promoting inclusion of those teacher behaviors and skills most directly linked to available training resources and the characteristics of the ongoing instructional environment.

All three sources of influence, internal, external, and contextual, play an important role in establishing the metatheory, which underlies and guides the further development of the appraisal system. Each source is therefore critically examined in order to determine the legitimacy of its influence in relation to that of all other sources, the values implied by the behaviors and skills it promotes, and the consequences of measuring those behaviors and skills.

Examining the Validity of Theoretical Predictions Implicit in the Appraisal System

Steps:

1. Search research literature for significant relationships between teacher behaviors and pupil outcomes.
2. Select promising behaviors and skills.
3. Arrange behaviors and skills in terms of antecedent, intervening, and terminal constructs, i.e., build a nomological network.
4. Test validity of hypothesized relationships in the network.

A *theory* is a schema for interrelating a set of conceptual or descriptive constructs. In simplest terms, it is a symbolic construction designed to bring facts, concepts, or variables into systematic connection. These facts, concepts, or variables are then used to make predictions about behavioral events.

Theories are employed in this second stage of system development to suggest relationships among teacher behaviors or between teacher behaviors and pupil outcomes. The selection of teacher behaviors to be appraised is often made on the assumption that these suggested relationships are causal. For example, an appraisal system may choose to measure intrapersonal teacher variables, such as self-confidence and anxiety, on the assumption that these constructs affect interpersonal behaviors (the teacher's interactions with the child), and that these interpersonal behaviors, in turn, affect pupil outcomes. The validity of such an assumption determines the effectiveness of the appraisal system. Therefore, the behaviors and skills selected for the appraisal are revised periodically according to the extent to which theoretical relationships between variables are empirically supported.

The validity of these assumed relationships is determined by correlating teacher and pupil variables selected for appraisal and then subjecting those found to be related to experimental study in order to determine whether or not the relationships are causal.* This process is simplified by the creation of

* It is important to note the danger of searching for significant relationships by correlating many teacher behavior variables with many pupil outcome variables in

a nomological network of the type pictured in Fig. 5.2 in which behaviors assumed to be antecedent, intervening, or terminal in relation to others are schematically linked according to theoretical predictions. The developer uses this network of relationships to revise and refine the appraisal system.

A nomological network is used to substantiate the effects of the teacher's behaviors (*B* through *I* in Fig. 5.2) on pupil outcomes (*A*). Correlations define relationships between antecedent and intervening teacher variables, on the one hand, and between intervening teacher variables and pupil outcomes, on the other hand. In the network depicted, relationships stronger than those expected by chance are hypothesized between antecedent, intervening, and pupil variables according to the theory upon which this particular appraisal subsystem was based.

Nomological networks are also used to verify predicted or poorly defined behaviors. A nomological network can, for example, confirm effects upon a terminal behavior (e.g., construct *A* in Fig. 5.2) by enabling the developer to retrace the path (moving from construct *A* to *B* to *F*) which led to that behavior. In this case a relationship can be confirmed by simply defining it in terms of its known antecedents (*B* and *F*). However, if one wishes to extend and verify the definition of, say, *B*, this can be done by discovering new paths to *F* via other constructs (e.g., *D* and *G*). The original link to pupil achievement (*A*) becomes less tenuous when relationships expand the network of hypothesized causal agents and at the same time more precisely define variables by associating them with other, known constructs.

The analytical activities described above provide an important transition from the evaluation of metatheoretical influences to the examination of model development. Validating relationships among the behaviors selected for appraisal serves two important functions. First, the information obtained from the nomological network can be used to revise the initial selection of variables prior to the development of an appraisal model, to reject untenable theories, and to construct new, more pragmatic ones.

The same information can also be used to further define antecedent behaviors, which then may be examined and linked to other variables in the nomological network. As noted above, retracing the direct and indirect connections between antecedent and intervening behaviors allows the developer to more concretely define and confirm the importance of the teaching skills and behaviors included in the appraisal theories. The outcome of this process aids in designing instructional resources and training experiences intended to teach the antecedent and intervening skills and behaviors.

---

the absence of *a priori* rationale. One should have sound theoretical or intuitive reasons for expecting certain relationships between teacher behaviors and pupil outcomes to be significant. In any large, indiscriminate matrix of correlations, some relationships will, by chance alone, appear significant when they, in fact, are not. Even in the correlational stage of validation, then, there is no substitute for selecting, prior to analysis, the specific relationships to be studied on the basis of theoretical predictions.

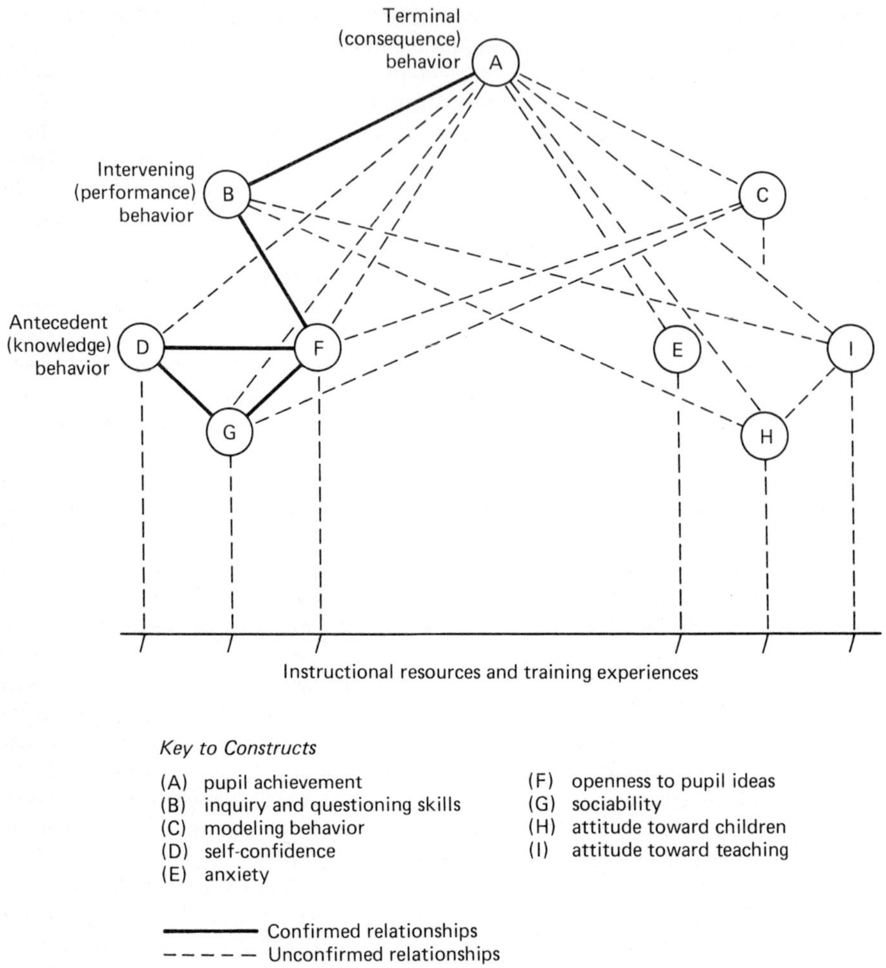

Terminal
(consequence)
behavior
A
Intervening
(performance)
behavior
B
C
Antecedent
(knowledge)
behavior
D
F
E
I
G
H
Instructional resources and training experiences
Key to Constructs
(A) pupil achievement
(B) inquiry and questioning skills
(C) modeling behavior
(D) self-confidence
(E) anxiety
(F) openness to pupil ideas
(G) sociability
(H) attitude toward children
(I) attitude toward teaching
Confirmed relationships
Unconfirmed relationships

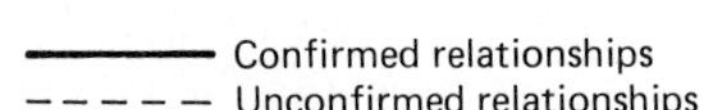

Fig. 5.2. Example of a hypothesized nomological network of behaviors for an appraisal subsystem.

Examining the Validity of the Appraisal Model

Steps:

1. Sequentially order teaching behaviors and skills.
2. Construct a taxonomy or hierarchy of behaviors and skills.
3. Develop individual teacher profiles of competency attainment.
4. Plan instructional resources and training experiences to match profiles.

After the theoretical relationships among variables have been analyzed and confirmed, a prototypic *model* of the appraisal system can be constructed and validated. The model incorporates all previous work at the metatheoretical and theoretical stages of development, thus providing an inclusive, up-to-date "picture" of the appraisal system. The model, therefore, combines the conceptual and descriptive parts of the appraisal process into a single, coherent whole, which serves as the basis for subsequent field testing and evaluation conducted to validate the entire system.

The model is a master plan for the appraisal system, indicating the final selection of teacher and pupil variables and specifying the desired sequence in which teacher behaviors and skills are to be attained and measured. According to theoretical predictions from the nomological network, selected behaviors are arranged in a taxonomy, or hierarchy, which indicates those considered prerequisite to the more crucial and complex skills measured at later stages in the appraisal process. This hierarchy is used to order the teacher's professional development program in such a way that instructional resources and training experiences are provided first for those behaviors at the lowest levels of the taxonomy. The sequential ordering of teacher behaviors and skills implies that those at lower levels of the hierarchy must be attained before those at higher levels become the subject of either training or appraisal. This pattern of attainment and its corresponding training requirements can be depicted in terms of proficiency levels expected of the teacher in his or her professional development sequence, as shown in Fig. 5.3.

Three behavioral domains—antecedent, intervening, and terminal—are represented in sections A and B of Fig. 5.3. A series of training components and related behaviors corresponds to each of these domains. Completion of a specific training activity and the attainment of the corresponding behavior is indicated by a plus sign, while nonattainment is shown by a minus sign. Sections A and B represent the performance of two different teachers, one of whom (B) has reached criterion performance at the product (pupil) level of assessment, and one of whom has not. It is clear that level-4 behaviors represent a stumbling block to teacher A, since no behaviors at or beyond this level have been acquired. The failure of teacher A to attain the criterion behavior does not necessarily indicate that the sequence of training components is unreasonable. Instead teacher A might simply require additional instruction, perhaps in smaller units, between levels 3 and 4. However, teacher B's pattern of attainment clearly indicates errors in the sequential arrangement of antecedent and intervening behaviors leading to the terminal behavior. Although teacher B achieved the terminal behavior, he did so without attaining any behaviors at levels 3 and 4. He achieved the terminal objective of the professional development program without acquiring all of the behaviors *assumed to be prerequisite to it.* Teacher B's pattern of achievement indicates a need to reconceptualize the training and assessment sequence, particularly with regard to levels 3 and 4.

Schematizations such as these represent the descriptive development of an appraisal model while nomological networks of antecedent, intervening, and terminal behaviors illustrate its conceptual development. The two processes are closely related. Theories associating teaching behaviors with pupil outcomes

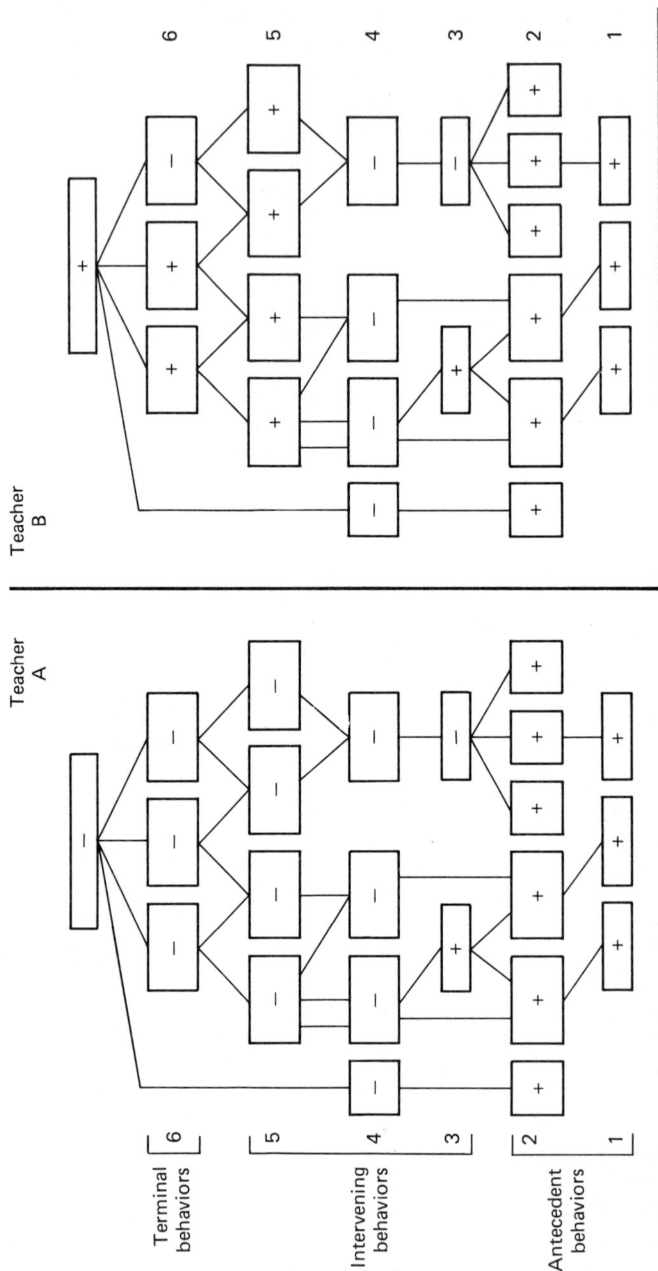

Fig. 5.3. Examples of the pattern of attainment of behaviors and skills for two teachers.

are conceptualized via nomological networks during the theoretical development phase. These relationships are then used to sequentially order behaviors and skills during the model-building stage. This sequential ordering, or hierarchy, of behaviors is in turn used to guide and record the teacher's pattern of attainment, which itself serves as a basis for revising theories or modifying training experiences. The continued failure of teachers to achieve certain proficiencies in the taxonomy should lead school personnel to question the sequential arrangement of behaviors or the theoretical predictions responsible for the selection of those behaviors.

Whether or not initial theories are altered, the cycle from theory development to sequential ordering of behaviors is an important step in building an appraisal system. This cycle provides a means of identifying areas in which instructional resources and training experiences need revision in order for the teacher to advance from one level of the taxonomy to another.

Examining the Validity of Examples of the Appraisal Process

Steps:

1. Select a subset of behaviors and skills for trial.
2. Select a related subset of instructional resources and training experiences.
3. Pilot test the subsystem.
4. Judge the efficiency and effectiveness of the subsystem for purposes stated and revise accordingly.

The final and most concrete element in the development and validation of a teacher appraisal system is the *example*. Examples, derived directly from models and indirectly from theories and metatheories, serve as a microcosm or subsystem of the appraisal process, which is used to test on a limited scale the cost and practicality of the system as a whole. Examples constitute short-term trials that test the feasibility of assessing selected behaviors and specify the techniques by which to measure these behaviors. If the metatheory, theories, and model are sound, the example is likely to be an effective demonstration of the system's potential for assessing teaching effectiveness. An example of the appraisal system need not represent every behavior in the model but may instead selectively focus on a few.

An example of the appraisal system is tested in three steps. The initial step involves data collection for the purposes of (a) validating the psychometric instruments to be employed by the appraisal system, and (b) determining the extent to which teachers actually use the training resources recommended. To achieve the first of these purposes, measurement devices are employed in one or two classrooms, with teachers typical of those to be appraised. Results are examined to insure that measurement procedures provide meaningful feedback to the teacher and yield data congruent with the table of specifications. Such an examination involves not only inspection of the data obtained, but also discussion with teachers, a review of the original design for the appraisal system, and an evaluation of the instruments' validity.

To achieve the second purpose—determining the extent to which teachers consult instructional resources and training experiences—data are systematically collected to indicate which training experiences are being used when a number of alternatives are available. Deviations from and substitutions for intended training are noted and used in revising the original set of training experiences proposed for the appraisal system.

The second step in evaluating the appraisal system involves pilot testing on a greater scale. A larger subset of behaviors and training experiences, including any revised as a result of the procedures described above, is tested in a number of schools on many different teachers. Here, the appraisal system's application across different pupil characteristics, school resources, and administrative personnel is determined. Variations in the system's performance and problems specific to particular instructional environments are noted for the purpose of revising or expanding the appraisal to make it more adaptable to diverse school contexts.

The final evaluation step is an extended field test of the completed appraisal system, covering a year or more. The purpose of this field test is to judge the longitudinal effectiveness of the system in increasing teacher proficiency across the complete list of behaviors measured and to assess long-term training experiences not adequately examined by earlier evaluation procedures. Field-test data are also used to supplement previously collected evaluative information in altering the theoretical basis of the appraisal system and rearranging the sequential order of the behaviors measured.

Three criteria are used in the field-test stage to evaluate the system: feasibility, effectiveness, and usability. The criterion of feasibility is concerned with questions of management, cost, and alternative measurement possibilities. Administrative efficiency and resource allocation are of primary importance here. The criterion of effectiveness is related to the accuracy of the entire appraisal model and the system's overall success in strengthening teacher performance within the school district or training institution. Finally, the usability criterion involves the system's flexibility and the extent of its application.

We now turn to the readings selected to illustrate and expand the appraisal concepts discussed thus far.

PART II

The Appraisal of Teaching: Selected Readings and Advanced Concepts

Chapter 6

Selected Readings: Toward Defining Teacher Competencies

The following selections describe the results of five large-scale teacher-effectiveness studies. These studies represent relatively recent projects which have employed large numbers of teachers across schools and, usually, school districts. The general intent of this research has been to find relationships between teacher behaviors and pupil outcomes, relationships which can then be submitted to experimental investigation in order to derive teacher competencies in the manner described in Chapter 1. The following selections were chosen for this volume because they represent the most recent efforts to define teacher-pupil relationships and the most sophisticated methodologies for conducting correlational studies of teacher effectiveness.

Before turning to these selections, however, it first will be helpful to study the results of other research efforts which have attempted to define relationships between teacher and pupil behaviors. Many early studies of teacher effectiveness were ably reviewed by Rosenshine and Furst (1971), who identified from all relevant research to that date, eleven teacher variables that have shown promising relationships to pupil gains in cognitive achievement. Five of these variables, the authors contend, have strong support from correlational studies, while six have less support but appear to warrant further study. The five teacher variables that have yielded the strongest relationships to pupil achievement and the number of studies supporting these variables are listed below:

1. *Clarity:* the cognitive clarity of a teacher's presentation (seven studies);
2. *Variability*: teacher's use of variety or variability during the lesson (eight studies);

3. *Enthusiasm:* teacher's vigor, power, involvement, excitement, or interest during classroom presentation (six studies);
4. *Task-oriented or businesslike behavior:* degree to which teacher is task-oriented, achievement-oriented, and/or businesslike (seven studies);
5. *Student opportunity to learn criterion material:* relationship between material covered in class and criterion pupil performance (four studies).

The six variables of secondary importance are:

6. *Use of student ideas and general indirectness:* acknowledging, modifying, applying, comparing, and summarizing students' statements (eight studies);
7. *Criticism*: criticizing or controlling the pupil, extent to which the teacher shows hostility, strong disapproval, or a need to justify authority (seventeen studies);
8. *Use of structuring comments:* the extent to which the teacher uses statements designed to provide an overview of or cognitive scaffolding for completed or planned lessons (four studies);
9. *Type of questions asked:* usually categorized as "lower cognitive" or "higher cognitive" (seven studies);
10. *Probing:* teacher responses that encourage the student (or another student) to elaborate upon his or her answer (three studies);
12. *Level of difficulty of instruction:* student perceptions of the difficulty of the instruction (four studies).

Rosenshine and Furst compare these "promising" variables to other variables that have not yet (as of 1971) shown significant or consistent relationships to pupil achievement. These "unpromising" variables, which also have been popular foci for research, are: nonverbal approval; praise; warmth; ratio of indirect to direct teacher behaviors; flexibility; ratio of teacher talk to student talk; student participation; number of teacher-student interactions; student absence; teacher absence; teacher time spent on class participation; teacher experience; and teacher knowledge of subject area.

The reader may use the studies presented in this chapter to amend Rosenshine and Furst's list of promising variables. A summary chart is provided at the conclusion of this introduction to assist the reader in relating these earlier findings to the more recent work presented in the following selections.

The first article in this chapter, by Brophy and Evertson, discusses the results of a four-year study to identify behaviors employed by teachers of known effectiveness. Brophy and Evertson's research is unique in that teachers were chosen not randomly but on the basis of previously established records of consistency in producing student gains on the Metropolitan Achievement Tests (MAT). Metropolitan Achievement Test scores for four consecutive years were obtained for pupils in the second and third grades. Teachers who had consistently produced student gains on the MAT were identified and selected for observation. As the authors point out, these teachers were particularly appropriate subjects for a process-product study designed to reveal the correlates of effective teaching as defined by the teachers' ability to produce learning gains.

The Brophy-Evertson research is also characterized by separate data analyses for low- and high-SES schools. This approach allowed the researchers to identify relationships between teacher behaviors and pupil outcomes which occurred in one type of school, but not the other. Differential findings such as these indicated that for some variables the kind of teaching associated with pupil gains in low-SES schools is quite different from that associated with gains in high-SES schools. The Brophy-Evertson research provides new data on the Rosenshine and Furst variables as well as information on variables untouched by Rosenshine and Furst.

In the second selection in this chapter, Soar presents parallel results of four studies with similar research designs. These results suggest that relationships between teacher behaviors and pupil outcomes may not be linear. That is, a given teacher behavior may benefit the pupil up to a certain point, beyond which continued use of that behavior may actually reduce pupil learning.

Soar's method of data analysis allowed discovery of differential outcomes, i.e., curvilinear relationships and teacher behavior by teaching objective interactions. And Soar did in fact find different outcomes associated with highly structured versus relatively unstructured teacher activities. According to his research, less-structured activities are more appropriate for teaching abstractions and generalizations, and more tightly structured activities for concrete learnings—knowledge and comprehension objectives, for instance, as opposed to higher-order objectives that call for analysis, synthesis, and evaluation. The reader should note the relationship between Soar's findings and those reported by Rosenshine and Furst and Brophy and Evertson.

The third selection, by Stallings, uses Project Follow Through classroom observation data to examine relationships between instructional processes and child outcomes. This rich source of geographically diverse data provides an abundance of information from which to study process-product relationships. The author, who amply mined these data, reports interrelationships among twenty-six instructional variables and multiple pupil behaviors, including pupil-process variables (independence, task persistence, cooperation, and child questions) and pupil-product variables (problem-solving ability and cognitive achievement in reading and math). By holding pupil achievement constant, Stallings was able to determine relationships between instructional variables and pupil outcomes unaffected by differences in the pupils' prior learning.

The importance of the Stallings research lies primarily in the richness and the diversity of the instructional variables measured—including traditionally investigated as well as heretofore unexplored behaviors. Among the latter are instructional-process, as opposed to teacher-process, variables (e.g., use of instructional materials, audio-visual equipment, and exploratory materials). The richness of these data is due primarily to the observation instrument used, an instrument constructed especially for this study and designed to record the intensity, quality, and complexity of classroom instruction.

The fourth selection in this chapter is a summary comment by Rosenshine, which attempts to interrelate the findings of Brophy and Evertson, Soar, and Stallings. Rosenshine notes that the studies of Brophy and Evertson, Soar, and Stallings utilize the same achievement criteria on similar subjects: primary-grade reading and math among low-SES children. Focusing on eleven variables measured by all three studies, he finds a reasonable amount of congruence among the three sets of findings, and offers useful generalizations about effective teaching in that particular context. A similar attempt to relate variables across all of the selections in this chapter appears at the conclusion of this introduction.

The fifth article, by Good and Grouws, resembles the Brophy and Evertson research; both sets of authors divide teachers into "more effective" and "less effective" categories according to pupil achievement gains. While Brophy and Evertson base this division on Metropolitan Achievement Test scores, Good and Grouws use pupil gain on the Iowa Test of Basic Skills. They correlate teacher behaviors and pupil test scores to indicate: first, differential pupil performance associated with the nine teachers considered most effective and the nine considered least effective; and, second, the extent to which teacher competence interacts with student achievement (i.e., the degree to which different teachers have different effects upon high-, low-, and middle-achieving pupils).

Good and Grouws conclude from these data that no single method is used by effective teachers to produce pupil gain, and that no single group of students benefits most from contact with more effective teachers, or suffers most from contact with less effective teachers. It is interesting to compare the findings of Brophy and Evertson to those of Good and Grouws in regard to variables investigated by both. As is often the case when such comparisons are made, some findings replicate and others do not. In the main, however, Good and Grouws find a number of congruent patterns between their data and the Brophy and Evertson findings.

The final selection in this chapter, by McDonald, summarizes the results of Phase II of the California Beginning Teacher Evaluation Study. An important feature of this study is its long-term character. Correlational relationships between teacher-process variables and pupil-product variables are studied over consecutive years and then submitted to cause-and-effect validation via experimental studies. Phase II of the project consists of measuring pupil pre- and postperformance in reading and mathematics, systematically observing teachers' classroom performances during the intervening period, and relating these observations to the differential achievement of pupils.

McDonald's study utilizes the best methodological features of the four previous studies. First, McDonald eliminates the influence of teacher interventions on pupil performance by measuring achievement at the beginning and the end of the school year. Thus, pretest performance is controlled. Second, by statistically controlling the influence of pretest scores upon posttest performance, he removes the effect of socioeconomic status to the extent that it correlates with the pretest scores of pupils. Third, McDonald analyzes teachers by class and therefore permits examination of the differential effectiveness of individual teachers. He then uses a step-wise regression procedure to determine the contribution to pupil posttest performance of each teacher variable, separately and then in combination with other teacher variables. The results are complex, perhaps the most complex of the six studies presented. However, they warrant close attention since they indicate that *the method of organizing instruction* is a critical domain of teaching variables related to pupil outcomes.

McDonald's results also indicate that the most effective pattern of teacher behavior differs according to subject matter and grade level. This finding is somewhat similar to Soar's conclusion that teacher effectiveness can be determined in part by the complexity of the material being taught and the extent to which the teacher structures or focuses the instruction.

The reader should carefully consider McDonald's structural model depicting the variables that influence teacher performance and pupil learning. This model represents a causal theory similar to those discussed in Chapter 5 under the topic nomological networks, relating teacher variables (such as aptitudes, attitudes, knowledge of the subject matter or teaching methodology) and environmental variables (such as organizational climate of the school) to pupil learning.

Because the presentations in this chapter are excerpts of more comprehensive reports, Table 6.1 summarizes the contextual characteristics of each of the included research studies. The reader is encouraged to consult the original reports for answers to specific questions or for a more complete discussion of the issues presented.

Table 6.2, as previously indicated, attempts to interrelate findings involving variables studied in two or more of these investigations. It is important to note, however, that the process of summarizing and accumulating findings from different research studies is usually fraught with problems. In this case, grade level, subject matter, and the operational definitions of the variables investigated differ across studies. For this reason, the names given to variables by individual researchers have been used in place of a single generic variable subsuming related findings. We believe the reader will find that the value of such summaries in producing new hypotheses and fresh conceptualizations outstrips their inherent problems.

The papers that have been selected for this chapter deal with teacher competencies only to the degree to which they identify teacher behaviors and translate these behaviors into teacher variables. The important step of specifying optimal levels of proficiency for each teacher variable, as described in Chapter 1, is not the primary intention of the studies presented here. These research findings provide the reader with a promising foundation upon which to *begin* the process of translating teacher variables into desired levels of performance and confirming via experimental studies the efficacy of these performance levels.

Reference

Rosenshine, B., and N. Furst. "Research on Teacher Performance Criteria." In B. O. Smith, ed., *Research in Teacher Education: A Symposium*. Englewood Cliffs, N.J.: Prentice-Hall, 1971, pp. 37–55.

Table 6.1. Some contextual characteristics of the research reported in Chapter 6.

Researchers	*Grades*	*Content*	*Sample size*	*Sample selection method*	*Criterion measures**
Brophy-Evertson	2nd, 3rd	Reading, math	1st year: 17 (2nd); 14 (3rd) 2nd year: 15 (2nd); 13 (3rd)	Self-selected + consistency in producing learning gains over a four-year period	Residualized gain, MAT
Soar	1st, 3rd, 4th, 5th, 6th	Reading, math	Study 1: 55 (3rd-6th) Study 2: 20 (1st) Studies 3 & 4: 22 (1st); 59 (5th)	Self-selected	Residualized gain, ITBS, MRT, MAT
Stallings	1st, 3rd	Reading, math	105 (1st) 58 (3rd)	Self-selected	Raven's, MAT with WRAT as covariable, IAR, SRI observation instrument
Good-Grouws	4th	Math	41	Self-selected + top and bottom on residualized gains	Residualized gain, ITBS
McDonald	2nd, 5th	Reading, math	44 (2nd) 53 (5th)	Self-selected + three years experience	CAT as covariable

* Key to criterion measures: MAT = Metropolitan Achievement Test; ITBS = Iowa Test of Basic Skills; MRT = Metropolitan Readiness Test; WRAT = Wide Range Achievement Test; IAR = Intellectual Achievement Responsibility Scale; SRI = Stanford Research Institute; CAT = California Achievement Test.

Table 6.2. Selected congruent and discrepant findings for the research studies reported in Chapter 6.

Brophy-Evertson	*Soar*	*Stallings*	*Good-Grouws*	*McDonald*
Teacher responds to each question + L*		Provides information/ asks question (systematic instructional pattern) +		
Making sure student understands + L*				
		Use of small groups +	Teaching whole class +	Teaching whole class +
Specialized materials + L		Use of textbooks and workbooks +		Variety of instructional materials −
Praise after student answers opinion questions + L		Praise**	Praise −	
Student initiated praise − L				
Flexibility of rules +		Flexible classrooms +		
Controlling student responses + L, − H	Direction and control of learning ∩ ***			Time organizing instructional activity −
Teacher structuring and feedback − L	Unobtrusive structuring behavior − L, + H			
Interacting with individuals during group lessons +	Teacher-pupil interaction at high cognitive level −		Teacher afforded contact with students −	
Teacher affect + L, 0 H	Teacher affect + L, − H			
Keeping students actively engaged +				Maintaining task involvement −
			Time teaching whole class +	Content covered +
Student initiated questions +			Student initiated interaction +	
Clarity 0			Clarity +	
Getting groups' attention +			Alerting behavior +	

Table 6.2. (continued)

Brophy-Evertson	*Soar*	*Stallings*	*Good-Grouws*	*McDonald*
Giving student correct answer +			Process feedback −	
Responding to substance rather than form +				
Failure to give feedback −				

Note: + indicates positive relationship to pupil achievement, − indicates negative relationship, 0 indicates no relationship.

* L indicates finding for low-SES pupils only, H indicates finding for high-SES pupils only.

** The effect of praise on achievement in math in first grade was variable: in classrooms where children had relatively low entering ability, pupils profited more from a high rate of praise than they did in classrooms where students had higher entering ability.

*** Soar's inverted U, indicating a curvilinear relationship between direction and control of learning and pupil achievement.

JERE E. BROPHY and
CAROLYN M. EVERTSON
University of Texas at Austin

Teacher Behavior and Student Learning in Second and Third Grades

Process-product research in which the investigator observes classrooms and tries to relate process measures of teaching to product measures of student outcome appears to be the most direct way to identify successful teaching behaviors. However, until relatively recently, such research has failed to establish clear relationships between teaching behaviors and student outcome measures (Rosenshine and Furst, 1973; Dunkin and Biddle, 1974). The results from process-product research have been more promising recently, however, because of improvements in observational systems and in research designs. Yet, the number of teaching behaviors established as correlates of teaching effectiveness is still limited to a handful.

These results of process-product classroom research have led many to conclude that teaching is a complex and mystical art, rather than an applied science that can be analyzed and measured objectively. In contrast, the position taken in this research was that the problem lay not in the phenomenon itself but in several identifiable and correctable weaknesses in the research approaches used. The Texas Teacher Effectiveness Project[1] was planned explicitly to test these assumptions in a two-year study designed to discover teacher characteristics associated with teachers' success in producing student learning gains on the Metropolitan Achievement Tests. These tests were used as the criterion for student learning because they had been administered for several years in the

This paper was especially prepared for this volume and was supported by the National Institute of Education Contract OEC 6-10-108, Research and Development Center for Teacher Education, and by Contract NIE-C-74-0089, Correlates of Effective Teaching. The opinions expressed herein do not necessarily reflect the position or policy of the National Institute of Education and no official endorsement by that office should be inferred.

[1] The authors wish to acknowledge and thank the following individuals who made special contributions to the research described herein and/or to the preparation of this report: W. John Crawford, Carol King, Nancy Moore, Gwen Newman, Brian Peck, Dr. Teresa Peck, and Dr. Donald Veldman.

school district and were thought to be reasonably representative of the curriculum goals of the second and third grade teachers involved, although it is recognized that they do not measure all goals, and that in some cases they might not have been the most accurate measures of student learning for a particular school or classroom. The second and third grades were selected for study because we are especially interested in young children, believing, as the results showed, that teaching in the early grades is different in many ways from teaching at higher grades, requiring different teacher behaviors for the best results. The first grade was omitted, however, because only readiness tests, and not achievement tests, were available to provide prescores on the students. Because readiness tests are so strongly influenced by the experiences the child has had in his home and elsewhere prior to entering school, they are not reliable or stable enough to be used as prescores for first graders.

SAMPLE SELECTION

Most previous studies used student teachers, first year teachers, teachers involved in implementing a new curriculum, or random samples of teachers which included some percentages of these teacher types. Such teachers are known to be changing almost daily, so that process measures taken from their classrooms have little validity. They do not reflect an established style or pattern that is characteristic of the teacher across time and situations. To avoid this problem, our research used a specially selected teacher sample.

Rather than randomly, teachers were chosen on the basis of their previously established records of consistency in producing student learning gains on the Metropolitan Achievement Tests. Metropolitan Achievement Test scores for three consecutive years were obtained for 165 second and third grade teachers in an urban school system, for each of five subtests for which data were available. Each student's raw gain score (grade level equivalent) was converted to a residual gain score by adjusting it to take into account his score on the pretest. This was done for each subtest, analyzing within sex and within each year. Then, these residual or adjusted gain scores from individual students were collated by class, and a mean residual gain score on each subtest was computed for each of the 165 teachers for each of the three years studied. These data revealed that about half of the subjects were stable across years, sexes, and subtests, while the other half were not (Brophy, 1973). In general, stability coefficients were higher than those reported in previous studies (presumably because of the specially selected, experienced sample), and thus we were able to select from the total of 165 a subsample of teachers who were notably consistent across subtests, sexes, and years in the relative achievement gains that they produced in their students (Brophy, 1973; Veldman and Brophy, 1974).

Thus, the teachers selected for observation in this study had established a record of *relative consistency* in producing student learning gains on the Metropolitan Achievement Tests. This made them particularly appropriate for a process-product study designed to reveal the correlates of effective teaching (as defined by the teacher's ability to produce student learning gains).

MEASUREMENT

Many previous studies were limited by the fact that behavioral process measures were confined to single, limited, systems. Some involved only low inference coding of discrete behaviors. This can lead to measures which are highly objective and reliable but rather trivial. Other studies used only high inference ratings, which often are more meaningful and interpretable but suspect because of halo effects, logical errors, and other sources of rater bias. Because of these problems, and also because of the lack of an established set of teaching behaviors acknowledged as effective, we took a broad-band approach to measurement, measuring presage variables with interviews and questionnaires and process variables with both high and low inference instruments.

Low inference measures involve coding the presence or absence of discrete, separate, and easily observable units of behavior (teacher asks question; student gives correct answer). The behaviors to be coded are so obvious and so clearly defined that little or no judgment or inference is required on the part of the observer-coder, and observer agreement usually is very high. With a low inference system, the observer-coder only needs to note the occurrence of a behavior of interest whenever it appears.

At the other end of the continuum (and it is a single continuum, not two mutually exclusive methods), are high inference measures. Here, the observer-coder rates the teacher on global characteristics such as affectionateness or organization. The rating must be made by drawing inferences about these general traits on the basis of observation of specific behaviors. By considering everything known about the teacher from observing overt behavior, the observer-coder comes to a general conclusion or inference about the teacher's general characteristics. Thus, teacher characteristics reflected on high inference measures are not seen directly and tabulated, like those on low inference behaviors; they are inferred. Consequently, there is more room for error due to bias or other characteristics of the observer-coder which might interfere with their objectivity in drawing inferences about teachers, although some behaviors or characteristics such as warmth are more easily and reliably coded with high rather than low inference measures.

Low inference coding instruments were used whenever possible, to maximize the objectivity of the data. However, high inference ratings were used to assess general teacher variables that are not easily measured through low inference coding of discrete teacher-student interactions. The major low inference observational system was a complex and multifaceted one, based upon the Brophy-Good Dyadic Interaction System (Brophy and Good, 1970), but supplemented to take into account classroom management styles and other variables not included in the original system. The expanded system measured most of the major variables stressed in other widely used observation systems, although not always in precisely the same way.

This coding system involved coding each *dyadic* interaction that the teacher had with an individual student, and keeping track of whether the teacher or the student initiated the interaction, the type of interaction (academic, procedural, or behavioral), the quality of the student's response (when a response was involved), and the nature of the teacher's feedback or other behavior during the interaction. An important feature of the system was that it retained the *sequence* of action and reaction. This feature made it possible to compile various percentage scores (such as the percentage of correct answers followed by praise or the percentage of behavioral contacts involving criticisms rather than mere warnings) which allow direct comparison of teachers and students who did not have the same numbers of relevant interactions. Thus, the system avoided one of the major problems of systems based on simple frequency counts: it allowed determination of whether a given finding was due primarily to the teacher or to the student.

The system also took into account *context variables* usually ignored in other systems. Included were such variables as whether the teacher or student initiated an interaction, whether the interaction occurred during small group or general class activities, whether the student called out an answer or whether the teacher gave him permission to speak, and whether the student's contribution to a discussion was relevant or irrelevant to the topic at hand. The expanded system also included provisions for coding several aspects of teacher classroom management, based on the observations of Kounin (1970).

A second process measure was specifically constructed to assess teacher behavior during structured teaching and lesson presentation. This system focused on lesson presentation variables such as advance organizers, sequencing, use of media, and time spent in various aspects of teaching lessons. In addition, observers used a variety of high inference ratings and percentage estimates to measure teachers on more general variables such as warmth, clarity, enthusiasm, and credibility. Presage variables were assessed through collection of background information on each teacher and administration of lengthy interviews and questionnaires covering teaching philosophy and practices. Some teachers were also given the COMPASS battery, a collection of pencil and paper tests of teacher concern levels, coping styles, and personality attributes. The COMPASS battery was developed by the Research and Development Center for Teacher Education at the University of Texas at Austin (Veldman, 1972), and is used as the basis for counseling future teachers. Relationships between presage variables measured on the COMPASS battery and teaching effectiveness as measured by student learning gains are discussed by Peck and Veldman (1973).

In addition, an attempt was made in the second year of the study to collect information about student attitudes by having the students respond to a brief questionnaire covering attitudes about teachers and school in general. These data were not used, however, because they were confusing, contradictory, and internally inconsistent. Apparently, the children were too young to fully understand the directions and respond to them meaningfully and consistently. Consequently, the present report deals only with the relationships between teacher practices and student learning gains. This should be kept in mind, because, as will be noted, some of the teacher behaviors associated with high learning gains may have interfered with the promotion of student self-concept or positive student attitudes.

DATA ANALYSES

Data are available from about ten hours of classroom observation on 31 teachers the first year, and from about 30 hours of observation of 28 teachers the second year (19 teachers were included both years). Using a combination of correlational analyses and multilinear curve fitting procedures, presage and process variables for each teacher were related to criterion scores for each of five subtests of the Metropolitan battery (word knowledge, word discrimination, reading, arithmetic computation, and arithmetic reasoning). For each teacher, the criterion score on a given subtest was the average (mean) of her classes' mean residual (adjusted) gain scores on that subtest across three consecutive years.

These analyses yielded voluminous results. Readers interested in the specifics should consult Brophy and Evertson (1973a, b); Evertson and Brophy (1973); Brophy and Evertson (1974a); Brophy and Evertson (1974b); Evertson and Brophy (1974). The present report is confined to those relationships which were among the strongest and most consistent across multiple measures and criteria. Numerous findings of borderline or questionable significance, and others which failed to replicate across years, have been omitted.

Following the suggestions of Soar (1972), teachers were selected from the full range of effectiveness scores, rather than only from the extremes, and assessment of process-product relationships included regression analyses of non-linear relationships in addition to the more typical Pearson *r*'s (to assess linear relationships). Also, in addition to an interest in the relationships between teacher practices and general student learning gains, we were interested in differential behavior that might work well with one type of student but not another. Consequently, the data also were analyzed for differences by student sex and social status (SES). The sex difference analyses revealed very little of consequence, but the SES difference analyses revealed that the kinds of teacher behavior associated with the greatest learning gains in low SES schools frequently differed from the kinds of teacher behavior associated with the best learning gains in high SES schools. Many behaviors related positively to effectiveness in one group were unrelated or negatively related in the other group.

RESULTS

Two general points should be kept in mind in considering the results. First, as mentioned above, the data usually make more sense when considered separately by low and high SES schools than they do for the total group, indicating that the kind of teaching associated with the best gains in low SES schools often was quite different from the kind associated with the best gains in high SES schools. There were many commonalities, but it was more typical for a given teacher behavior to be more important in one type of school than in the other than it was for it to be equally important in both types of schools. Second, the data came from the second and third grades, where children are still learning fundamental tool skills, and where the nature of teaching is considerably different from what it is later. We believe that this is the biggest single reason for the discrepancies between some of our findings and those of previous studies which have been conducted at higher grade levels.

GENERAL FINDINGS

The majority of significant relationships with learning gain scores were negative. In short, we found out more about what *not to do* than we did about what *to do*. Furthermore, many of the positive relationships were non-linear, indicating that increases in the teacher behavior involved led to increases in student learning only up to a certain point. Beyond this point, further increases in the teacher behavior did not improve student learning, or perhaps even *decreased* it. The upshot of all this is that teaching involves orchestration of a large number of different behaviors which the teacher must have mastered to at least a certain minimal level and can adapt to different situations, as opposed to application of a few basic teaching skills that are "all-important." These behaviors were many and complex rather than few and simple. There are no magical "keys" to successful teaching.

Classroom Management

Of the variables which did show general relationships across SES groups, the most important area by far was *classroom management* or control. This was not surprising, because, other things being equal, it seems obvious that children will learn more when most classroom time is spent teaching and learning than when significant portions are spent dealing with misbehavior or other problems. However, the findings go beyond this obvious fact, providing strong support for Kounin's (1970) statements about classroom control.

In brief, Kounin stressed that teacher behavior which is effective in keeping students *actively engaged* in productive work is much more important for maintaining good classroom atmosphere and control than teacher success in dealing with crises or misbehavior. Among the important behaviors cited by Kounin were: general alertness in knowing what is going on in the classroom, so that potential problems can be nipped in the bud before they become serious; providing assignments which are interesting and appropriate in difficulty level, so that students stay actively involved in them; keeping lesson pacing sufficiently brisk, so that "dead spots" and periods of inactivity (which are especially likely to lead to trouble) are minimized; and having well developed management procedures, to minimize the time spent in everyday housekeeping activities that can be done efficiently and quickly but can take up a lot of time if not done properly (collecting money, arranging for use of the washroom, getting coats and lunches, etc.).

A variety of variables dealing with these teacher behaviors consistently correlated with student learning gains in both high and low SES schools. Also, variables dealing with teacher punishment methods and other aspects of reaction to misbehavior proved relatively *unimportant,* so that Kounin's general conclusion was strongly supported in our research: successful classroom management involves *preventing problems before they get started,* not dealing with problems *after* they get started.

Another classroom management variable of general importance was the dimension of strictness versus flexibility versus "anything goes" with regard to *classroom rules* concerning free time activities, movement around the classroom, talking to friends, and the like. In general, teachers who had a relatively small number of rules (necessary to maintain classroom order), but who at the same time were *flexible* in allowing students to move about during free periods without first getting specific permission, tended to be more successful than teachers who were either too strict (requiring the children to get permission to do virtually anything) or too lax (having few if any rules, and a somewhat chaotic classroom).

Reward and Punishment

The data on *punishment methods* revealed, as expected, that teachers who used milder and more informative types of punishment, such as keeping the child after school to discuss the incident, were more successful than teachers who were physically punitive or who relied on threats. Isolation from classmates and removal from the classroom, two techniques often recommended by behavior modification theorists, did not correlate with learning gains one way or the other. Apparently, these methods were effective for some teachers but not for others.

Some of the reward methods suggested by behavior modification theorists did receive support, however. The use of symbolic rewards such as smiling faces or stars and the use of rewards such as special privileges were positively associated with learning gains. In contrast, "rewarding" students by having classmates clap or cheer or by assigning them jobs or monitor duties was negatively associated with learning gains. Apparently, these "rewards," although meant as rewards by the teachers, were not experienced as rewards by the children and thus were ineffective for motivating them. The same was true for verbal praise (most correlations for praise were at or near zero). It should be noted, however, that the praise data were based on frequency alone. If qualitative aspects of praise, such as its appropriateness, genuineness, and/or degree of elaboration had been measured, praise might have shown the expected positive relationships.

Role Definitions and Expectations

Teacher expectations and role definitions were important in both SES groups, too. Teachers who were more successful in producing student learning gains tended to have high expectations and to assume personal responsibility for making sure that their students learned. If they encountered difficulties, they viewed them as obstacles to be overcome by discovering teaching methods that would succeed, not as indications that the student was incapable of learning. They did not hesitate to use supplementary or even alternative methods and materials when they thought it was necessary. This quality was especially important for teachers working in low SES schools. Apparently, considerable adaptation of the curriculum and use of substitute books and materials more suited to the interests and achievement levels of the students was necessary in these schools.

Individualization

Another general finding concerned what Hunt (1961) has called "the problem of the match." This refers to the problem of matching the *difficulty level* of the lesson to the *present ability levels* of the students. In contrast to the theories of errorless learning advocates who believe that learning proceeds most easily when there are as few errors as possible, our data suggested that there is an optimal error rate associated with maximal learning. Teachers who maintained the difficulty level of their questions and lesson content at this *optimal level* were more successful in producing student learning gains than teachers who taught at either too easy or too difficult a level.

Although this was a general finding across SES groups, there also was an SES difference in optimal levels, suggesting that low SES students needed to get material in smaller chunks and with more repetition, redundancy, and opportunities to practice than higher SES students, who responded better to the challenge of more difficult material. One indication of this was the percentage of teacher questions which students answer correctly. In low SES schools, learning was optimal when about 80% of the teachers' questions were answered correctly. In contrast, learning was optimal in high SES schools when about 70% of the questions were answered correctly. Because SES is a general indicator of student ability, the upshot of these findings is that bright and well motivated students (regardless of SES) will tend to respond best to relatively difficult and challenging questions and assignments, while students of limited ability and motivation (regardless of SES) will respond better to a somewhat less demanding and slower paced program of instruction. All students tend to do better when new demands are mild enough to allow relatively easy assimilation, but there must be new demands if there is to be forward progress. Learning should be "painless," but not so redundant and repetitious as to be errorless.

Group Lessons

Data on organized lessons, particularly reading groups, showed that the more successful teachers tended to get the whole group's attention *before* beginning a lesson; to call on the children in some *pattern* rather than randomly (this was unexpected; we now think that the advantages this method provides in minimizing anxiety and making sure that all children get equal opportunities to recite outweigh any disadvantages it might involve in reducing attention because students know when they are going to get their turn); to spend time interacting with *individuals* even during group lessons; and to spend most of the lesson giving the children *opportunities to practice* the new learning and get *feedback* (as opposed to spending the time lecturing or discussing). These findings appear to result from the fact that children at this grade level are learning fundamental tool skills which require considerable physical practice. A certain minimum amount of introductory explanation and demonstration is necessary to make the students clear about what they are supposed to do and how they are supposed to do it, but then it is important to let them start practicing it and to provide them with feedback so that they can gradually perfect their skills.

Teacher Feedback

Measures dealing with teacher reactions when students failed to answer questions correctly or stumbled over words in reading group revealed that the more successful teachers tended to give the students the answer rather than call on someone else or pump the student to try to get him to come up with the answer himself. This finding was somewhat unexpected. We had thought that teachers who stayed with students and tried to get them to come up with answers on their own would be the most successful. However, the vast majority of questions at these grade levels were factual questions to which the student either did or did not know the answers. Therefore, there was little chance that a student would be able to reason through to a response or otherwise figure out the answer if he was not able to give it after a few seconds. Under the circumstances, then, it appears that the best thing for the teacher to do when the student did not know an answer was to give it to him. Calling on other students generally was not successful, probably because this involved embarrassment for a student who could not respond correctly. This method also tends to encourage students who already are prone to call out answers out of turn, and thus may increase management problems.

The more successful teachers tended to respond to the *substance* rather than the *form* of student responses. Thus, they credited students when they had the general idea or answered a question partially correctly, and they did not focus attention on minor inaccuracies. They may have briefly corrected a mispronunciation or expanded a partial response to make it complete, but they did this quickly in order to move the lesson along and provide the student with a feeling of at least partial accomplishment, rather than dwelling upon the mistake by calling specific attention to it and taking time to correct it in detail.

Teacher *failure to give feedback* to student answers correlated negatively with learning gains. This indicates that it is important for the teacher to acknowledge each student response and to indicate whether or not it is correct. Failure to do so may leave the student confused about whether or not he was correct, and may make him feel that the teacher is interested only in hearing answers to her questions and not interested in him as an individual.

Student Initiation

Student initiated questions were positively associated with student learning gains. The frequency of such questions probably indicates general student motivation and interest. In contrast, *student initiated comments* showed a mixed pattern. When such comments were made after the student first got permission to speak by raising his hand, and especially when comments were relevant to the discussion, they tended to relate positively to student learning gains. In contrast, student initiated comments which were called out without permission tended to be negatively related to learning gains. Apparently, classrooms in which such comments were especially frequent tended to be classrooms which had many management problems.

Negative Findings

The final set of general findings across both SES groups includes unexpected negative findings revealing that *teacher behavior stressed in textbooks as important tended to be uncorrelated with student learning gains* in the present study. Although some of the following were more important for one SES group rather than the other they did not correlate positively for the total sample. Such variables included indirect vs. direct teaching; teacher talk vs. student talk; use of student comments and integration of such comments into the discussion; warmth; enthusiasm; clarity; ratings of student attentiveness; and teacher task orientation vs. student orientation. None of these variables was correlated with student learning gains one way or the other.

This also was true of teacher praise for the most part, although an exception will be noted below. We were surprised to a degree by certain of these negative results. However, it should be noted that most of the studies which have supported them have been done at higher grade levels, and there are several reasons to believe that these teacher behaviors would be more important with older students than with students in the early elementary grades.

LOW SES SCHOOLS

The preceding findings dealt with variables that were important in both low and high SES schools. Besides these general findings, there were certain teacher practices that were especially important in low SES schools (or, by extension, with low ability students).

Teacher Affect

One of the more important of these was a general attitude of *warmth and encouragement* (although not so much specific verbal praise). As will be noted later, the more successful teachers in high SES schools were not especially warm or encouraging towards their students, but the more successful teachers in low SES schools were. They tended to have good rapport with their students and to motivate through positive and encouraging behavior, letting the students know that they expected them to be able to do the work but also expected to help them do it.

Student Responses

It was especially important in low SES schools for the teacher to make sure that she got some kind of *response from a student each time she asked a question,* even if the response was "I don't know." Thus, in low SES schools, it was especially important for the teacher to stay with the student who was asked the original question and not move on to someone else if he failed to answer correctly. We believe that this was partly a matter of conditioning the students to understand that they would be expected to respond and that the teacher would insist upon a response when they were asked a question, and partly a matter of expressing confidence in the students' ability to respond through such behavior as being willing to wait for a response and insisting that other students remain quiet and give the respondent a chance to answer. Thus even if the teacher could not get the answer from the original respondent, it was still beneficial to get it from someone else even in the form of a call-out.

Indirect Teaching

Because of these considerations, variables related to Flanders' concept of *indirect teaching* (Flanders, 1970) were especially *inappropriate for low SES classrooms at these grade levels.* Attempts to teach in such classrooms through methods such as promotion of discussion rather than lecturing and providing structured practice or attempting to get frequent pupil-to-pupil interaction during discussion sessions instead of more teacher structured lessons were unsuccessful. The more successful teachers in these schools were more directive, although, as noted above, they combined this directiveness with warmth and encouragement.

Overteaching and Overlearning

As noted at the beginning of this report, there was a general finding to the effect that there was an optimal level of difficulty for teacher questions and for student assignments in both SES groups. However, *the low SES students profited most when learning was presented in smaller and more redundant chunks and at a somewhat slower pace providing more opportunities for practice.* Teachers who tried to teach too much too fast, progressing through the curriculum too quickly before the students had a chance to really master things as they went along, were less successful than teachers who "covered" less but taught thoroughly the material that they did teach. Overly difficult assignments in low SES schools tended to lead to student frustration and failure to complete assignments, and ultimately to poor learning gains.

Teacher Structuring and Feedback

The use of *peer tutoring* correlated *negatively* with learning gains in low SES schools. This finding fits with several others suggesting that low SES students at these grade levels require directed instruction from the teacher and are not yet capable of profiting much from learning situations based on the attempt to see that they learn from one another. Assignment of *homework* in addition to seatwork also was *ineffective* in low SES schools. There are many possible reasons for this, although the most likely one appears to be that the students did not profit from it because they did not have the teacher available to provide feedback.

Classroom Interaction

Other teacher variables that correlated positively with learning gains in low SES schools were teacher stress on factual *realism* and avoidance of childish idealism; *monitoring the classroom* regularly to continually make sure that the teacher knows what is going on; *smooth and efficient transitions* that waste little time; and well established routines which *minimize interruptions* for housekeeping matters (i.e., a system of classroom monitors which would insure that necessary tasks were taken care of "automatically" without the teacher having to interrupt the flow of things in order to give instructions). Most of these measures are related to the classroom management principles put forth by Kounin and discussed previously.

When students needed help with their seatwork, the most successful teachers in low SES schools provided help *as soon as possible on request* (as opposed to delaying the student or encouraging him to try to figure it out on his own), and spent time with the student to *make sure that he understood the instructions* and could carry on on his own (as opposed to merely giving him an answer or very brief feedback which might have helped with one problem but not have enabled him to complete the assignment). Thus, work related interactions with individual students in low SES schools were most successful when the teacher took time to make sure that the student understood the assignment and could continue on his own.

When a child in a low SES school was stuck on a word during reading group, giving a phonics clue was helpful, while giving a clue unrelated to the sound or meaning of the word (such as, "It's one of our new words today.") was not helpful. In general, phonics clues (and word attack skills generally) were especially important for the low SES children.

Individualization

The teacher's willingness to supplement the standard curriculum materials with *special individualized materials* to meet the needs of individual students was especially important in low SES schools. So was the use of audio-visual aids and other multi-media approaches to teaching. These, in combination with some of the teacher expectation data, indicate that teacher determination to find a way to teach the students one way or another was an especially important key to teacher success in the low SES schools.

Praise and Criticism

The one place where teacher *praise* correlated positively with student learning gains was when it followed student answers to *opinion questions*. It is not clear why praise in response to answers to opinion questions should correlate positively with learning when praise for factual answers or for good seatwork was unrelated to learning. Perhaps the praise given in these instances was more spontaneous and genuine and thus more motivating to the students. Another possibility is that opinion questions themselves and teacher praise in response to answers to opinion questions may have encouraged students to become more accustomed to responding to teacher questions and to gain some self confidence in answering questions. In any case, teacher praise correlated positively with student learning gains in low SES schools when it was given in response to student answers to opinion questions. In contrast, teacher praise given in student initiated contacts (in other words, when the student came up to the teacher to show his work and appeared to be seeking praise) was *negatively* related to learning gains. Apparently, praising students in this situation is *not* effective.

Teacher criticism of student work was negatively associated with learning in low SES schools, again indicating that the more successful teachers in these schools worked through encouragement and patience rather than demandingness and criticism.

HIGH SES SCHOOLS

In contrast to the above, a number of variables were important for learning in high SES schools but not low SES schools, or were correlated in an opposite direction with learning gains from the way that they correlated in low SES schools.

Praise and Criticism

One of the most general and surprising series of relationships concerned teacher praise and criticism. Teacher praise failed to correlate significantly with student learning in high SES schools in any and all circumstances. This could be because all of the teachers were praising sufficiently; because the teachers were not praising effectively or appropriately; because teacher verbal praise simply is not very important; or for some other reason. In any case, contrary to expectations, teacher verbal praise was *unrelated* to student learning in high SES schools.

At the same time, and also unexpectedly, teacher criticism of poor answers or poor work by students was *positively* related to student learning gains in the high SES schools (only). The most successful teachers in these schools not only had high expectations (like the most successful teachers in low SES schools); they also were highly *demanding* of their students and *critical* when the students failed to perform. It should be noted that this criticalness was restricted to academic responses; the teachers were *not* generally hypercritical or negativistic towards the students. However, when students failed to answer appropriately (or at least failed to measure up to the teacher's expectations), the teachers did not hesitate to criticize them. This critical demandingness was related to the highest learning gains in high SES schools, in contrast to the pattern of patience and encouragement which was associated with the highest learning gains in low SES schools.

This finding, and certain other ones associated with it raised the question of the relative importance of student achievement gains as contrasted with affective criteria in high SES schools. It may be that the greatest learning gains in high SES schools are achieved by teachers who may be sacrificing some gains in the *affective* area.

Student Variables

Student *withdrawal and passivity* were negatively correlated with learning gains in high SES schools, indicating that student motivation was important. Other indicators of student motivation, such as the frequency with which students came to the teacher for help with their work and the frequency with which they called out answers, also supported the importance of student motivation in high SES schools.

In fact, some data suggested that *high* student motivation in high SES schools might have been something of a problem; in many classrooms, the majority of students might have been motivated to the point of being *overly competitive.*

Individualization

As with the low SES schools, optimal learning in the high SES schools occurred in conjunction with an *optimal level of question difficulty.* However, high SES students responded best to relatively difficult questions and assignments which provided *challenges* for them. Teachers who stayed in a given lesson or on a given topic too long, to the point where the children had overlearned it and were beginning to become bored, were less successful than teachers who moved on before they reached this point.

In high SES schools, *sticking with the prescribed curriculum* tended to be correlated with learning gains, contrasting with the findings in low SES schools. This indicates that the curriculum was more appropriate for high SES students than for low SES students. Also, in high SES schools greater learning was associated with teacher activities such as assigning *homework* in addition to seatwork and spending relatively more amounts of time on curriculum related activities and less on personal matters and managerial matters. Thus, in high SES schools, learning gains were directly related to the *time and emphasis directed on teaching.*

Classroom Management

The most successful classroom management was somewhat looser in high SES than in low SES schools. Here, the successful teachers were somewhat more *flexible,* granting students more autonomy in taking care of their own needs and moving about freely without permission. There also was an implicit expectation that students would take care of themselves and communicate their needs if they had any. The most successful teachers in the high SES schools were those who *let the students come to them* if they needed any help (as opposed to systematically checking with all of the students to find out whether they needed help), and who expected the students to handle their classroom equipment and other everyday housekeeping needs on their own. Furthermore, when students did come to the teacher to seek help, the most successful teachers in high SES schools frequently delayed them or *encouraged them to figure out the answer on their own* rather than providing help. When they did provide help, it tended to be a brief interaction rather than an extended explanation of the sort that was most helpful for low SES students. Here again, we see a general pattern of demandingness and expectations that the students will take as much responsibility as possible for managing their own learning experiences in the high SES schools.

Controlling Student Responses

In reading groups, phonics clues and other *word attack skills* that were important in low SES schools were *relatively unimportant* in high SES schools. However, the method of having the child start the sentence or paragraph over again was positively associated with student learning gains, suggesting that the high SES students benefited more from *context clues* compared to the low SES students who benefited more from *phonics clues.* This probably represents a difference in the levels of reading skills in the two sets of students.

Unauthorized *calling out* of answers was especially maladaptive in high SES schools, probably indicating both management problems and a degree of overcompetitiveness on the part of the students.

In contrast to low SES schools, where it was important for the teacher to stick with the original respondent and get some kind of response, in high SES schools this appeared to be relatively unimportant. Instead, in these schools it was important to *keep the lesson moving at a brisk pace,* so that if one student did not give the answer the teacher would either give it herself or quickly move on to another student (giving it herself was preferable to calling on someone else). In any case, in the high SES schools it did not seem to be particularly important for students to respond personally; they seemed to learn just as well from watching and listening to the teacher interact with other students as they did from interacting themselves. Low SES students, in contrast, seemed to require personal participation. Apparently, the difference here reflects a difference in the two types of students, with a significant portion of the low SES students being inhibited or unwilling to respond, but the vast majority of high SES students showing no such problems.

Because of the competitiveness problem, it was especially important in high SES schools for the teacher to insist that students keep quiet and allow the respondent to answer, rather than call out answers themselves.

Verbal Activities

Measures of the relative amounts of class time spent in questions and answers and verbal discussions (as opposed to seatwork and other non-verbal activities) were positively related to learning gains in high SES schools. This indicates that these students were more able to profit from verbally oriented instruction, suggesting that they were beginning to move away from concentration on mastery of tool skills toward the more verbally oriented types of learning that are typical at higher grade levels.

References

Brophy, J. "Stability of Teacher Effectiveness." *American Educational Research Journal* **10** (1973): 245–252.

Brophy, J., and C. Evertson. "Low-Inference Observational Coding Measures and Teacher Effectiveness." *JSAS Catalog of Selected Documents in Psychology* **3** (1973a): 97. (Ms. No. 436)

Brophy, J., and C. Evertson. "Appendix to First Year Data of Texas Teacher Effectiveness Project: Complex Relationships between Teacher Process Variables and Student Outcome Measures." *JSAS Catalog of Selected Documents in Psychology* **3** (1973b): 137. (Ms. No. 502)

Brophy, J., and C. Evertson. *Process-Product Correlations in the Texas Teacher Effectiveness Study: Final Report* (Res. Rep. 74–4). Austin, Texas: Research and Development Center for Teacher Education, 1974a.

Brophy, J., and C. Evertson. *The Texas Teacher Effectiveness Project: Presentation of Non-Linear Relationships and Summary Discussion* (Res. Rep. 74–6). Austin, Texas: Research and Development Center for Teacher Education, 1974b.

Brophy, J., and T. Good. "The Brophy-Good Dyadic Interaction System." In A. Simon and E. Boyer, eds., *Mirrors for Behavior: An Anthology of Observation Instruments Continued, 1970 Supplement* (Vol. A). Philadelphia: Research for Better Schools, Inc., 1970.

Dunkin, M., and B. Biddle. *The Study of Teaching.* New York: Holt, Rinehart and Winston, 1974.

Evertson, C., and J. Brophy. "High-Inference Behavioral Ratings as Correlates of Teaching Effectiveness." *JSAS Catalog of Selected Documents in Psychology* **3** (1973): 97. (Ms. No. 435)

Evertson, C., and J. Brophy. *The Texas Teacher Effectiveness Project: Questionnaire and Interview Data* (Res. Rep. 74–5). Austin, Texas: Research and Development Center for Teacher Education, 1974.

Flanders, N. *Analyzing Teacher Behavior.* Reading, Mass.: Addison-Wesley, 1970.

Hunt, J. *Intelligence and Experience.* New York: Ronald Press, 1961.

Kounin, J. *Discipline and Group Management in Classrooms.* New York: Holt, Rinehart and Winston, 1970.

Peck, R., and D. Veldman. "Personal Characteristics Associated with Effective Teaching." Paper presented at the meeting of the American Educational Research Association, New Orleans, February 1973.

Rosenshine, B., and N. Furst. "The Use of Direct Observation to Study Teaching."

In R. Travers, ed., *Second Handbook of Research on Teaching*. New York: Rand McNally, 1973.

Soar, R. "Teacher Behavior Related to Pupil Growth." *International Review of Education* **18** (1972): 508–526.

Veldman, D. *Comprehensive Personal Assessment System for Teacher Education Programs*. Research and Development Center for Teacher Education, The University of Texas at Austin, 1972.

Veldman, D., and J. Brophy. "Measuring Teacher Effects on Pupil Achievement." *Journal of Educational Psychology* **66** (1974): 319–324.

ROBERT S. SOAR
University of Florida

An Integration of Findings from Four Studies of Teacher Effectiveness

Teacher effectiveness research has produced a wealth of what Biddle terms "isolated curiosities," which are of interest in themselves, but which often disagree, and cannot be brought together into a coherent basis for change in teacher education. Differences in measures of classroom behavior, measures of pupil outcome, differences in methods of analysis, and differences in the groups studied, to name a few sources of differences, make integration of the results of different studies difficult. In contrast, this paper is an attempt to integrate results from four studies of ours in which there were greater degrees of parallelism across studies than is usually found.

We will first describe briefly the several studies from which findings will be reported; and then describe several findings which seem to appear with some consistency across the four studies, and attempt to identify concepts which seem basic to effective teaching.

I would like to make clear that when I talk about "we" or "our" data this is not a use of the editorial we; rather, it refers to my wife, with whom I have collaborated for about 15 years now, in the series of researches that I'll be describing.

THE STUDIES

There are four studies whose basic designs are similar, whose results seem to be parallel and which we will attempt to integrate. A fifth study, our third year of data collection in Project Follow Through (Soar, 1973), will not be reported because we are unable to integrate the results with those of the other four studies.

This paper was presented at an invitational conference on research of effective teaching sponsored by NIE and the California Commission on Teacher Preparation and Licensing, San Diego, August 26–29, 1975. Used with permission of the author.

The first study was carried out in central South Carolina in four elementary schools, in grades 3 through 6, and involved 55 teachers for most of the analyses (Soar, 1966). The observation measures included Flanders Interaction Analysis, and an additional instrument, the South Carolina Observation Record, which was specially developed to fill what seemed to be gaps left by the Flanders system, primarily as a consequence of its focus on verbal behavior. It was assembled from sources such as the original OScAR (Medley and Mitzel, 1958) and later unpublished work of Medley's; and an observation schedule for recording affect, positive and negative, teacher and pupil, verbal and non-verbal, developed by a graduate student (Fowler, 1962), and a number of original items were also generated. The measures which were obtained from pupils included the Vocabulary, Reading, Arithmetic Concepts, and Arithmetic Computation subtests from the Iowa Tests of Basic Skills, a number of personality and attitude measures, and a number of creativity measures from Torrance's battery.

The second study was carried out the first year of Planned Variation in Project Follow Through (Soar and Soar, 1972). Consistent with the other projects, the primary objective was the identification of dimensions of behavior across programs which in turn were related to pupil gain. (A secondary objective which was unique to the Follow Through effort was testing whether or not classrooms in different programs did, in fact, differ in observed behavior.) The primary objective was based on the expectation that no program would, as a complex, be likely to be functional for the growth of pupils in all respects, but rather that each program would be a mix of behaviors, some of which would be functional but some of which would be less than maximally functional for pupil growth. The diversity of classroom behavior in the variety of programs observed was expected to be an unusually useful "laboratory," in which classroom behavior would have maximum variance, in which to search for relations between classroom behavior and pupil gain.

In this study, eight teachers from each of seven experimental programs were observed, along with two comparison teachers from the same sites as the experimental teachers, for a total of 70 K-1 teachers. They came from a number of states, and represented both large cities and remote rural areas. The data which will be referred to here are from 20 first grade classrooms on which we had pre- and postachievement measures.

It seemed useful to consolidate the pupil outcome measures since they were one-third length versions of previously developed tests and since reliable test performance would be difficult to obtain from young, disadvantaged pupils. We sought to consolidate the subtests into composites differing in cognitive levels since the first study had suggested that different cognitive levels responded differently to a given teacher behavior. Therefore, we factored the subtests. Dimensions of this sort did not emerge from factor analyses of the pretest or the posttest data, but did emerge from analysis of the gain data.

The third and fourth data sets are both from north central Florida—a first grade sample of 22 classrooms, and a fifth grade sample of 59 classrooms. The observation measures in these two samples, as well as the Follow Through sample, included a revision of the observation instrument developed in the first study, in order to focus on the classroom management behavior of the teacher, the response of pupils to that management behavior, and expression of affect as the original instrument recorded it. These latter three studies also included the Teacher Practices Observation Record (Brown, 1968) which looks at the classroom through the eyes of Dewey's experimentalism, recording such items as who is central in classroom activities, the teacher or the pupil; who chose the problem being worked on, teacher or pupil; who evaluates whether a question has been answered adequately, the teacher or the pupil; whether activities in the classroom are differentiated; is the motivation extrinsic or intrinsic; are pupils involved in identifying and selecting sources of information or are the materials brought in "prepackaged." An extension of the Flanders system was also used, the Reciprocal Category System (Ober, Bentley, and Miller, 1971) which records pupil interaction with as much variety as the original system did teacher behavior. And in each of the three samples a version of the Florida Taxonomy of Cognitive Behaviors was used, one developed by Brown and others for use in all grade levels, and an additional version which we developed especially for use in kindergarten, first, and second grades. In the fifth grade sample, spelling was added to the achievement battery in order to obtain a relatively simple concrete achievement measure, Vocabulary and Reading were used as more complex verbal skills, and Arithmetic Comprehension was used as a complex measure of quantitative achievement. Again, a variety of attitude and personality measures were used, including a measure of self-concept.

PARALLEL FINDINGS

The Inverted "U"

All four studies support the idea that measures of teacher behavior which represent direction and control of pupil learning tasks show greatest pupil gain at intermediate levels; with the extremes of either high or low control being associated with smaller amounts of pupil gain. We suspect that good teachers have always known this, but researchers have been slower to recognize it, and to judge from popular writing, the critics of education have been even slower. Probably the two innovations in education which have received the most attention in the past few years are open classrooms, in which teacher control is minimized [as advocated in Silberman's *Crisis in the Classroom* (1970)], and the movement toward behavior modification, contingency management, behavior analysis, precision teaching, or whatever term is used to refer to the application of operant conditioning principles and programmed learning to classroom instruction.

The inverted "U" phenomenon in education seems to be well enough established now to leave little question of its meaningfulness and its implication for teaching. Other studies include Solomon, Bezek, and Rosenberg (1963) who found such a relationship for permissiveness, Coats as reported by Flanders (1970) for indirectness and Brophy and Evertson (1974) for structured time in a number of activities.

The Differentiated "U"

This finding is less clear, but there is some support for it in three of our studies. The sense of the concept is that pupil learning of low cognitive level objectives proceeds best under relatively tightly structured, closely focused learning conditions, whereas more complex kinds of learning proceed best in settings in which pupils have more freedom to explore and interact with subject-matter, that is, more freedom in their thinking processes. This concept was suggested in our 1966 report, and analyzed and reported shortly after (Soar, 1968) from the same data; some suggestions of it were found in the first year of Follow Through (Soar and Soar, 1972), and a partial replication found in the recent fifth grade sample (Soar and Soar, 1973).

In the last study pupil achievement measures were chosen to span the range of cognitive levels, from spelling as a simple concrete measure, to vocabulary as a complex abstract measure, with reading at a slightly less abstract level, with the order of the latter two based on the 1968 results. The prediction was made that greatest growth in spelling would take place under closest control, vocabulary under least control, and reading at an intermediate level. Spelling did indeed grow best under closest control (significantly different from both reading and vocabulary), but the order for reading and vocabulary was reversed from the prediction, although the difference between them was not significant. In attempting to understand the difference from the predicted order (in the event it was meaningful) we recalled that the sample in the first study, which included third through sixth grades, was a grade level advanced in reading achievement on the average, so that the mean for the total sample was a grade equivalent of about 5.5 at the pretest, whereas our more recent fifth grade sample was about a grade level below norms, with a pretest mean of about 4.0. If, as seems reasonable, reading is a complex abstract task as it is being learned, but becomes a lower cognitive level task after it is well learned, then these results also seem reasonable. In the earlier sample of better readers, reading was interpreted to be at a lower cognitive level than vocabulary; whereas for the later sample, which read less well, reading was interpreted as a more complex activity, and more complex than vocabulary. Given this interpretation, the results do not contradict the idea that the more complex the learning objective, the less the teacher control which is optimal for growth, although they did not fit our prediction.

There is additional support for the same idea, however. In analyses of pupil data from our second year in Follow Through (Soar, 1971) the contingency management program which was included in our sample showed greater pupil gain than any other program for the measures of low and intermediate complexity, but was at the bottom for gain produced in the most complex measure. Cline (personal communication), in an early description of results of the Abt analyses of more recent Follow Through data indicates that pupils in that same contingency management program showed rapid growth early in the development of reading skill, but fell behind at the next grade level when manipulation of concepts began to be measured.

Some evidence, then, suggests that when a teacher is concerned with students having the facts at their fingertips—the multiplication table, today's list of fifteen spelling words, or dates in history—she would probably do well to organize tightly structured activities such as a drill session. But when a teacher is concerned with students learning complex problem solving, understanding concepts or developing abstractions or generalizations, she should use less structured activities in which pupils have some degree of self-direction, but within a framework established by the teacher and with the teacher available as a resource.

The inverted "U" and differentiated "U" need to be seen as theme and variation: the theme is that neither extreme of freedom or control is likely to be most functional for learning; the variation is that the precise balance between them which will be optimal is likely to shift with the complexity of the learning objective.

What is Controlled?

The differentiated "U" suggests the importance of the teacher's distinguishing between objectives and adapting degree of control to abstractness of objective. But we suspect that it is also functional for a teacher to distinguish *what* is controlled. The distinction which needs to be made is among three separable aspects of classroom activity: teacher management and control of pupil behavior; teacher assignment of the subject-matter task; and teacher control of pupil thought processes. These are not typically separated, but can be. For example, pupils may have little freedom to leave their seats or move about in the room and little freedom to talk to one another, may be working on a task assigned by the teacher, yet may still have considerable freedom in their thinking processes, or may even be engaged in creative activities. The usual (unstated) assumption is that pupils must be free in all three respects to grow in creativity, but the limited evidence we have suggests that this is not so—that creative development proceeds best under classroom conditions in which the distractions of noise and physical movement of pupils are limited. Data from our first study indicated that a factor titled "Freedom of Physical Movement" related negatively to a measure of creativity growth, but another factor which reflected indirectness of teacher style in interaction with pupils related positively to the same outcome measure. The first factor was a relatively clear measure of physical activity in the classroom—of freedom of behavior, that is; and it seems probable that the second factor reflected teacher behavior which supported pupil freedom in the development of thought, while maintaining a necessary degree of organization.

Although it is little more than a hunch, we suspect that the concepts of the inverted "U" and the differentiated "U" apply particularly to teacher control of pupil thinking processes, rather than to teacher control of behavior. What *is* clear in the data is that a high degree of freedom of behavior for pupils is *not* a necessary condition for complex cognitive growth or creative growth. It may even be, as adults assume for themselves, that demanding mental work proceeds best for children in an environment in which distraction is at a minimum.

The data also make clear that teachers do not generally make a distinction between control of behavior and control of the thinking process. In several sets of data, factors emerged which seemed to reflect control of behavior and others which appeared to reflect control of thinking and subject matter; when this happens, the two factors are strongly positively related—correlations from the high .70's to the high .80's. So it seems clear that if the typical teacher permits little freedom of behavior she also permits little freedom in the thinking process, and if she frees one, she frees the other. Even though it is not at this point well established in the data, this seems to us to be a distinction of considerable usefulness, since what evidence there is suggests that control in the three areas relates differently to pupil growth.

The cognitive level of interaction can be too high. Three of our samples (Soar and Soar, 1972, 1973), all that have studied the question, show negative relations between the amount of teacher-pupil interaction at a high cognitive level and pupil achievement gain, even for complex measures. Dunkin and Biddle (1974) also report a study which finds the same results. In some of our data the results appear not just for measures from the cognitive taxonomy, but also for a factor from the Teacher Practices Observation Record. The factor is one in which the pupil is given a difficult problem, asked to go beyond the data he has been given, and encouraged to "sit, think, and mull." The negative relation sometimes appears for pupils across all SES levels, but sometimes as an interaction with SES indicating that achievement gain is decreased more for low SES pupils than for high.

We have difficulty concluding that teachers ought not to involve pupils in higher cognitive level activities, but the findings do seem to raise serious questions about the "universal prescription" that teachers ought to involve pupils in more of this sort of activity. Although our interpretations are speculative, we wonder whether the findings may represent the lack of "the match" between the task and the pupil's ability to cope successfully. Two bits of evidence support this interpretation: high level teacher-pupil interaction interacts in the statistical sense with both teacher choice of activity and activity in which the teacher is central. Both of these may be situations in which it is easy for the teacher not to realize that a mismatch has occurred. It would not be surprising, then, if the setting were one in which the teacher works at a high cognitive level with a small number of pupils, ignoring the rest or unaware that they are not coping successfully. We suspect the cues which would give the teacher feedback on where the pupils are must be quite subtle, since many teachers apparently do not read them correctly; and the literature which urges this activity on teachers, but does not raise cautions, concerns us.

INTERACTIONS BETWEEN PUPIL ENTRY CHARACTERISTICS AND CLASSROOM PROCESS AS THEY RELATE TO GAIN

Only in the two most recent studies have we examined interactions of this sort with any frequency, but in both of these data sets, socio-economic status, crude proxy measure though it is, interacted more often than any other with classroom process. The interaction of SES with affect expression in the classroom parallels the findings of Brophy and Evertson (1974) in indicating that positive affect is more functional, and negative affect is more dysfunctional, for low SES pupils than for high SES pupils. To carry the point a step further, plots of the interaction suggest that for high SES pupils, positive affect may be slightly negatively related to gain. The relationship is so small as to invite the assumption that the true relationship is zero, except that it has emerged in similar fashion from several sets of data, two of ours, and the Brophy and Evertson results.

Another interaction with SES was one in which the teacher provides a relatively high amount of gentle, unobtrusive structuring behavior. Large amounts of this structuring behavior were functional for low SES pupils, but disfunctional for high SES pupils.

A final result which appeared in the only study in which the relevant pupil characteristics were measured was an interaction between SES and change in internality of control and motivation during the school year. Socioeconomic status accounted for 35% of the variance in change in internality during the school year, with low SES being associated with a decrease. Parallel results were found for a measure of motivation, accounting for 18% of the variance. Since SES was unrelated to change in either of these measures across the following summer, it seems reasonable to hypothesize that the decrease in internality and motivation for low SES pupils may be a function of school experience. These are correlational data and causation cannot be concluded, but it seems reasonable to expect lower internality and motivation if school is perceived as a failure experience. And if there *is* a causal relationship, cumulating its effect across a number of years of school experience suggests a problem with serious social consequences.

A CONCLUDING COMMENT

These findings suggest that an intermediate amount of different kinds of teacher behaviors are best for a particular goal and for a particular group of pupils, but they don't begin to answer the question of the classroom teacher—how much of a certain behavior is best for which goal for which pupil?

What we have so far is an organizing principle which can be used by the teacher and the researcher in thinking about effective teaching; we do not have specific answers for the teacher's question. This will require a more detailed research methodology than we have used, but it seems to be a very logical next step.

In all probability the answer when it comes will involve the additional research question of how the teacher can know when her behavior is at the "intermediate optimum level." What are the cues in the classroom? This, too, is a formidable research effort. But the consistent findings we do have should point to some of the kinds of classroom behaviors for which it might be profitable to ask these additional questions.

References

Brown, B. B. *The Experimental Mind in Education.* New York: Harper & Row, 1968.

Brophy, J. E., and C. M. Evertson. *The Texas Teacher Effectiveness Project: Presentation of Non-Linear Relationships and Summary Discussion,* Report No. 74–6. Austin: Research and Development Center, University of Texas, 1974.

Dunkin, M. J., and B. J. Biddle. *The Study of Teaching.* New York: Holt, Rinehart and Winston, 1974.

Flanders, N. A. *Analyzing Teacher Behavior.* Reading, Mass.: Addison-Wesley, 1970.

Fowler, B. D. "Relation of Teacher Personality Characteristics and Attitudes to Teacher-Pupil Rapport and Emotional Climate in the Elementary Classroom." Ph.D. dissertation, University of South Carolina, 1962.

Medley, D. M., and H. E. Mitzel. "A Technique for Measuring Classroom Behavior." *Journal of Educational Psychology* **49** (1958): 86–92.

Ober, R. L., E. L. Bentley, and E. Miller. *Systematic Observation of Teaching: An Interaction Analysis–Instructional Strategy Approach.* Englewood Cliffs: Prentice-Hall, 1971.

Silberman, C. *Crisis in the Classroom: The Remaking of American Education.* New York: Random House, 1970.

Soar, R. S. *An Integrative Approach to Classroom Learning.* (NIMH project numbers 5-R11 MH 01096 and 7-R11 MH 02045). Philadelphia: Temple University, 1966. (ERIC Document Reproduction Service No. ED 033 749)

Soar, R. S. "Optimum Teacher-Pupil Interaction for Pupil Growth." *Educational Leadership Research Supplement* **1** (1968): 275–280.

Soar, R. S. *Follow Through Classroom Process Measurement.* Contract #OEG-0-8-522471-4618(100) to the University of Florida, and OEG-0-8-522394-3991(286) to Florida Educational Research and Development Council, Gainesville, Florida, Institute for the Development of Human Resources, University of Florida, June 1971.

Soar, R. S. *Follow Through Classroom Process Measurement and Pupil Growth (1970–71) Final Report.* Gainesville, Florida: Institute for the Development of Human Resources, University of Florida, 1973. ERIC No. ED 106 297.

Soar, R. S., and R. M. Soar. "An Empirical Analysis of Selected Follow Through Programs: An Example of a Process Approach to Evaluation." In I. J. Gordon, ed., *Early Childhood Education.* Chicago: National Society for the Study of Education, 1972.

Soar, R. S., and R. M. Soar. "Classroom Behavior, Pupil Characteristics, and Pupil Growth for the School Year and for the Summer." JSAS *Catalog of Selected Documents in Psychology* **5** (1975): 200. Gainesville, Florida: Institute for the Development of Human Resources, University of Florida, 1973. (Ms. No. 873).

Solomon, D., W. E. Bezdek, and L. Rosenberg. *Teaching Styles and Learning.* Chicago: The Center for the Study of Liberal Education of Adults, 1963.

JANE STALLINGS
Stanford Research Institute

How Instructional Processes Relate to Child Outcomes

The purpose of the Follow Through classroom observation evaluation was to assess the implementation of seven Follow Through sponsor models and to examine the relationships between classroom instructional processes and child outcomes. The Follow Through Program was established by Congress in 1967 under the Office of Economic Opportunity when it became apparent that a program was needed in the early grades of public school to reinforce and extend the academic gains made by economically disadvantaged children enrolled in Head Start or similar preschool design; that is, the goal was to examine the differential effectiveness of programs based on divergent educational and developmental theories. The program began when researchers and other educational stakeholders were invited by the government to submit plans for establishing their various programs in public schools in order to test whether their individual approaches could improve the educational achievement of economically disadvantaged children. The seven programs selected for study in this analysis represent a wide spectrum of innovative educational theories represented in Follow Through.

While the Follow Through evaluation was planned to answer several questions, the following excerpt addresses the question: how do classroom instructional processes used in the various programs impact upon the growth and development of children?

The present summary represents highlights of the full report prepared by Stanford Research Institute, Menlo Park, California—*Follow Through Classroom Observation Evaluation 1972–1973* (Stallings and Kaskowitz, 1974). A brief description of the sample and measuring instruments for this study appears below.

Excerpted from a paper presented at the Conference on Research on Teacher Effects: An Examination by Policy-Makers and Researchers, The University of Texas at Austin, November 3–5, 1975. Used with permission of the author.

SAMPLE

Four first-grade and four third-grade classrooms were observed in 36 cities and towns. This represented five projects for six Follow Through educational models and six projects for a seventh model. One first-grade and one third-grade Non-Follow Through classroom were selected for comparisons at each project. These Non-Follow Through classrooms were combined to form a pooled comparison group. The projects included in the sample represented all geographic regions, urban and rural areas, and several racial and ethnic groups.

MEASUREMENTS

Classroom Processes

The SRI Classroom Observation Instrument was employed to gather data about classroom environment and processes. The instrument was initially developed in 1969 with the assistance of eight Follow Through sponsor representatives with a goal of being flexible enough to record the salient features of a variety of program components.

The instrument consists of five sections:

1. *Classroom Summary Information (CSI)*—The CSI is filled out once each day. It identifies the sponsor and teacher and provides information on the number of teachers, aides, volunteers, and students, and the class duration.
2. *Physical Environment Information (PEI)*—The PEI is filled out once each day. It provides information on the seating patterns and on the presence and use of equipment and materials.
3. *Classroom Check List (CCL)*—A CCL is filled out about four times an hour. It provides information on the grouping of children and teaching staff and activities in the classroom.
4. *Preamble (PRE)*—A Preamble is filled out subsequent to each CCL. It contains information about the activity and role of the person who is the focus of the FMO interactions.
5. *Five-Minute Observation (FMO)*—The FMO is filled out subsequent to each Preamble. It contains information in the form of coded sentences concerning the type of interactions occurring in the classroom. The information includes the parties to the interaction, the type of interaction, and the quality of the interaction.

Child Measures

The entering ability of the children was assessed by the Wide Range Achievement Test (WRAT) which was administered to the children when they first entered school, either at the kindergarten or first-grade level.

Reading and math skills were assessed by the Metropolitan Achievement Test (MAT) in both first and third grades.

Problem-solving skills (perceptual) were assessed in third grade only, using the Raven's Coloured Progressive Matrices (Raven's). This test was designed by John C. Raven (1956) as a culture-fair test of nonverbal reasoning, or fluid problem-solving ability in visual perceptual tasks.

The Intellectual Achievement Responsibility Scale (IAR), used in the third grade only, assessed the extent to which the child takes responsibility for his own successes or failures or attributes his achievements to the operation of external forces (e.g., luck or fate).

Child behaviors were assessed through systematic observations recorded on the SRI Observation Instrument. The behaviors reported here are independence, task persistence, cooperation, and question asking.

Absences from school were determined from school records.

READING ACHIEVEMENT RESULTS

Out of a possible 340 correlations between reading achievement and classroom processes, 118 were significantly related at the .05 level. Of these, the most strongly correlated variables suggest that the length of the school day and the average time a child spent engaged in a reading activity were related to higher reading scores in both first grade and third grade. When the school day is longer, the children have more opportunity to engage in reading. The length of the school day for the classrooms in the evaluation varied among schools by as much as two hours. Higher reading scores were also found in classrooms where there was more reading or discussions of reading between adults and children. Thus, opportunity and exposure to reading had an important relationship to good performance on tests.

Higher reading scores were obtained in classrooms using systematic instructional patterns where the teacher provides information and asks a question about the information. The child responds and the teacher immediately lets the child know whether the response is right or wrong. If he is wrong, the child is guided to the correct answer. If he is correct, he receives praise, a token, or some form of acknowledgment. These preliminary findings suggest this type of positive reinforcement contributed to higher reading test scores in both first and third grades.

Small groups were most effective for teaching first grade reading, while large group instruction worked well in the third grade. In classrooms where children worked by themselves and were task persistent (maintained their attention on their studies without teacher guidance), they also achieved higher reading scores. In classrooms where textbooks and programmed workbooks were used most often, the reading scores were higher. Also, in classes where a greater-than-average amount of time was spent on social studies, the reading scores were higher. Obviously, reading skills are used in social studies projects, but it is of interest to note that experience in social studies was related to reading scores.

It is noteworthy that the University of Oregon and the University of Kansas, both of which are models that use the classroom procedures described here, showed greater gains in first grade reading than the other five sponsors and greater gains than Non-Follow Through classes.

MATH ACHIEVEMENT RESULTS

Out of a possible 340 correlations between math achievement and classroom processes, 108 were significantly related at the .05 level. Of these, the most strongly correlated variables suggest that, as in reading, the length of the school day and the average length of time each child spent in math activities were related to higher math scores in both first and third grades. Thus, the opportunity a child had to engage in math, either in formal instruction or in less formal exploratory activities (e.g., working with, or just "messing with," weights and measuring tools) contributed to higher scores in math. Also, in classrooms where adults and children more often discussed or talked about mathematical problems and concepts, the test scores in math were higher. The value (in terms of math scores at the end of the third grade) of spending large amounts of class time on math was especially marked for the children whose numerical ability was weak when they entered school.

The effect of praise on achievement in math in first grade was variable: in classrooms where children had relatively low entering ability, the children profited more from a high rate of praise than they did in classrooms where the students had higher entering ability. This type of information could be useful in planning educational programs to enhance the learning of children with differing abilities at different age levels.

As in reading, children had higher math scores in classrooms where teachers used systematic instructional patterns; that is, the teacher provides information and asks a question about the information. The child responds and the teacher immediately lets the child know whether the response is right or wrong. If he is wrong, the child is guided to the correct answer. If he is correct, he receives praise, a token, or some other form of acknowledgment. This positive reinforcement contributed to higher scores on math tests in both grade levels.

In classrooms where textbooks and programmed workbooks were used frequently, the test scores on math were especially high. In addition, the use of instructional materials such as programmed materials, Cuisenaire rods, or Montessori materials contributed to higher math scores.

In first grade classrooms where children were taught in small groups, the math scores were higher. In third grade, large group instruction contributed to higher scores. When children could work by themselves some of the time and could persist at a task, they were also more likely to have higher scores in math achievement.

University of Kansas, which used the classroom procedures described here as contributing to higher math scores, had higher scores in first grade math than the other six sponsors and Non-Follow Through classes. University of Oregon, which also used these instructional processes in their classrooms, had higher scores in the third grade math than the other six sponsors and Non-Follow

Through classes. These findings strongly suggest that classroom procedures used in University of Kansas and University of Oregon classrooms contributed to child achievement in math.

RAVEN'S PROBLEM SOLVING TEST RESULTS

Out of a possible 340 correlations between the Raven's Problem Solving Test and classroom processes, 114 were significantly related at the .05 level. Of these, the most strongly correlated variables suggest that high scores on Raven's Coloured Progressive Matrices (a test of nonverbal perceptual problem solving) tended to be earned by children in the more flexible classrooms where a wide variety of materials is used, many different activities occur, and children are allowed to select their own groups and seating part of the time. In these more flexible classrooms, children have more opportunities to manipulate materials and discover the relationships between items to see how things fit together. In these classrooms, adults interact with children on a one-to-one basis, more open-ended questions are asked, and children show more verbal initiative. Far West Laboratory, University of Arizona, Bank Street College, High/Scope Foundation, and Educational Development Center use these processes, and the classrooms in these models had higher scores on the Raven's than did the classrooms in the University of Kansas and University of Oregon models.

RESPONSIBILITY SCALE RESULTS

Out of a possible 340 correlations between the Intellectual Achievement Responsibility Scale and classroom processes, 106 were significantly related at the .05 level. Of these, the most strongly correlated variables suggest that children in the more open classrooms earned higher scores on the Intellectual Achievement Responsibility Success Scale. Our results indicate that children from the more flexible classrooms took responsibility for their own success but not for their failure. Children from the more highly structured classrooms took responsibility for their own failure but attributed their success to their teacher's competence or other forces outside themselves. Only the classrooms of Educational Development Center had scores indicating that the children took responsibility for both their success and failure.

DAYS ABSENT RESULTS

The absence rate is important for several reasons; e.g., many school budgets are determined by the average daily attendance. Also, days absent can be used as an indicator of attitude toward school. It is well known to parents and teachers that if a child enjoys school, he may attend even if he does not feel very well. If he does not like school, he is more likely to stay home whenever he feels any discomfort.

Out of a possible 340 correlations between days absent and classroom processes, 102 were significantly related at the .05 level. Of these, the most strongly correlated variables suggest that in both first and third grade classrooms, children are absent less frequently in open classrooms—that is, in classrooms where there is a high rate of child independence, child questioning, adults responding, individualized instruction, and open-ended questioning. Also, in classrooms where children and adults smiled and laughed more often, the children were absent less often.

Children in both first and third grade were absent more frequently from classrooms where they worked in large groups more often and where adults used direct questions in academic work and frequent corrective feedback. Findings for the third grade indicate that in classrooms where children were punished they also were absent more often. In addition, classrooms with a higher rate of negative, harsh, or demeaning statements on the part of teachers and students showed a higher absence rate.

The findings in this report of absence rate indicate that at the first grade level, children in classrooms of sponsors who used more highly structured environments, materials, and interactions also had a higher absence rate. Classrooms of three sponsors, Far West Laboratory, University of Arizona, and High/Scope Foundation, models which used a wide variety of activities and materials, had children who had lower absence rates than children in classrooms of other sponsors and Non-Follow Through classrooms. As might be expected, the absence rate for all sponsors and Non-Follow Through diminished from first grade to third grade.

CHILD BEHAVIOR RESULTS

Table 1 presents the results of the partial correlations for child independence, task persistence, cooperation, and question asking.

Independence

In our study, independence is defined as a child or children engaged in a task without an adult. This type of independent behavior is more likely to be found in classrooms where teachers allow children to select their own seating and groups part of the time, where a wide variety of activities is available, and where an assortment of audiovisual and exploratory materials is available. The adults provide individual attention and make friendly comments to the children.

Our investigations indicate that children in the classrooms of Educational Development Center and Far West Laboratory showed more independence than did the children in Non-Follow Through and the other five sponsors' classrooms.

Task Persistence

For this study, task persistence is defined as a child engaged in self-instruction over a few minutes or more. If the child becomes engaged in a conversation with someone else during the task, the observer no longer codes task persistence.

Table 1. Partial correlations of instructional variables and child behaviors (Fall 1971 WRAT partialed out).

Instructional variables	*Independence*	*Task persistence*	*Cooperation*	*Child questions*
		Correlations		
Child/adult ratio	.23*	.09	.02	−.15
Children select groups and seats part of the time	.36‡	−.22*	.19*	.03
Instructional materials used	−.01	.11	.09	−.07
Audiovisual equipment used	.13	−.25†	.15	−.12
General equipment and materials	.22*	−.08	.09	.005
Total resource materials used	.13	−.23*	.18	.03
Wide variety of activities occur concurrently	.22*	−.12	.15	.09
Wide variety of activities occur during the day	.43‡	−.36‡	.32†	.14
An adult with one child	.57‡	−.16	.08	.14
Use of TV	−.03	−.10	−.11	−.03
Audiovisual equipment used in academic subjects	.24†	−.25†	−.01	−.04
Exploratory materials used in academic subjects	.34‡	−.22*	.27†	−.11
Math or science equipment used in academic subjects	−.18	.17	−.18	.11
Textbook and workbooks used in academic subjects	−.33‡	.31†	−.49‡	−.04
Puzzles and games used in academic subjects	.16	−.07	.09	−.07
Adults asking children questions	−.17	.03	−.17	−.04
Adult instructs an individual child	−.09	.23*	−.17	.22*
Adult comments to children	.22*	−.12	−.13	.36‡
Adult task related comments to children	.12	−.24*	.39‡	−.16
Adult acknowledges children	−.16	.15	−.11	.04
Adult praises children	−.60‡	.20*	−.21*	.02
Adult speaks to one child	−.01	.13	−.06	.38‡
Adult speaks to two children	.29†	−.13	.28†	−.03
Adult speaks to a small group	−.15	.19*	.01	−.32‡
Adult asks direct question about subject matter	−.41‡	.07	−.28†	.03
Adults ask open-ended thought-provoking questions	.16	−.12	.13	−.07

* $p < .05$
† $p < .01$
‡ $p < .001$
Number of classrooms used in the correlation computations = 105 first grades.

The highest positive relationships indicate that task persistence occurred most often when textbooks and workbooks were used in the classroom. Where adults instructed one child at a time, the children were also likely to be more task persistent. This may be because young children often have difficulty understanding group instructions. However, in settings where adults work with children on a one-to-one basis, children can have a question answered or directions clarified and then go ahead independently with the task at hand.

University of Arizona and University of Kansas had higher scores on task persistence than did the other five models and Non-Follow Through.

Cooperation

For this study, cooperation is defined as two or more children working together on a joint task. This kind of cooperation is more likely to be found in classrooms where a wide variety of activities occurs throughout the day, where exploratory materials are available, and where children can choose their own groupings. If the adults interact with two children, asking questions and making comments about the task, the children seem to be encouraged to join each other in cooperative tasks.

The children in the Bank Street College, High/Scope Foundation, and Educational Development Center programs more often joined each other in a cooperative task than did children in the other four models and Non-Follow Through children.

Question Asking

Educators have long recognized the value of a child's asking questions as a primary means to gain information. Previous research indicates that question asking is positively related to test scores.[1] In our study, we found that first grade children asked more questions where there was a one-to-one relationship of adult with child in classrooms, where adults responded to children's questions, and where adults made general conversational comments to children.

Children in classrooms using Far West Laboratory, Bank Street College, University of Kansas, High/Scope Foundation, and Educational Development Center programs asked questions more often than did children in the Non-Follow Through classrooms.

CHILD OUTCOME SCORES EXPLAINED BY ENTERING ABILITY[2] AND CLASSROOM PROCESSES

Whether or not classroom procedures affect the growth and development of children has been seriously questioned by other research (Coleman, Jencks, Herrnstein, Moynihan, and Mosteller). Their research has indicated that a child's entering aptitude is of primary importance and, in fact, governs what the child will achieve in school. The study reported here, however, found that

[1] Stallings, Baker, and Steinmetz (1972) and Stallings (1973) report that an increased frequency of children asking questions is related to higher scores on achievement tests and attitudinal tests.

[2] Measured by the Wide Range Achievement Test administered when the child entered school.

observed classroom procedures contributed as much to the explanation of test score differences as did the initial ability of children.

In both first and third grades, child behavioral outcomes were only slightly explained by entering aptitude. As might be expected, these behaviors were much more related to classroom processes.

Very little of the absence rate was explained by entering ability, in either first or third grade. Approximately 60 percent of the variance was explained by the instructional procedures used in the classroom, suggesting that what occurs in classrooms is related to whether or not the child stays away from school.

The achievement of a child in math at the end of first grade can be attributed in part to his ability as it was measured when he entered school, but even more so to the instructional practices used by his teachers. In first grade, entering ability accounts for approximately 40 percent of the achievement. By the third grade, less of the achievement can be attributed to entering school ability and more to classroom practices.

In first grade we found that a variable which describes a stimulus/response/feedback (S/R/F) sequence of interaction entered the regression equation after the WRAT and explains 13 percent of the variance of the math scores. Eight of the 10 variables which entered the equation are related to this S/R/F sequence.

In third grade, 25 percent of the test score variance is explained by the process variables which describe adults asking children questions about academic subject matter. The WRAT only explains 17 percent of the variance.

Approximately 50 percent of first grade reading achievement can be attributed to the entering ability of the children. The instructional procedures used by teachers account for approximately 25 percent of the reading achievement.

In the first grade, the total number of verbal interactions which were related to reading accounted for 12 percent of the variance in first grade reading scores. The other variables which entered the equation were primarily related to average amount of time spent in reading and stimulus/response/feedback variables.

In third grade, reading success can be attributed about equally to the instructional procedures used by teachers and the entering ability of the children.

An adult working with a large group of children accounts for 16 percent of the third grade reading score variance. Total academic verbal interaction accounts for less of the variance (4 percent) in third grade than in first grade. This may be explained by the fact that third grade children may not need as much interaction with adults about reading and work more on their own.

One of the most important findings centers around the Raven's test of nonverbal reasoning or perceptive problem solving (considered to be a culture-fair test of fluid intelligence). The abilities required to function well on this test have not been considered to be influenced by environment. This study found that ability to perform well on the Raven's test was related to the classroom environment and strongly suggests that children who, for a period of three years, have been in classrooms that use a wide variety of activities and provide a wide variety of manipulative materials have learned to see the relationship between parts and wholes. At any rate, they learn to see spatial relationships similar to those tested on the Raven's.

CONCLUSION

A study of the instructional procedures used in classrooms and the achievement of children indicates that time spent in reading and math activities and a high rate of drill, practice, and praise contribute to higher reading and math scores. Children taught by these methods tend to accept responsibility for their failures but not for their successes. Lower absence rates, higher scores on a nonverbal problem solving test of reasoning can be attributed in part to more open and flexible instructional approaches in which children are provided a wide variety of activities and materials and where children engage independently in activities and select their own groups part of the time.

Classroom instructional processes predicted as much or more of the outcome score variances than did the entering school test scores of children. Based upon these findings, we conclude that what occurs within a classroom does contribute to achievement in basic skills, good attendance, and desired child behaviors.

References

Stallings, J. *Follow Through Program Classroom Observation Evaluation 1971–1972.* Menlo Park, California: Stanford Research Institute, August, 1973.

Stallings, J., P. Baker, and G. Steinmetz. "What Happens in the Follow Through Program: Implications for Child Growth and Development." Paper presented for the American Psychological Association convention, Honolulu, Hawaii, September 1972.

Stallings, J., and D. Kaskowitz. *Follow Through Classroom Observation Evaluation 1972–1973.* Menlo Park, California: Stanford Research Institute, 1974.

BARAK ROSENSHINE
University of Illinois

Review of Teaching Variables and Student Achievement

Research relating teaching variables to pupil achievement consists of two major steps: (1) obtaining a count (or an estimate) of the frequency of a number of instructional events, and (2) correlating the frequency of these events with measures of student learning or attitudes. An example would be counting the frequency of teacher "higher order" questions in 20 or so classrooms and then correlating these frequencies with student learning in each of the classrooms.

Although studies of this type have appeared since 1940, the "modern era" of this research began with the work of Flanders in 1957. The popularity of his "Interaction Analysis" procedures led to the development of hundreds of observation instruments of varying degrees of complexity. The major part of all these instruments is in the interaction section. Here, some of the major categories are:

teacher structuring procedures
teacher questions
student responses
teacher reactions
warmth
criticism
managerial activities
groupings of students

Most of the instruments have been used to describe teaching—to give the frequencies and percentages of different events along with commentary on the "goodness" and "badness" of such behaviors. (That is, one frequently reads that teacher talk is "bad" and pupil talk is "good," and similar judgments are

---

Excerpted from a paper presented at the Conference on Research on Teacher Effects: An Examination by Policy-Makers and Researchers, The University of Texas at Austin, November 3–5, 1975. Used with permission of the author.

made about higher level questions, praise, criticism, and whole-class teaching.)

There have been only a handful, perhaps no more than 75, correlational and experimental studies which have attempted to determine the relationship between classroom events and pupil outcomes. The number of studies on any single variable is extremely small. One cannot find more than 25 studies on teacher criticism or on teacher questions. Indeed, there have been far more modules and materials on how to train teachers to ask "higher level questions" than there have been studies on higher level questions. Unfortunately, the number of studies on any variable of interest does not begin to cover the number of grade levels and subject areas which are taught, and if one subdivides these studies according to SES, student prior achievement, and geographic setting, then there are a large number of blank spaces. If one wishes to learn about the effects of teacher praise in 6th-grade reading with low SES pupils, one can find, at most, two or three studies—if that many. And, when these studies are located, one frequently learns that the results are not consistent across the two or three studies.

In sum, even if the studies were well-designed, well- executed, and consistent and significant in their results, there would still be too few to support policy decisions about desirable instructional behaviors. In practice, the design and analysis of many studies is easily criticized, results are frequently nonsignificant, and consistent and significant results are hard to come by. What we have learned, to date, is offered more as hypotheses for further study than as validated variables for the training and evaluation of teachers.

REVIEW ON SELECTED VARIABLES

Between 1972–1976, six major correlational studies have been reported (those by Brophy and Evertson, 1974; Soar, 1973; Stallings and Kaskowitz, 1974; McDonald, 1975; Tikunoff, Berliner, and Rist, 1975; and Good and Grouws, 1975) along with three major experimental studies (Ward and Tikunoff, 1975; Gall et al., 1975; Stanford Program on Teaching Effectiveness, 1976). Yet, it is hard to summarize these studies because of differences in topic and particularly in the SES background of the students studied. Three of these studies (those by Soar, Stallings and Kaskowitz, and Brophy and Evertson) covered the same context—primary grade reading and mathematics for children from low SES backgrounds—and because of this common focus only those studies were selected for this review. The variables common to this subset of studies were grouped into eight categories and the major results are presented in Table 1. Although the results from other studies are included whenever relevant, the generalizations in this review are limited to the above context.

Time

The amount of time spent directly on instruction appears to be significantly related to student achievement. For example, Stallings and Kaskowitz coded the *observed time spent* on reading and mathematics activities and obtained

Table 1. Summary of results on common variables in recent studies on primary grade low SES in reading and math.

Variable	*Stallings Kaskowitz*	*Soar*	*Brophy Evertson*	*Others*
Direct time on academic activities	+			+
Time on noncurricular activities	−	−	−	
Allotted time for school or instruction			0	+
Content covered				+
Direct, narrow questions	+	+	+	+
Higher order, open questions	−	−	−	0
Student attention to task	+	0,+	0	0,+
Student inattention, misbehavior		−	−	−
Student in large group	+	+		
Students in independent study without teacher	−	−		
Students in supervised independent study		+		
Praise, and adult positive feedback	+	+	0,+	0
Criticism, and adult negative feedback	+	−	0,−	−
Accepting student comments	+		+	
Student comments—relevant	0	0	+	
Student comments—irrelevant	−	0	0	
Student questions—relevant	−	0	0	
Student questions—irrelevant	−	0	−	
Teacher initiation		−,+	−,0	
Teacher management requests, requests for order		0	−	

+ = positive and significant correlations
0 = nonsignificant and mixed correlations
− = negative and significant correlations

significant and positive results. In addition, all three investigators coded time spent on non-academic activities (such as dramatic play, games, or questions about home and family) and all three obtained consistent negative correlations. Wiley and Harnischfeger (1974) also found that the average number of hours of schooling per year in a school was positively and significantly related to achievement in reading and mathematics.

Other recent studies also support the importance of direct time. For example, the coding of *content covered* has yielded significant positive correlations with achievement (see Rosenshine and Furst, 1973). Similarly, in a review of studies comparing different curriculum programs, Walker and Schaffarzick

(1974) concluded that the outcomes of different curriculum programs mirrored the content that was taught. That is, new curriculums were more effective when the post-test measured content relevant to them, whereas traditional curriculums were slightly superior when traditional post-tests were used.

Overall, then, both direct instructional time and content covered have been positively related to achievement whereas time on non-academic activities has been negatively related.

Questions

The results on questions suggest that for this context (primary grade students from low SES backgrounds) it may be preferable to proceed in small steps and ask factual questions at the child's level. In all three studies, the frequency of factual, single-answer questions was correlated positively and significantly with achievement, whereas the frequency of more complex, or difficult, or divergent questions had negative correlations. Brophy and Evertson also found that for low SES students, the percentage of correct answers was positively and significantly related to achievement.

However, in two well-designed experimental studies using randomly selected students, (Gall et al., 1975 and the Stanford Program on Teaching Effectiveness, 1975) a high frequency of higher order questions *did not* improve student post-test scores, not even on higher level questions. The lack of significant results for complex or higher level questions has puzzled all the researchers, and led us to conclude that we need to rethink what is meant by types of questions and their effects.

Student Inattention

Student inattention was consistently, significantly, and negatively related to achievement in all three studies. Similar negative results have usually also been obtained in other studies (e.g., McDonald et al., 1975). The results for student attention or on-task behavior were positive but the correlations were not as high or consistent as those for inattention; again, similar results were obtained in other studies.

Thus, student disruptive behavior, off-task behaviors, and inattention appear to be consistent negative correlates with achievement.

Work Groupings

For both Stallings and Kaskowitz and for Soar, positive and significant correlations were obtained for students *working in groups* or doing seatwork under supervision. Both investigators also found *negative* correlations for children working independently without supervision of a teacher. The researchers agreed that independent study without supervision does not appear successful unless students are first taught how to work independently.

Adult Feedback: Praise and Criticism

Overall, teacher praise showed consistent, positive, but low correlations with student achievement and praise of student academic responses had higher correlations than praise for student behavior. However, the results were *not consistent* for academic criticism—criticism following a student answer. Stallings and Kaskowitz found that criticism following an incorrect answer had positive correlations with achievement, whereas Brophy and Evertson found significant negative correlations for the same variable, and Soar obtained negative but low correlations.

Student-Initiated and Teacher-Initiated Comments

With one exception (see Table 1) all types of student-initiated talk, whether academic or nonacademic, yielded negative or low correlations. Student-initiated talk does not appear to be as important for this type of achievement as was once thought.

The frequency of teacher-initiated comments did not show consistent results in these studies—sometimes yielding significant positive and sometimes significant negative correlations. Coding the probable cause of a teacher's comment (e.g., management, clarification, feedback, or motivation) might be helpful in future research.

Management and Control Requests

There were no consistent results for teacher management or control statements. Brophy and Evertson found that such statements (e.g., "silence," "get to work") were negatively related to achievement. However, Stallings and Kaskowitz found significant *positive* correlations (in third grade) both for adult punishment of children and for negative corrective feedback on academic matters, while Soar found nonsignificant relationships between control statements and achievement.

DIRECT INSTRUCTION

Across the studies by Brophy and Evertson, by Soar, and by Stallings and Kaskowitz, there are consistent elements which can be assembled into a "direct instruction" model. The elements would describe a small-step instructional procedure which is under the control of the teacher, which provides students materials at their level, and provides fairly quick feedback. Some of the elements would be:

1. Time is structured by the teacher, and a large portion of time is spent on a number of reading activities. There is a predominance of seatwork in academic workbooks which the students do in groups supervised by the teacher. Materials are broken into small steps.

2. Questions are narrow, direct, usually with a single answer, and structured to obtain a high percentage of correct answers.

3. Teachers or materials provide *immediate feedback* using praise and acknowledgement of student answers. In oral interaction, there is little discussion of the answers—correct answers are followed by another question and incorrect answers are followed by the teacher giving the answer.

4. Students work in *small or large groups* supervised by the teacher for instruction or for seatwork. There is little free time or independent-unsupervised activity.

5. There is *less off-task* student behavior. This may occur because of the systematic, structured, supervised setting and the management system.

In addition to the above, the following may be reasonable extrapolations, although they appear in only one or two studies: The teacher is the dominant *leader* who decides which activities will take place. The learning is approached in a direct *business-like manner* and is organized around questions posed by the teacher or the materials. The materials and the instruction are systematically organized, proceeding within *small steps. Goals* are clear and known to the students. Yet, within this task setting the teacher is *warm and convivial,* frequently giving praise and encouragement to the students for academic work.

Despite publicity given to open-space classrooms, variations of direct instruction may be the model instructional approach in the U.S. and elsewhere. For example, in the ethnographic studies done by the Far West Laboratory (Tikunoff, Berliner, and Rist, 1975) the descriptions of both the most effective and the least effective teacher resembled direct instruction. Furthermore, an inspection of curriculum materials—the reading programs and materials packages used in primary grades—reveals the same small-step, immediate feedback, materials-oriented direct learning approach described above. The direct instruction approach—using conventional materials—also appears in the identified successful remedial programs for low SES children (Tallmadge, 1974).

In practice, direct instruction need not be the joyless, highly regimented authoritarian sweatshop that some critics imagine. In the Follow Through studies praise was more frequent in the direct instruction programs than it was in the flexible programs (Stallings and Kaskowitz). Kindness, concern, and consistency were part of the environment in the structured and successful Follow Through programs, in the structured classrooms of the most successful teachers in the Far West Laboratory study (Tikunoff, Berliner, and Rist, 1975), and in the structured classrooms of successful compensatory reading programs (Tallmadge, 1974).

Future Research on Direct Instruction

If direct instruction is pervasive, then the research strategy becomes one of identifying effective and ineffective direct instruction. These steps would include developing a tentative list of major implementation variables, identifying discrepancies between the implementation ideal and actual practice, and, most important, identifying which implementation variables are critical for student achievement and which can be dropped. Perhaps the important part of future research on direct instruction is that we would be looking for patterns rather than single variables.

References

Brophy, J. E., and C. M. Evertson. *Process-Product Correlations in the Texas Teacher Effectiveness Study: Final Report.* Austin, Texas: The University of Texas, 1974.

Gall, M. et al. *Teacher Questions.* San Francisco: Far West Laboratory for Educational Research and Development, 1975.

Good, T. L., and D. A. Grouws. *Process Product Relationships in 4th Grade Mathematics Classes.* Columbia, Missouri: College of Education, University of Missouri, 1975.

McDonald, F. J. et al. *Beginning Teacher Education Study, Phase II: Final Report.* Princeton, N.J.: Educational Testing Service, 1975.

Rosenshine, B., and N. F. Furst. "The Use of Direct Observation to Study Teaching." In R. M. W. Travers, ed., *Second Handbook of Research on Teaching.* Chicago: Rand McNally, 1973.

Soar, R. S. *Follow Through Classroom Process Measurement and Pupil Growth (1970–71): Final Report.* Gainesville, Florida: College of Education, University of Florida, 1973.

Stallings, J. A., and D. H. Kaskowitz. *Follow Through Classroom Observation Evaluation (1972–1973).* Menlo Park, California: Stanford Research Institute, 1974.

Stanford Program on Teaching Effectiveness. *A Factorially Designed Experiment on Teacher Structuring, Soliciting, and Reacting.* Stanford, California: Stanford Center for Research and Development in Teaching, 1976.

Tallmadge, K. *The Development of Project Information Packages for Effective Approaches in Compensatory Education.* Technical report UR-254. Mountain View, California: RMC Research Corp., 1974.

Tikunoff, W. J., D. Berliner, and R. Rist. *An Ethnographic Study of Forty Classrooms.* Technical Report Nr 75–10–5, San Francisco: Far West Laboratory for Educational Research and Development, 1975.

Walker, D., and J. Schaffarzick. "Comparing Curricula." *Review of Educational Research* 44 (1974): 83–111.

Ward, B. A., and W. J. Tikunoff. *Application of Research to Teaching. Report A75–2.* San Francisco: Far West Laboratory for Educational Research, 1975.

Wiley, D. E., and A. Harnischfeger. "Explosion of a Myth: Quantity of Schooling and Exposure to Instruction, Major Educational Vehicles." *Educational Researcher* 3 (1974): 7–12.

THOMAS L. GOOD and
DOUGLAS A. GROUWS
University of Missouri—Columbia

Teaching Effectiveness in Fourth-Grade Mathematics Classrooms*

Table 1 presents the significant findings from a study to determine process-product relationships in fourth-grade mathematics classrooms. A complete discussion of all results is available elsewhere (Good and Grouws, 1975). The data suggest that more effective teachers (highs)† spend more time teaching the whole class as a group, with more clarity, and appear to strike an interesting combination of engaging the entire class on similar tasks while maintaining a relatively relaxed classroom climate. High teachers' ability to present material clearly and to keep students' attention is no doubt part of the reason that teaching the whole class (as a unit) works for them.

In a relative sense, it appears that less effective teachers (lows) are poor classroom managers. This can be seen in the fact that they ask more discipline questions (i.e., teacher requests a student to respond to a question because he or she was misbehaving), as well as warning and criticizing students more frequently than do highs. No doubt such behavioral criticism and warnings work against the creation of a relaxed learning environment. Higher alerting and accountability scores in the context of frequent criticism and warnings may take on an adversive quality (e.g., students may fear failure).

In general, we see that students initiate much more interaction in high classrooms. In particular, students in high classrooms are more likely to *ap-*

Excerpted from T. L. Good and D. A. Grouws, *Process-Product Relationships in Fourth-Grade Mathematics Classrooms* (Final Report, NIE Grant #NEG-00-3-0123, 1975). Reprinted by permission.

* See note at end of excerpt.

† For purposes of the following discussion, more effective and less effective teachers represent the 9 teachers (out of a sample of 41) whose pupils had the highest positive residual gain scores and the 9 teachers whose pupils had the highest negative residual gain scores over two consecutive years on the Iowa Test of Basic Skills (total math subscale). A residual gain score for a particular teacher represents his pupils' level of achievement over (positive residual) or under (negative residual) the average gain for all classrooms.

Table 1. Significant or near-significant process variables from an analysis of variance across the top and bottom nine teachers.

Variables	*p Value*	$\bar{X}$ *High*	$\bar{X}$ *Low*
Number of students	.0001	26.70	21.34
Time teacher taught "whole" class	.1001	40.47	30.18
Time going over homework	.0656	4.98	8.19
Classroom climate*	.0771	2.00	2.26
Clarity	.0135	4.06	3.53
Average accountability	.0424	3.46	3.15
Average alerting	.0350	3.90	3.59
Discipline question	.0656	0.11	0.35
Direct question	.0113	14.07	28.26
Process question	.0131	2.72	7.53
Correct response	.0533	38.70	50.98
Wrong response	.0017	5.39	11.39
No response	.0058	1.37	3.26
Student response followed by teacher praise	.0046	2.74	14.09
Negates wrong	.0088	1.51	3.29
Repeats question	.0295	1.39	2.78
Student-initiated work-related contact; teacher gives process feedback	.0654	4.41	1.56
Student-initiated work-related contact; teacher gives feedback	.0004	17.65	9.30
Teacher-initiated work-related contact; type feedback unknown	.1072	0.02	0.24
Teacher-initiated behavior-related contact; teacher gives warning	.0081	1.75	3.37
Teacher-initiated behavior-related contact; teacher gives criticism	.0548	0.30	0.67
Total teacher-initiated work-related contacts	.0383	3.01	5.96
Total teacher-initiated behavior-related contacts	.0853	4.22	5.85
Total teacher-initiated contacts	.0129	7.23	11.83
Total student-initiated work-related contacts	.0004	23.44	11.80
Total student-initiated contacts (work and procedural)	.0003	25.35	13.41
$\frac{\text{Direct questions}}{\text{Total response opportunities}}$	.1089	28.13	36.54
$\frac{\text{Total teacher-initiated contacts}}{\text{Total student-initiated contacts}}$	.0058	54.10	116.41
$\frac{\text{Process questions}}{\text{Total questions}}$	.0518	7.44	14.56
$\frac{\text{Correct responses}}{\text{Total responses}}$	.0051	82.80	76.17
Total process feedback	.1005	6.51	3.04

* This scale was reversed such that a higher score corresponds to a more intense, less enjoyable classroom climate.

proach the teacher for information or feedback than are students in low classrooms. This finding is coupled with an interesting form of complimentary teacher behavior: the provision of process feedback. Highs do not ask many process questions. (Process questions call for a student explanation rather than a simple one or two word answer.) Apparently, these teachers prefer to provide process feedback when students are ready to listen to process explanations.

In public settings highs spend proportionately more time on developmental activities (explaining the process publicly to all students) than do lows, but keep the ball moving rather than frequently calling upon students. When highs do call on students in public settings, they are most likely to ask product questions (questions that call for a straightforward correct answer), presumably followed by a quick student response.

The public presentations of high teachers are interrupted by student questions and call-out responses more frequently than in low classrooms. Hence, these may be mechanisms through which teachers allow students to get feedback in public settings.

TOP THREE AND BOTTOM THREE TEACHERS

Table 2 presents yet another way of looking at the question: what classroom process behavior correlates with student learning performance? Table 2 presents the results of an analysis of variance run across the top three and bottom three teachers. Hence, these results report comparisons across the highest and lowest classes in the sample. In general, these data do not contradict or extend the data that we have reviewed above.

Again, we see that highs teach the class as a class* more frequently than do lows and that they are successful in constructing a more relaxed classroom atmosphere. Lows engage in more alerting and accountability behaviors than do highs. Highs ask fewer discipline questions and fewer process questions than do low teachers. However, highs are more likely to provide process feedback to their students than are low teachers.

In general, highs are less likely to stay with students by providing sustaining feedback when students do not make a response or indicate that they do not know how to respond. In such situations, high teachers are less likely to repeat the question, to give a clue, or to expand upon student responses. However, as previously noted, the 9 high teachers were more likely to stay with students when they give a partially correct response. The means for the top 3 and bottom 3 teachers are in the same direction (highs sustained 3.40 part right responses per hour; whereas, lows sustained 1.60 per hour), but the p-value does not approach significance and the behavioral frequency of part right responses is low. Still, given that these teachers are proportionately asking more product questions, the strategy appears to make sense. That is, students are asked questions that they either know or do not know and when they indicate

* Most teachers who basically teach the class as an intact group would have a few students (1–4) working on individual tasks.

Table 2. Significant or near-significant process variables from an analysis of variance across the top and bottom three teachers.

Variables	*p Values*	$\overline{X}$ *High*	$\overline{X}$ *Low*
Number of students	.0027	27.90	20.33
Time teacher taught "whole" class	.0284	37.90	25.50
Classroom climate	.0082	1.85	2.53
Average accountability	.0190	3.47	2.78
Discipline question	.0317	0.00	0.59
Process question	.0511	1.89	5.31
No response from student	.0353	0.74	2.06
"No response" or "don't know" response followed by sustaining feedback	.0988	1.88	4.54
Student response followed by teacher praise	.0382	1.92	7.75
Repeats question	.0876	0.48	1.21
Gives clue	.0819	0.78	1.67
Teacher expands student's response	.0683	0.00	0.25
Student-initiated work-related contact; teacher gives feedback	.0003	26.08	9.08
Student-initiated procedural contact; teacher gives feedback	.0719	1.08	2.67
Teacher-initiated work-related contact; teacher gives praise	.0706	0.19	0.89
Teacher-initiated work-related contact; teacher gives feedback	.0024	0.95	5.86
Teacher-initiated work-related contact; teacher criticizes work	.0205	0.00	0.46
Teacher gives behavioral warning	.0023	1.08	4.93
Teacher gives behavioral criticism	.0028	0.00	1.14
Total teacher-initiated work-related contacts	.0016	1.52	8.41
Total teacher-initiated behavioral contacts	.0022	2.65	8.34
Total teacher-initiated contacts (work and behavior)	.0002	4.17	16.75
Student-initiated work-related contacts	.0012	30.26	13.03
Student-initiated procedural contacts	.0431	1.08	2.88
Total student-initiated contacts (work and procedural)	.0030	31.34	15.91
Direct questions / Direct questions plus open question	.0121	21.44	48.63
Direct questions / Total response opportunities	.0210	19.05	40.60
Open questions / Total response opportunities	.0172	72.88	47.29
Student-initiated work contacts / Total student-initiated contacts (work and procedural)	.0064	96.22	81.17
Total teacher-initiated contacts / Total student-initiated contacts	.0004	26.02	122.30
Teacher process feedback / Teacher product feedback	.0965	6.44	2.15

that they cannot respond the teacher moves on to someone else or provides a process explanation.

Lows are much more likely to praise students than are high teachers. This is strong evidence that excessively high praise rates are *not* necessarily associated with student learning. We suspect that in this sample the high praise rates are indicative of an inability to cope with managerial demands. That is, teachers through the use of praise are attempting to "buy off" and control students: a strategy that does not appear to work. Part of this problem may be that teacher training programs encourage teachers to use praise liberally. Some teachers respond to this plea indiscriminantly and do not make praise contingent upon good performance. It is clear from these data that high praise rates are not necessary for learning and may be detrimental (e.g., may communicate low expectations). Data in Table 2 also make it clear that low teachers have more discipline problems. This can be seen in the fact that they ask more discipline questions, give more behavioral warnings, and more behavioral criticisms. The tendency to criticize the behavior of students even spills over into the criticism of academic work. Table 2 also shows that lows are more likely to criticize students when *they approach* students in work situations.

Perhaps this is one reason why teacher afforded contact (teacher goes to student desk without being requested by the student) with students is negatively associated with student achievement. If students are unduly concerned about teacher praise and/or criticism, the presence of the teacher moving around the room may have a detrimental effect upon student performance.

Table 2 results emphasize the importance of student initiated work contacts (students go to teacher or request that the teacher come to their desk) and the relatively detrimental effects of teacher afforded contacts. Presumably, in classroom situations that involve children from middle class homes (at least in a focused academic subject like mathematics) it is better to allow students to approach the teacher when they need help. Interestingly, in this teaching context process feedback appears to be important in facilitating student progress even though process questions are not.

PATTERNS AND EFFECTIVENESS

Teaching effectiveness (as operationally defined in this study) appeared to be strongly associated with the following clusters: (1) *student-initiated behavior;* (2) *whole class instruction;** (3) *general clarity of instruction,* and *availability of information as needed (process feedback in particular);* (4) a *nonevaluative* and generally *relaxed learning environment;* (5) *higher achievement expectations;* (6) *classrooms that were relatively free of major behavioral disorders.*

Several different behavioral measures consistently demonstrated that high teachers were approached by students more than teachers in low classrooms.

* This variable did not differentiate high and low classrooms as both utilized whole class instruction. However it was the instructional mode in high classrooms and these teachers obtained better results than teachers who taught mathematics via groups.

Presumably when students in high classrooms wanted information or evaluative input they felt free to approach the teacher. Even when the teacher dealt with the entire class in a public format, students in high rooms were able to participate through their own initiative. Students in high rooms asked the teacher more questions, called out more answers, and proportionately were asked more open questions (questions which students indicate they want to answer: they raise their hands, etc.).

In this context, student initiated behavior appears to make good sense. For example, students' call-out rates per hour are not excessive. Given a general population of middle class students, it appears appropriate to allow them to approach the teacher as they need help. Teachers who choose to rotate around the room will find the one or two students who are having difficulty (and not approaching the teacher) but may delay several students who want teacher feedback. In a class setting filled with students who possess at least minimal self-management skills, the general policy of allowing and encouraging students to approach the teacher is a good one. Teachers may profitably seek out the few students who don't come to them without developing systematic routines of circling the room.

A second general finding of these data was that students in high classes received instruction as a unit. They were given the same in-class assignments and identical homework assignments. However, students in low classes also were basically taught as a whole group. But low teachers also worked with individuals or groups of students much more frequently than did highs.

Perhaps if the variance of learners within a class is not too great, it makes more sense to gear instruction toward a particular mode (whole class or group: not both). Interestingly, those teachers who taught mathematics via groups in this particular study, fell into the middle effectiveness range. The data clearly suggest that teaching the class is not a poor or good strategy categorically. If the teacher possesses certain capabilities it may be an excellent strategy, if not, the whole class instructional mode will not work.

One of the necessary skills for effective whole class instruction is the ability to make clear presentations. Highs regularly exceeded lows in clarity scores. They generally introduced and explained material more clearly than did lows. Interestingly, in whole class settings highs asked more product questions and appeared to keep the "ball moving." However, when students did experience difficulty, highs were more likely to give process feedback than lows. In contrast, lows were more likely to ask process questions and less likely to give process feedback. It seems that highs did not focus upon process as a ritual, but rather, they used process responses when student responses indicated some error or misunderstanding.

The data demonstrate that high praise rates do not categorically enhance learning. Indeed, in this study, praise is negatively associated with both achievement and climate. Consistently, high teachers were found to praise less than low teachers. Interestingly, despite their high praise rates, lows were much less likely than highs to praise students when they approached them about their academic work. Presumably, low teachers prefer to go to students (rather than being approached by them), a strategy that proved to be ineffective in this study. High teachers were basically non-evaluative. They did not criticize or praise academic work as frequently as did low teachers. The evaluative stance of lows coupled with their high rates of approaching students may have interfered with learning progress as well as creating a "heavy" climate. High classrooms were regularly described more favorably by students, despite the fact that high teachers did not praise much.

Highs also appeared to demand *more* work and achievement from students. They tended to assign more homework and moved through the curriculum more briskly than low teachers (Good, Grouws, and Beckerman, 1976).

Low teachers seemed to have more frequent managerial problems than did high teachers. However, the data here are not as clear as for the five clusters described above. Several measures show little difference between high and low teachers (e.g., percent of students not involved in lesson). Suggestion of discipline problems stems from the fact that lows issue many more behavioral warnings and criticisms than do highs. This may be a comment upon differential teacher reaction to similar behavioral events (lows are more threatened by the same noise levels, etc.), but we suspect that there are more managerial problems in low classrooms. In part, we feel this way because students are often left sitting waiting for the teacher to come to them, and because they receive unclear and incomplete directions (as reflected in the high rates of teacher afforded contacts that were recorded in lows' classrooms and as reported in observers' summaries).

CONCLUSIONS

In general, our data correspond to the linear process-product findings in high SES schools reported by Brophy and Evertson (1974) and described earlier in this chapter. Probably the most basic correspondence is the pattern of results. In both data sets there are numerous weak correlations rather than a few big relations that seem to be of critical importance. The data in both studies suggest that successful teaching is based upon a large number of variables (that must be present to a minimum degree) rather than upon two or three critical factors.

Among the agreements in our data and the Brophy-Evertson high SES data are: calling on volunteers correlates positively with student achievement, student initiated questions correlate positively with achievement, teacher afforded work contact (going to students' seats) correlates negatively with student achievement, the positive relationship between process feedback and student achievement, the positive relationship of homework and achievement, and the negative value of using materials in instruction.

Both sets of findings suggest that it makes sense to allow students (who are capable of self-direction) to work semi-autonomously during seat work assignments, but also to allow these students the freedom to seek out the teacher when they need feedback. In public settings, both sets of findings suggest that within limits it is a reasonable strategy to call on volunteers, and that student initiated questions appear to be a sign of appropriate involvement.

However, our data seem to go a little further in supporting the concept of student assertiveness and initiative than do the Brophy-Evertson data. For example, student eagerness to respond (call-outs) correlated negatively in the Brophy-Evertson study but our data show a positive relationship. Perhaps this finding is because of age (older children are less likely to over respond) or because of subject matter (call-out is more appropriate in a focused subject like mathematics than other subjects).

For whatever reason the two studies provide conflicting results on this point. But again both data sets suggest that child *initiative* appears to be a generally good index of learning in middle SES classrooms. This form of initiative should not be confused with indirect teaching. . . , a variable that has frequently been interpreted to mean: the less teachers talk the better. In general, we refer here to student initiative in seeking out the teacher during seat work and in seeking feedback during public discussion (by asking questions). These data say nothing about the frequency of student talk *per se* and in the context of the data presented in this study it appears that less frequent teacher questioning (and presumably less public student talk) seems to be a more preferable instructional style.

There are other variables as well that appear to be in conflict when the present data and the Brophy-Evertson process-product data are examined. For example, clarity of teacher presentations seem to be an important variable in our study but it draws little support in the Texas data. In contrast one of the interesting variables in the Texas project (percent of correct answers) draws little confirmatory support in our data.

But as a set the findings appear to hang together reasonably well and provide a number of agreement "points" that can be directly translated into treatment research allowing the value of these correlational relationships to be directly tested. Obviously, points of conflict can also be studied in treatment research but initially they may need to be reexamined in other naturalistic settings as well.

Although the data do suggest a set of findings that are internally consistent and a set of clusters that draw solid replication support from the Texas Teacher Effectiveness Project, the data do not provide a base for accountability purposes. The data are interesting and have clear treatment implications; however, until experimental work has been completed the process-product relationships reported here are appropriately viewed as hypotheses to be tested.

A NOTE ON INTERPRETING THE RESULTS

In reacting to the data that follow, it is important to realize that different metrics are being utilized. First, time measures are reported in terms of a mean score across all observations. The means for teaching "whole" class, the second variable listed on Table 1, are correctly interpreted as follows: the 9 high teachers, as a group, averaged 40 minutes and 47 seconds in teaching "whole" class *each observation;* whereas, the 9 low teachers, as a group, averaged 30 minutes and 18 seconds *per observation.*

Second, low inference behavioral measures are reported in terms of rates per hour. To control for unequal length and number of observations, the frequency of each behavioral measure was divided by the number of minutes in the observation and multiplied by sixty. One variable reported from the Brophy-Good Dyadic is Teacher Asks Direct Question (see Table 1). The means here are interpreted as follows: the 9 high teachers initiated, on the average, 14.07 direct questions *per hour;* whereas the 9 low teachers initiated, on the average, 28.26 direct questions *per hour.*

High inference measures are represented by a mean score across observations. Four high inference variables (organization, alerting, accountability, classroom climate) were rated *once* at the end of each observation. Hence the rating is a single global estimate, and the means that appear in Table 1 for these variables represent the average of the ratings that were made at the end of each observation.

However, several high inference variables (general thrust of homework; student attention; clarity; enthusiasm; average accountability; average alerting; percent of students probably involved; and percent of students definitely not involved) could be measured several times during an observation. Here a mean is computed for separate ratings within an observation and then the mean score for an observation is combined with the mean score of other observations to yield a general mean.

One intriguing question that the present study raises concerns the relationship between student achievement and classroom climate. In an initial study involving 130 teachers (from which eventually the observation sample was picked), the correlation between climate and residual achievement on the Iowa Test of Basic Skills was about zero. The correlation varied from subtest to subtest but all correlations were quite low. However, in the year in which observational data were collected (two years after the first study) the obtained correlation between residual achievement on the total math score on the Iowa and the same climate scale was .50.

We suspect two reasons account for this major difference. First, perhaps, by studying teachers who were stable and relatively high or low in achievement we biased the sample systematically. The second and, we suspect, the more important reason is that during the year of observation, students rated the teacher with particular reference to mathematics instruction. Earlier, students had rated the teacher and classroom instruction generally. This may have been a confusing task given that some students in the large sample spent part of their instructional day with different teachers. In contrast, the observational study specifically targeted student reaction to instruction during mathematics.

References

Brophy, J., and C. Evertson. *Process-Product Correlations in the Texas Teacher Effectiveness Study: Final Report* (Res. Rep. 74–4). Austin, Texas: Research and Development Center for Teacher Education, 1974. (ERIC No. ED 091 394)

Good, T., and D. Grouws. "Teacher Rapport: Some Stability Data." *Journal of Educational Psychology* **67** (1975): 179–182.

Good, T., D. Grouws, and T. Beckerman. *Teaching Effectiveness: A Study of Teachers' Curriculum Pacing in Fourth-Grade Mathematics.* Technical report. Columbia, Missouri: Center for the Study of Social Behavior, 1976.

FREDERICK J. McDONALD
Educational Testing Service
Princeton, New Jersey

Research on Teaching: Report on Phase II of the Beginning Teacher Evaluation Study[1]

The Beginning Teacher Evaluation Study, Phase II is one component in a long-term study of teaching effectiveness. This first phase was a field study, that is, a study of teaching conducted in actual classrooms and schools. An important feature of this study is its long-term character. In this respect in conception the total project is unique, and is a marked departure from the history of research on teaching.

Phase II of this project consisted of the following major operations:

1. Children's performance in reading and mathematics was measured at two points in time.
2. In the intervening period, teachers' classroom performances were observed.
3. These observations were related to the differential achievements of the pupils.

A design of this type was used to answer the question, "Is there a correlation between teaching performance and gains in learning?" There are several unique features to this design. First, the measurements of pupil performance were made at the beginning and the end of the school year. This feature of the design enables us to eliminate one major source of effects on pupil learning, namely, the interventions of many different teachers. We know where a student or a class began and where they ended in terms of achievement. During this period of time, the class had one teacher.

Second, the measure of the pupils' achievement at the beginning of the year is an index of previous influences on learning. The correlation between socioeconomic status and total fall reading scores, for example, was $r = .35$ for

---

Excerpted from a paper presented at the Conference on Research on Teacher Effects: An Examination by Policy-Makers and Researchers, The University of Texas at Austin, November 3–5, 1975. Used with permission of the author.

[1] The Beginning Teacher Evaluation Study is being conducted by the California Commission on Teacher Preparation and Licensing and is supported by the National Institute of Education.

the second grade. When, therefore, we partial out the fall reading scores we are "removing" to some degree the relation of socioeconomic status to these scores.

Third, the data are in a form that we may analyze them by class, that is, by individual teacher. If the correlation between fall and spring scores is essentially the same for all teachers, we suspect that all the teachers are contributing about equally to changes in learning. If there are differences in this correlation among the teachers, then we suspect that different teachers are contributing differently to changes in learning. We may then ask the question, "Are these teachers teaching differently?"

To study patterns of performance we ran stepwise regressions on the significance of the relation. The result of this analysis is a prediction equation that specifies the contribution of each variable to predicting pupil performance. In such analyses some teaching performance variables will turn out to be positive predictors; others will be negative predictors. This information is in itself useful. But one may also look at the set of positive predictors and at the set of negative predictors to see if there is a pattern in the set and if the contrasts between the two sets makes sense. In this analysis the following results were obtained (McDonald *et al.,* 1975).

1. *For Grade 2 Reading:* Use of a variety of instructional materials was a positive predictor. This methodological procedure is related to group teaching and providing feedback individually.

   It seems that in teaching reading increasing the amount of direct instruction per pupil may be the underlying variable that accounts for improved pupil performance. Direct instruction can be increased in two ways: by teaching in groups and by interacting more frequently with students, and in doing so, by monitoring their performance and by providing corrective feedback on it.

   In this analysis, having a variety of instructional purposes, particularly when the teacher is the principal source of instruction is a negative predictor.

2. *For Grade 2 Mathematics:* Variety of skills taught, maintaining task-involvement, and covering a wider range of content are positive predictors of pupil performance. Teaching the class as a whole or in groups, a variety of instructional activities, unsystematic questioning, and a variety of instructional materials are negative predictors.

3. *For Grade 5 Reading:* Independent work and a variety of instructional techniques are positive predictors whereas a variety of instructional materials, time spent organizing the instructional activity, and variety of materials are negative predictors.

4. *For Grade 5 Mathematics:* Teaching the class as a whole or in groups and a variety of instructional techniques are positive predictors. Variety of materials is a negative predictor.

These results in and of themselves may seem confusing and inconsistent but interpretations can be made of them by considering the teaching performance variables in terms of larger categories such as *instructional time, instruc-*

tional content, instructional material, instructional organization, instructional activity, teacher-pupil interaction, and *pupil behavior.* If the positive and negative predictors are grouped in such categories the following hypotheses seem to be consistent with the data:

1. In second grade reading a variety of instructional material is related to increased pupil performance. In the second grade instructing in a group and more monitoring of individual performance with corrective feedback are positively related to pupil performance. *Thus, it appears that the critical domains of teaching performance in teaching reading in the second grade are those related to the amount and kind of interaction with individual pupils, how pupils are organized for instruction and the variety of instructional materials that are used.* As I suggested earlier, I suspect that the critical factor underlying these results is the amount of direct instruction provided by the teacher; therefore, procedures which increase the amount of direct instruction are related to increased improved pupil performance. This result should not be surprising because students still have not highly developed reading skills in the second grade and are more dependent on the teacher for direct instruction.

This result also suggests where one ought to look for greater specificity about the character of the organizational pattern. It was apparent to us on the basis of our observations that some teachers, while teaching some of the students in a group, did not maintain sufficient control over the task-involvement of individual students, whereas others were able both to teach a group and at the same time monitor the performance of other children working outside the group. We suspect it is the combination of maximizing direct instruction by using group procedures and maintaining a high level of interaction with individual pupils that is a highly effective instructional pattern.

2. In second grade mathematics the critical domains are different. In second grade mathematics the amount of *instructional content* is a critical variable and *amount of time spent* in teaching mathematics was also directly related to pupil performance. These results are probably related to the fact that the total amount of time spent in teaching mathematics was relatively low on the average across this group of teachers, so that the positive effects of spending more time when also covering more content became apparent.

The data also suggest that attempting to teach mathematics in second grade by using groups or teaching the class as a whole is an ineffective system of instructional organization. The learning of mathematics requires the making of a large number of specific responses in the second grade; for example, consider the number of responses involved in adding a column of numbers. At any point errors can be made. Therefore, much closer monitoring of these performances is probably necessary if students are to learn mathematics well. Instructing the class as a whole or instructing in groups does not provide the opportunity for a large amount of individual monitoring of pupil performance.

The results for Grade 2 Mathematics and Grade 2 Reading present an interesting contrast. The results suggest that an organizational pattern combining group instruction and individual monitoring of performance is effective in teaching reading, but more individual monitoring and less group work is more likely to be an effective instructional pattern in teaching mathematics.

3. For Grade 5 Reading the major domain related to improved pupil performance is the domain characterized as *instructional activity,* whereas instructional materials characterized by variety are negative predictors. In general, the character of reading activity in Grade 5 is continuous reading of more complex materials that require thinking, the understanding of concepts and principles and the analysis of meanings. Such learning is most likely to occur if teachers spend considerable time discussing, explaining, questioning, and in general, stimulating cognitive processes. The results of this study suggest that teachers characterized by large amounts of such teaching performances have classes which make greater gains.

The variety of materials as a negative predictor is somewhat puzzling since many educators believe that a variety of materials is likely to be an effective teaching procedure; however, the data suggest that a variety of materials in and of itself is not related to improved pupil learning. It may be that either the materials are inappropriately chosen, which suggests that the teacher's diagnostic skills need to be improved, or that trying to manage a variety of instructional materials may in some way inhibit the teacher's ability to interact with students in ways that stimulate their thinking about the reading. Whatever the explanation may be, it is obvious that one needs to study seriously those teachers who use a variety of materials and are also producing significant gains in reading, and also study those teachers who, although they are using a variety of materials, are not producing such gains.

4. For Grade 5 Mathematics the critical domains of teaching performances seemed to be the methods of *instructional organization,* and the range of *instructional content* covered. In general, group instruction is more effective than individual instruction in the fifth grade. It may be that by the time students have reached fifth grade they have mastered a sufficient number of the essential responses to be made in mathematics that the performance of students does not have to be monitored as carefully as it does in the earlier grades.

Independent work, however, is an ineffective teaching procedure. The reason for this may be that under such circumstances the teacher has greater difficulty maintaining on-task behavior. Or it may be that when such a procedure is used the teacher is relying more heavily upon the instructional materials and if the performance of students is not carefully monitored, then the students make a large number of errors which remain uncorrected.

It should be of interest that at both the second and fifth grade the *amount of mathematics covered* is a critical factor. This result should not be surprising. Mathematics is an organized body of content, and tests constructed to measure what students learn in mathematics are organized around this content. If students have not been taught percentages or some other concept or procedure, they simply do not do well on those portions of the test relevant to that topic. Teaching procedures which maximize the range of content covered are teaching procedures likely to be effective.

Several general comments seem appropriate at this point. It appears to us that the *method of organizing instruction is a critical domain of teaching per-*

formances. In general, the appropriate pattern differs by subject matter and grade level. There is no one method of organizing instruction that is effective across both reading and mathematics and across both second and fifth grade. But there are methods which are effective for each subject area and each grade level.

Another general observation is that any teaching performance that increases direct *instructional time* tends to be a positive predictor across the variety of analyses. This conclusion, however, should be considered in light of the previous statement. Grouping students for direct instruction is more effective in second grade reading but is not effective in fifth grade mathematics. Such differences are probably related to the character of what is being learned. In second grade reading where group techniques are effective, processes are being learned and presumably the learning of these processes can be stimulated by direct instruction in a group; whereas, in second grade mathematics where discrete responses are being linked together, close individual monitoring of pupil performance is required.

It should be noted, however, that any instructional activity that decreases direct instructional time is almost invariably negatively related to pupil performance. Amount of time spent in organizing instruction generally decreases the amount of direct instructional time, and therefore the students have less time to acquire concepts and skills, less time to practice them, and there is less time for the teacher to provide corrective feedback.

We also suggest that the character of effective interactive techniques varies by subject matter and by grade level. In second grade reading where skill processes are being acquired (the skills of decoding), specific prompts and questions requiring identifications, or questions that ask the student to attempt a response, are the relevant procedures to be used. Whereas in fifth grade reading where the higher or cognitive processes are being developed, the questioning techniques probably should be more of a thought-provoking kind. We have not explored these differences in detail in this study but some of the results suggest that an analysis of those two different interactive patterns would be a profitable area for further investigation.

One surprising result appeared in this study. Because we observed individual pupils, we were able to keep a record of the amount of task-involvement of the pupils and the amount of productive work in class. In general these pupil variables did not relate significantly to learning. This result may seem surprising. But it should be noted that the teachers who we were observing were experienced teachers and we did not have any teachers in the sample whose classes were disorderly.

There is a general level of inattentiveness that is characteristic of most classes, which is not surprising because sustaining attention in young children is a difficult task. But the amount of this inattentiveness in the classes in this study was not a negative predictor of pupil learning nor was a greater amount of on-task behavior a positive predictor. In general, it seems reasonable to assume that on-task behavior is a necessary but not a sufficient condition for improving learning. Only at the extremes of inattentiveness are we likely to find a severe deficit in learning.

In summary, the major domains of teaching performance that appear to be critical are those related to how *instruction is organized* and *how the materials are used.* Relatively few specific teaching techniques appeared significant, and these seemed to be effective when they were part of a complex of techniques.

FACTORS AFFECTING TEACHER PERFORMANCE

Although the major purpose of this study was to relate teaching performances to student learning, the study was designed to analyze the relations between a number of factors and teaching performance. These factors included measures of teachers' aptitudes, attitudes, knowledge of the subject being taught, knowledge of teaching methodology and characteristics of the environment of teaching such as the organizational climate of the school. Figure 1 presents a model of the relationships among these factors that was tested in this study.

This model is a structural model. It represents a "causal" theory of relations among variables related to teaching performance and student learning. In this diagram a straight-line arrow indicates a prediction was made that there is a "causal" connection between the domain from which the arrow is drawn and the domain to which it is drawn. Each of the boxes represents a domain of variables. The analyses made by using this model answered such questions as, "How do teacher cognitive and perceptual aptitudes affect teaching performances?"; "How does knowledge of teaching methodology affect teaching performances?"; "How does the organization of instruction in the school affect teaching performance?" and similar questions.

Although there are a number of interesting specific relations, it would be most useful for our purposes here to give a summary of where the largest number of relationships was found. The largest number of relationships between these domains and the teaching performance variables was found with the domain of teachers' aptitudes. In this domain we had four major aptitude factors, verbal flexibility, verbal fluency, reasoning, and memory. The *verbal flexibility* factor was frequently found related to teaching performances which required a large number of interactions with students which had to occur more or less simultaneously. For example, verbal flexibility is highly correlated with teaching the class-as-a-whole. When the teacher teaches the class-as-a-whole, a certain amount of time is devoted to explanation, but a substantial portion of time is directed to asking and answering questions. This latter procedure requires the teacher to process a considerable range of information more or less simultaneously and to interrelate one item of information to another and to develop a meaningful pattern of questioning. It is not surprising, therefore, that teachers who are more adept at interrelating concepts, ideas, and information may use this technique of teaching the class-as-a-whole more frequently.

What is of greater interest is the general hypothesis that is suggested by the relatively large number of relationships found between the aptitude domain and the performance domain. It may be that teachers develop per-

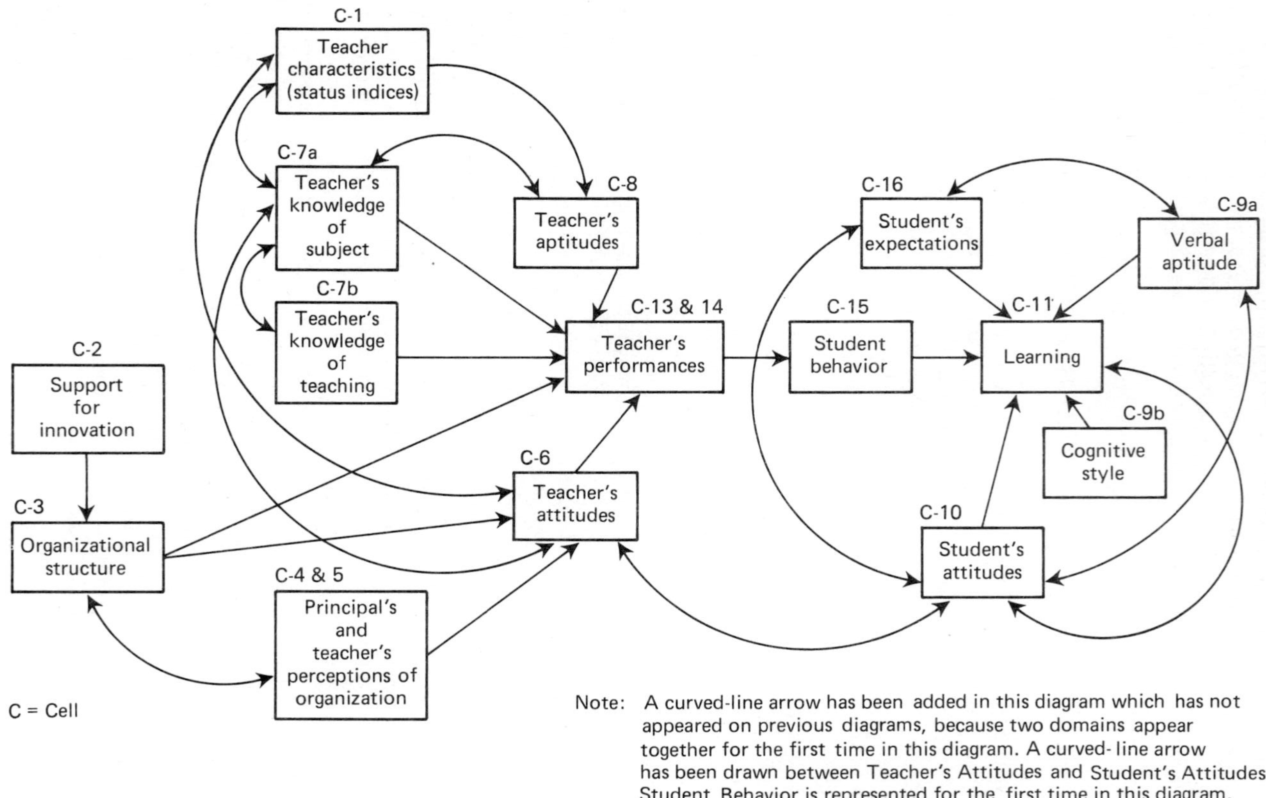

Fig. 1. A structural model of the domain of variables influencing teaching performances and children's learning.

formance styles because they have characteristic ways of relating to the world, perceptually and cognitively. Aptitudes are stable habit structures used in a variety of situations for organizing the stimuli of the phenomenal world. Presumably these aptitudes are acquired because their acquisition has been rewarding in some way to a person. Therefore, a person is likely to act in a way that maximizes the use of his aptitudes. If this hypothesis has validity, then the problem of modifying teacher behavior becomes more complex. It may be that some of these aptitudes are so stable and so well learned that it will be very difficult if not impossible for some people to develop new teaching styles. Or, even if the styles can be modified, a strong relationship between aptitude and performance suggests that different types of training procedures will be needed for people with different aptitudes if they are to acquire new teaching skills. Thus, for example, attempting to teach a teacher who prefers to use instructing the class-as-a-whole the techniques of individual instruction will require that we teach this teaching procedure in such a way that the teacher's verbal flexibility habits are maximized in some way.

Several interesting relations were found between characteristics of the teaching environment and teacher variables; for example, teachers with more positive attitudes towards teaching and higher aspirations for achievement in teaching and with longer term commitments to teaching generally perceived their principals more positively. They also perceived students as more potentially autonomous and had more positive views of their students. This particular analysis does not permit us to say what is cause and what is effect among these variables. We can assume that the teacher's attitudes are determined by a variety of factors other than the events occuring in school, and their existing attitudes lead them to perceive principals and students in certain ways.

The advantage of using a structural model of the kind employed in this study is that analyses of this kind are frequently used in policy research. A structural model is a description of potential causal relations. Each prediction assumes that if a variable in a domain is increased or decreased in amount, it will produce corresponding changes in another variable.

Such models are particularly useful when it is difficult to manipulate variables experimentally. It is difficult to manipulate aptitudes experimentally. Before we attempt experiments involving aptitudes we ought to know if aptitudes are related strongly enough to performance to consider experiments involving them. Also through simulation techniques we can estimate how much of a difference in aptitudes will make a significant difference in teaching performance. Similar estimates can be made of the effect of increasing teachers' knowledge of the subject.

Reference

McDonald, F. J., P. Elias, M. Stone, P. Wheeler, N. Lambert, R. Calfee, J. Sandoval, R. Ekstrom, and M. Lockheed. *Final Report on Phase II Beginning Teacher Evaluation Study*. Prepared for the California Commission on Teacher Preparation and Licensing, Sacramento, California. Princeton: Educational Testing Service, 1975.

Chapter 7

Selected Readings: Measuring Teacher Performance

This chapter begins by acknowledging that much information is needed about how to reliably and validly measure teacher effectiveness. While Chapter 2 focused on the problems and cautions inherent in measuring teacher performance, the following readings place these problems and cautions in a broader perspective by relating them to the planning of appraisal systems.

An appraisal system must rest on the assumption that the teaching behaviors measured relate to meaningful pupil change. Yet, as noted in Chapter 1, few strong empirical relationships have been identified between teacher-process and pupil-product variables. Borich and Madden (1977), reviewing empirical studies of teacher effectiveness, posed four measurement problems that may account for this dearth of identified process-product relationships:

1. a narrow range of measurements frequently employed in individual studies of teacher behavior;
2. lack of a generic framework or guide from which to select behaviors to be measured in the classroom;
3. use of instruments with inadequate psychometric characteristics to measure these behaviors; and
4. inconsistent use of specific instruments across studies measuring the same or similar hypotheses.

While these problems are dealt with elsewhere (Borich and Madden, 1977), the first three relate directly to the readings selected for this chapter.

The first problem became apparent from an examination of literally hundreds of empirical studies investigating relationships between teacher behaviors and pupil outcomes. This review revealed that an inordinate number of research studies measured only a single criterion behavior. While it was apparent that a single outcome provided investigators with a parsimonious research design and a "clean" interpretation of results, the large number of nonsignificant findings produced by studies of this kind suggested that such simplistic methodology represented too narrow and theoretically vacuous an approach to measuring classroom behavior. A number of studies defined teacher behavior, treatments, or instructional programs so broadly that the reader was led to expect wide ranging effects upon pupils. Yet in many of these studies only one treatment or teacher effect was actually measured. Even when multiple outcomes were measured, they often represented only one area of behavior (e.g., classroom interaction variables) or closely related areas (e.g., self-, pupil, and supervisor evaluations of the teacher). Rarely did researchers employ instruments that captured a range of both pupil and teacher affective and cognitive behaviors. Surprisingly, concurrent measurement of teacher-process and pupil-product variables was infrequently incorporated into research designs, and few investigators focused on *causal sequences of behavior* which might have accounted for the effects of classroom instruction.

This limited scope might have been avoided had researchers utilized a multivariate approach to the study of classroom behavior, perhaps similar to that illustrated in Fig. 7.1. Most of the research encountered in this review dealt with only a "slice" of the classroom behavior shown in the model; relatively few studies investigated the sequence of classroom behaviors, taking into account the interactive effects of context, classroom, school, pupil, and teacher variables.

The second problem apparent in the literature was the absence of an overall framework or model to guide researchers in selecting the teacher and pupil behaviors to be measured. Few investigators provided rationale for the kinds of teacher behavior they assessed, and even fewer showed interest in (or knowledge of) the causal sequences of behavior possibly prerequisite to the single variable they did measure. Although promising process-product relationships (Rosenshine, 1971) sometimes encouraged researchers to collect both teacher and pupil

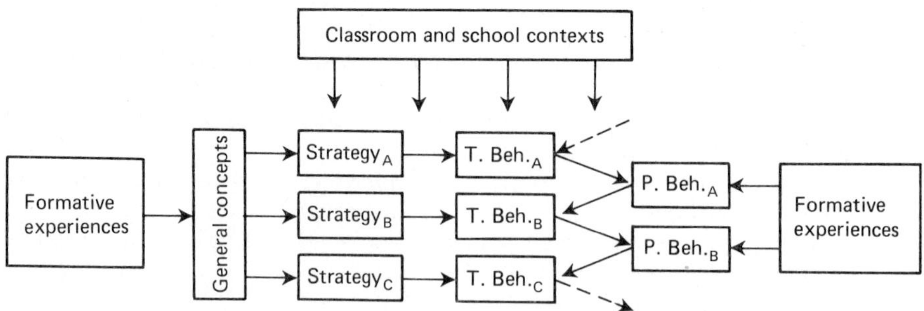

Fig. 7.1. A multivariate model of classroom behavior. (After Biddle, Good, Hall, and Bank, Institute for Research on Teaching: A proposal in response to RFP-NIE-R-76-0001, Teaching Division, National Institute of Education, Washington, D.C., 1975.)

data within the same study, other variables (e.g., context, ethnographic, presage, and affective) were often ignored. Researchers seemed averse to studying those behaviors that were prerequisite to teacher-process variables or that were likely to complicate the interpretation of student achievement data. Chapter 2 presented the general type of framework from which investigators must work in order to assure that classroom, school, context, teacher, and pupil variables, as well as the relationships among these variables, are included in the appraisal design. The reader will recall that this framework included preoperational, immediate-process, intermediate-process, and product variables, as well as affective and cognitive, low-inference and high-inference behavior—all necessary for the composite appraisal of classroom instruction.

Both of the problems cited above have particular meaning for the appraisal of teaching and both proffer the same warning: a single type of behavior or a single set of variables cannot provide an adequate picture of classroom instruction for appraisal purposes. As the following selections illustrate, many problems in the appraisal process stem directly from the complexity of classroom instruction, i.e., the multitude of behaviors (both teacher and pupil) and influences (classroom, school, context) which affect a teacher's performance. While problem one (the narrow range of measurements employed in studies of teacher behavior) suggests that the appraisal of teaching consider the interrelationships among and causal sequence of variables, the second problem (lack of a generic framework or guide from which to select behaviors to be measured) suggests that multiple behaviors be chosen for appraisal according to some systematic scheme depicting the interaction of teacher and pupil behaviors in the context of instruction.

The third problem relating to the readings in this chapter concerns the psychometric inadequacy of most tests and measures used in teacher effectiveness research. The literally hundreds of instruments employed in this field have been subjected to little critical assessment, and in the rare cases when such assessment has been conducted and reported in a journal article or test manual, researchers seem unaware of or indifferent to it. In addition, when psychometric evaluations are available, the instruments are generally judged according to absolute, rather than relative standards. Few sources currently exist whereby one can judge the reliability and validity of an instrument in relation to the reliability and validity of other instruments with similar objectives. Therefore, researchers commonly choose an instrument with relatively low validity and reliability without realizing that a more reliable and valid instrument is available and suitable for measuring the same construct. Revision and further development of an existing instrument is in many cases more appropriate and productive than construction of still another instrument of equal, or more questionable, reliability and validity. The inadequate psychometric properties characterizing many of the instruments in the studies reviewed, and the apparent availability of other more appropriate measures, suggests that instruments are not being selected in a systematic way.

These, as well as other specific measurement problems, are the focus of the five readings in this chapter. Whether a particular selection addresses problems of instrumentation, measurement of multivariate outcomes, or assessment of change, the reader will note that the three above-mentioned problems—i.e., the narrow range of measurements frequently employed, lack of a generic framework, and psychometrically inadequate instrumentation—are at the root of every issue.

The first selection, by Berliner, addresses a potpourri of measurement problems, many relating to the instrumentation concerns highlighted in a later reading by McNeil and Popham. Berliner maintains that the various difficulties in measuring teacher effectiveness are responsible for the many nonsignificant results generated by studies that have attempted to correlate teacher behaviors with pupil outcomes.

Two major areas of concern are identified: instrumentation and methodology. Problems of instrumentation include choosing or designing instruments to assess multivariate outcomes. Berliner advocates the measurement of multivariate outcomes, so that many kinds of achievement and affective responses can be used as indicators of the quality of classroom life. His point is best exemplified by returning to the multivariate model of classroom behavior illustrated in Fig. 7.1. Berliner's approach considers *simultaneously* all of the inputs and outcomes of the classroom, including school, context, teacher, and pupil variables.

But this approach brings up a second problem—that of determining the unit of analysis for the independent variable. Berliner asks, "Is the single teacher question the unit of analysis, is the question along with the wait time the unit, or is the teacher question, wait time, and student answer the unit which best characterizes the independent variable?"

Berliner's methodological problems are of course related to the multivariate nature of the classroom and the need to adequately measure it. Once we admit that there are simultaneous influences upon both teacher and pupil (e.g., SES, grade level, subject matter, prior experiences), then we must also admit that causal links between teacher and pupil can be long and circuitous, i.e., mediated by classroom and school context as well as attitudinal, personality, and achievement variables of both teacher and pupil. This, as Berliner appropriately indicates, complicates the measurement process considerably. Berliner's selection, however, should be viewed optimistically as well as realistically, for the many problems he and others have identified are now being subjected to intensive investigation in a number of national research projects.*

In the next article, Robert Soar indicates some additional obstacles to measuring teacher behavior and a procedure by which at least one of these might be eliminated. He traces many of these measurement problems to the use of pupil achievement scores as an index of teaching effectiveness. While Soar takes exception to several of the traditional teacher rating techniques, such as supervisory and administrative ratings, he does suggest the measurement of teacher

---

* These projects, funded primarily by the National Institute of Education, are those represented by the selections in Chapter 6, Table 6.2. The Evaluation of Teaching Project at the Research and Development Center for Teacher Education, The University of Texas at Austin is devoted to the examination of methodological issues related to the appraisal of teaching.

process as a substitute for student gain, but only when systematic observations of teacher behavior are made with an objective record and when relationships between teacher process and pupil achievement can be empirically confirmed.

Soar's disenchantment with pupil gain is based primarily on the difficulties surrounding the measurement of behavioral change, which have admittedly complicated the reliable assessment of pupil growth. However, the reader should consider the disadvantages of Soar's teacher-process approach. Interestingly enough, his position actually may serve as a straw man, for much of his research, reported in Chapter 6, has employed *both* teacher-process and pupil-achievement data—an approach that seems to avoid the measurement problems inherent in using any single index of teacher effectiveness.

In the third article, Popham distinguishes the terms "process" and "standards" as they relate to the implementation of California's Stull Act (see Preface). Popham's selection provides a link between the popular use of instructional objectives and the appraisal of teaching process. He believes that instructional objectives offer one approach to the appraisal process, if the problems that have plagued their implementation in the past can be resolved. These problems include: (1) determining the appropriate level of specificity for teaching objectives; and (2) selecting suitable objectives to be used for the appraisal process. Popham suggests that the latter problem can be resolved by having various individuals with an interest in the appraisal process set priorities among a large list of possible objectives. This process, commonly referred to as "needs assessment," is also described by Scriven in another selection in this chapter.

Popham's discussion is noteworthy since it introduces the qualitative concepts of values and judgments into the otherwise quantitative process of teacher appraisal. Popham reminds us that we never completely escape value judgments as long as we are selecting objectives for appraisal and levels of specificity at which to measure these objectives. And, as he notes, judgments also play a role in the assessment of teachers who are affected by situational and context variables associated with a particular school and the behavioral antecedents (e.g., prior achievement) of pupils, both of which can bias the appraisal process. Though Popham does not resolve these issues, he suggests procedures that may eventually lead to solutions.

The fourth selection, by Scriven, confirms the need for and expands the meaning of "needs assessment," a procedure used to determine which objectives are most appropriate for appraisal. Unlike Popham, Scriven draws a sharp distinction between needs and goals, defining goals as the substance from which needs are derived. Differences between Scriven and Popham on this point, however, may involve form more than substance, since both authors apparently agree that the setting of priorities among goals (Scriven) or instructional objectives (Popham) by individuals involved in the appraisal process is the most useful way to determine the behaviors for which the teacher will be held accountable.

While describing several of the methodological difficulties involved in assessing teacher performance, Scriven presents a "parsimonious" model for the appraisal of teaching, which includes evaluative data from peer groups, administrators, and students. Scriven's aim is to use as "lean" a data base as possible, while still sharply focusing on six particular functions of teacher evaluation. These functions correspond closely to the diagnostic, formative, and summative purposes for appraisal described in Chapter 3.

Finally, Scriven takes issue with process appraisal of teacher behaviors via classroom visits or even systematic classroom observation techniques. He charges that these procedures are unrelated to the ultimate summative purpose of appraisal, i.e., the assessment of pupil growth. It is interesting that Scriven criticizes those appraisal schemes that focus primarily on teacher process as opposed to pupil product, while his own "parsimonious" appraisal model includes "estimates of classroom justice, e.g., appropriate exams, appeal procedures, etc." and "nonclassroom contributions to teaching." This and other apparent contradictions are clarified by Scriven as he describes his model of appraisal.

The last selection, by McNeil and Popham, evaluates criteria widely used to assess teacher competency. While the authors refer to the first two measurement problems noted by Borich and Madden (1977), they give particular emphasis to the third—use of instruments with inadequate psychometric characteristics to measure classroom behaviors. Interestingly, the authors focus on instrument types which are in popular use *today*.

McNeil and Popham discuss two kinds of psychometric inadequacy: first, the inadequacy inherent in the instrument itself, i.e., poor reliability and validity; second, the inadequacy that results from selecting the wrong instrument for a particular appraisal purpose, i.e., diagnostic, formative, or summative. They suggest six psychometric characteristics that can be used to distinguish various forms of instrumentation for various purposes of appraisal. As McNeil and Popham state, "At times we want data that simply state what was seen and heard in the classroom, while at other times it would be useful to gather information—interpretations—which illuminate the nature of the instructional tactics." The authors' primary point is that no single type of instrumentation can serve all assessment purposes. Instead, an intelligent selection of multiple forms of measurement is the most promising approach to accurate teacher assessment.

McNeil and Popham refer to "contract plans" and "performance tests of teacher effectiveness," methods that employ pupil achievement as a final criterion of teaching success. The contract plan depends on the development of a carefully selected set of objectives for the pupil. Supervisors and teachers agree in advance what will be accepted as evidence of the teacher's success in changing the skills, competencies, or attitudes of the students, and data are collected to see how well the learners achieve these stated objectives. Teacher competency is judged according to pupil learning rather than teaching techniques used.

The second procedure, performance tests of teaching effectiveness, assumes that teacher effectiveness cannot be validly judged when instructional conditions vary from teacher to teacher. Consequently, performance tests require that a number of teachers be given one or more identical objectives and a sample of the measures (based on those objectives) that are to be administered to pupils following the instruction. Often the objectives are novel to both pupils and teacher, thereby eliminating "contamination" due to the learner's previous exposure to the subject. As in the contract plan, the achievement of learners is the ultimate criterion for judging the effectiveness of the teacher.

Reference

Borich, G., and S. Madden. *Evaluating Classroom Instruction: A Sourcebook of Instruments.* Reading, Mass.: Addison-Wesley, 1977.

Rosenshine, B., *Teaching Behaviors and Student Achievement.* Windsor, Berkshire, England: National Foundation for Educational Research in England and Wales, 1971.

DAVID C. BERLINER
Far West Laboratory for Educational Research and Development

Impediments to Measuring Teacher Effectiveness[1]

Advocates of performance or competency based teacher education, state mandated evaluation programs such as the Stull Bill in California, and teacher accountability systems, all suffer to some degree from ostrichism. Ostrichism is a common disease often afflicting education. Its etiology is in a premature commitment to a particular educational movement. Behavioral symptoms include the practice of sticking one's head into the sand when problems appear, in the hope that the problems will go away.

The particular educational movement which is inducing the current epidemic of ostrichism is the commitment of educators to competency training and evaluation without the existence of empirical evidence linking teacher behavior to student outcomes in classroom settings. The Coleman report (1966), and its offshoots (Jencks, 1972; Mosteller and Moynihan, 1972), have minimized the role of the teacher in accounting for educational outcomes. These investigators claim that family background, socioeconomic status, ethnicity and the like, are the major causal variables affecting between school differences in achievement. They imply that teachers only minimally affect student achievement. Heath and Nielson (1974) reached the same conclusion in their review of the studies of teacher clarity, use of student ideas, criticism, enthusiasm, and other variables commonly accepted as skills or competencies. They concluded first that there is no established empirical relation between teacher behavior and student achievement. Second, that the flaws in the research are due to nonsensical statistical analyses, weak research designs, and sterile operational definitions of teacher

---

This paper was presented at the Conference on Research on Teacher Effects: An Examination by Policy-Makers and Researchers. The University of Texas at Austin, November 3–5, 1975. Used with permission of the author.

[1] The ideas presented in this paper have emerged from discussions with the staff of the Beginning Teacher Evaluation Study of the Far West Laboratory for Educational Research and Development. This is a project of the California Commission of Teacher Preparation and Licensing, funded by the National Institute of Education.

behavior and student outcomes. And third, that because of the strong association between omnibus measures of student achievement and socioeconomic and ethnic status, the effects of teachers and techniques of teaching on achievement are bound to be trivial.

These are serious criticisms of the effects of teaching on student achievement. They have serious consequences since *the heart of the performance and competency based approaches to teacher education, teacher evaluation and teacher accountability has to be the empirically established relationship between teacher behavior as an independent variable and student cognitive and affective outcomes as dependent variables.* Whether we are interested in effective social or natural science teaching, or effective mathematics or home economics teaching, establishing empirical relationships between teacher behavior and student outcomes has to be our goal. Unless replicable findings relating teaching behavior to student achievement in natural classroom settings can be found, the performance and competency based teacher education, evaluation, and accountability programs will not be believable.

Ferment exists because performance and competency based education, in all its forms, has been sold before it really exists (cf. Shanker, 1974). Those who use research to criticize teachers, teaching, and performance based teacher education, as well as those who defend teachers, teaching and performance based approaches have all taken positions before they have the necessary empirical backing. There is not now, and there will not be for some time, any empirical evidence on which to take a firm position on these issues. Extremely important problems hamper the study of teachers and teaching in all subject matter areas. It will take years before these problems can even be understood well enough to do classroom research properly.

An important step in the systematic study of any phenomena is the recognition of what problems exist in that research area. Addressing these problems, rather than assuming they will go away, or that they do not apply, will enhance the likelihood that studies of teacher effectiveness will be fruitful. The problems can be loosely grouped into two categories concerned with the instrumentation and methodology used in studying how teachers affect the achievement of students.

INSTRUMENTATION PROBLEMS

There are serious instrumentation problems connected with both the independent and dependent variables commonly used in research on teacher effectiveness. Six of the problems are discussed here.

Dependent Variable Problems

Our work at the Laboratory has been hampered by an inability to satisfactorily resolve three problems connected with development of dependent variables. These problems are connected with standardized testing, tests of special teaching units, and development of multivariate outcome measures.

Standardized Testing. In studies of how teachers affect students, standardized achievement tests are extensively used as criteria or outcome measures. These tests are, as a group, highly reliable instruments. They usually have adequate curriculum content validity, and seem predictive of future academic success. These tests have, however, one overwhelming flaw. They simply may not reflect what was taught in any one teacher's classroom. The tests are designed to be used in all kinds of courses within a curriculum area, and therefore cannot be completely sensitive or appropriate for any one teacher's teaching (Gall, 1972). They simply lack content validity at the classroom level.

The standardized achievement tests are also highly correlated with standardized intelligence tests, thus causing us to wonder exactly what kinds of items are really used in these tests. Furthermore, the tests are usually group administered multiple-choice tests. When working with young, bilingual, or lower socioeconomic status children, there is a serious question about whether many of the children are being appropriately tested.

In our own work, when standardized tests must be used, we try to refine the items in a number of ways. We try to choose items where there is evidence of substantial change in difficulty level over some instructional period. In this way we hope to identify items that are reactive to instruction. We try to pick items that correlate weakly with a measure of general intelligence, like the Raven's Progressive Matrices test, rather than picking those items with higher saturations of general intelligence. We try to have teachers rate items on how much time it would take them to teach that idea, or, how much emphasis they put on material like that addressed by the item. Unless items on a standardized test are put through a systematic screening of this type, the test is not going to be particularly reactive to teaching. Off-the-shelf standardized tests make poor dependent variables for studies of teaching. This is part of the difficulty in interpreting the Coleman report. The tests they used in that study were more reactive to family background and ethnicity than they were to instructional events within the school. It does not directly follow from this kind of evidence that teachers have no effect on student achievement.

Tests for Special Teaching Units. To insure the use of tests that are content valid for a particular classroom, many investigators of teaching have created special teaching units, or content vehicles to study teaching (Berliner and Ward, 1974; Joyce, 1975; Popham, 1971). An experimental unit of this type contains curricula materials, objectives, and sample test items. The teacher is asked to teach to the objectives. The unit could be a single 30-minute lesson, or require daily work over three weeks. Under these conditions every teacher has similar materials and objectives to work with. Students are pretested and posttested with carefully constructed tests designed to tap many dimensions of the material in the experimental teaching unit. The dependent variable in this situation is much more valid and much more reactive to classroom teaching. In comparative studies of teaching effectiveness, these experimental teaching units, and their tests, have much to commend them. Each teacher has a similar chance to try to produce gains in student achievement. Some teachers will be better at this than others.

Unfortunately, at this time in our research efforts, we do not know if the measures of teaching effectiveness arrived at over a short period of time provide an estimate of teacher effectiveness over a longer period of time. This methodology, which is used in our research on teaching, allows us to use tests of high content validity that seem to accurately reflect classroom practice for a short period of time. But this methodology may not always show strong predictive validity. The ranking of teachers on effectiveness, as determined by the relationships between student pretest and posttest scores associated with an experimental teaching unit, is only moderately correlated with a ranking of those teachers based on gains over the whole school year. Studying teacher effectiveness with dependent measures tied to special teaching units may not be a fair characterization of teaching over the long haul. But it certainly may be one way to identify teachers who differ in measured effectiveness when teaching a common curriculum, to common objectives, for controlled amounts of time.

Multivariate Outcomes. There are at least two dependent variables in any instructional interaction that should be of interest to us. One of these is the achievement of the learner in the situation. This has been a commonly used measure of instructional outcomes. The other, less often examined, is the learner's feelings about the instructional situation. Students are not always asked questions which probe their liking for their teacher or the subject matter. Researchers often overlook inquiring about a student's enjoyment of their classmates, the degree of threat felt in the class, and whether or not they would take more courses in that area. Moreover, when such issues are addressed in research studies, the affective set of dependent measures is kept separate from the achievement measures.

The problem in the research we do is to find ways to use multivariate outcomes so that many kinds of achievement and affective responses are used as indicators of the quality of classroom life for a child. The problem is something like the difficulties in teaching reading. You can get high comprehension at slow reading rates. Or you can get low comprehension at high rates of reading. But it is obvious that there must be some optimum multivariate outcome that simultaneously considers both reading comprehension and speed. The same kind of multivariate outcome measures, simultaneously considering both achievement and affective outcomes is needed for research on teaching. If researchers in this area do not consider what is learned and what is felt about that learning, *simultaneously*, they will continue to fractionate school learning into pieces that do not resemble the students' view of reality.

Independent Variable Problems

Research has also been hampered by problems connected with the independent variables used in studies of teacher effectiveness. A major difficulty is the "appropriateness" of particular teacher behavior in a given situation. A second issue is the determination of a unit of analysis for the independent variable. A third issue is the stability of teacher behavior.

Appropriateness of Teacher Behavior. Researchers have spent a good deal of time counting teacher behaviors. We know something about the number of higher and lower cognitive questions asked per unit time; we have counted the rate of positive verbal praise, the number of criticisms made, the number of probes, the frequency of explaining links, etc. For many of these variables a low correlation with some student outcome measure is found. But in classroom observation one becomes acutely aware of the difference between a higher cognitive question asked after a train of thought is running out, and the same type of question asked after a series of lower cognitive questions has been used to establish a foundation from which to explore higher-order ideas. Teachers sometimes ask inane questions. Teachers sometimes direct questions to what we believe was the wrong child. We have seen positive verbal reinforcement used with a new child in the class, one who was trying to win peer group acceptance, and whose behavior the teacher chose to use as a standard of excellence. We watched silently as the class rejected the intruder, while the teacher's count in the verbal praise category went up and up and up. Teachers have been seen responding to student initiated questions with irrelevant information. Teachers sometimes achieve a high rate of probing student responses to questions, seemingly without regard for the student or the kind of initial response given to a question. Some students are embarrassed by the probing, with other students probes occurred at inappropriate times, and sometimes probes were not used when the situation seemed to cry out for them. Similarly, skillful probing has been observed. A student's knowledge about an issue was brought out and shared with the class, after a weak first response was given by that student. The teacher's probing questions may have been as skillful as Plato's, but only their frequency was recorded.

All these events have led us to reassess our strong behavioristic stance in the study of teaching. We still regard frequency counts as very useful information. But we now feel quite strongly that the *qualitative* dimension, dealing with value judgments about appropriate use of skills, must enter into our observations of teaching. Researchers must address the appropriateness issue in order to study the information processing and decision making skills of human teachers. It is precisely these skills that provide the most important rationale for having human teachers in the classroom.

The Unit of Analysis for the Independent Variable. Something else we have become acutely aware of in our studies of teacher effectiveness is the problem of the unit of analysis for characterizing the independent variable. Is the single teacher question the unit of interest? Is the question, along with the wait-time, the unit? Or is the teacher question, wait-time, and student answer the unit which best characterizes the independent variable? And if the latter is most appropriate, does that transaction become part of an episode or strategy of even more complex dimensions and longer duration? Teachers follow strategies of questioning and of discussion. In an inductive lesson the meaningful unit of analysis may be a one-hour or one-week episode that is concerned with the conservation of matter. The individual questions, reinforcers, probes and student responses may be trivial aspects of the overall episode. New conceptions for the units underlying independent variables used in studies of teacher effectiveness are clearly needed.

Something else about the nature of an instructional episode is perplexing. Very little data are available describing the nature of the instructional activities and episodes a child engages in each day. Since instructional time appears to be an important variable in the learning process (Wiley, 1973; Harnischfeger and Wiley, 1975), accurate records of how time has been allocated to the various instructional activities and episodes are needed. The work of Gump (1967) and the techniques of Barker (1968) on obtaining accurate descriptions of the time a child spends in various activities may be useful starting points for obtaining these kinds of data. The time and type of activities can be treated as independent variables and may be causally related to various types of student outcomes.

Stability of Teacher Behavior. Before an observer enters a classroom to code teacher behavior in any sensible way, he has to be sure of two things. First, that the event must occur frequently enough to observe during the observation period. Second, the behavior should be representative of the teacher's *usual* and *customary* way of behaving. Only if these conditions are met can a teacher's behavior be sensibly characterized by the frequency count or rating scale description obtained in observation of classroom activities. These basic requirements for observation must be examined closely.

Many studies relating teaching behavior to student outcome have examined teacher behavior that did not occur frequently. For example, among 32 primary-grade science teachers the use of questions calling for identifying relationships, hypothesizing, and testing hypotheses is an extremely rare event on any given occasion of observation (cf. Moon, 1969; 1971). Another case of low frequency events, in an important area of teaching, has to do with the management skills of teachers. In some communities classroom management is not too difficult. The students are motivated and parents exert tight behavioral control at home, so that traumatic disturbances in classrooms are quite infrequent. In other communities serious management problems exist all day long. So we find that to observe instances of teacher behavior in the area of classroom management, ecological factors must be taken into account. Furthermore, even in settings where management problems usually occur with high frequency, certain teachers are so quick to establish a non-disruptive social system, that by the time the observer enters the class, particular kinds of events have been precluded from occurring.

How then can one study teacher behavior when important variables in the study rarely occur? One answer, of course, is in denser observation than is customary. Five one-hour observations of teacher behavior, which is unusually high for most studies of teaching, may simply not provide all the information an investigator may want. In addition, part of the answer is in knowing when and where to observe. For example, the first two weeks of schooling would be important for a study of management skills in inner city schools. Simply trying for denser observation later in the year and in other types of schools might be wasted effort.

The problem of estimating behavioral stability is partly related to the problem of the frequency of occurrence of behavior. When the frequency of a behavior is low, the correlations between the frequency of occurrence for certain events, over occasions (that is, a coefficient of stability for the behavior), will be low. But part of the problem in looking at stability of teacher behavior is quite distinct from the frequency issue. Think for a moment about the characteristics you prize in a teacher. Usually, people think of "good" teachers as flexible. Such teachers are expected to change methods, techniques, and styles to suit particular students, curriculum areas, time of day or year, etc. That is, the standard of excellence in teaching commonly held implies a teacher whose behavior is inherently unstable. Needless to say, this poses a problem for an observer trying to observe a teacher's customary and usual ways of teaching.

For our study of teaching we have reviewed teacher stability, over occasions, for a great many variables (Shavelson and Dempsey, 1975). The results are fascinating. On the laughable side are coefficients of stability from Campbell's (1972) analysis of science teaching at the junior high school level, over two occasions. The Flanders Interaction Analysis System was used. The stability coefficient (that is, the correlation between a teacher's standing on a measure across two occasions) was −.90 for a measure of indirectness in teaching (the i/d ratio). On five occasions Moon (1969; 1971) studied 32 primary grade science teachers trained in the Science Curriculum Improvement Study (SCIS). The stability coefficient for the Flanders indirectness measure went all the way up to +.18; for the frequency of fact or recall questions, the stability coefficient was −.12; and for amount of teacher talk, only +.12. In Borg's (1972) study, the behavioral stability of teachers was measured after training in questioning techniques had taken place. The stability of the ratio of higher-order to fact questions was .07. The rather large number of low and even negative stability coefficients which exist in the literature confirms our belief that the independent variables we often work with in studies of teacher effectiveness are not fair indicators of a teacher's typical behavior. Researchers are so eager to capture variables for data analysis with rating scales and frequency counts, that they seem to have forgotten to check if their methodology is appropriate to the phenomena they are interested in studying!

Of course there are many exceptions to the trend for teacher behavior to be unstable. We have found *ratings* of variables over 10 occasions that yield high stability coefficients. These include stability coefficients of .92 for teacher warmth; .79 for teacher enthusiasm; and .83 for teacher sensitivity (Wallen, 1969). We have found *frequency counts* demonstrating that a global variable composed of all types of reinforcement is reasonably stable over occasions, yielding a stability coefficient of .64 (Trinchero, 1974). In the latter study, however, there is considerable evidence pointing to the lack of generalizability of stability coefficients across different teacher populations, curricula areas and student populations. For example, the stability coefficient over two occasions for the frequency of positive verbal teacher behavior was .04 for English teachers, and .57 for social studies teachers.

By examining the stability of teachers' behavior which is used as the independent variable in studies of teacher effectiveness, we conclude that: (1) some teacher behaviors that we think are important to study occur infrequently. To study them requires extensive observation in particular settings at appropriate times; (2) some teacher behaviors that we think are important to study are basically unstable over occasions. No practical amount of observation will result in a reliable estimate of a teacher's use of these behaviors. Perhaps we need to develop measures of variance instead of measures of central tendency to describe these behaviors; (3) some teacher behaviors are stable over occasions. In general, but not always, ratings or high inference variables, rather than frequency counts or low inference variables, are the more stable; (4) stability coefficients for many teacher behaviors will not demonstrate ecological or population validity. Teacher behavior is moderated, *as it should be,* by the kinds of students and the variety of settings that teachers work in. Until more is known about which teacher behaviors fluctuate, and how and why they fluctuate over time, settings, curricula, and populations, studies relating teaching behavior to student outcomes must remain primitive.

METHODOLOGICAL PROBLEMS

A loosely related set of issues has been grouped under the title problems in methodology. Each of the problems and issues mentioned is in some way hampering the development of reliable knowledge about the relationship between teacher behavior and student outcomes.

Student Background and Teacher Effectiveness

One problem in studying the teaching process is estimating how much can legitimately be expected of teachers or schools as an influence on student growth. This problem is debated in educational philosophy, sociology and economics, as well as educational psychology. And this issue has already been mentioned when it was noted that procedures were needed to reduce the influence of intelligence and ethnicity on test performance in studies of teacher effectiveness. But the problem is even more pervasive. Can a teacher be held accountable if a perfectly appropriate prescription is given, and then not followed by students? Suppose a teacher says, "read this chapter and come to my office so we can discuss it." Among sub-cultures that see schools as hostile or useless, students will not read the chapter and will not come in to discuss it. Classes of such students may show minimum growth in achievement at the end of the year. And these low achieving classes may very well be made up of lower socioeconomic status children and ethnic minorities. Under these conditions, how much responsibility is to be placed on teachers for the low student performance?

On the other hand, with children of high intelligence and high socioeconomic background, growth in achievement takes place almost in spite of teachers and teaching. Can the achievement of students in those settings be attributable to teachers, or is it a product of genetic and environmental advantage, relatively unaffected by what teachers do?

Since some children, often whole groups of children, may be unwilling to learn in the institutions now used to educate them, and some children learn in those institutions regardless of what happens to them, how do we go about attributing student achievement to what teachers do? In the case of low achieving students teachers may have to be evaluated against some other criteria than student achievement. Yet to do so denies that teachers can and should make a difference in the achievement of lower socioeconomic and minority children. There may not be solutions to this problem. But the problem exists and must be thought about as people naïvely discuss teacher effectiveness without qualifying what they say by noting the students' background characteristics, particularly socioeconomic status and intelligence.

Subject Matter and Teacher Effectiveness

That student background characteristics influence test performance and almost all other aspects of schooling is well established. What was not so well understood, until recently, is that student performance in different curriculum areas is differentially affected by those background characteristics. In the International Education Association's (IEA) cross-cultural study of student achievement (Postlethwaite, 1973), the variance accounted for by student background characteristics, such as intelligence and social class, was estimated for a number of subject matter areas. Clearly highlighted, around the world, was that home influences on subjects like reading and social studies are very powerful. Those influences are so powerful in accounting for student achievement that there may not be enough variance unaccounted for in the performance of students to attribute to the influence of teachers.

But in other curriculum areas, student background accounts for much less variance. Physics, chemistry, French, Spanish, geometry, and trigonometry are not typically learned at home, and therefore the schools account for more variance in these measures of achievement than for achievement measures in reading, social studies or language arts. This does not mean that socioeconomic status and intelligence are not related to performance in science, foreign language or mathematics. It simply means that the influence of those background factors is much less, thus leaving more variance to potentially attribute to school and teacher effects.

If teaching behavior in natural settings is to be studied in a correlational manner it should be studied in those areas of the curriculum where we are most likely to be able to attribute an effort to teachers, after the influences of test unreliability and home background have been removed. Instead researchers typically study teaching in those subject areas where they will be hardest pressed to causally relate teaching behavior to student outcomes. New approaches are called for.

Normative Standards and Volunteer Samples in the Study of Teacher Effectiveness

Much of the research on teacher effectiveness is, in simplest form, a comparison of the post-instruction test scores of classes that had similar pre-instruction test scores. These comparative differences in outcomes are believed to discriminate between more and less effective teachers. This research approach is entirely normative. And in a norm referenced research study some teachers will always appear to be better than others. In fact, the whole sample of teachers in any study may be quite poor when judged against some absolute standards, and we would never know.

More likely, since studies of teacher effectiveness in natural environments require the informed consent of volunteer teachers, research is likely to be conducted with a sample of self-confident, relatively open teachers, almost all of whom may be superior to a non-volunteer sample on an unknown number of unidentified dimensions. But in a norm referenced system, where teachers are evaluated against other teachers, some of our sample will be judged to be less effective than others. This is a silly research strategy, but one that is not easily changed. To bring about change in this approach we would need to impose criterion referenced achievement standards for teachers, and require all teachers to participate in research on teacher effectiveness. Until that can be done (though I doubt it ever will be done) we should *never* talk of effective and noneffective teachers. At best the research sample can be described as more and less effective teachers, which is quite different from the absolute criteria implied by the terms effective and noneffective: And because norm referenced research is conducted with volunteer samples, statements about teacher effectiveness should also include some reference to the fact that these are more or less effective teachers from a sample of teachers that are themselves probably superior to the average teacher in an unknown number of ways.

Individual Differences among Students and Teacher Effectiveness

All teachers know that some of the things they do will not be effective with some of the children they teach. There is no feeling of failure when this occurs, that's just the way things are. Most teachers recognize this problem and modify instruction accordingly. They customize their behavior, as best they can, to fit the individual styles of students. Research on teacher effectiveness, however, usually ignores this phenomenon. Rarely are enough data about individual differences among students collected to find out if particular teaching behaviors are differentially effective with different types of children. For example, from what is known about how aptitudes and treatments interact (cf. Berliner and Cahen, 1973), it can be expected that a highly structured course in, say, science, taught by a well organized somewhat dominant teacher, will yield greater achievement for high anxious students than for low anxious students. On the other hand, the low anxious student will probably perform better than the high anxious student in the class of a science teacher providing only small amounts of guidance and using an inductive approach. Research on teacher effectiveness ordinarily finds no relation between student achievement and teacher behaviors that helps to define constructs like inductive or deductive teaching style. Relationships may not appear because it is not yet known how to partition students into meaningful sub-groups for whom the two different treatments might be uniquely applicable. If students could have been divided into high and low anxious individuals, to follow our example, it might have been found that teacher behaviors within each teaching style had important effects on student achievement.

I have no doubt that the styles of teaching and teaching behavior recommended by, say, the curriculum guides accompanying new science curriculum projects are appropriate recommendations for some teachers, when interacting with some students. But not all students! By not focusing on the individual aptitudes, styles, personality, and traits of the students, the effects of teachers are masked thus making it almost impossible to establish empirical relations between teaching behavior and student outcome.

An equally important reason to use the aptitude-treatment interaction approach is to find teacher behaviors that in general have positive relationships with student outcomes, but are, in fact, negatively affecting the performance of small numbers of students. Research on teacher effectiveness has to begin searching for interactions as it continues trying to establish more general links between teacher behavior and student outcomes.

Mediation of Teacher Effectiveness through the Student's Behavior

A fact of classroom reality that must be brought into designs for research on teaching is that teacher behavior does not influence student achievement directly. A teacher's indirectness, or questioning, or reinforcement does not simply result in greater mathematics, reading, or science achievement. The link that must be considered is the behavior of the student in the instructional setting. We are now convinced that the mediating link so necessary to consider is a student's active time-on-task. If teacher questions, reinforcement, warmth, and clarity are to affect outcomes, they can only do so by engaging and then keeping the student's attention. If the student will attend, the possibility of learning exists. Teacher behaviors that affect student active learning time must be examined carefully. To do so means putting much more effort into clinical studies. In this way an investigator can work one-to-one with students, trying to understand how the student allocates his attention, and how nominal stimuli emitted by the teacher, become effective stimuli for that student. To think that there is a direct link between, say, a teacher's questions which require the generation of hypotheses by students, and the student's achievement on an achievement test is overly simple. Intermediate links in that causal flow require us to examine the student's attending and information processing behavior.

Another aspect of the student that must be thought about for research in teaching is the student's perspective of the events that impinge upon him in classrooms. Researchers do not know how much of what is called skilled teaching is even perceived by the learner. From the learner's perspective, perhaps "analysis" and "synthesis" level questions are not distinguishable. Students may differentiate only "memory" and "thinking" questions. From the learner's perspective the rate of reinforcement may be irrelevant. The teacher either is "nice' or "not nice" to students. I believe that some variables thought to be quite important by educational theorists are in fact unimportant, unperceived, or unperceivable by students (cf. Winne, 1974). Students exposed to variables they cannot perceive or to variables they believe to be unimportant, may be unaffected by such variables. Researchers certainly need to follow Snow's (1974) advice that urges more detailed accounts of what learners do in response to experimental treatments.

Construct Validation and Teacher Effectiveness

Through the writings of the logical positivists, and particularly the physicist Bridgeman, social scientists became aware of the critical nature of language and operations in science. An initial development to further scientific understanding of some phenomena is a descriptive language that uses concepts having common meaning among the scientists working in the same area. The intensive and extensive meaning of key concepts needs to be shared by the members of the scientific community. The less the overlap of shared meaning, the less rigor the science can develop. A case in point would be a term like "withitness" from the study of teaching by Jacob Kounin (1970). The teacher who can spot trouble before it begins has "withitness." Such a teacher can be working with one group of students and call out a student's name at the other end of the room because he is beginning to cause a disturbance. That is "withitness." I recently went into a classroom and one of the concepts that helped me organize what I saw was the concept of "withitness." I felt perfectly at home using the concept. It helped me make sense out of the different styles of two teachers I was observing. Yet the concept itself cannot be rigorously defined and relies upon very subjective interpretation of phenomena. The construct of "withitness," like many of the concepts we work with, is useful, but inadequately defined.

One way to increase the preciseness of our concepts is to tie them through clear operations to the measurement of their occurrence. For example, a concept like teacher warmth can be defined as the number of times per day the teacher smiles. But is that what is wanted when warmth is to be measured? It seems that the phenomena of interest are fragmented beyond recognition when the occurrence of some molecular behavior is used to operationally define our terms.

What is needed in the study of teaching is to begin incorporating multiple methods of measurement into the studies we do (Campbell and Fiske, 1959). If one chooses to work with the concept of "withitness" or "warmth," there is a need to measure the concept from as many different perspectives as we can. For example, a teacher's warmth can be measured by self-report, student report, observer rating, frequency count of smiles, percent of gestures regarded as affectionate, and anything else that can be thought of. Then, from the intercorrelations of the various imprecise and imperfect measures of warmth, one can begin to understand the construct that is so glibly used, but cannot clearly be defined. Extensive construct validation must take place or the impreciseness of our language for describing the phenomena of interest will keep the empirical study of teaching at its present primitive level.

The Generalizability of Measures of Effectiveness

If teachers are to be characterized as more or less effective, in order to see if the behavior of those teachers differs, knowledge about whether the teachers maintain their rank ordering on measures of effectiveness over time and over subject matter areas is needed. As part of our research we reviewed studies that addressed this problem. There are about eight studies of teacher effectiveness over lengthy periods of time (see Shavelson and Dempsey, 1975). From those studies it is estimated that the mean correlation between measures of teacher effectiveness obtained two or more times is about .30. This estimate is based on data from predominantly primary age children tested with standardized reading and mathematics achievement tests. Brophy's (1973) study presents some interesting data to consider. Residual gain scores over 3 years were examined for 165 elementary teachers. Twenty-eight percent of the teachers were consistent in their effects on students three years in a row. Approximately 14 percent of the teachers in the study were consistently effective in producing higher than predicted reading and math achievement. And 14 percent of the teachers were consistent in being associated with classes that had scores lower than predicted in reading and mathematics three years in a row. Thirteen percent of the teachers showed linear increases in residual gains over the three years. That is, they appeared to be getting more effective in their teaching. Similarly, 11 percent of the teachers showed a linear decrease over that time period. They seemed to be getting less effective over time. Forty-nine percent of the teachers in this sample were inconsistent in the patterning of their residual scores over time.

In our review of short term studies of teacher effectiveness, ranging across grade levels and all kinds of curriculum areas, it was found that when the same content is taught to similar students (for example, teaching and reteaching an ecology lesson to two samples of urban students), moderately stable estimates of teacher effectiveness are obtained. But when different content is taught to two or more groups of similar students, the effectiveness measures are not stable. Similarly, when different content is taught to the same students, effectiveness from occasion to occasion is unstable. In recent research, involving 200 elementary school teachers, each of whom taught a two week, specially designed teaching unit in reading and mathematics, similar data were obtained. Residual gain scores for each subject matter were calculated. These measures of effectiveness using different content and the same students were correlated. From these data we find that measures of effectiveness in the two curriculum areas correlate about .30.

It appears that teachers do not, by and large, remain in a stable ordering on measures of teacher effectiveness. If, as has been discussed, the independent variables typically looked at are often unstable, and measures of teacher effectiveness also show instability, the possibility of correlating teacher behavior with student achievement to determine effective teaching behavior is quite limited. In fact, *unless we reconceptualize much of what we do in this research area, our research will be ludicrous!*

CONCLUSION

Stated above was the belief that the heart of performance and competency based teacher education, evaluation and accountability programs is the establishment of empirical relationships between teacher behavior as an independent variable and student achievement as a dependent variable. But before researchers can adequately establish those relationships they need to deal with the problems of instrumentation and methodology. Workers in this area must come to grips with the inadequacy of standardized tests, the unknown predictive validity of tests from special teaching units, the problem of building multivariate outcome measures, the problems of measurement of appropriateness of teacher behavior, the lack of experience in choosing an appropriate unit for analysis for describing teaching behavior, and the lack of stability of many teacher behaviors.

Time must be taken to consider the problems of how student background affects measures of teacher effectiveness, what subject matters should be examined, how normative standards and volunteer teachers affect what can be said about teachers and teaching, how individual students react to teaching skills, and how students monitor and interpret a teacher's behavior in ways which may or may not coincide with how educational theorists interpret the phenomena. Time and resources are needed to do construct validation and studies of the generalizability of measures of teacher effectiveness.

Finally, guidance is needed in choosing techniques to use for measurement of change in the achievement of students in natural classrooms.

When we have finished examining this potpourri of problems, issues, and concerns, we will be ready to begin the scientific study of teaching. And if we cannot deal with all of these problems, perhaps we should simply acknowledge that teaching is, after all, a very complex set of events which cannot be easily understood.

References

Barker, R. G. *Ecological Psychology: Concepts and Methods for Studying the Environment of Human Behavior*. Stanford, California: Stanford University Press, 1968.

Berliner, D. C., and L. S. Cahen. "Trait-Treatment Interactions and Learning." In F. N. Kerlinger, ed., *Review of Research in Education, 1*. Itaska, Illinois: Peacock, 1973.

Berliner, D. C., and B. A. Ward. *Proposal for Phase III Beginning Teacher Evaluation Study*. San Francisco, California: Far West Laboratory for Educational Research and Development, 1974.

Borg, W. R. "The Minicourse as a Vehicle for Changing Teacher Behavior: A Three-Year Follow-up." *Journal of Educational Psychology* **63** (1972): 572–579.

Brophy, J. E. "Stability of Teacher Effectiveness." *American Educational Research Journal* **10** (1973): 245–252.

Campbell, D. T., and D. W. Fiske. "Convergent and Discriminant Validation by the Multi-Trait-Multimethod Matrix." *Psychological Bulletin* **56** (1959): 81–105.

Campbell, J. R. "A Longitudinal Study in the Stability of Teachers' Verbal Behavior." *Science Education* **56,** no. 1 (1972): 89–96.

Coleman, J. S. *et al. Equality of Educational Opportunity*. Washington, D.C.: U.S. Government Printing Office, 1966.

Gall, M. D. *The Problems of "Student Achievement" in Research on Teacher Effects*. San Francisco, California: Far West Laboratory for Educational Research and Development (Report A73–2), 1973.

Gump, P. V. "The Classroom Behavior Setting: Its Nature and Relation to Student Behavior." Mimeographed. U.S. Office of Education, Dept. of Health, Education and Welfare. Final Report, Project No. 5-0334, Contract No. 0E-4-10-107. Lawrence, University of Kansas, 1967.

Harnischfeger, A., and D. E. Wiley. "Teaching-Learning Processes in Elementary School: A Synoptic View." Mimeographed. Beginning Teacher Evaluation Study, Technical Report No. 75-3-1. San Francisco, California: Far West Laboratory for Educational Research and Development, 1975.

Heath, R. W., and M. A. Nielson. "Performance-based Teacher Education." *Review of Educational Research* 44 (1974): 463–484.

Jencks, C. *et al. Inequality: A Reassessment of the Effect of Family and Schooling in America.* New York: Basic Books, 1972.

Joyce, B. R. "Vehicles for Controlling Content in the Study of Teaching." Paper given at the meeting of the American Educational Research Association, Washington, D.C., April 1975.

Kounin, J. S. *Discipline and Group Management in Classrooms.* New York: Holt, Rinehart and Winston, 1970.

Moon, T. C. "A Study of Verbal Behavior Patterns in Primary Grade Classrooms during Science Activities." Ph.D. dissertation, Michigan State University, East Lansing, Michigan, 1969.

Moon, T. C. "A Study of Verbal Behavior Patterns in Primary Grade Classrooms during Science Activities." *Journal of Research in Science Teaching* **8** (1971): 171–177.

Mosteller, F., and D. P. Moynihan. *On Equality of Educational Opportunity.* New York: Vintage Books, 1972.

Popham, W. J. "Performance Tests of Teaching Proficiency: Rationale, Development, and Validation." *American Educational Research Journal* **8** (1971): 105–117.

Postlethwaite, T. N. *A Selection from the Overall Findings of the IEA Study in Science, Reading Comprehension, Literature, French as a Foreign Language, English as a Foreign Language, and Civic Education.* Paris, France: International Institute for Educational Planning, 1973. (mimeographed report no. IIEP/STU/MISC/73.3 [Rev. 1])

Shanker, A. *Competency-Based Teacher Training and Certification: Acceptable and Unacceptable Models.* QuEST Consortium Yearbook. Washington, D.C.: American Federation of Teachers, 1974.

Shavelson, R. S., and N. Dempsey. *Generalizability of Measures of Teacher Effectiveness and Teaching Process.* San Francisco, California: Beginning Teacher Evaluation Study, Technical Report #2, Far West Laboratory for Educational Research and Development, 1975.

Snow, R. E. "Designs for Research on Teaching." *Review of Educational Research,* 44 (1974): 265–291.

Trinchero, R. L. *Three Technical Skills of Teaching: Their Stability and Effect on Pupil Attitudes and Achievement.* Ph.D. dissertation, Stanford University, Stanford, California, 1974.

Wallen, N. E. "Sausalito Teacher Education Project." Annual Report. Mimeographed. San Francisco, California: Division of Compensatory Education, Bureau of Professional Development, San Francisco State College, 1969.

Wiley, D. E. "Another Hour, Another Day: Quantity of Schooling, a Potent Path for Policy." *Studies of Educative Processes,* No. 3. Chicago, Illinois: University of Chicago, July 1973.

Winne, P. H. "Teacher Effectiveness and Student Perceptions of Teacher Cues." Mimeographed. Dissertation proposal, Stanford School of Education, Stanford, California, 1974.

ROBERT S. SOAR
University of Florida

Teacher Assessment Problems and Possibilities

Logically, there appear to be three major strategies contending for a role in the evaluation of teaching skills. The traditional and most widely used strategy to date has been an assessment of the quality of the program within which the teacher was trained (Elam, 1971). The aspects of that strategy have led to the movement for competency-based teacher education (CBTE). As a part of traditional evaluation in teacher preparation, measurement of the teacher's knowledge continues to be relevant.

Two other strategies appear to be viable ones within the broad context of evaluation of teacher competence: measuring the growth of pupils taught by the teacher and measuring the teaching behavior of the teacher.

MEASUREMENT OF PUPIL GROWTH

This is an assessment strategy which is immediately appealing to many. Probably there are a number of reasons for this. Since the business of schools is to produce change in pupils, it seems reasonable to assess the success of the school by measuring the growth of pupils. In some instances, businesses pay workers in terms of production; why not pay teachers on the same basis? Such a solution is immediate and compelling, but examination of this possibility raises questions.

The Influence of the Classroom

A major difficulty in evaluating the teacher is the amount of influence the classroom can have in relation to other influences on the pupil. A series of papers published by the Office of Education (1970) concluded that the relative influence of the teacher or the school is not great. A documented example of a

From *Journal of Teacher Education* 24 (1973): 205–212. Reprinted by permission.

specific non-school effect, the relations between attitudes and expectations of parents to intelligence and achievement of their children, has been found to be strong. The relations hold even within a single socioeconomic group and have been demonstrated in a number of ethnic groups (Wolf, 1964; Keeves, 1970; Garber, 1972). Similarly, the peer group influence has been demonstrated.

Presumably these are only a few effective non-school influences. If the teacher is only one of a number of influences on pupil growth, the correlation of growth for one pupil group with another the following year should *not* be high. This turns out to be the case. One study (Soar, 1966) showed a correlation of .08 for successive years of pupil growth in pooled achievement measures for a group of 55 teachers. Rosenshine (1970) has summarized a series of studies indicating relations typically in the .30's for growth for successive years. Brophy (1972) has reported successive year data which are highly variable, with correlations ranging from low negative to high positive, but with a median in the .30's. As test-retest reliabilities, correlations like these would not be acceptable.

To lay the pupil's growth, or lack of it, at the teacher's door, seems a major oversimplification considering the many other factors involved.

Measurement-Statistical Problems

The solution of measuring pupil growth looks so simple—yet involves a series of problems. Specialists in educational and psychological measurement have labored with the difficulties for a generation or more, without final resolution. As Bereiter (1963) comments:

> Although it is commonplace for research to be stymied by some difficulty in experimental methodology, there are really not many instances in the behavioral sciences of promising questions going unresearched because of deficiencies in statistical methodology. Questions dealing with psychological change may well constitute the most important exceptions. It is only in relation to such questions that the writer has ever heard colleagues admit to having abandoned major research objectives solely because the statistical problems seemed to be insurmountable.

These problems are not widely recognized except by measurement specialists; a few of them will be outlined below.

The procedure of only measuring pupils' standings at the year's end would be inadequate. Whatever growth may have occurred would be such a minor element in the total amount of pupil knowledge that this possibility is easily dismissed. The alternative is testing pupils in the fall and again in the spring to determine the change made while with a given teacher. This is where the booby traps are important.

One such is the regression effect. Figure 1 illustrates fictitious data on weight measurements for a group of people weighed three months apart, assuming no weight gain or loss on the average. The ellipse in the figure represents the outline of a plot of hypothetical points, each of which represents the weight of one person on both occasions. The cross-hatched areas at the ends of the distribution represent the lightest and the heaviest individuals at the first weighing, and the cross-hatched areas at the top and bottom of the distribution represent the extreme weights at the second weighing. Since the areas at the ends of the ellipse only overlap slightly with the areas at the top and bottom of the ellipse, the highest and lowest weight people must, to a considerable degree, be a different group on the two occasions.

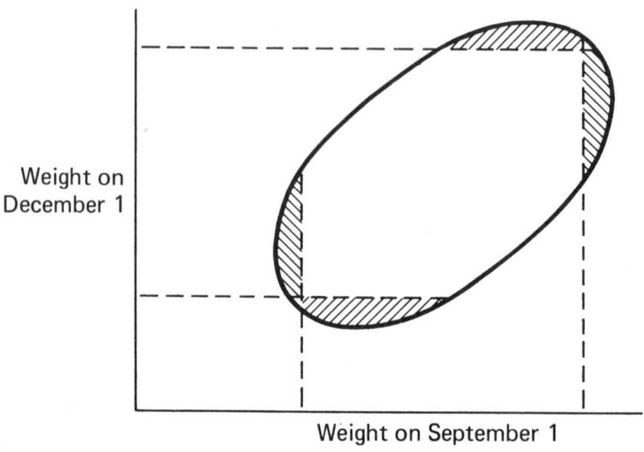

Fig. 1. An illustration of regression effect.

Presumably, there are at least two reasons for this: one is error of measurement when the scales were not read accurately on one or more occasions. The other is that weight changes occur for individuals from one occasion to the other. It is easy to imagine the person who discovers his weight is higher than usual and goes on a diet as well as the person whose weight is less than he assumed and affords an occasional dessert. Perhaps it would be easy to imagine parallel influences on some pupils as a consequence of knowing their standing on achievement test scores. In any case, the effect will be present any time the two sets of scores are less than perfectly correlated.

The next point to be developed from the figure is the realization that if the people who were in the heaviest 10 percent on the first weighing were not in that same group in the second, they must have lost weight. Similarly, the people in the lightest 10 percent must have gained weight. Since initially heavy people tend to gain weight, there must be a negative correlation between initial weight and change in weight.

The same negative correlation will routinely be found between the fall scores that students make on achievement tests and the change they make during the year. This runs so counter to the expectation that high achieving pupils will grow most during the year that it is hard to accept, but it is true. In our past work, for example, these correlations have ranged from the –.30's to the –.50's for full-length subtests of the Iowa Test of Basic Skills, for third through sixth graders, and typically from the –.40's to the –.60's (with some higher correlations) for specially assembled subtests with kindergarten and first graders.

We recognize that the year-end score a pupil makes on an achievement test represents his knowledge before he entered the class, but we do not readily recognize the gain a pupil shows during a year is also related to his standing at the beginning of the year. Although true, the relationship is negative rather than positive, as is the correlation between pretest and post-test.

To correct for this spurious effect, another kind of gain measure is used with some frequency—regressed gain. The logic of this gain measure is that of correlating pretest scores with post-test scores for the total group; then, for each individual, predicting the post-test score that he would be expected to earn on the basis of his pretest score, and subtracting that predicted score from his actual final score. In effect, what this does is to create a measure of gain which is independent of the pupil's initial standing, so it more freely represents the change which has occurred in him during this year in the classroom. The procedure parallels the use of analysis of covariance to hold the effect of pretest scores constant, except that scores for individual pupils are created which can be used in further analysis.

This apparently simple solution is only a beginning toward the solution of the problem. In order for a regressed gain score to be independent of pretest score, the adjustment made must vary with how extreme the prescore is. Students with initially high scores have their gain scores increased, and students with initially low scores have their gain scores decreased.

The next question, then, is to what group a pupil reasonably belongs. A group of low social status pupils, for example, will have a lower mean score than a group of high social status pupils. If the two groups are combined in one analysis, then the adjustment made to the gain score for each individual will be made from the mean of the combined group. Low pupils will stand relatively lower than they would from the mean of their own group, and as a consequence their gain scores will be reduced more than they would be if they were compared to the mean of their own group. Similarly, gain scores of the high standing pupils will be increased more than if they were compared with the mean of their own subgroup. Since the amount of the adjustment made to the gain to make it independent of initial standing depends on how extreme the pretest score is from the mean of the group being analyzed, the amount of the adjustment which is made depends on a proper grouping of pupils. What groups should be created in order to compare each pupil with his own group? Since there are no very clear bases for deciding this question, the gain score which the pupil will be assigned is uncertain.

At least occasionally, further problems exist. In our own work, we have often found that even on well-developed standardized tests it is not unusual for pupils to show ceiling effects. That is, the extent to which a pupil can show growth is limited by the number of items he missed in the fall. High scoring pupils will be penalized since they can't show the real gain they have made on a test with this ceiling effect. In some of the data we are currently analyzing (subtests assembled out of standardized tests), we have found relatively strong nonlinear relationships between pupils' initial scores and the gains they show. Pupils who initially make low scores gain little, pupils who make initially moderate scores gain greatly, and pupils who make initially high scores also gain little. So the classroom which happened to contain pupils who tested toward the middle of the scale will show considerably more gain than a classroom would in which pupils initially scored low or high. If pupils were ability-grouped, the teacher with the middle group would have a material advantage.

The general conclusion from these measurement problems is that the growth a pupil shows is a function both of the growth he actually made and the test items which are used to reflect that growth as well as the kind of score used to represent the growth. Since it is difficult to know the relative contribution of each of these sources, the measurement of gain remains uncertain. Also, it is relevant to note that the tests cited above are probably better developed than those to be used in state accountability programs.

Problems of Rate and Growth

Still further problems may exist. It seems reasonable to expect that at least some characteristics of pupils grow slowly enough that change during the school year would not be measurable. (An AACTE task force on performance-based teacher education has developed this point.) As examples, it seems likely that learning sets toward complex problem solving and responsible citizenship behavior probably change too slowly to be measurable within a single year.

Problems of Teaching and Test Administration

The St. Petersburg Times (Orsini, 1972) reported on two other problems cited by teachers in the initial application of Florida's accountability program. One is the tendency for some teachers to concentrate on teaching the eight or ten children in the class who were tested in the fall and will be tested again in the spring. Small (1972) documents the parallel problem of teachers concentrating on low-standing pupils in an application of accountability measurement in England a century ago. In addition, the problem of teachers concentrating on the material to be tested also was reported in both articles. Of course there is always the problem of teachers "helping" pupils take the spring test to enable them to do well. The alternative of having a disinterested outsider do the testing raises cost-feasibility problems.

Problems of Levels of Complexity

If the competence of the teacher is to be assessed by measuring growth in pupils, it seems important to measure pupil growth at all levels of the Taxonomy of Cognitive Objectives (Bloom, 1956). Current evidence (Soar, 1972; Soar and Soar, 1972) suggests the teacher behavior which supports relatively simple-concrete kinds of pupil growth is different from the kind which supports relatively complex-abstract pupil growth. It also would seem important to judge the competence of the teacher on his ability to promote higher level objectives as well as lower level ones.

In the accountability program which the state of Florida is developing, the intent is to develop test items to measure objectives at all cognitive levels, at each grade level, and in all subject matter. This appears to be a very ambitious undertaking, considering the difficulties measurement specialists have encountered in developing measures of higher level objectives. The program probably will be forced to go into the field because of legislation which requires only the development of measures of lower level objectives because of the difficulty of developing the higher ones. In that event, it would seem reasonable to expect the result to be accountability testing which would emphasize lower level objectives and underrepresent higher level ones, if they are represented at all. The consequences would be that teachers who stress lower level objectives would do well by the accountability criteria, and teachers who teach to facilitate the growth of higher level objectives would appear to be less satisfactory. It would not be surprising if this led, in turn, to greater numbers of teachers stressing low level objectives.

Another reasonable expectation is that the teacher who feels the accountability movement looking over his shoulders may very well "turn the screws" a bit by putting pressure on the pupils to achieve, so the teacher will make a satisfactory appearance in the spring testing. This is generally the sort of teacher behavior which is destructive of higher level objectives. A number of pressures converge on the teacher to teach for immediate effects—for low level objectives—and to concentrate on low-achieving pupils.

While it certainly is not conclusive, it may be suggestive to recognize that the current generation of alienated college students have spent most of their years in public education in the post-Sputnik era when concentration on subject matter learning was stressed.

In summary, the measurement of teacher competence by way of pupil gain appears to be an uncertain route to travel. While there are problems in the use of pupil measures for lower level objectives, these problems are perhaps manageable. The attempts to measure teacher competence through pupil gain in higher level objectives appears to be exceedingly difficult and probably impossible in many cases.

THE MEASUREMENT OF TEACHER BEHAVIOR

Having recognized some of the difficulties in pupil measurement as an assessment strategy, we will consider the measurement of teacher behavior. The long history of negative results which have been produced by the use of traditional teacher ratings is almost certainly one of the reasons why the observation of teacher behavior as an assessment strategy is not viewed more favorably than it is.

Medley and Mitzel (1959) comprehensively reviewed studies in which ratings of teacher effectiveness, made by supervisors or administrators, had been related to any reasonably objective measure of pupil growth. The findings from numbers of studies consistently showed no relation between ratings of teacher effectiveness and measures of pupil growth. It is only reasonable that this dismal literature has led many people in education to assume that effective teaching was not identifiable.

This research literature has changed materially since about 1960. Numbers of identified measures of teacher behavior appear to hold real promise for clarifying the nature of teacher effectiveness, although it is becoming increasingly clear that the nature of the phenomenon is very complex (Soar, 1972). These promising findings come from the application of systematic observation, as distinguished from rating procedures. Systematic observation is a way of observing classrooms in which the observer is made a recorder insofar as possible, rather than an evaluator. That is, he looks for specific items of behavior from a standardized form and checks the occurrences of these behaviors. He does not combine the behaviors into sums or composites; he does not make judgments based on them. The data are then treated statistically so that composites are created with known weights, and with the possibility of trying different combining schemes, or "scoring keys."

Another characteristic of data of this sort is that they tend to be "low inference" rather than "high inference." They stay closer to the original behavior. When the effectiveness of the teacher is rated, for example, there is no way of knowing what behaviors entered this rating. If a teacher is rated as "warm," the field is sharply restricted; but there are still numbers of possible behaviors which may have been involved. But if an observer counts the number of times a teacher smiles, pats a child, or praises a child's behavior or work, the behavior which entered the measure has considerably greater specificity. These, then, are examples of behavior measures ranging from high to low inference.

Recent studies using ratings of intermediate levels of inference, such as "clarity" or "enthusiasm" have produced considerably more promising results than the earlier high inference ratings (Rosenshine, 1971). Before these results can be used maximally, the low inference behaviors which enter the ratings need to be identified.

There are also hopeful results from the application of systematic observation which suggest that presently identified classroom behaviors are related to pupil growth (Soar, 1972; Rosenshine, 1971). Parenthetically, it may seem contradictory to refer to measures of pupil growth as criteria against which measures of classroom behavior are validated, when they are dismissed as a basis for evaluating teachers. There are many differences. The small number of pupil measures which assess higher cognitive levels of growth may be adequate for research directed at identifying teacher behavior which is associated with complex pupil growth but probably is not adequate for wide scale teacher evaluation. The problems of measuring gain can be better dealt with in research studies in which intensive analyses of data are carried out than in wider scale evaluation studies in which analyses of data are likely to be simpler. Uncontrolled influences are spread over a number of teachers, with general trends sought, rather than affecting the evaluations of individual teachers.

A parallel with medical practice seems relevant. If the only criterion of a physician's effectiveness were the mortality rate of his patients, then he could scarcely afford to take terminal patients. If the criterion is whether he prescribes the treatment which is known to be the most effective, then the evaluation becomes a fairer one. Similarly, the teacher appears to be more fairly evaluated if the judgment is made on what he does, rather than on the outcome of what he does. The first is under his control and the second is not (or at least not nearly so much so).

Admittedly, the results of research to date are not completely clear and consistent. There are suggestions that some teacher behaviors are more likely to produce valued outcomes. The following generalizations are among those which might be cited. Indirectness of teacher behavior tends to be associated positively with assessment growth, favorableness of pupil attitudes, and creativity growth. Teacher flexibility tends to be associated positively with achievement gain. Teacher criticism tends to be negatively related to achievement gain. Subtle rather than obvious aspects of teacher behavior tend to be related to pupil growth. The cognitive level of pupil interaction tends to follow the levels used by the teacher, up to intermediate levels; but pupil interaction involving the higher levels tends to occur only in the presence of supportive interaction by other pupils.

The conclusions which seem appropriate begin to become complex before the findings of various studies are pursued very far. For example, several studies suggest that pupil growth increases as freedom and self-direction increases, but only up to a point. Beyond that point, less growth rather than more appears to take place. Further, the point at which maximum growth takes place appears to be a function of the complexity or abstractness of the learning task—the more abstract the task the greater the freedom which is optimal; the more concrete the learning, the greater the teacher control which is optimal.

Figure 2 presents an integration of the relationships suggested by various studies conducted by Soar and Soar (1972). There are also suggestions that different pupil groups (dependent vs. independent, low vs. high anxious, low vs. high ability) respond differently to the same classroom behavior, but the clearest conclusion in this case is the need for further research.

The use of systematic observation could meet the requirements that student

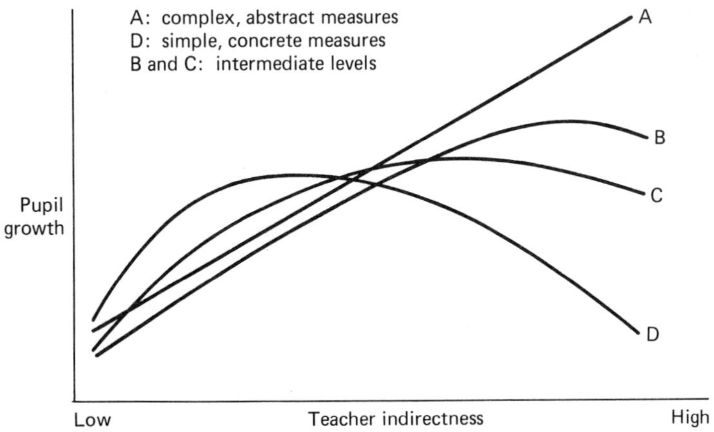

Fig. 2. Hypothesized relation between teacher indirectness and pupil growth across a broad range.

teacher competencies be derived from explicit conceptions of teacher roles, be stated to make assessment possible, and be made public in advance (1971). Systems provide explicit, behavioral, low inference measures of teaching behavior and, as such, provide a vocabulary and a set of concepts for communicating about teaching as well as a metric for measuring it. It is hard to see how these requirements could be met without procedures such as these.

SOME POSSIBLE APPLICATIONS

Measuring teacher behavior is certainly applicable to teacher preparation programs. In fact, such applications have been made for some time now. For some years, Hough, in a program at Ohio State University, has been teaching a methods course in which students are given a series of prescriptions for behavior which they must be able to produce in simulated teaching to complete the course. As examples, each student teacher must teach a lesson in which at least half of the talk in the lesson is produced by students; he must teach a lesson in which at least one-third of his own talk is indirect, as defined by the categories of an observation system. If the student can produce all of the prescribed behaviors at the beginning of the course, he has completed it. If it requires several quarters for him to produce the behaviors, then he has not finished the course until he has produced those behaviors. If he is never able to produce the behaviors, he never completes the course. This is a measurement of exit competencies which Elam (1971) identifies as being desirable.

An important issue is the need to represent teacher behavior through the use of multiple systems in order to gain a broader view of the classroom behaviors important to pupil growth. A course such as Hough's is surely a pioneering effort.

When all student teachers are routinely observed the economic problems of observational procedures do not appear to be great, even if each graduating teacher is to be certified on this basis. If the goal is to certify a program, then perhaps it would be appropriate to observe a sample of teachers to evaluate the program rather than the individual teachers.

There are promising beginnings in researching aspects of teacher behavior which are important for pupil growth. The use of such observational measures is a preferable way to proceed, even when the goal is to measure the implementation of theory which is still unverified by empirical research. Of course, some measures of classroom behavior might be seen as measures of objectives in and of themselves, quite apart from their relation to other measures of the growth of pupils. For example, it would seem reasonable to value a classroom in which a smaller rather than a larger proportion of the teacher's efforts is directed toward controlling the behavior of pupils instead of "teaching." Similarly, it seems desirable for a teacher's management of a classroom to take place through directions which are gentle and noncoercive, rather than ordering and commanding. The classroom in which moderate amounts of positive affect are expressed and relatively small amounts of negative affect occur, would probably be valued by many.

Observation also offers the possibility of measuring the attainment of pupil objectives which would probably be difficult to assess in any other way. How better to measure pupil responsibility and self-direction than to record the ability of pupils to carry out a task without teacher direction? How better to measure the socialization of young children than to code the interactions that occur between members of small groups as they work together in the classroom?

SOME CONCLUDING COMMENTS

Measuring teacher effectiveness by measuring change in pupils is probably only feasible for simpler, lower level objectives.

For the attainment of higher level objectives, or more slowly developing objectives, the more appropriate procedure appears to be to measure the behavior of the teacher and compare it to behavior which is thought to be related to the development of higher level objectives in pupils. Such a procedure appears feasible, both for the assessment of competence of individual teachers and for the certification of programs.

While much research and development work remains to be done, the beginnings appear to be promising. In contrast, however, both as research on teacher behavior suggests and as Small (1972) and the *Times* article attest, the attempt to measure the attainment of all objectives by measuring growth of pupils is likely to be a disaster. It could foreclose the possibility of implementing a procedure which in the long run would represent a real advance in teacher education, certification, and evaluation.

The caution of the researcher about implementing a procedure which still needs extensive work is surely appropriate; yet in comparison to the alternatives, observational methods seem the most hopeful. They do not create pressure for the teacher to stress low level objectives. They avoid a series of measurement problems which are difficult, if not disabling. They measure the performance which is most directly under the control of the teacher. They permit the faculty and administration of a school or system to agree on valued teaching behaviors with a minimum of misunderstanding. They give the teacher feedback on his teaching behavior. They permit the teacher to apply the research findings which do exist relatively directly. If programs of accountability on competency-based teacher education are to be implemented, systematic observation appears to be one of the more promising assessment procedures for measuring teaching skill.

This article has only considered the problems of how to hold the classroom teacher accountable and for what. There is a broader context and the teacher's accountability is only part—the reciprocal responsibilities of the schools to society, and vice versa. A few examples are cited. Is there any limit to the pupil objectives for which schools are to be held accountable? A role in helping solve an imposing array of social problems has been given to the schools in the past generation. Concern about traffic safety has resulted in driver education in the schools. Other problems, in turn, have led to the addition of such programs as those concerned with sex, drugs, and now "parenting." It is hard to imagine any other agency of society which has been as involved in working to eliminate minority discrimination. Are there any old responsibilities for which schools are no longer accountable? Or has the list simply kept extending?

Is the family accountable in any way for the readiness or socialization of the child when he starts to school? Is a teacher of a regular kindergarten or first grade, for example, accountable for usual grade achievement for a child who begins school with little or no language, cleanliness habits or toilet training, safety, etc.? Is the interest and effort the child brings to his work solely the teacher's responsibility? Again, is there any limit to the objectives for which the teacher and the school are to be held accountable?

Does the school system and the society it represents have responsibility to the teacher for a variety of kinds of support? Are these measured in any ways but money? As only an extreme example, how is the society held accountable for the physical safety of the teacher? Who pays the penalty when it fails?

Superintendencies in large cities seem increasingly to have become "revolving door" positions. Is accountability for the problems involved placed anywhere but with the succession of incumbents?

Is society accountable for the support of research to improve the quality and efficiency of the educational process in the schools?

Illustrative questions such as these, which are only a few of the possible ones, seem not to be included in discussions of accountability. Are they relevant, or is only the teacher accountable?

References

Bereiter, C. "Some Persisting Dilemmas in the Measurement of Change." In C. W. Harris, ed., *Problems in Measuring Change.* Madison: University of Wisconsin Press, 1963.

Bloom, B. S., ed. *Taxonomy of Educational Objectives Handbook 1: Cognitive Domain.* New York: McKay, 1956.

Brophy, J. E. *Stability in Teacher Effectiveness* (R & D Report Series 77). Austin: The Research and Development Center for Teacher Education, The University of Texas, July 1972.

Elam, S. *Performance-Based Teacher Education: What Is the State of the Art?* Washington, D.C.: American Association of Colleges for Teacher Education, 1971.

Garber, M., and W. B. Ware. "The Home Environment as a Predictor of School Achievement." *Theory into Practice* **11** (1972): 190–195.

Keeves, J. P. *The Home Environment and Education Achievement.* Australian National University Research School of Social Sciences, Dept. of Sociology, October 1970.

Medley, D. M., and H. E. Mitzel. "Some Behavior Correlates of Teacher Effectiveness." *Journal of Educational Psychology* **50** (1959): 239–246.

Office of Education, U.S. Dept. of Health, Education, and Welfare. *Do Teachers Make a Difference?* (Cat. No. HE 5.258:58042). Washington, D.C.: U.S. Government Printing Office, 1970.

Orsini, B. "Perspective." *St. Petersburg Times,* 19 March 1971.

Rosenshine, B. "The Stability of Teacher Effects upon Student Achievement." *Review of Educational Research* **40**, no. 5 (1970): 647–662.

Rosenshine, B. *Teaching Behaviours and Student Achievement.* London: International Association for the Evaluation of Educational Achievement, 1971.

Small, A. A. "Accountability in Victorian England." *Phi Delta Kappan* **53** (1972): 438–439.

Soar, R. S. *An Integrative Approach to Classroom Learning.* NIMH Project Nos. 5-R11 MH 01096 to the University of South Carolina; and 7-R11 MH 02045 to Temple University, Philadelphia, Pa., 1966.

Soar, R. S. "The Classroom: Teacher Pupil Interaction." In J. S. Squire, ed., *A New Look at Progressive Education, Yearbook 1972.* Washington, D.C.: Association for Supervision and Curriculum Development, 1972.

Soar, R. S., and R. M. Soar. "An Empirical Analysis of Selected Follow Through Programs: An Example of a Process Approach to Evaluation." In I. J. Gordon, ed., *Early Childhood Education.* Chicago: National Society for the Study of Education, 1972.

Wolf, R. M. "The Identification and Measurement of Environmental Process Variables Related to Intelligence." Ph.D. dissertation, University of Chicago, 1964.

W. JAMES POPHAM
University of California at Los Angeles

Measurement Problems in Implementing the Stull Act

The architects of the recently enacted California teacher evaluation law left the implementers of that law with far more slack than is typical in the building industry, where architectual specifications must be both comprehensive and detailed. Whether, in the case of the Stull Act, this latitude represented political sensitivity to local educational prerogatives, or merely shoddy architectural planning, remains to be seen. Motives aside, California educators now have a ton of required explicating to do if they are to implement the new law.

This paper will focus on implementation problems associated with defining educational objectives and standards for the now required district personnel evaluation systems. The analysis will be restricted to considerations of teacher evaluation, rather than the evaluation of non-teaching certified personnel.

The impetus for this particular analysis stems from two specific *binding* sections of the Stull Act which, rather than allowing local district implementation schemes, require local educators to include the following elements in their teacher evaluation procedures:

a. The establishment of standards of expected student progress in each area of study and of techniques for the assessment of that progress.
b. Assessment of certificated personnel competence as it relates to the established standards.

There are two key terms in these stipulations which must be inspected further, namely, *progress* and *standards*. Dealing with the easier analysis first, the term *standard* shouldn't pose much difficulty in interpretation since the technical denotations and connotations of the term pretty much parallel popular usage. When most people use the term *standard* they refer to a level or degree of proficiency. In educational parlance the term generally describes *how well* we

From N. L. Gage, ed., *Mandated Evaluation of Educators* (Washington, D.C.: Capitol Publications, 1973), pp. 111–132. Reprinted by permission.

expect a person or a program to perform. Later in this paper an attempt will be made to consider alternative techniques for establishing educational standards.

The second term, *progress*, is more vexing. For some people it means pretest to posttest growth. For others it simply means *how are the kids doing*. Some educators equate progress with the degree of objectives-attainment. To some it merely represents the *substance* of whatever we apply standards to. The possibilities of disagreement over basic terms and of resulting confusion are rife with respect to the term *progress*. An operational definition is clearly required.

Although attempting to infer legislative intent from actual legislation is as risky as reading pharmacy prescriptions—upside down from a mirror—it appears that the California legislators responsible for the Stull Act were using the term *progress* to describe *what* students were learning. They reserved the term *standards* to get at how well the students were learning whatever it was they were supposed to.

Thus, rather than assuming that there is an automatic equivalence between *progress* and *instructional objectives,* it makes more sense to examine alternative *indicators of progress,* then see how instructional objectives might relate to such indicators.

INDICATORS OF EXPECTED STUDENT PROGRESS

By and large the indicators of student progress which will be employed to implement the Stull Act will be learner performance on measuring instruments. Although theoretically consisting of a wide variety of assessment procedures, not just paper and pencil tests, it is very likely that the measurement schemes initially selected will generally be paper and pencil tests. This will occur less from the lack of imagination of Stull Act implementers than from the astonishing imposition by the legislators of a statewide teacher evaluation enterprise *without providing adequate financial resources* to give that enterprise a decent chance to succeed. Financially frantic districts will be hard put to provide any other measurement mechanics than those which can be acquired or developed inexpensively.

Before considering several of the measurement acquisition options open to Stull Act implementers, it may be useful to remind ourselves that a local district can pursue at least four sources of measurement devices. There are, of course, commercial firms which distribute tests of various types. Second, if a district has sufficient financial resources *plus* measurement expertise, then local development of tests is an eligible contender. Third, for affluent districts all or part of the test development effort can be contracted to one or more of the private consulting groups springing up to satisfy this type of need. Finally, a cooperative interdistrict test development enterprise might be undertaken, for example, involving a number of small or middle sized districts within a particular county.

While there are other sources of good measuring instruments (e.g., truly desperate Stull Act implementers may wish to rub old lamps vigorously, then look for a large, turban-wearing stranger.), those listed above represent the most common ways of acquiring the needed tests. In the next section of the paper, as we examine three different types of measurement procedures, remember that any of these acquisition routes can be employed, that is, (1) purchases from commercial firms, (2) local development, (3) contracted development, or (4) interdistrict cooperative development.

Norm-Referenced Measures

The treatment of alternative types of measurement approaches will be given short shrift in the present paper (have you ever met a tall shrift?) because this topic has been treated elsewhere (See Glass, 1972). Nevertheless, a word or two about norm-referenced tests is in order.

Generally speaking, norm-referenced tests, such as commercially distributed achievement tests, suffer from two major deficiencies which render them unsuitable for Stull Act implementation. First, they are by design so general (in order to serve an entire nation) that there is often little congruence between the emphases of the test and the emphases of a particular teacher (or school district). Mismatched measurement and instruction doesn't give the instructor a fair break.

Second, certain psychometric requisites of norm-referenced tests, such as the necessity to produce considerable score variance, may lead to the elimination or modification of the very test items that would be most sensitive to detecting the instructional impact of a truly effective teacher. Thus, typical standardized achievement tests will penalize the high quality teacher while perhaps not identifying the teacher most in need of improvement.

Finally, and I believe this is perhaps the most important deficiency of standardized tests for use in evaluating an instructional program (or an instructor), norm-referenced measures offer few cues to those teachers who, upon failing to perform satisfactorily, wish to improve themselves. For the vast majority of norm-referenced measures, there is no attempt made to delimit with precision the types of learner behaviors measured by the tests. As a consequence, the teacher only has a fuzzy notion of what the test really measured, other than that his/her students couldn't do it very well. An implicit assumption of evaluation programs is that we want to improve the efficacy of those instructional efforts identified as inadequate. The ill-defined boundaries of most norm-referenced tests are not compatible with this assumption.

Criterion-Referenced Measures

Advocacy of criterion-referenced tests, in contrast to norm-referenced tests, is becoming very fashionable these days. One of the problems with this position, however, is that different people mean different things by the phrase, "criterion-referenced measures." For Robert Glaser, who has been instrumental in popularizing this distinction, a criterion-referenced test measures the degree to which a student has achieved a given competency (often described in terms of an instructional objective). To others, a criterion-referenced test indicates whether a student has reached a given criterion *level,* that is, a *standard* of performance.

These people very frequently harken back to classical prediction approaches where the task was to forecast whether an individual would reach a given level of competence. To others, the criterion involved in a criterion-referenced test is not test behavior but some external, real-world behavior such as the individual's ability to cope satisfactorily with the price computation problems presented in a typical supermarket. And for still others, a criterion-referenced test simply refers to any kind of measure that is *not* a norm-referenced test.

These distinctions become important, of course, in that they influence how the evaluator proceeds with respect to the development and refinement of such measures. For purposes of this discussion, the interpretation supplied by Glaser will be followed whereby a criterion-referenced test is designed to measure whether a learner has mastered a particular type of intended behavior.

Now the advantages of criterion-referenced tests for purposes of evaluation are several. In the first place, since they are not hobbled with the requirement to produce considerable score variance, but merely to discern whether a given behavior falls within an individual's repertoire, the tests can more readily pick up those post-instruction behaviors which are achieved by most learners. Second, a criterion referenced test is generally wedded to a more circumscribed description of learner behavior than a norm-referenced test and, consequently, provides those evaluated with a better notion of what is actually being assessed. This increased clarity of description can lead to important instructional advantages. A key advantage of criterion-referenced tests is that typically they can be constructed so that they are more congruent with local curricular emphases. Because there are few such tests existing now, they will generally have to be devised locally and can therefore be tailored more directly to the instructional emphases within a given district.

Thus, the use of criterion-referenced tests seems to offer the teacher a better chance in Stull Act implementation schemes. They will generally be more sensitive to change and more consonant with local curricular foci. But there are some problems with criterion-referenced tests which should be recognized. First, if they are to be constructed locally, and this will frequently be the case, they will probably be generated by individuals who have less measurement sophistication than personnel preparing commercially distributed tests. Furthermore, if the tests are constructed too narrowly, that is, so that only performance on a few test *items* rather than a *class* of learner behaviors is being measured, then there are dangers of the teacher instructing precisely to a test rather than a range of eligible learner behaviors. Finally, because these tests will characteristically be "home grown," they may not induce the same degree of confidence on the part of the public that can be enlisted by standardized tests. In spite of these dangers, however, it still appears that for Stull Act implementation criterion-referenced tests would, in general, be preferable to their norm-referenced counterparts.

Domain-Referenced Tests

While technically only a variation of criterion-referenced tests, the domain-referenced test scheme devised by Wells Hively and his associates has much to commend it for purposes of teacher evaluation. According to Hively's approach, inordinate attention is given to identifying the domain of eligible test behaviors assessed by a given measuring instrument. In other words, the measurement designer goes to great pains to clarify the eligible stimulus elements within that domain, the possible learner response options, the distinguishing criteria of correct and incorrect responses, the content limits to be included in the domain, etc. By thus explicating the nature of the domain to be assessed via a pool of test items, both the test developer and the individual being evaluated have a much more definitive idea of the boundaries of the measures involved.

THE RELATIONSHIP OF ALTERNATIVE INDICATORS TO STATEMENTS OF INSTRUCTIONAL OBJECTIVES

Just what is the relationship between the kinds of measures described above and statements of instructional objectives? As many California educators initiated efforts this year to make implementation plans for the Stull Act, there was an obvious gravitation toward instructional objectives as a way of describing how students would display "progress." While this is only natural, considering the national emphasis on measurable instructional objectives during the past ten years, it is by no means necessary. Statements of objectives can, in a shorthand fashion, capture much of the meaning of a set of test items. In other words, rather than looking over a set of ten or twenty items designed to measure a particular kind of mathematics skill, the inspection of a well-formed instructional objective can save the educator much time in determining what is really involved in the test. Since educators are beginning to use objectives more frequently for curriculum decisions and instructional planning, it is only natural that statements of objectives will often be used to conceptualize the nature of expected student progress.

But consider for a moment the three main operations of education, i.e., curricular decision-making, instructional decision-making, and evaluation decision-making. Whereas objectives can prove useful in the first two of these without measurement devices, when it comes to the evaluation operation, use of objectives without measurement is meaningless. Accordingly, in evaluation enterprises such as those designed to implement the Stull Act, measurement procedures must be constructed. Objectives may or may not be used to describe those measures. This is the primary role of objectives in connection with the Stull Act, that is, they can serve as economical descriptors.

PROBLEMS OF DEFINING OBJECTIVES

Assuming that statements of objectives may be used as a way of helping teachers and others involved in Stull Act implementation define the nature of student progress, there are clearly alternative ways whereby a useful set of objectives can be derived. Some of these should be examined. It must be noted that while the language of the Stull Act emphasizes the assessment of learner progress in each area of study, implementers of the new law should not overlook those easily ignored but terribly important affective goals that most of us hope our schools are promoting.

Local Generation of Objectives

One procedure for the identification of objectives which has been followed by many school districts in the past decade is to have district teachers and administrators participate in the development of measurable objectives suited for that district. The chief benefits of this approach are that (1) the objectives can be explicitly tied to the curricular emphases of the district and (2) local educators feel they have a vital role in determining the objectives. The disadvantages, however, appear to outweigh the advantages.

In the first place, many teachers and other district education personnel are not particularly expert in the generation of objectives. Hence, one can anticipate a fair number of ambiguous, non-measurable goals as well as more than the necessary number of low-level, trivial objectives. Furthermore, most district educational personnel are already far too busy with their ordinary educational responsibilities to spend much time in the generation of objectives. Finally, there is something intrinsically debilitating in realizing that you are engaged in a wheel reinvention enterprise, for since so many measurable objectives have already been generated in various parts of the country for such evaluation efforts, it seems unfortunate to ask any individual to create anew that which has already been born.

Interdistrict Sharing

A way of partially avoiding the problems associated with local generation of objectives is to engage several districts, perhaps a whole county, in the task of generating appropriate objectives. Even assuming that there would be some differences among districts with respect to instructional emphases, these could be more readily accommodated thereafter by a local district. The advantage of pooling resources in this manner, of course, is that it reduces inadvertent duplication of effort and can capitalize on the most capable representatives of several districts.

The Use of Objectives Depositories

In the past few years several objectives depositories such as the Instructional Objectives Exchange[1] have been created which make available to educators collections of measurable objectives from which selections can be made for local purposes. It would seem clear that if objectives are to serve as the rubric around which Stull Act implementers will organize their thinking, then an inspection of the objectives available from such depositories should be undertaken.

---

[1] Instructional Objectives Exchange, Box 24095, Los Angeles, California 90024.

Technical Difficulties

It would be unfortunate not to alert Stull Act implementers to several technical problems associated with the use of objectives which have not been satisfactorily resolved. One of these deals with the level of specificity at which the objectives should be written. One can conceive of extremes along a continuum of specificity in which at one end we find a highly explicit objective that is essentially equivalent to a test item (the student will list the names of six U.S. presidents) and at the other end an extremely imprecise objective written in nonbehavioral form (the student will appreciate the importance of good citizenship). Unfortunately, the appropriate point between these two extremes has not been identified. We do not currently possess any techniques for replicably generating precise levels of specificity for measurable objectives. Those districts involved in the selection and/or generation of objectives, even though they be measurable, must anticipate considerable latitude in the degree of specificity associated with those objectives.

A second problem deals with the appropriateness of the objective selected. Although we might wish for more definitive guidelines regarding whether the objectives chosen for such evaluation operations as the Stull Act are, in fact, appropriate, these kinds of decisions still rest largely on personal judgment. We don't yet have a defensible technology for deciding what ought to be taught, even though the use of objectives clarifies far better than any previous technique exactly what the nature of a goal intention really is.

These two problems only illustrate the point that whereas the use of measurable objectives adds much to the promotion of clarity, the technical difficulties associated with using such objectives statements are considerable. Stull Act implementers who employ objectives may be better off than those who employ nebulous goal statements, but the techniques of formulating objectives statements are not as advanced as we might wish.

Needs Assessment Strategies

Once it has been decided that objectives can prove a serviceable descriptor for Stull Act implementation, then the question arises as to how decisions will be made with respect to what the final objectives really ought to be. There have been several attempts in recent years to tackle this problem in a technical manner through the use of educational needs assessment approaches. According to this general strategy, preferences are secured from a variety of individuals associated with the educational enterprise, for example, students, community representatives, teachers, etc. Either by ranking or rating extant sets of objectives or by generating new goals themselves, different inputs from various representative groups are secured. These preferences are then translated, sometimes by highly quantitative techniques, into overall indicators regarding the relative priority of different objectives. The technical procedures for employing such multigroup preference determination schemes are outlined in some detail elsewhere (Stake, 1972; Popham, 1972).

Summary

In review, if instructional objectives are to serve as descriptors for thinking about Stull Act measurement operations, then a local district may secure such objectives by one or more of the schemes described above, then decide in some way which of those objectives are more important.

Care should be taken when adopting objectives as a descriptive vehicle not to generate so many objectives statements that the result is an intellectually unmanageable collection. In 1971, for example, the Wisconsin legislature enacted a law requiring an annual statewide assessment. Designers of the plan to implement that law have adopted statements of instructional objectives as the descriptive language for conducting the assessment. Yet in the field of mathematics (grade K-8) they are now working with somewhat in excess of 400 objectives, and will be assessing student performance at the end of the third grade with over 300 of those objectives. Now most human beings simply cannot comprehend the educational meaning of 300 disparate objectives. Although no empirical studies have been conducted on this point, one suspects that being able to cognitively process many more than 15 or 20 objectives per academic year probably represents sufficient detail for most educators. As a consequence, objectives must be stated at a greater level of generality and, perhaps, only a few objectives should be emphasized.

DECIDING ON DEFENSIBLE STANDARDS

We now turn to the super-sticky problem of determining the standards of expected student progress against which teacher competence is to be appraised. Here, of course, the quantitatively oriented methodologist starts to perspire a bit, for there will have to be something other than numbers and test scores involved, there will have to be—judgment. Because no matter how many numerical machinations we employ during the process of determining how well we want youngsters to perform, there will necessarily be abundant doses of personal estimates regarding how much to weigh various factors in order to spell out a desired level of learner proficiency.

A fair amount of discussion has been carried on in evaluation circles recently regarding the merits of a distinction between relative and absolute standards. Perhaps such discussions have merit at a theoretical level, but from the practitioner's plateau it is hard to visualize a decision regarding where to establish an educational standard that is not heavily dependent on experience-based comparisons. For example, once a given type of learner behavior has been isolated, our notions of how well we want learners to display that behavior are contingent on previous experience regarding how well we or others should be able to do with respect to that behavior under typical or, possibly, ideal conditions. How perplexing it would be if someone defined an innovative type of cognitive skill for learners, one which bore little relationship to skills with which we were familiar, then asked us to specify how well 12-year-old children should be expected to perform the skill. Unless we had some experience to call on in conjuring up performance standards, we'd probably draw a blank. For several of the procedural suggestions to be offered in the following paragraphs, a conscious effort has thus been made to bolster the decision-maker's experience base.

Another general point needs to be made regarding standards, one that is so obvious it almost need not be mentioned, namely, *realistic standards must take into consideration the entry behaviors of the learners involved.* Clearly, for example, we would expect a different level of proficiency in reading for first graders than for high school seniors. Just as clearly, youngsters from an environment in which the merits of intellectual achievement have systematically been praised should be expected to perform at a different level of proficiency than children from an environment in which intellectual achievement is ignored or degenerated. There should not be one standard—statewide or nationwide—for children at a given point in their lives. Defensible levels of expectation must involve the tailoring of standards to situational variables and personal antecedents.

This raises an interesting question regarding diversity of standards, that is, should we lower our expectations for educationally disadvantaged youngsters to the point where we will require no more of them than second class studentship? Definitely not! What we may have to do is move more slowly toward desired standards of excellence. Whereas a fourth grade teacher may not be evaluated adversely if his/her ghetto-background students are reaching only 25 percent on a given skill dimension when children of the same age from an economically advantaged suburb are reaching 50 percent, we can not be satisfied with the proficiency levels of the disadvantaged children. To correct such deficits will undoubtedly require either far greater expenditures of the nation's resources for education or a major reallocation of current resources. In the meanwhile, as far as evaluating a teacher according to specific standards of learner progress, the standards must be predicated on what the learners bring into the instructional situation.

Let's examine some alternative procedures for deciding on the kinds of standards which might be involved in a Stull Act teacher evaluation program.

The Estimated Percentage Method

One rather common procedure which dates back to the early days of programmed instruction involves the evaluator's making a judgment about what percentage of the learners should perform with what percentage of proficiency. An expectation of a 90-90 percentage proficiency standard might be set for a given test which signifies that at least 90 percent of the learners are expected to earn scores of 90 percent or better on the test. Often these percentage estimates are made almost arbitrarily, sometimes on the basis of more systematic data. But generally this procedure requires the estimator(s) to make pretty intuitive judgments regarding expected levels of learner proficiency.

A Needs Assessment Analog

As described earlier in the paper, one of the identifiably new activities in educational planning during recent years has been an activity referred to as educational needs assessment. Stemming largely from a requirement in the distribution of ESEA Title III funds which stipulates that each state must conduct such a needs assessment, these operations have become well known throughout the nation. Many states have chosen needs assessment strategies which consciously attempt to be responsive to the preferences of those groups with a legitimate interest in the educational enterprise. There are, of course, important procedural considerations, e.g., (1) should different groups' preferences be given different weightings in determining the final statement of needs, or (2) to what extent should data regarding learners' current status be used in the analysis. But regardless of the procedural variants, the key to these needs assessment strategies is that different groups are allowed inputs in the mechanism for the identification of educational needs.

It only takes a modest extension of the approach involved in goals or needs determination strategies to apply an analogous scheme to the determination of standards. Various groups could be apprised of the need for such standards, then allowed to proffer their views regarding how well students should be expected to perform various tasks, goals, etc. While this approach might well involve estimated percentage techniques, it reflects a more systematic, diverse-input scheme.

A Simple Improvement Technique

Although apparently too simplistic for consideration, a straightforward scheme for deciding on standard might consist of merely expecting the progress of learners during a particular year to be better than it was during the preceding year. For instance, if a posttest minus pretest equals gain model is employed, then a standard involving no more than the following could be used: gain this year greater than gain last year.

In the absence of more defensible standards-determination schemes, a simple improvement technique may prove helpful as an interim solution. It seems certain that whatever resources can be used by a district to implement the Stull Act will, at the outset, more likely be expended on decisions regarding what types of progress to identify and how to measure it. A simple improvement technique can serve as a satisfactory temporizing vehicle.

One of the practical difficulties associated with such methods is that if there is no history of the previous performance of district pupils on certain measures, then it is difficult to establish the baseline on which improvement can be predicted. One method of playing this kind of game is to use standardized test grade level equivalents, i.e., one academic year's expected growth, as a *guide,* not a definitive quantity. By inspecting standardized tests themselves, plus the accompanying normative data per grade level, some limited extrapolations can cautiously be made to guide a local district.

An Asymptote Option

One of the requirements of the Stull Act which has yet to receive the attention it warrants is a provision that each district's implementation plan incorporate an assistance program for those teachers being evaluated. In other words, the new law mandates not only a teacher appraisal system but also a staff development program. Now assuming that a district is serious about this improvement requirement, and does invest a substantial amount of resources in an effort to improve the effectiveness of its teachers, we might reasonably expect some kind of payoff, albeit modest perhaps, in staff effectiveness. This improvement would undoubtedly have to peak at some point, for it is unlikely that staff improvement would occur ad infinitum. Thus we might find, *if a substantial staff improvement program is present each year,* learner performance gains such as those seen in Figure 1. Now at the asymptote of the improvement curve we could identify a level of expected learner performance based on more substantial evidence than mere guesswork. Quite clearly, this approach represents little more than a refinement of the simple improvement technique. But in districts where a major effort to improve staff competence is underway, it is an option worth considering.

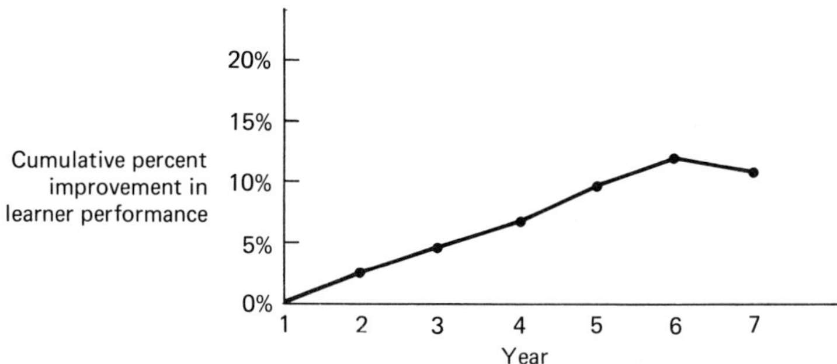

Fig. 1. Fictitious levels of improvement in learner performance based on a substantial staff development program.

A Regression Solution

In a recent paper Klein and Alkin (1972) have reminded us of a familiar but not widely employed procedure for establishing standards, namely, regression analysis. This approach involves the administration of a pretest (any of the indicators of student progress described earlier) at the beginning of the year and a comparable or identical test at the close of the year. Based on the relationship between these two sets of data, an *expected* posttest score can be computed for each learner. By inspecting, teacher by teacher, the proportion of actual posttest scores which are equal to or above the *expected* score, we can calculate a per-teacher index of the degree to which the teacher is able to promote predicted (by the regression analysis) achievement. The Klein and Alkin article, because it offers a simple step-by-step explanation of this procedure along with easy to interpret examples, should be consulted by those interested in exploring this alternative further.

FINAL THOUGHTS

It is evident somebody has to decide on what the areas of content/behavior are in which learners will be measured to reflect teacher competence. Statements of instructional objectives are a handy way of talking about such learner performance. Then somebody has to decide on the kinds of measurement procedures needed to provide indicators of this performance. Next, somebody has to figure out a scheme for deciding how well students ought to perform so that such standards can be employed in contrast to actual teacher performance. Finally, somebody has to coalesce all of these data and report them in an accurate and readily interpretable form.

I have attempted to set forth options, with a bit of implicit and explicit preferences, for the chief phases of such an operation. Because the Stull Act, with all of its shortcomings, represents an effort to consider the worth of instructors in terms of learner results, I am supportive of the general intent of the new law. I hope that new analyses of the issues will help promote the kind of educational improvements anticipated by Assemblyman Stull and his colleagues.

References

Glass, G. V. "Statistical and Measurement Problems in Implementing the Stull Act." Paper presented at the Conference on the Stull Act, Stanford Center for Research and Development in Teaching, October 1972.

Klein, S. P., and M. C. Alkin. "Evaluating Teachers for Outcome Accountability." *Evaluation Comment* 3, no. 3 (1972): 5–11.

Popham, W. J. "California's Precedent-Setting Teacher Evaluation Law." *Educational Researcher* 1, no. 7 (1972): 13–14.

Popham, W. J. *An Evaluation Guidebook: A Set of Practical Guidelines for the Educational Evaluator*. Los Angeles: Instructional Objectives Exchange, 1972.

Stake, R. E. *Priorities Planning: Judging the Importance of Objectives*. Los Angeles: Instructional Objectives Exchange, 1972.

MICHAEL SCRIVEN
University of California at Berkeley

The Evaluation of Teachers and Teaching

INTRODUCTION

I here react to the usual practices in the evaluation of teaching, and propose an alternative approach. The treatment is conceptual, not experimental.

The crucial feature of this evaluation problem is the failure of research to establish useable connections between (classroom) process variables and the outcome variables which—for the most part—define or serve as criteria for what we identify as "good teaching." Hence there are some possibilities of generalizing the line of approach here to other evaluation problems where there is the same absence of "linkage" research.

GOOD TEACHING

One does not have to be able to give a fully general definition of good teaching in order to be able to identify it in particular cases, or to contrast it with its converse (cf. "good answer," "good student," "good test"). Nevertheless, one can indicate some directions to go and some to avoid.

It is clear that good teaching cannot be defined simply in terms of achieving the goals of the teacher or the student since these may be—and often are—trivial or indefensible. Good teaching must make significant contributions to meeting the educational needs of the student and society and must be reasonably effective by comparison with the teaching alternatives available—e.g., must not make a much smaller contribution than could be made by another teacher, or by using other teaching strategies (reading a text). This definition does not exclude the possibility that non-teacher educational technologies might be more

This article is an extensively revised version of a paper with the same title published in the *California Journal of Educational Research* **25,** no. 3 (1974): 109–115. Alan Walworth's comments were very helpful. Used by permission of the author.

(cost-) effective than teaching by (human) teachers; good teaching may not be the best way to educate people in all (or most) situations. Good teaching may achieve the acquisition of needed knowledge, cognitive, perceptive, or psychomotor skills, and attitude/value changes; and it may achieve them temporarily or for life. Achieving such changes if they were not needed would be a less valuable contribution, but might still be a notable accomplishment, as long as the changes were not harmful. A type of harm is involved if this kind of teaching displaces teaching to needs; and a good deal of it does. Hence, in a broad sense, one cannot identify good teaching without some reference to what is taught, to content or curriculum, and to the students' needs for that content.

NEEDS ASSESSMENT

The introduction of needs as the basic currency instead of goals doesn't make evaluation easier, but it shifts the difficulty to the right place; instead of making the teacher's goals unassailable, it makes them just an intermediate means to the proper end. Who is to judge needs? *Not* just the teacher, who is scarcely in an unbiased position; not just the student, for the same reason; nor the administrator, nor the parent, nor the counselor, minister, or school psychologist. But most of these are likely to have something relevant to say about the needs of students, or of a particular student. Needs-assessment is probably the weakest component in most evaluations, but it is not *always* hard, especially K–12. For example, there is—by definition—a need to achieve mastery level on a valid functional literacy test. Here then is a criterion for the merit of a remedial reading teacher: does (s)he make a significant contribution to that need (whether or not it is his or her goal)? Notice that no one can be shown to have a need to reach *grade* level on a standardized reading test, since (a) the connection between that performance and functional literacy is unknown (one might be *at* grade-level and still have reading-skill needs, or below it and have none); (b) variations in the developmental rates between individuals make deficits of a year or so insignificant; and (c) the unreliability of the tests is serious. Still, a *three* grade-level deficit, achieved by a steady decline over five years of reading and testing, *would* suggest a need for remedial reading. And the simple discovery that a particular tenth-grader cannot read the word "Poison" on a medicine bottle label, or "Go Back: You Are Going the Wrong Way" on a freeway on-ramp, or pick up the gist of news stories on Watergate does identify a need. Finally, the needs to be considered are those of the population actually affected, not just the target (intended) audience. This includes students in other classes (through "leakage"), fellow teachers (especially in team teaching situations), parents, visitors, siblings, etc.

Now of course there are situations in which what a teacher has to teach is fairly tightly defined and beyond his/her control. But there is nearly always some leeway, and usually a great deal—more than the teacher at first is inclined to suppose. It isn't just teachers of reading that should be teaching reading—it's all those teachers (going well into college) who can do some teaching of reading for students who need it. To take another and simpler example: *Most* social studies teachers, *most* of the time, are bad teachers (or not as good as they should be) because what they are teaching is not what their students most grievously need, even within the area of social studies (as the NAEP results tell us).

EVALUATING TEACHERS VERSUS EVALUATING TEACHING

Teachers do more than teach, and they teach other than by "teaching" to a class. When they are evaluated in personnel review procedures it is sometimes appropriate and sometimes quite wrong for a particular extra-classroom activity to be taken into account. Their public, private, and professional services to students and to education should be acknowledged; their political and personal activities should, by and large, be ignored if within the legal boundaries.

It is helpful to distinguish three evaluation processes or procedures that involve the teacher, and the associated personnel, although in practice there is often some compression. First, students may evaluate teachers: let us call the form used for this, the S-form. Second, administrators or peers or specialists may evaluate the *teaching* of a particular teacher; *one* of their several inputs might be (and should be) the data from the S-form. Let's call the "form" they use, in reality or as a reconstruction from their practice, the T-form. Some of the other considerations that should be rated on the T-form are discussed below, and we've already stressed one—responsiveness to student needs. Third, administrators (etc.) will use the data from T-forms as *part* of the input for *personnel*-evaluation of the teacher, using what we can call a P-form. They will also consider, e.g., the public and administrative service of the teacher. It is poor evaluation methodology to look at any one of these without at least considering the others in the system under study, since the use of each (and hence criticism of it) is determined by its interaction with the others.

THE FUNCTIONS OF TEACHER EVALUATION

Major uses for the evaluation of teaching need to be distinguished before one can evaluate proposed procedures. These include:

a. Evaluation for self-improvement
b. Evaluation to assist an adviser or supervisor in the process of improving someone's teaching
c. Evaluation to advise other possible "consumers," especially other students
d. Evaluation for personnel decisions (hire, fire, promote, etc.) by present or potential employers or superiors
e. Evaluation by external audiences interested in, e.g., cost effectiveness or accountability considerations or the success of a particular project
f. Research to identify process ("style") variables that correlate with good teaching.

Types (a) and (b) are often called formative evaluation; (c), (d), and (e) are called summative evaluation.

Notice that the audience in (c) will have other interests besides the evaluation of teaching; prospective students will often be interested in the workload imposed by a teacher or the cost of texts, etc., whether or not these bear on the quality of teaching (in *some* cases they will). It is common, in the usual sloppy approaches to the evaluation of college teaching, to toss all questions of any possible interest to any audience onto the S-form. This leads to information overload for the evaluators using the form. They tend to free-associate to the shapeless mass of data and comments and essentially to treat it as a kind of Rorshach test in which they find what their prejudices want or their fancy impels them to find. A major aim of this paper is to recommend extreme parsimony in the data-gathering, combined with extreme care in identifying the use to which the data will be put. Parsimony is advocated, not for the sake of economy in evaluation costs and to increase return rates by decreasing the load on the respondents (both being very desirable side-effects, however) but for the sake of validity. The Principle of Parsimony for evaluation might be expressed thus: gather data only when you can demonstrate its connection with merit, and only when you have arranged a legitimate market (use) for it.

The power of this principle with regard to the evaluation of teaching is immense; its credentials are based on the halo effect at the methodological end and the threat of legal action (based on the possibility of the halo effect) at the other. This is a simple extension of the point about barring racial data or photos on application forms. The main reason for ignoring this principle to the extent it has been ignored in practice so far is the confusion of evaluation with research. Most of the work on form-development (which means S-forms) has been done by researchers like Bob Wilson (then at the Research and Development Center for Higher Education) or the ETS team or the University of Illinois group, who were looking for interesting correlations, which is of course not the task in evaluation. By and large, the research function item (f in the list) needs to be kept out of the way of most evaluation of teaching. Which is not to say we don't need the research. We need it desperately. But much of what has been done is not what I'd call primary evaluation research—the kind we need—which identifies the process variables which could improve teaching. Usually, it's just open-season correlation-hunting, and even where one of the correlated variables *is* student gains (a necessary condition for primary evaluation research) the others are not appropriately restricted.

For primary evaluation research, aimed to give a legitimate basis for formative evaluation, the correlated variables must be restricted to "*improvement*" variables, not just any (i.e., "indicator") variables. Even for summative evaluation, the latter group is too inclusive to be legitimate. The best indicator of learning gains is probably student intelligence, but you can't use it for evaluation, certainly not for self- or other-improvement. Improvement variables are a *sub*-set of the causal factors, hence this is not the usual "cause vs. correlation" distinction. It is in general undesirable to use factors as criteria of merit which when emulated would not produce benefits or which cannot *in principle* be generally emulated, since the instrument then sows the seeds of later invalidity. Hence "having the highest proportion of science students enrolled" is a dubious criterion of teaching merit (i.e., it's not an improvement variable—probably) even if it is at present the best statistical indicator of learning gains in philosophy classes. So, research is needed, but a very definite kind of research is needed most. And before then, we need better evaluation, using what we can already get.

Another pressure in (partly) the wrong direction has been that of student consumers, who have often been the only group keeping S-based evaluation of teaching going on a campus and who have interests going beyond mere evaluation of teaching, some just mentioned and one that deserves more extensive comment.

THE EVALUATION OF COURSES VERSUS THE EVALUATION OF TEACHERS

A crucial concern for a prospective student involves the merit of courses rather than teachers; indeed, at the college level, the relevant publications are often called "course guides," though they normally consist to a substantial extent of teacher evaluations. The problem is that it's difficult for students to distinguish between the teacher and the course, especially with regard to compulsory courses, but it's obviously improper to lump the two together in the evaluation of teaching, since it means lower evaluations for teachers who are obliged to teach unpopular required courses. Here is one of several points where some training of the evaluators (in this case the students), e.g. by conceptual discussion or by going over 'calibration' examples, is essential, and can eliminate a good deal of error variance. The same applies to distinguishing between personality assessment and teaching assessment; some interaction is sure to occur, but it is known not to be very serious, and it can almost certainly be greatly reduced by discussion of the distinction and examples. Training of the instructors in the construction of the questions that they wish to place on the S-form and interpretation of the responses; and of administrators in interpretation, is also much needed to reduce the farcical errors that even highly intelligent teachers and administrators make when they begin work on these things. (I speak from reviewing administrative files at the college level, and from intensive discussions with several hundred school administrators taking my doctoral training seminar in evaluation.)

In case this kind of training should be thought of as a diversion of valuable energy, it should be realized that for teachers and administrators it involves probably the most important professional skill they can acquire, and for students *one* of the most useful intellectual skills of all, the improvement of evaluative judgments.

THE RELEASE OF INFORMATION AND ANONYMITY

At the college level, either one releases the S-form data to students, or they may recommend a parallel evaluation with consequent questionnaire overload problems. I regard it as morally objectionable and probably contrary to current guidelines governing research on human subjects to gather data from subjects who want it but then refuse it to them. I hope to see this practice explicitly forbidden by enlightened administrations in the near future.

In the high school, the same arguments apply, though they may well be less widely accepted. But in lower grades there might be some question; and by the time we get to the primary grades, the use of the S-form may be somewhat inappropriate in the first place, though I do not take that to be as obvious as is often assumed.

Teachers often would prefer that S-forms be signed. This simply shows they are incredibly naive: with all the power of retribution, do they expect to get honest negative responses? The request is often defended by reference to the greater importance of responses from 'good' students. But that defense is no more than implicit elitism; the needs of poorer students are often greater and their perception of the reasons for their failure may be made more acute by the extremity of their position.

PROCESS EVALUATION OF TEACHING

The usual procedure for evaluation of teaching in the United States K-12 system uses sporadic classroom visits [Dale Bolton, *Selection and Evaluation of Teachers* (Berkeley, Cal.: McCutchan, 1973)]. Except in truly bizarre cases, this is essentially impossible to defend. Such visitors are producing their more-or-less immediate reactions to charactistics of style and/or personality, and the research linking this with any gains by the students, let alone need-related ones, is simply not enough to support such an approach. Snapshot process evaluation of this kind suffers from major handicaps. First, it is based on too small a sample of the teacher's performance. Second, that sample is atypical because of the effect of the visitor's presence. Third, the visitor's head is not where the students' heads are at (by several decades). Fourth, the visitor's judgment is highly prone to personal bias due to non-classroom interactions with the teacher. And, given all these a priori handicaps, there is nothing to fall back on in the way of observable qualities of the "good teacher." Even Rosenshine in his definitive review of the research, does not deny this [e.g., p. 175, *Second Handbook of Research on Teaching,* ed. R. Travers (Chicago: Rand McNally, 1973)] and Heath and Nielsen's critical re-review of the studies on which Rosenshine's modest conclusions are based ["The Research Basis for Performance-Based Teacher Education," in *Review of Educational Research* 44, no. 4 (1974): 463] makes even those conclusions look shaky. The hundred and fifty available classroom observation instruments are thus totally unproductive of evaluation criteria. But that—we see from Bolton—is exactly what they get used for in schools with some pretension at sophistication. And Bolton himself is taken in by them (e.g., p. 9, p. 33, *Selection and Evaluation of Teachers*). One need hardly add that the millions of hours of advising or supervising devoted to advocating or implementing these systems are mostly wasted. And of course the usual alternative employed at the college level, which consists of de facto evaluation of teaching by looking at research and/or at anecdotal evidence, is even less defensible.

If process evaluation is invalid, what can we use instead?

PERFORMANCE-BASED EVALUATION OF TEACHING

Readers of the recent literature will not need reminding of the difficulties with this approach, both logistical and research-based. It has a solitary merit by comparison with process observation. It does refer to a defensible criterion (student learning), albeit one that is sometimes oversimplified in a given experiment. In short, this is the only way to travel, but the road lies mostly ahead. We have not yet succeeded in stabilizing the results from teachers sufficiently to distinguish good from poor teachers in micro-experiments (Popham-Glass, informal consensus), and macro-experiments are in short supply and still open to multiple interpretations. Moreover, one can't squeeze evaluation out of either raw or reduced gain scores. One must have comparisons with previous efforts by the same teacher, and/or with other teachers dealing with comparable students and curriculum. Not impossible—in fact, in two or three years any large department could build up the norms and estimates needed in some courses—but it's not automatic.

What is there for the evaluator in this great desert of null hypotheses? Why, common sense and a compass! And that is enough to point to procedures vastly superior to the present ones.

A DEFENSIBLE SYSTEM

There are several legitimate inputs for the instrument that we are hypothesizing will be used for evaluating teaching, the T-form. These are

a. student estimates of teaching merit
b. learning gains due to the teacher
c. subject-matter choice and coverage, treatment, testing and feedback
d. estimates of classroom justice, e.g. sexism in appropriate examinations, no appeal procedures, etc.
e. non-classroom contribution to teaching.

And the best feasible way to get these inputs is as follows:

a. from an S-form with a single question, calling for an evaluation of the teaching skill on a simple A-F scale
b. from a controlled study using pre- and post-tests, etc.; done by teacher with advice of evaluation specialist
c. from subject-matter specialists, e.g. department members, and the S-form: they must look for the needs-assessment used by the instructor, his/her procedures for evaluation of possible alternative materials, grading procedures, up-to-date content, etc.
d. from the S-form plus detailed study of materials, quizzes, returned assignments, etc.—can use peers or specialists
e. administrators plus peers, and possibly students.

Under extreme political pressure, one might have to allow (d) to *include* an estimate of teaching merit, i.e., merit of style, in which case it would be exceptionally important to have it done by someone *not* involved in the frictions of a department or campus. I suggest this as a role for a 'teaching specialist' ('master teacher' was the pre-liberated term). Such a person would ideally be providing only formative feedback, and certainly mostly this. They should be identified from amount of training *and* acceptability to staff; they should have a half-load at most, and service about five to six teachers; they would represent the commitment to development in a defensible form. Failing this, a *visiting* administrator might do it on a trade-off basis.

Lest this looks as if (d) would be a revival of the present system, let me stress that (1) it *should* only be used for formative evaluation, and (2) it would only have at most 10% of the weight if it *were* used for summative evaluation of teaching. (And the P-form would bring in other factors, so its effect on the personnel decision might only be 5%, which is negligible.)

How did we get the 10% figure? Simply by halving an equal weighting of all five scales. Methodological research has now amply supported this parsimonious approach in all cases where a regression equation cannot be exactly fitted. If we have grounds for supposing that each of the inputs contributes *something* in the direction that seems apparent (e.g., if it's plausible to suppose that better ratings by students *in general* indicate better performance by a teacher, rather than worse), then the optimal model is the equally weighted one. If we have *no* data on e.g. learning gains, we average across the rest (and we should penalize 5–10% of the total score).

There are many details one can add—for example, one might say that a high performance score should expunge and not just count against a low student-rating. One can explore costs in order to show that there are several ways to handle this approach without significant direct cost increases and with considerable hidden gains. One can point with pleasure at the low test-load on students involved (a single-item questionnaire, a post-test they'd have to have anyway, and a pre-test that is defensible as a pedagogical device anyway).

But above all, for a suggestion like this one which *should* be criticized, there is one main claim to fame. It includes nothing that can't be tied to merit and it excludes nothing that can. Let's hope—it's a modest enough hope—that in the years to come, educational research will enable us to leave this primitive instrument behind. But meanwhile, let's not use something worse.

JOHN D. McNEIL and
W. JAMES POPHAM
University of California at Los Angeles

A Critique of Widely Used Criteria in Assessing Teacher Competency

DESIRABLE ATTRIBUTES OF TEACHER COMPETENCY CRITERIA

In surveying the numerous measuring approaches which have been employed to identify the effective teacher it becomes apparent that for given purposes some criteria are better than others. Perhaps the best way to promote a better fit between one's purpose and the selection of a criterion measure will be to isolate a reasonable number of attributes on which the available criterion measures differ, then rate the measures according to these attributes. One should be able to make a more defensible selection among competing criterion measures by deciding which of the several attributes are important to his particular operational decision or research investigation, then contrasting alternative measures according to whether they possess these attributes.

General Attributes

Ideally, of course, all measuring devices would possess certain positive attributes such as *reliability*. We would always want to devise classroom observation schedules, for example, which were quite reliable. Obviously, in selecting among alternative measures one should be attentive to whether the approach yields a relatively consistent estimate of teaching competence.

There are other general attributes which can or cannot be built into measuring devices. General attributes may be present or absent in particular members of a class of criterion measures, such as administration rating scales, but not in all members of that class. Such an attribute would be whether the measure possessed an essentially *neutral orientation,* that is, could be profitably used by educators with a variety of instructional viewpoints. Certain measuring instru-

---

Excerpted from John D. McNeil and W. James Popham, "The Assessment of Teacher Competence," in *Second Handbook of Research on Teaching,* ed. R. M. Travers (Chicago: Rand McNally, 1973), pp. 131–147. Reprinted by permission.

ments, e.g., observation schedules and rating scales, are so wedded to a particular view of instruction that anyone with a contrary view would find it difficult if not impossible to use the instrument. For instance, one might conceive of a classroom observation form designated so that the observer was to attend only to operant conditioning methods. Such a form would not possess a neutral orientation and, therefore, would be less serviceable to a large number of those who must attend to many other factors. Not that highly partisan measures have no value, especially for certain research purposes, but generally criterion measures that are more neutrally oriented are to be preferred.

Another general feature which should be sought whenever possible in teacher competence measures is that it yields information about the types of instructional situations in which a given teacher functions best. This attribute can be described as an *assignment indicator* and, if present, would obviously be helpful for researcher and decision-maker alike. One could conceive of performance tests which might be designed so that we could discover what types of instructional objectives a teacher can best achieve for particular kinds of learners. Criterion measures which would permit this identification of the optimal role for a given teacher would be most helpful indeed.

There are other attributes of useful criterion measures which are a function of particular measures rather than a given class of measures, for example, initial cost, reuseability, etc. But if a measure possesses *reliability*, a *neutral orientation*, and an *assignment indicator*, it has a running start toward being a useful measure for a variety of situations.

Six Attributes for Discriminating among Criterion Measures

We can turn now to several attributes which are often present or absent in an entire class of criterion measures, for example, in (almost all) contract plan measures (see the introduction to this chapter for a description of "contract plans"). These attributes are not always needed by all who are seeking a criterion measure, but for given situations one or more of these attributes will usually be requisite. Without implying any hierarchy of import, we shall briefly examine six such attributes, thus attempting to rate classes of criterion measures according to their possession of each attribute.

1. *Differentiates among teachers.* For certain situations it is imperative to discriminate among teachers. Who is best? Who is worst? Is teacher X better than teacher Z? Under what conditions will teacher A perform best? What are the separate effects of teacher A? To answer such questions a criterion measure must be sufficiently sensitive to differentiate among teachers. There are decisions where we do not have enough knowledge merely by knowing that a teacher has met a minimal level of proficiency. Both administrators and researchers, for instance, often encounter situations where they need a measure sensitive enough to assess variance in teachers' skills.

2. *Assesses learner growth.* The thrust of frequent discussions in this chapter has been to emphasize the necessity to produce criterion measures which can

be used to assess the results of instructional process, not merely the process itself. In certain limited instances we may not be interested in the outcomes of instruction as reflected by modifications in the learner, but these would be few in number. Certain classes of criterion measures are notoriously deficient with respect to this attribute.

3. *Yields data uncontaminated by required inferences.* An attribute of considerable importance is whether a measure permits the acquisition of data with a minimum of *required* extrapolation on the part of the user. If all observations are made in such a way that beyond human frailty they have not been forced through a distorting inferential sieve, then the measure is better. A classroom observation system which asked the user to record the raw frequency of teacher questions would possess the attribute more so than a system which asked the user to judge the warmth of teacher questions.

4. *Adapts to teachers' goal preferences.* A desirable feature of teacher competence measures for certain selections is that they can be adjusted to the differing estimates of teachers regarding what should be taught in the schools, indeed, what schools are for in the first place. In our society there are divergent viewpoints regarding the role of the schools, and in given subject fields even more disagreement about the best goals for that subject. A measure of teaching skill will be more useful for given situations if it can adapt to such dissimilarities in goal preferences.

5. *Presents equivalent stimulus situations.* For some purposes we would like to have criterion measures which could produce results not easily discounted because certain teachers were at a disadvantage due to deficiencies in the situations in which they were operating. If we use gross achievement scores of learners as an index of one's teaching skill, then it is not surprising that a ghetto school teacher would be perceived as being in a less advantageous position than a teacher from a wealthy suburban community. There are times when we might like to use a measure which would permit the measurement of teaching proficiency when the stimulus situations were identical or at least comparable.

6. *Contains heuristic data categories.* In a sense this final attribute is the reverse of attribute number three above which focused on the collection of data uncontaminated by required inferences. At times we want data that simply state what was seen and heard in the classroom. At other times it would be useful to gather information—interpretations—which illuminate the nature of the instructional tactics. For the unsophisticated individual, in particular, measures which would at least in part organize his perceptions regarding strengths and weaknesses in teaching would in certain situations be most useful. Theoretical concepts which suggest linkages between events are cases in point. The teacher or supervisor who learns to both recognize instances of the psychological principle of reinforcement (a class of events which modify responses) and to apply this principle in classroom situations should be able to generate more alternative teaching strategies than before.

Now these six attributes should be considered by those requiring teacher competence measures to see which attributes are particularly important for the situation at hand. Thus an inspection of Table 1 may be useful when we have arranged the classes of certain measures previously considered along with the six attributes just examined. In the table a minus indicates a deficiency with respect to the attribute, a plus indicates that the attribute is well satisfied by that class of criterion measures. Absence of a plus or minus reflects no predominant presence or absence of the attribute in the class of criterion measures. The following instances are offered as illustrations of how the table might be used. Principal X wants to know which of several teachers can best teach the children in his school to pronounce given vowel sounds in unfamiliar words. He therefore will select a performance test that measures the ability to teach this reading skill, for differentiation sensitivity is necessary to answer the question. Supervisor Y wants to know how successful a teacher is in achieving a certain instructional objective of great importance to that particular teacher, and how to help the teacher in the event the objective is not attained. The supervisor could use both a contract plan which allows for selection of an individual goal and a systematic observation which promises to provide a more meaningful record of teacher-pupil interaction patterns.

Table 1. Classes of teaching competence criterion measures with respect to six desirable attributes of such measures.

	Classes of criterion measures							
Desirable attributes of teacher competence criterion measures	*Systematic observation*	*Administrator ratings*	*Student ratings*	*Peer ratings*	*Self ratings*	*Personal attributes*	*Contract plans*	*Performance tests*
1. Differentiates among teachers	+					+		+
2. Assesses learner growth	−	−	−	−	−	−	+	+
3. Yields data uncontaminated by required inferences		−	−	−	−		+	+
4. Adapts to teachers' goal preferences	−				+		+	−
5. Presents equivalent stimulus situations		−	−	−				+
6. Contains heuristic data categories	+							

CONCLUDING REMARKS

An evaluation of a teacher is not equivalent to determining the teacher's instructional competency, i.e., the ability to effect desired changes in learners. Defensible decisions concerning teachers rest on many kinds of data. However, it is essential that among these data appears valid information about teacher competencies. There is evidence that this latter kind of information is now overlooked in favor of subjective impressions of the teacher which are concerned primarily with the teacher's personal attributes and instructional techniques. Effectiveness in teaching is best evidenced by criterion measures which detect pupil growth as a result of the teacher's instruction. Contract plans and performance tests are two promising tools for collecting information about instructional effectiveness. There should be more inquiry centered on these tools, their development, uses and limitations. Measures of long- and short-range instructional objectives for a variety of outcomes are very much needed if two key purposes of assessment are to be fulfilled: instructional accountability and improvement.

It is clear that investigators have shown a lack of balance by directing most of their inquiries toward development of schemes for analyzing teaching and the conduct of studies that correlate process and product. In order to confirm the power of instructional variables derived from theory, analysis and statistical associations, we now need experiments showing that the teacher's use of these variables can indeed produce predicted effects in learners.

This is not to say that we expect scientific findings about teaching to be valuable as rules for action in the classroom. On the contrary, evidence cited in the previous chapter suggests that practice has been seriously weakened by the false belief that there are scientific conclusions which correspond to good teaching. Teacher educators err when they promote teaching skills that are approximately consistent with scientific conclusions as if these skills were certain, confirmed answers about how a teacher should proceed to effect desirable consequences in learners. Instead, such skills should be regarded as hypotheses to be tested. The practical utility of research should be seen as allowing all students of teaching—teachers, administrators and researchers—to be more flexible in planning, executing, analyzing and evaluating the teaching act.

Chapter 8

Selected Readings: Applications of Performance Appraisal Systems

The selections in this chapter describe models illustrating the design and implementation of appraisal systems. Each of these models is suitable for one or more of the appraisal applications discussed in Chapter 3. Thus, while Chapter 3 explained the various purposes of appraisal (diagnostic, formative, and summative), the accompanying readings present models designed to achieve these purposes. The models of Knezevich and Coleman, for example, serve all the functions of appraisal, while those of Klein and Alkin, Dyer, and Barro are intended primarily for summative purposes. Before turning to these selections, we shall briefly consider the nature of models in general, and in relation to the assessment of classroom behavior.

A model is a methodological tool used to guide and focus inquiry. Many different types of models exist, and their functions vary. For the mathematician, chemist, or physicist, for example, a model is a precise tool, often technical in nature, used to study a well defined and usually minuscule event, such as the outcome of a specific experiment. For the evaluator, it is a general plan or guide used to study a vaguely defined, often large and complex event, such as teacher performance.

Models, particularly those used in the sciences, have at least three identifiable characteristics. They are *precise:* they are basically quantitative in nature and usually employ elaborate measurement techniques to describe the phenomena of interest. Second, they are *specific:* models deal with only a select number of phenomena, purposely avoiding complex summary or aggregate characteristics. Third, they are *verifiable:* hypotheses are posed to check the precision of the model, and empirical evidence is collected to determine its accuracy and usefulness. Scientists and evaluators alike have over the years constructed many different models, all of which exhibit these characteristics to varying degrees.

Three different types of models can be constructed. The first of these is an iconic model, which is either a large- or small-scale representation of the "real thing." Iconic models resemble what they represent; they are replicas. The molecular structure of an atom is often illustrated by an iconic model.

A second type is the analogue model, which uses one property to represent another. A thermometer is an analogue model since temperature (one property) is measured indirectly by the height of mercury (another property).

A third type is the symbolic model, which describes properties in coded—usually mathematical—terms. The psychologist Kurt Lewin, for example, used a symbolic model to describe behavior, so that observations such as "the child chose the toy he liked best" were expressed with symbolic formulae. The formula, $F_p\ (G_1) > F_p\ (G_2)$, meant that the child liked goal one (G_1) better than ($>$) goal two (G_2) and that personality characteristics (p) of the child could account for his behavior.

Common sense tells us, however, that less-sophisticated models are used in the appraisal of teaching. For example, in the model in Fig. 8.1, relationships between the formative preconditions for teaching and the use of specific classroom strategies, and between these strategies and child outcomes, are depicted graphically, not mathematically. We are not told which precondition most relates to or determines which classroom strategy. Models such as this, and the model depicted in the introduction to Chapter 7, are most helpful when they are: (1) precise—i.e., quantitative; (2) specific—i.e., detailed; and (3) verified—i.e., validated. To the extent that a model is not precise, specific, and verified, it will be of less use in designing and implementing an appraisal system. In the appraisal of teaching we are usually less concerned with the type of model being used (e.g., analogue vs. symbolic) than its accuracy in portraying relationships among classroom variables.

Models for the appraisal of teaching are usually not strictly iconic, analogue, or symbolic, but rather a combination of the three. While appraisers strive to construct models that are precise, specific, and verifiable, their results often fall short of the stringent standards expected in the hard sciences. Much of the discrepancy between appraisal models and scientific models, however, is by design and not by chance. Because of the complexity of the events requiring description, the appraiser is usually cautious about using a model that applies to only one set of phenomena. Even though the appraiser attempts to be precise, it is difficult to describe with a great deal of precision all of the many inputs at work in the classroom. Also, in contrast to the scientist, the appraiser usually spends much less time verifying a model than using it. Much like the traveler who finds that a soiled and outdated map has guided him successfully to his destination, the appraiser sees the model primarily as a means to an end. If a model works reasonably well in achieving that end, the appraiser rarely takes time to document its effectiveness.

The appraisal models presented in the following selections can be grouped into two general categories: planning models and data analysis—or quantitative—models. In the first category are models described by Knezevich and Coleman. Klein and Alkin, Dyer, and Barro present more specific—symbolic—models which, in essence, are quantitative schemes for appraising teacher performance at the school-district level.

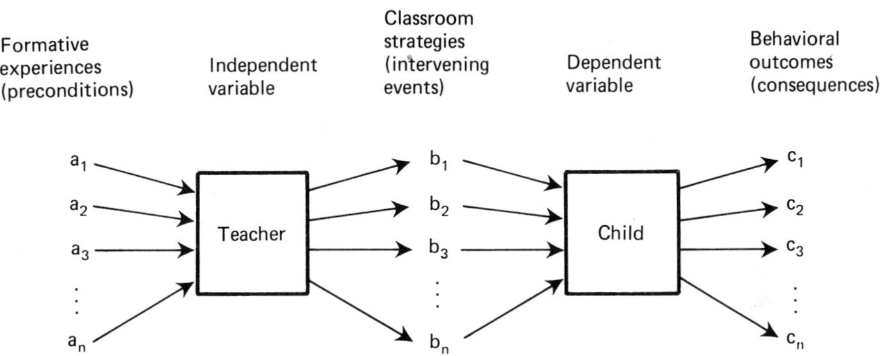

Fig. 8.1. A general model showing the interdependence of classroom variables.

The two types of models are related: Knezevich and Coleman provide the foundation for the specific empirical procedures illustrated by Klein and Alkin, Dyer, and Barro. Both planning and quantitative models are needed to resolve two of the problems of teacher appraisal described in Chapter 7: (a) the narrow range of measurements frequently employed in studies of teacher behavior; and (b) the lack of a generic framework or guide from which to select behaviors to be measured in the classroom.

The first selection, by Knezevich, presents a nonquantitative "planning" model that offers a four-phase conceptual framework for designing performance appraisal systems. Knezevich states that his is "an evaluation systems model," which considers appraisal a *positive* method of personnel and organizational improvement, rather than a measure to prevent deterioration of existing effectiveness levels. Knezevich points out that the latter approach is neutral with respect to improving or upgrading teacher competence and, therefore, is clearly less desirable.

The four phases in Knezevich's model are: (1) determination of the purpose and effectiveness of the system; (2) development of monitoring procedures; (3) data collection and treatment; and (4) decision making and actions. The first phase is of particular note since previous selections in this volume have also emphasized the importance of identifying the basic assumptions as well as the goals and objectives of the appraisal system. Defining effective teacher performance is a long and arduous task, which Knezevich tackles head-on in phase 1 of his model. As Scriven and Popham noted in Chapter 7, appraisers cannot escape their own values and judgments. Knezevich suggests, however, that these values and judgments be exposed to analysis by others in an attempt to arrive at a group consensus regarding those behaviors for which the teacher will be held accountable. Though lacking the mathematical sophistication of quantitative models, Knezevich's framework incorporates a logical flow of events and includes all major process steps needed to design an appraisal system. Therefore, as Knezevich points out, his model is particularly noteworthy for incorporating all of the concepts that comprise an operational appraisal system.

The Coleman selection also describes a planning model for the design and implementation of a teacher appraisal system, this time aimed specifically at the school-district level. While Knezevich's model cannot be described as specific, precise, or verifiable, Coleman's model is at least precise and specific. That is, Coleman specifies a limited number of teacher behaviors and suggests methods for measuring them.

Coleman's approach to the appraisal process is an optimistic one that builds on current knowledge of relationships between teacher behavior and pupil outcomes. From the research literature, Coleman chooses four variables, warmth, indirectness, cognitive organization, and enthusiasm, as *examples* of the type that can be employed in teacher appraisal. It is interesting to note that empirical support for two of these dimensions, enthusiasm and cognitive organization, is provided by earlier selections in this volume. Enthusiasm, for example, is included among Rosenshine and Furst's five most promising variables derived from process-product studies of teacher effectiveness, while cognitive organization is among their six secondary but still promising variables. Cognitive organization also receives support from both the Brophy-Evertson and the Soar studies. Coleman's other variables, warmth and indirectness, do not fare as well, at least in terms of the research reported in this volume. However, Coleman's variables are merely examples; the approach he suggests is applicable to a wide variety of teacher behaviors. The reader will find Coleman's model a useful prototype, regardless of whether he or she agrees with the selection of teacher variables.

Coleman applies his model to decisions regarding teacher selection, development, retention, and assignment, all of which were identified in Chapter 3 as typical appraisal purposes. He suggests that these decisions be made using the diagnostic, formative, and summative data generated by the appraisal system. Illustrating the application of appraisal data to teacher assignment decisions, he presents a "mini" model designed to match teachers and pupils. The concept of matching, already addressed in Chapter 3 in relation to teacher experience and contextual characteristics of the school district, is particularly important since appraisal data can be contaminated by the teacher's preference for certain students, subjects, or grade levels.

Klein and Alkin, in the third selection in this chapter, describe one of the three quantitative appraisal models presented. They begin by explaining what an appraisal model *should not* look like, suggesting that it should exclude subjective judgments of teachers (such as those described under the topic of personal judgment in Chapter 1), variables unrelated to student performance, and nationally normed tests. An appraisal system *should* incorporate an objectives-based approach that samples a large number of behaviors and measures them with performance tests, or "job samples."

The importance of this particular reading involves its quantitative approach to appraising teacher performance—an approach similar to those discussed in the next two selections. Klein and Alkin's model incorporates the regression approach to the appraisal of teaching by comparing the performance of one teacher's pupils (on a test carefully constructed to match the teacher's objectives) with the average gain of all pupils of all teachers being appraised. The most important characteristic of this particular technique is its ability to adjust pupil posttest scores to take into account different levels of entering behavior, i.e., pretest scores of pupils. As the authors point out, other variables such as SES, verbal ability, and contextual factors (i.e., characteristics of schools and school districts) can be used in addition to pretest scores to adjust pupils' posttest performance to eliminate confounding effects from the appraisal of teacher performance. The rationale underlying the regression approach is the belief that the teacher's performance should be judged solely on that portion of the pupils' performance which is directly related to classroom instruction. All other variables are therefore considered contaminating influences.

One final comment should be made in regard to the Klein and Alkin selection. The authors indicate the importance of differentiating the terms "assessment" and "measurement" from the word "evaluation." The latter, they point out, includes not only assessment, but also a judgment of the quality of the obtained measurement. Therefore, regardless of the mathematical precision of the measurement process, our own values and judgment are used in determining the adequacy of the objectives evaluated and the quality of the measurements obtained.

The fourth selection, by Dyer, describes an appraisal model that has been employed in the schools of New York City. After considerable revision and refinement, Dyer presents a practical—though highly quantitative—scheme for measuring teacher competence.

Dyer's approach involves four groups of variables, which he contends must be recognized and measured if acceptable criteria are to be developed for staff accountability. These four groups are: *input* variables—the characteristics of the pupils as they enter a particular level of schooling; *output* variables—the characteristics of pupils as they emerge from a particular phase of schooling; *educational-process* variables—the school activities expressly designed to bring about desirable changes in pupils; and *surrounding conditions*—the contextual constraints within which the school operates. The importance of Dyer's conceptualization, however, lies not so much in the specification of these particular groups of variables, but in the recognition of their interaction. Dyer's model circumvents one of the generic problems of appraisal, i.e., the narrow range of measurements frequently employed in studies of teacher behavior, by viewing the classroom and the school as a multivariate interacting environment.

Aside from its multivariate nature, Dyer's model incorporates two additional features. The first is a capacity to adjust pupil outcome measures with those variables beyond the teacher's control. That is, the Dyer model allows one to appraise the influence of the teacher, unaffected by variables unrelated to the instructional process. The model also has the capability to focus on behaviors that are easy to change. For example, school personnel may not be able to alter "surrounding conditions," such as the classroom footage per pupil, but they can develop inservice training programs to improve the morale and competence of the staff. The identification of "easy-to-change" surrounding conditions is of primary importance in providing objective criteria for appraisal. Dyer contends, appropriately, that the staff of a school can hardly be held accountable for changing those factors over which they have little or no control.

The culmination of Dyer's model is the generation of school effectiveness indices, or SEI's. These indices are signs by which the staff of a school can judge the success of their efforts to produce pupil change. Dyer computes SEI's using regression analysis—the same technique employed by Klein and Alkin—and uses them to answer questions such as, "In teaching reading over a three-year period, has the school done a better job with pupils who entered grade four reading poorly than it has with those who entered reading well?" This approach is designed for the general appraisal of *groups of teachers* within a school or school district rather than individual teachers. While it may be unresponsive to the spirit of California's Stull Act, this model nevertheless offers a particularly powerful (and nonthreatening) method for use in states that do not require the individual appraisal of teachers.

The final selection, by Barro, presents a model which, like those of Klein and Alkin and Dyer, is quantitative in nature. Mathematically, Barro's model is the most sophisticated of all and is therefore intentionally presented last. Hopefully, the Klein and Alkin and Dyer models will have familiarized the reader with the "regression approach" to the appraisal of teaching.

Barro lifts this approach to a higher level of sophistication by extending its application to many more dimensions of educational process and surrounding conditions. Klein and Alkin simply include the pretest behavior of pupils as a surrounding condition, while Dyer adds several variables, such as pupil SES in addition to pretest performance. Barro provides an extensive list of variables to be considered in the analysis of teacher performance. Among these are: individual pupil characteristics (ethnicity, SES, home-family characteristics, etc.); teacher characteristics (age, training, experience, etc.); school characteristics; staff characteristics; and factors such as resource availability, class size, amount of instructional support, amount of materials, condition of physical facilities, etc. All three models provide quantitative techniques for making comparisons among teachers and between teachers and criterion levels of performance, comparisons uncontaminated by factors falling outside of the teacher's instructional domain. Thus, the primary characteristic of all three models is their attempt to separate teacher effects from nonteacher effects that might account for pupil performance—with Barro achieving the highest level of sophistication.

The reader will also notice that Barro's model, like the others in this chapter, is multivariate in nature. The selections in this chapter, and in this volume, generally attempt to resolve the appraisal problems arising from a narrow range of measurements and the absence of a theoretical or conceptual framework guiding the selection of behaviors to be measured. It is no coincidence that Barro's model confronts both of these problems by (a) utilizing a diversity of teacher, pupil, and contextual variables; and (b) using research data to select variables leading to the highest payoff. While the Barro article will be difficult for those unfamiliar with the statistical approach used, a rereading of the Klein and Alkin procedure and careful scrutiny of Barro's proposal should help readers understand the insights he offers.

STEPHEN J. KNEZEVICH
University of Wisconsin at Madison

Designing Performance Appraisal Systems

Evaluation of instructional and administrative personnel has been pursued with varying degrees of diligence, objectivity, and sophistication since the very first time specialized personnel and educational institutions joined the home and family in the instruction of children, adolescents, and adults. As one looks at the historical records, evaluators change from ministers concerned about religious orthodoxy to lay board members to selected professionals in the hierarchy. Appraisal of teachers and administrators has challenged scholars and practitioners alike and, as Bolton indicated, triggered a half-century of prodigious research. Nonetheless, few appear to be satisfied with the state of the art. Although 90 percent of school systems with sixteen thousand or more pupils have formal assessment procedures, more school systems than ever before are committed to improving existing evaluation methods. This paper describes a general approach to designing the relevant personnel appraisal systems so essential to operational educational accountability systems.

Researchers and writers have tended to focus on a single dimension of performance appraisal, such as what constitutes teacher effectiveness, how to design and use a rating scale, or the role of the principal in evaluation. Such topics dominate the literature. In contrast, little is written about how to put it all together into an operational evaluation system.

My emphasis here is on a conceptual framework, or model, with which educational institutions can integrate the complex elements and actors in what is called performance appraisal. Implementation may vary from one type of organization to another, but the basic design features will be evident in all. Likewise, this evaluation model may be adapted for all types of personnel: those concerned primarily with instruction (such as teachers); those who provide special support for instruction (such as librarians, counselors, and supervisors); and those engaged in administration and supervision (such as princi-

---

From *New Directions for Education* 1, no. 1 (1973): 37–50.

pals and elementary school supervisors). In short, this article is directed to the practitioner who is responsible for personnel evaluation and, therefore, must blend each of the complex elements, which separately attract the interests of researchers, into an operational system.

A SYSTEM AND THE SYSTEMS APPROACH

This approach is related to what is referred to as systems management or systems administration. A brief description of systems and systems administration is therefore in order. A system can be defined in many ways, but for our present purposes it is an array of resources focused on achieving a set of objectives according to plan. Within it a number of interrelated elements attempt to achieve one or more objectives. These elements are unified and interact with each other as well as with the "outside" environment. An open system, by definition, is in communication with its environment and is influenced by what happens outside as well as within it. Stated another way, a permeable boundary encloses the interlocking elements of an open system and separates it from its environment. Since meaningful exchanges are necessary between internal elements and those in the surroundings, an open system remains relevant and extends its period of survival by adjusting to pressures from without. An open system is thus an evolving unit committed to change.

In contrast, a closed system is encased in a hard boundary which inhibits interplay with environmental factors. It remains either ignorant of or insensitive to external messages. The breakdown in communication, or reduced receptivity, means the closed system very soon gets out of tune with its environment. In the long run closed systems are unstable and will be destroyed by the accumulations of unresolved pressures generated by a dynamic environment.

Volumes have been written on systems management or administration. The essential characteristics of this approach as it applies to educational administration would include the following:

1. The school is viewed as a delivery system for providing educational services desired by the society.
2. All systems are goal-seeking mechanisms. Administrative practice starts with identification of goals and continues by designing an organizational structure and management techniques which facilitate achievement of predetermined objectives.
3. Missions, goals, and objectives are not eternal verities. Recycling objectives, refining and generating new ones as needed, and reordering priorities are essential.
4. The environment surrounding a system is dynamic; therefore, change is considered normal. The introduction and management of innovations are considered essential operational skills.
5. The search for alternative strategies for reaching objectives is continual.
6. Competence in generating and using rational models is essential for attacking and solving problems confronting the delivery mechanism.

7. Quantitatively oriented problem-resolving tools are emphasized.
8. Top executives give high priority to planning and programming as opposed to total immersion in the daily grind.
9. Since complex problems demand a variety of talents, interdisciplinary teams are often chosen to attack problems.
10. Complexity also calls for the use of scientific or highly rational decision-making approaches.

Performance appraisal becomes a specialized set of procedures within a delivery system that produces significant evaluative data relating to the productivity of the total educational enterprise.

GENERAL EVALUATION SYSTEMS MODEL

A diagram of the essential elements, as well as the interrelationships among them, for the performance appraisal of educational personnel is shown in Figure 1. The ideas behind it, which I developed initially in 1968, influenced the design of teacher evaluation seminars sponsored by the AASA National Academy for School Executives.

Phase I: Evaluation Theory, Missions, and Effectiveness Model

Space limitations permit only limited exposition of the various elements in each major dimension of the evaluation systems model, but two contrasting theories of personnel evaluation may be outlined as follows.

Theory P: Evaluation is a positive factor in personnel and organizational improvement. (A) Personnel evaluation is the analysis of performance outcomes leading to additional coaching of personnel to achieve greater effectiveness. (B) Expected outcomes of this interpretation of an evaluation system are: identification of specific performance capabilities or competencies of all personnel; determination of present performance levels in the light of selected criterion measures; use of evaluative data to design relevant professional development programs; improved performance following completion of inservice activities; higher morale; identification of personnel with very limited competence (usually a small percent of the total); and objective data (documentation) to justify the orderly dismissal of personnel with limited capabilities and who could not be helped sufficiently through additional coaching.

Theory N: Evaluation is a neutral force with respect to personnel and organizational improvement but can be used to prevent deterioration of existing effectiveness levels. (A) Personnel evaluation is primarily a mechanism for identifying the weak and incompetent and documenting dismissal actions for them. It is a means of labeling personnel, that is, discriminating between the effective and ineffective. (B) Expected outcomes of this interpretation are: discrimination between "good" and "bad" performers; identification of incompetent performers; collection of objective data for the orderly dismissal of incompetents as soon after labeling as is legally possible; little effectiveness gain for the majority judged to be competent in varying degrees; greater fear of personnel evaluation; lower morale; and little relationship between evaluation and professional development program.

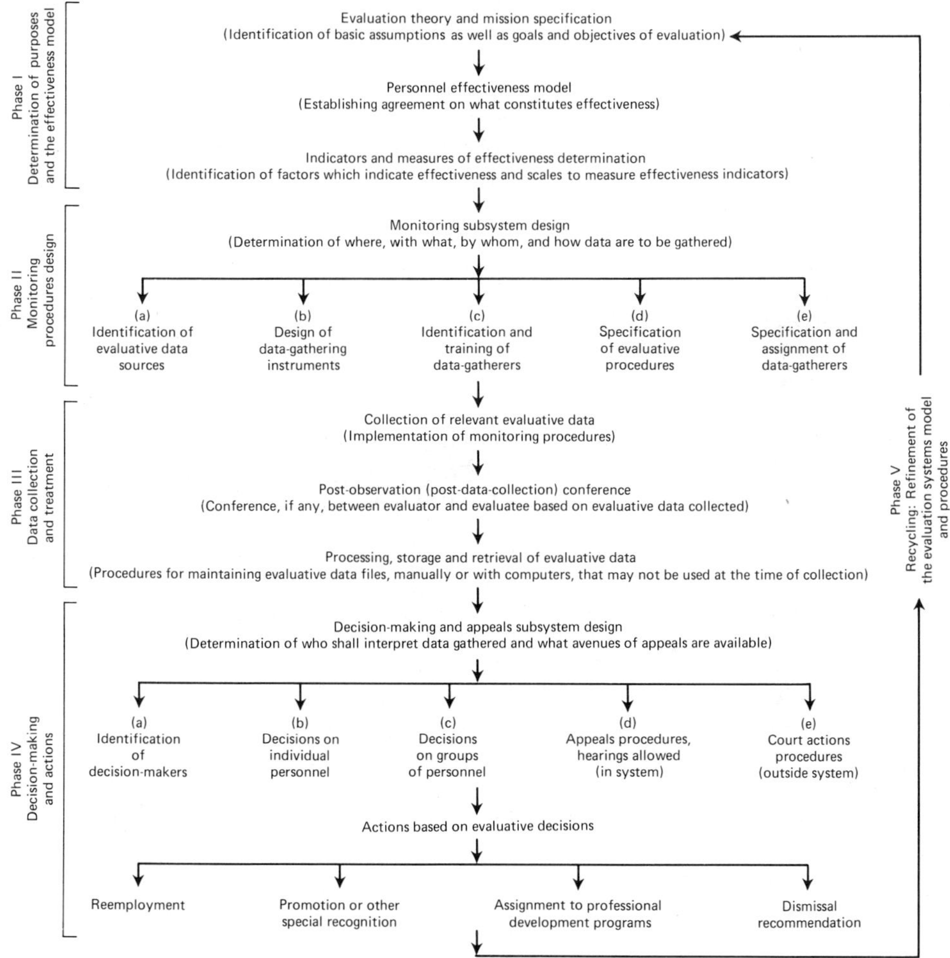

Fig. 1. General evaluation systems model.

The dichotomies outlined are obvious oversimplifications. Nonetheless, the attitudes expressed or reasons given for demanding personnel evaluation, no matter how phrased, may be classified under either Theory P or Theory N. Implementation of Theory P is clearly more difficult and time-consuming than N; it also demands greater resources. The general evaluation systems model is more closely related to the expected outcomes of Theory P. Likewise, it embodies much of the spirit of management by objectives (MBO) as well as what is being identified as competency-based evaluation (CBE). More will be said about these later on.

Another issue to be determined in Phase I is what are the purposes, or objectives, to be served by the system? The most frequently written, but not necessarily realized, purposes for teacher evaluation are (in order of frequency) to: stimulate improvement of performance, decide on reappointment of permanent teachers, and qualify teachers for regular salary increments. (Using personnel evaluation to establish a case for merit pay or salary acceleration for other reasons appears to be relatively rare.) The typical goals of evaluation may thus be classified into two broad areas: improving instruction and determining the employment status of personnel. It is no exaggeration to state that in many operational appraisal systems there is only a casual relationship between avowed purposes and what is actually attained with the evaluative procedures followed. But the systems approach demands that the evaluation procedures actually implemented do indeed fulfill stated purposes.

The model described here also requires that what constitutes effectiveness, under various conditions, must be specified as yet another outcome in Phase I. Models of teacher or administrative effectiveness are rarely explicitly described in existing school or university appraisal efforts. Such models can only be inferred from the type of evaluative data sought. How to identify those factors and behaviors that produce successful teaching and administration continues to puzzle and challenge researchers. Until more definitive data are available, there can only be inferences or opinions about what constitutes effective teaching or administration. Table 1 summarizes various teacher-effectiveness models implied in existing appraisal efforts or recommended in the literature. A similar list may be developed for administrators.

Teachers, community leaders, and even students may participate in determining what model of effectiveness will undergird the institution's evaluation system. But their involvement does not spell out what indicators of effectiveness will be used and how these are to be measured or scaled, factors which must also be clearly specified in the model.

Phase II: The Monitoring Subsystem

Agreement on purposes, effectiveness model, indicators, and measures gives direction to the search for data.

This phase is concerned with the operational problems of collecting such information. Tradition has it that the ultimate reviewer of what a teacher does in the classroom is the independent observer, sometimes called the evaluator. Additional sources of significant data could be students, professional peers, parents, or any person inclined to offer an opinion on a teacher's or administrator's performance. This proliferation raises the issue of what weight or significance should be attached to formal versus informal, professional versus nonprofessional, or in-school versus out-of-school sources.

The classic data-gathering instrument is the ubiquitous rating scale, which

Table 1. Alternative models of teacher effectiveness

Type A: *Input Models*
Effectiveness is:
1. a specified constellation of teacher traits (such as honesty, dependability, and intelligence).

Type B: *Process or Behavior Models*
Effectiveness is:
2. a series of specific teacher behaviors or roles performed in the classroom (such as presenting information, evaluating pupil progress, and motivating learning).
3. a series of specific pupil activities (such as group work, participation in discussions, and laboratory experiments).
4. a set of interactions between pupils and teachers.
5. a set of teacher skills utilizing media or technology (such as using sound films in teaching and employing computer-assisted instruction).
6. a set of instructional strategies or methods of motivating learning.

Type C: *Outcome Models*
Effectiveness is:
7. a set of pupil accomplishments as measured by specific instruments (this is the "pupil gain" model of effectiveness).
8. a given standard of classroom appearance (with some emphasis on bulletin board displays and appearance of chalk boards).
9. a specified level of classroom control.
10. a consensus of parental, student, or community reactions to or opinions of an individual teacher.
11. what the evaluator says is effectiveness.
12. attainment of any set of predetermined objectives or growth levels (management by objectives).

Type D: *Eclectic Models*
Effectiveness is:
13. any combination, in varying proportions, of two or more of models indicated in Types A, B, and C.

is intended to focus the rater's attention on the indicators of effectiveness and to help him measure the degree to which any factor is present. Its validity is derived from its relationship to the effectiveness model, and its reliability from the scales and measuring units. It is only as good as the person using it. Any rating scale in the hands of the untrained may be misused and perhaps result in distortion. The rating scale is only one element in the evaluation system and only one data-gathering instrument. Certain kinds of information, such as biographical data, aptitude scores, and gradepoint average of the person being evaluated and test scores for pupils instructed, are collected by other means.

To illustrate, a rating scale used to gather data on the teacher's instructional competence should focus the attention of the observer on at least three key questions:

1. *What is the teacher trying to do?* The observer should seek evidence or documentation that the instructional objectives for the day are clear and there is indeed an underlying rationale for the class activities.

2. *Are the teaching strategies being employed appropriate to: (a) students? (b) discipline or grade level? (c) situation? (d) the avowed objectives?* The teaching or instructional strategies are means for reaching objectives.

3. *How well are the teaching strategies being executed?* Thus, although purposes are clear and strategies clever, execution may be poor for a variety of reasons, such as low level of competence, lack of materials, and the "situation itself."

Performance appraisal is usually assigned to persons in particular positions in the educational hierarchy, such as the principal or personnel director. Appointment to such a position does not automatically qualify its incumbent as an expert data-gatherer or "evaluator." To improve the total process of performance appraisal, those charged with gathering and interpreting data should receive special training.

Note that the act of collecting data, by whatever instrument and persons, is not to be confused with interpretation. In other words, being a data-gatherer is not necessarily the same as being the "evaluator," the person who renders judgments. This important differentiation of roles means that department heads, supervisors, and even teaching peers who may hold the same degree of special knowledge and instructional expertise can be employed as objective data-gatherers, if trained to do so, and still remain separate from the act of rendering judgment. In complex educational centers where frequent readings on performance are desired a large number of independent or coordinate data-gatherers may be necessary.

Lastly, the design of the monitoring subsystem must specify who is evaluated, how often, and under what conditions. Thus, evaluation policy may call for annual assessment of all teachers or for cooperative or unilateral approaches. To illustrate, an appraisal-by-results approach consistent with management by objectives may be indicated for all administrators. The end product of Phase II is the design of an operational data-gathering subsystem. Various people and groups in and outside the institution may be involved in planning the monitoring subsystem as well as in Phase I.

Phase III: Data Collection and Treatment

Implementation of the designs produced in Phases I and II leads to Phase III. These activities require the attention of full-time and professional personnel. "Postdata-gathering," more often called "postobservation," conferences may be convened as specified. The only way large masses of evaluative data can be handled effectively is through computer-based information systems. Rating forms should allow appraisal information to be recorded in ways that facilitate information entry, processing, and retrieval in and from computerized data banks.

Phase IV: Decision-Making, Actions, and Appeals

Evaluative data are garnered to provide documentation for judgments about the performance capabilities (competencies) of professional personnel. The interpreters of appraisal information may be a panel or selected individuals with the expertise, position, and professional status to do so. Because such judgments may be questioned within or outside the system, appeals and hearings procedures must be specified. One reason why it may not be wise to have school board members serve on the initial evaluation decision councils is that their participation could compound problems in designing appeals procedures.

Appraisal judgments lead to actions such as recommendations for reemployment or special recognition. They provide the foundation for designing professional development programs. Dismissal is only one of several possible actions resulting from performance appraisal; in fact, it is the least likely outcome if there has been quality screening before employment. Past experience indicates that less than one percent of the teaching force will face dismissal in any one year. Dismissal is justified only when capabilities have so degenerated that learners may be harmed and when institutional resources are inadequate to rehabilitate the employee. Since dismissal is such a rare outcome, it is unfortunate that many policymakers and professional educators equate evaluation with dismissal.

Phase V: Recycling

The built-in capacity for corrective action is characteristic of systems administration. Error-free systems are not produced immediately, if ever. Initial efforts spell progress but not perfection. But continuing appraisal of the evaluation system should lead to continuing refinement as the result of experience.

COMPETENCY-BASED EVALUATION

Competency-based evaluation (CBE) is a relatively new development which is consistent with the spirit of the systems approach to performance appraisal and, of course, with competency-based education. CBE can be outlined as follows:

Step 1: Specification of objectives or results to be achieved by a person in a given position. Effective performance of responsibilities is equated with outputs. The first step specifies "competency for what?"

Step 2: Identification of professional competencies needed to satisfy predetermined objectives. In short, the skills or abilities related to objectives become the requisite competencies. Sometimes competencies may be classified around roles to be played.

Step 3: Conversion of competencies into performance or observed behaviors that can be measured. Indicators and measures must be specified for each competency.

Step 4: Design of an assessment system to measure competencies from at least two vantage points, namely, were objectives achieved and did the person have the skills necessary to meet the situation? Effectiveness is a matter of degree and not an all-or-none proposition.

Step 5: Determination of which competencies are lacking in order to improve performance by coaching.

Step 6: Operation of inservice or "coaching" clinics to improve effectiveness of personnel.

The flow of ideas may be summarized as: objectives ⟶ competencies ⟶ performance objectives ⟶ appraisal ⟶ coaching ⟶ effectiveness. The similarity in spirit between CBE and Theory P of personnel evaluation, described earlier, should be evident.

The emphases of conventional evaluation and CBE may be contrasted as follows:

Conventional	*CBE*
Do Things Right	Do Right Things
Emphasize Inputs	Specify Outputs
Identify Traits	Measure Competencies
Discharge Duties	Obtain Results
Solve Problems	Produce Creative Alternatives
Safeguard Resources	Optimize Resources

MANAGEMENT BY OBJECTIVES AND RESULTS (MBO/R)

I prefer the MBO/R to the MBO acronym because some people have a propensity to stop with the generation of objectives and thus fail to emphasize results. Relatively few school systems operate in the MBO/R mode. Most of those few see MBO/R as a results-oriented appraisal system in which goals and objectives replace personality traits as evaluation criteria. Most writers, however, recognize that there is more to MBO/R than appraisal of the managerial staff.

As the first step in MBO/R appraisal, superior and subordinate agree on a set of objectives for the subordinate. Some argue that MBO/R can become a "do-it-yourself hangman's kit" when the subordinate agrees to do more than he can deliver. Others cite the opposite danger of setting up "Mickey Mouse" objectives whose attainment is neither challenging nor meaningful for organizational development. Obviously neither extreme captures the true spirit of MBO/R as a participative evaluation style which seeks to establish clear expectations and which, ideally, stimulates increased productivity by all members of the organization. In the MBO/R model effectiveness is equated with results; its monitoring subsystem involves both the evaluatee and evaluator in gathering and interpreting data in light of jointly predetermined objectives.

It is apparent that operating in the MBO/R mode facilitates CBE and is consistent with the evaluation systems model. MBO/R was designed primarily for administrator evaluation. Whether teachers can be appraised by an approach designed primarily for management personnel is now the subject of considerable debate.

WRAPPING IT UP

The evaluation systems model describes the flow of ideas and actions necessary to produce a relevant and integrated approach to staff appraisal. It provides the operational system that practioners responsible for implementing personnel evaluation require. The model is less meaningful to researchers, who must restrict their focus to execute a manageable research topic. Each step along the way poses a special challenge because we are not sure how to measure human productivity or effectiveness in educational institutions. The model at least gives a framework for asking the right kinds of questions to fill the present knowledge voids.

Competency-based evaluation (CBE) and MBO/R are relatively new approaches to performance appraisal which are output- rather than trait-oriented. They are consistent in spirit with the systems model developed in this paper.

PETER COLEMAN

Manitoba Association of School Trustees

The Improvement of Aggregate Teaching Effectiveness in a School District

Any attempt to improve the effectiveness of teaching must recognize the relative lack of success of many thousands of such attempts which have been made in the past. In this proposal, teaching is defined as "the exertion of the behavioral influence," (Gage, 1972: p. 43) and more effective teaching as the exertion of behavioral influence in desired directions and in larger measure than before.

The notion that teaching can become more effective assumes that the behavior of teachers in classrooms can be changed. This is part of a general assumption about human behavior which is somewhat questionable at this time. In a recent article in a popular magazine, entitled "Human Beings are Not Very Easy to Change After All: An Unjoyful Message and Its Implications for Social Programs," Etzioni suggests that social scientists "have begun to reexamine our core assumption that man can be taught almost anything and quite readily" (1972: p. 45). However, there is a substantial body of research which demonstrates that teacher behavior can in fact be changed, at least in the context of formal teacher training programs. (For example see Turner, 1963 and Berliner, 1969).

A second major assumption being made here is that enough is known about the dimensions of effective teacher behavior to enable us to decide what represents more effective behavior. There is some real doubt about this (Morrison and McIntyre, 1969: p. 41). However, recent research seems to justify more optimism. The most recent review of the research on "teacher effectiveness" in the Encyclopedia of Educational Research suggests that

> the research which is reviewed herein permits cautious optimism and indicates that the tools long needed for the analysis of the teaching-learning process are gradually being developed. This optimism is in contrast with the conclusions reached in past reviews (Flanders & Simon, 1969: p. 1423).

From *Educational Administration Quarterly* **9**, no. 3 (1973): 28–45. Reprinted by permission.

The tentativeness of the conclusions arrived at so far in research on teacher effectiveness, and the lack of clarity about their applicability to specific school district situations, suggests the need for caution. However, the practical problem of evaluating teachers is so pressing that some uses of the research findings, however uncertain and tentative, seem essential. There is for the first time a reasonably well-established set of research findings on teacher effectiveness, they do offer some possibility of use in practice, and the main purpose of this paper is to describe briefly these findings and suggest how they might be used.

The dimensions of teacher behavior used here were identified originally by Gage. They are "warmth," "indirectness," "cognitive organization," and "enthusiasm." These do not exhaust the possibilities and they are really only representative of the things that research on teaching can presently support. What is important about these dimensions, Gage comments, "is their basis in empirical research. The ease with which others have told us such truths in the past is matched by their untrustworthiness" (p. 39). The reasons for selecting these dimensions, in very brief form, are that first, they are based on empirical research; second, reliable instrumentation for measuring these teacher behaviors generally exists; third, the desirability of these teacher behaviors has been demonstrated; and fourth, these behaviors can in fact be learned by teachers.

EVALUATING TEACHER EFFECTIVENESS IN A SCHOOL DISTRICT

The current status of teacher evaluation programs in large school systems in the United States was reported recently by the Educational Research Service of the American Association of School Administrators (1972). Based on a survey of school systems in the United States enrolling 25,000 or more pupils, and on returns from 155 systems, the survey showed that the four major purposes of evaluations are "to stimulate improvement of teacher performance," "to decide on reappointment of probationary teachers," "to recommend probationary teachers," "to recommend probationary teachers for permanent status," and "to establish evidence where dismissal from service is at issue." In the overwhelming majority of school systems, classroom observation of teachers by principals or supervisors is the standard method of evaluating. In a majority of cases, a check list or rating form is used.

On the basis of this survey, it seems reasonable to conclude that most large school systems in the United States will make use of evaluation schemes the basis for which has been rather thoroughly discredited over a substantial period of time. Morrison and McIntyre summarize the case against rating scales thus:

> Despite their popularity several objections can be raised against rating scales. One of their more serious limitations when used for assessing the classroom behavior of teachers is that an extensive amount of information about what has gone on has to be reduced to subjective and impressionistic endorsements on a few scales. Since they are heavily dependent upon the subjective impressions formed by the individual rater, their reliability from

> one occasion of rating to another by the same rater, or between two or more raters on the same occasion, is highly variable. Also, when the rater is presented with several supposedly distinct characteristics to assess he may in fact be unable to distinguish between them, leading to a tendency to rate an individual as 'high,' 'average' or 'low' on most of them. Finally the information available to the rater can vary very much from one characteristic to another and from one individual to another (1969: p. 22).

This is not to say that ratings of teachers are necessarily and invariably inaccurate. However, unless the set of guidelines proposed by Ryans (1960: p. 75) or something similar is observed, these ratings will not generally be very reliable. Such guidelines are not normally observed in actual teacher rating systems, as the ERS Survey shows.

Rating techniques have never been acceptable to teachers, who have strongly resisted, via their professional associations, any suggestion that either their salary or their job security should be determined by ratings. Their success in achieving job tenure and pay scales unaffected by judgments of their competence arrived at through classroom visitations is some evidence of the unspoken agreement by virtually all concerned that classroom visitation and rating is neither a reliable nor a valid means of evaluating teachers.

The model proposed here satisfies the definition adopted by the Center for Study of Evaluation of UCLA, which suggests that educational evaluation is

> the process of determining the kinds of decisions that have to be made; selecting, collecting, and analyzing information needed in making these decisions; and then reporting this information to appropriate decision-makers (Klein, 1971: p. 9).

The three kinds of decisions which the model proposed here provides information for are: teacher selection, teacher development, and teacher retention/release. Different kinds of information are required in each of these different decision areas, and thus the model provides for predictive, formative, and summative evaluation. This is summarized in the following chart.

The Evaluation of Teacher Effectiveness: An Administrative Model

Dimensions of teacher behavior	*Types of evaluation yielded*	*Decision area*
Warmth	Predictive Formative	Selection Development
Indirectness	Formative Summative	Development Retention/Release
Cognitive development	Predictive Formative Summative	Selection Development Retention/Release
Enthusiasm	Formative Summative	Development Retention/Release

A subsequent section of the paper discusses a fourth kind of decision, also important to improving aggregate teaching effectiveness, the assignment of teachers.

THE DIMENSION OF "WARMTH"

The dimension which Gage labels "warmth" has been identified by three different instruments, the Minnesota Teacher Attitude Inventory, the California Scale, and the Teacher Characteristics Schedule, and these three instruments correlate fairly closely. Furthermore, all of the instruments identify attitudes and behaviors which correlate positively with favorable assessments of the teachers by both students and objective observers, and with the achievement of students (Gage, 1972: p. 35).

If the desirability of warmth is accepted, the various instruments described here can then be used predictively, that is as selection devices in hiring teachers, with reasonable probability that the teachers with favorable scores will be effective teachers, both in terms of students' attitudes towards them, and the achievement of students.

In addition, there are further possibilities inherent in these research findings on the dimension of warmth. Since the M.T.A.I. has been shown to relate quite closely to favorable ratings of the teachers by their pupils (Yee, 1967), and since student ratings of teachers have been shown to be extremely useful in changing teacher behavior, this dimension can also provide formative evaluation.

Student ratings of teachers "have yielded useful evidence on teaching at levels as low as fourth grade and as high as medical school" (Gage, 1972: p. 172). In a long series of experiments in feedback from students to teachers, a number of researchers have demonstrated that student feedback, particularly in the form of written ratings, is a reliable and valid way of helping teachers improve their teaching, at least as it is perceived by students. The improvement here does not generally reflect in gains in student achievement, but only in more positive attitudes in students. This technique, it should be emphasized, is really a private transaction between students and their teachers. Nevertheless, it is a form of teacher development which has had good effects in a number of different contexts and could well be an important element in inservice training of teachers, provided the privacy limitation is clearly spelled out. This limitation necessarily rules out the use of student ratings for retention/release decisions.

THE DIMENSION OF "INDIRECTNESS"

Gage bases this dimension on two different but relatively closely related research areas. The first is usually identified as "interaction analysis," and is associated with the work of Flanders. One characteristic of teacher verbal behavior has been found in close association with both constructive student attitudes and favorable student achievement levels in a number of studies by different researchers:

> The percentage of teacher statements that make use of ideas and opinions previously expressed by pupils is directly related to average class scores on attitude scales of teacher effectiveness, liking the class, etc., as well as to average achievement scores adjusted by initial ability (Flanders and Simon, 1969: p. 1426).

The variety of studies, and of ways in which the interaction analysis data have been used, as reviewed by Flanders and Simon, suggests that such data enable one to train teachers to exhibit the apparently desirable verbal behavior, and to distinguish classrooms in which achievement and attitudes of students will be relatively poor. Thus, this dimension has formative and summative utility, and could be used to develop in-service training programs for teacher development and to evaluate teachers for retention or release.

THE DIMENSION OF "COGNITIVE DEVELOPMENT"

This dimension of effective teacher behavior is certainly the least understood and least immediately useful way of measuring teacher effectiveness. Since it has not yet been satisfactorily defined operationally, it will be necessary here to suggest the use of four proxies, or indicators, in place of direct measures of cognitive development. Unfortunately, three of these proxies are not "process variables" or even clearly related to such variables, and consequently do require the inference that the characteristics measured do affect teachers' classroom behavior. They have all been shown to correlate positively with student achievement levels; what is in question is the degree of causal relationship. Proposed are first, verbal facility; second, academic achievement; and third, recency of academic training. Each of these proxies requires some description and specification.

The importance of the teacher's verbal ability was clearly demonstrated by the Coleman Report, and is not currently questioned. (See, e.g., Guthrie, 1970: p. 37.)

The usefulness of this measure of teachers for administrative purposes is certainly debatable. Gage points out that this relationship is correlational, but not necessarily causal. Consequently, "we cannot proceed to improve student achievement by hiring teachers with greater verbal ability" (1972: p. 33). In addition, Mood suggests that:

> If we went about increasing the verbal ability of teachers, the increase that might result in student achievement would be far less than what would be calculated by using the equation that relates to achievement. The reason is that a specific increase in verbal ability would probably not be accompanied by a corresponding increase in all the other attributes that verbal ability is serving as a proxy for (1970: p. 3).

However, other writers disagree. For example, Lavin maintains that:

> Recruiting and retaining teachers with higher verbal scores is five to ten times as effective per dollar of teacher expenditure in raising achievement

> scores of students as the strategy of obtaining teachers with more experience (1970: p. 24).

The latter view is accepted here, at least tentatively, pending further research on the causal relationship, which the writer believes will substantiate that relationship.

The relationship between academic achievement of teachers and the achievement of students has been shown by many different studies at various times. However, the finding that recency of academic training is more closely associated with student achievement than the overall level of training obtained is relatively new, and is an outcome of a re-analysis of Coleman Report data (Hanushek, 1970: p. 92).

The dimension of "cognitive development" in teachers would be assessed in part by the development of three proxies, each of which has been shown to be associated with student achievement. It seems reasonable to infer that teachers with comparatively high scores on these proxies would then be relatively more effective than other teachers. It is suggested that the administrative use made of these proxies would be both predictive and summative. That is, at the teacher selection phase teachers would be selected in part on the basis of verbal ability scores, academic achievement, and recency of academic training. In the evaluation for retention or release phase, similar use would be made of new proxy scores, obtained subsequent to employment.

The fourth proxy, ability to explain, is a process variable, but its relationship to cognitive development is uncertain. It is drawn from a series of studies by Gage and colleagues based on the notion that teaching behavior consists of a group of technical skills, amongst other things, and that one such skill is the ability to explain. Studies of this ability in teachers showed that the differential effectiveness of teachers as explainers was perceptible to trained observers using a video and audio record of the explanations given by the teacher in the classroom. More interestingly, from the point of view of teacher development, a manual developed by Miltz on "how to explain," which was based on the previous research, increased the ability of teacher trainees to explain. Thus this proxy has formative value.

THE DIMENSION OF "ENTHUSIASM"

The distinction between "enthusiastic" or "stimulating" teaching and "indifferent" teaching has been used in a substantial number of research studies. In a recent review of these studies Rosenshine (1970) distinguished between high inference studies, which "require considerable inferring from what is seen or heard in the classroom to the labelling of the behavior" (p. 500) and low inference studies in which specific behaviors are carefully identified. The six high inference studies reviewed

> provide strikingly consistent results. They suggest that one of the patterns of effective teaching behavior identified by Ryans (1960), namely Pattern Z,

> described as "stimulating, imaginative, surgent versus dull, routine teacher behavior" is significantly related to pupil achievement (p. 506).

Reviewing the low inference studies, which are particularly useful for teacher training programs because they do give some indication of the specific behaviors which teachers should exhibit, Rosenshine identified a number of behaviors as components of "enthusiasm," and hence desirable:

> The teacher who scored high on the Energy factor appears to exhibit three types of related behavior. First, he is energetic, a rapid speaker, mobile and enthusiastic, but relaxed. Second, he asks varied questions, emphasizing questions of interpretation and opinion as well as factual questions. Third, he praises frequently (p. 506).

Clearly, the high inference studies above relate more generally to the summative element of the evaluation model used here; the low inference studies relate to the formative element. There seems little doubt however that the same general teacher behavior is being noted in both types of studies. Rosenshine's final summary of the studies on enthusiasm suggests that:

> The results of high inference studies provide evidence that ratings given to teachers on such behaviors as "stimulating," "energetic," "mobile," "enthusiastic," and "animated" are related to measures of pupil achievement. The results of low inference studies suggest that the frequencies of such variables as movement, gesture, variation in voice, and eye contact are related to pupil achievement (p. 510).

There is another research area which seems fairly closely related. Presumably enthusiastic and energetic teachers have differential impact on the attention level of the students. As Rosenshine points out, the result of the study described "may occur because animated behavior arouses the attending behavior of pupils," (p. 510) and in fact the attention level of the pupil is itself an area of investigation with a long history. This has been reviewed and summarized by Jackson (1968: p. 102). Given the existence of the relationship between enthusiastic teaching, the attention of pupils, and student achievement which is suggested by the research, and which certainly seems consistent with common sense and the experience of practitioners, the use of observer estimates of the attention of the class to the teacher does not seem an unreasonable evaluation technique. Furthermore,

> An estimate of pupil attention is commonly used by teachers to judge their personal effectiveness in the classroom. The possibility of massive inattention, signaling the loss of the teacher's authority, is frequently reported as a dominant fear among beginning teachers. Second, students also worry at times about their inability to remain focused on the task at hand. Boredom is one of the chief complaints of students who are having difficulty with school (Jackson, 1968: p. 102).

Thus there seems to be substantial justification for the use of observation of pupil attention as an element in formative evaluation as well. If the anxieties of teachers, particularly beginning teachers, and the boredom of students can be somewhat relieved by training teachers to be more enthusiastic or energetic, as the research suggests is possible, this could be a most useful contribution to teacher effectiveness.

TEACHER ASSIGNMENT: IMPROVING THE MATCH

The general issue of match or consistency between teachers and their work assignments can be considered in three different ways: first, the relatively simple question of the wishes of the teacher with regard to a teaching assignment; second, the more complex question of role expectations and role conflicts for teachers and students; and third, the even more difficult, and relatively unexplored question of what is the most productive match (or mismatch) between students and teachers for promoting student growth along psychological, social, or cognitive dimensions can be considered.

A recent study of the teacher workforce in British Columbia (Wallin, 1971) showed that only 57.57% of the teachers responding (n = 16,387) expressed satisfaction with their teaching assignment. The study found that perceived misassignment was relatively common, with 12.66% of teachers falling into this category. Misassignment seemed to be particularly common amongst rather well-trained teachers.

These data on assignment seem to indicate a concern amongst teachers regarding the misuse of talents, abilities, or training, and perhaps also to illustrate a resentment over lack of control of work which is common amongst professionals working in organizations, including teachers (Corwin, 1970: p. 46). Thus a reduction of misassignment may require two kinds of solution: a process of consultation, to increase the sense of control, and also a serious attempt by administrators to reduce mismatch between desired and actual assignments, and hence to alleviate concerns about the misuse of talents, abilities, or training.

The second version of matching can be based on the research on role behavior, particularly in organizational contexts. The theoretical model of factors in role conflict and ambiguity used here (see diagram) is that of Kahn *et al.* (1964).

The model is based on the notion of a role episode, "a complete cycle of role sending, response by the focal person, and the effects of that response on the role senders" (p. 26). In practice, conflict and ambiguity are experienced by the focal person through a series of such episodes. The notion of matching applied here suggests that appropriate teacher assignment might be able to minimize role conflict by ensuring a relatively high degree of congruence between student expectations and teacher expectations of appropriate role behavior. One caution is in order: although studies of expectations are common, studies of teacher-role performance are relatively uncommon, and it is quite possible that the continuity between role expectations and role performance will not be direct and straightforward, so that knowledge about expectations will not necessarily yield knowledge about classroom behavior. However, it seems possible that if there is a good match between student and teacher expectations, these expectations might more readily be translated into the expected behavior.

In order to achieve congruence in assignment, prior knowledge regarding the expectations of the teacher and the students is necessary. Although a good many test instruments for ascertaining role expectations of teachers and students exist, for example those used by Bogen, (1964) and Cheong and DeVault (1966), it would probably be necessary to develop a simple test for the purpose.

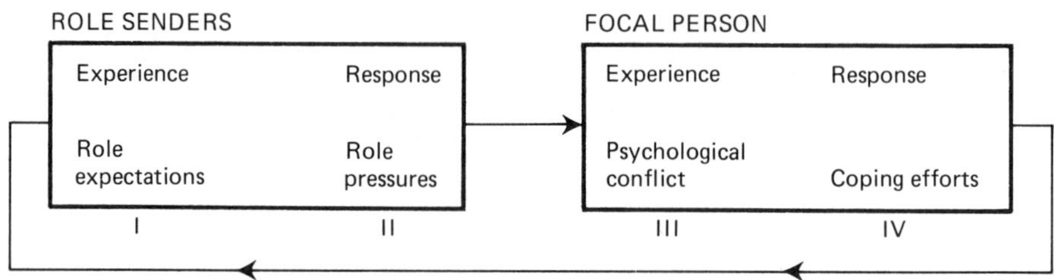

Another technique, which might be used together with or instead of the pencil-and-paper test of expectations, is simply to offer students a choice of teachers and assume that they possess enough knowledge to choose the teacher whose behavior will conflict least with their expectations. The obvious and commonsense reaction amongst educators to this suggestion is that the students would all wish to be taught by the least demanding teacher. However as is often the case research does not support the glib generalizations of common sense. A British study found

> wide agreement among pupils about the importance of firmness, justice, the avoidance of corporal punishment, friendliness, knowledge and, most of all, participation in class activities. Amongst junior school pupils, encouragement to work hard was stressed, as was politeness by the girls; and amongst secondary school pupils, cheerfulness and explaining the work was emphasized (Morrison and McIntyre, 1969: p. 109).

These findings lead one to expect that students might be quite capable of choosing the teacher who most appropriately satisfied their expectations through his teaching behavior, and indeed trials of this in other areas, which generally have been unsystematic and not reported in the research literature, have found that pupils did derive some satisfaction from the choice of teachers, just as university students do. At the university level, studies of student ratings of teachers have found that the fact that the course is elective, in other words that students chose a particular teacher, has a significant impact on the rating of the teacher by the students (Gage, 1972: p. 171).

Another approach, probably useful with elementary school students, derives from the work of Thelen and his colleagues on the "teachable group." After demonstrating the weaknesses of traditional grouping practices based on age, ability, or some other shared characteristic of pupils, Thelen records favorable results from teacher-constructed teachable groups. Allowing teachers to select their own classes, student by student, seems an eminently simple way of improving teacher feelings about assignments, and has demonstrably improved student attitudes (Thelen, 1967).

The third version of matching, developed by Hunt and his colleagues, might more accurately be described as constructive mismatch. They reject simple matching in terms of personality:

> We . . . disagree with some prevalent views of education, especially at the college level, which emphasize placing the student in the environment that is most congruent with his existing personality structure. In our view such procedures simply promote arrestation and thereby defeat the process of growth and progression, which should be the major goal of education (Harvey, Hunt, and Schroeder, 1961: p. 340).

Rather, their proposals rest on a value assertion: "abstract, conceptual structure and its associated characteristics of creativity, flexibility, stress tolerance, and broad-spectrum coping power is a desirable adaptive state. This value assertion stems from a concern with the person's capacity to adapt to a changing environment" (Hunt, 1971: p. 18). This conception emphasizes the need for a student-environment match which provides a challenge to stimulate growth. Ideally, this could be provided "in terms of a classroom of which the entire student population is homogeneous in stage of conceptual development" (Hunt, 1971: p. 25).

An earlier version of this work involved an exploratory study, intended to

> obtain some indication of the educational relevance of the model by exposing classroom groups of the same conceptual stage to the same educational environment. Students at a given stage are expected to share certain common characteristics based on conceptual level. They should respond favorably to certain forms of teaching and unfavorably to others, even though the environments may not necessarily be optimal for progression . . . in this study we ask, "do these classroom stage groups differ from one another in expected ways?" and if so, "do these differences make any educational sense to the teacher?" (1971: p. 26).

The success of the study led to further theoretical work and to the development of the most recent formulation, the Conceptual Level Matching Model, which involves specifying the desired change (educational objectives), a conception of the person (learner characteristics), a conception of the environment (educational approaches), and a conception of the interactive process (theory of instruction).

The early results of empirical work using this model have been quite interesting, and do suggest that the Conceptual Level of students can be a useful guideline for varying classroom groupings and educational approaches. Given that different teachers prefer different approaches, it also suggests the possibility of matching student requirements, based on conceptual levels, and teacher predilections, based on preferred educational approaches. However, the tentativeness of the empirical results to date, and the relatively small samples involved, require that some caution be exercised in applying this particular notion of matching. It remains one of the more interesting new approaches.

IMPLEMENTING THE PROPOSAL

A number of general points about evaluation and its impact on an educational system can be made, in the form of cautions to administrators wishing to implement an evaluation proposal such as this. The main point here is that evaluation in the context of educational organizations invariably has political implications, for the following reasons (based on Tumin, 1970):

1. It means different things to different people, because they have both different bases of judgment and aspire to different standards of competence.
2. Consensus agreements become a necessary way of proceeding with implementation and this consensus necessarily implies the need for some educational growth on the part of participants, and suggests that the whole evaluation process in an organization needs to develop by evolution rather than by fiat.
3. The evaluators need to be open to influence by all parties involved, not forgetting students, in the planning and implementation stages particularly.

Evaluation is inevitably an exercise of power, at the very least the power to discriminate levels of competence, and at the most the power to retain or release employees. It is thus intrinsically threatening to all concerned, although there is some evidence that better than average and non-tenured teachers have somewhat more positive attitudes towards evaluation than others (Wagoner and O'Hanlon, n.d.). Further, for students, evaluation may represent a shift in power in their favor: their participation in rating teachers often represents a gain in power. There is some evidence that this in itself is desirable, that

> by giving some power to students, perhaps in the form of choice of teacher, or voluntary attendance, or monthly ratings of teacher performance, one might well inculcate a higher priority for the goals of students and of the school system in the minds of teachers (Coleman, 1972: p. 46).

If these cautions are kept in mind, it is possible that the evaluation scheme can in fact contribute positively to the general health of the school district as an organization, since there is some evidence that the absence of control is relatively undesirable for all concerned. The desirable situation is participation in control. (See Tannenbaum, 1962). For example, a study of teachers and bureaucracy found, contrary to expectation, that the sense of power was higher in highly bureaucratic schools: "Teachers in highly bureaucratic systems had a significantly higher, not lower, sense of power than those in less bureaucratic systems" (Moeller and Charters, 1966: p. 458).

With regard to more immediate problems of implementation, two related points can be made: the selection, assignment, and retention-release decisions regarding teachers will generally be made by a superintendent or assistant superintendent, and consequently implementation of the program proposed here will depend a good deal on the ability of these people to administer pencil-and-paper tests, and to carry out careful classroom observation. Fortunately, interaction analysis has been quite highly developed, and instructional materials exist which make the skills readily teachable in in-service workshops. (See, for example, Amidon and Hunter, 1966.)

The second point concerns in-service programs for teachers. At present these are rather poorly developed, perhaps because there is no reasonable theoretical basis for these programs, and consequently they tend to be rather haphazard and only marginally effective. The technical skills approach to teacher training developed at Stanford University (Berliner, 1969) seems ideally suited for in-service work. The references here to evaluations used developmentally provide only very limited hints as to what the needs of teachers might be, but it does seem unlikely that a serious in-service program can be developed until after some relatively extensive and objective evaluation schemes have revealed the areas of greatest need. Teachers are not very likely to be aware of their deficiencies, although there seems little doubt that student rating schemes could help to enlighten them. Thus the implementation of the teacher evaluation program suggested here is seen as a necessary prerequisite to the development of an adequate in-service program.

Given the need to develop and implement the evaluation scheme in advance of determining in-service training needs and programs, and the requirement that in-service programs continue over a considerable period of time, the full implementation of the evaluation-based activities of selection, development, and retention/release may require five years. An anticipated timetable might resemble the following:

YEAR 1 Development of instrumentation for model.
Trials and modifications.
YEAR 2 Teacher selection based on model.
Evaluation of existing staff.
Planning of in-service programs.
YEAR 3 Re-evaluation of staff. Operation of in-service programs.
YEAR 4 Re-evaluation of staff. Operation of in-service programs. Release or placement on probation of weak staff.
YEAR 5 Re-evaluation of staff. Operation of in-service programs. Fully-informed release of weakest staff members.

Implementing the proposal for improving teacher assignment requires at least as much caution, in the opinion of the writer, as the evaluation-based proposals. Consulting teachers on their preferred assignment and consulting students on their preferred teacher both seem reasonable practices, well worth trying. However, reducing the discrepancies between actual and preferred educational contexts for teachers and students will not necessarily result in improved achievement. Careful evaluation of the outcomes would therefore be necessary. The Conceptual Level Model of Hunt and colleagues, which emphasizes constructive mismatch, seems likely to be more productive of desirable student growth. However, this model should be applied only under carefully controlled conditions and preferably with the assistance of competent consultants. In essence, all of these matching possibilities require rather careful testing before they can be unequivocally recommended.

CONCLUSIONS AND IMPLICATIONS

The approach to improving aggregate effectiveness proposed here purports to be timely in that a probable oversupply of teachers in North America makes it possible to replace released teachers, and also makes the problem of selecting and assigning teachers very much less difficult than previously. Rather than having one candidate who seems suitable for the required position, the administrator will probably have several candidates, and thus the problem of selection and assignment becomes one of applying more refined processes, far beyond the kind of gross matching which was possible in the past.

It is also maintained that the approach here is likely to be effective, in that the teacher behaviors and characteristics considered desirable here have had, in empirical studies in the past, positive relationships with good attitudes and achievement levels of students; unless evidence to the contrary exists, it seems reasonable to expect the positive outcomes to be replicated in districts adopting this approach.

In addition, it is also maintained that the approach proposed here is practical, in that it can be utilized without extensive retraining of supervisors or heavy expenditures for consultants and data analysis. Unquestionably, some additional topics for the in-service training of administrators are implied by the proposals made here; for example, few administrators have had exposure to verbal interaction analysis techniques for evaluating teachers, but this could easily be remedied in a school district wishing to adopt this proposal. The model can conveniently be summarized in a simple table.

Teacher Evaluation and Administrative Decision Making:
Data Needs and Administrator Responsibilities

Administrative decisions and evaluation data needed	*Sources of data*	*Persons responsible for collecting and utilizing data*
Selection	M.T.A.I.	Superintendent
(Predictive data)	Verbal facility test	Superintendent
Development	Student ratings	Teacher
(Formative data)	Interaction analysis	Principal
	Classroom behavior	Principal
Retention/Release	Interaction analysis	Principal, Superintendent
(Summative data)	Classroom behavior	Principal, Superintendent
	M.T.A.I.	Superintendent

Additionally, it is proposed that in teacher assignment matching models of three types are relevant to the improvement of teacher effectiveness: one, improving the match between teachers' preferences and training and their teaching assignments; two, improving the match between teacher and student expectations of role behaviors, and thus reducing role conflict; and three, improving the match between student needs for growth and teacher practices. The first two can be implemented to some extent by extending consultation and choice for teachers and students.

Close attention by administrators to the processes of teacher selection, assignment, development, and retention/release can, it is maintained, substantially increase the aggregate teaching effectiveness of the staff of a school district over a period of some years. Serious administrative attempts to improve teaching have not been common in recent years. They may well become more popular in response to demands for accountability, and to the improving supply of teachers.

References

American Association of School Administrators. "Evaluating Teaching Performance." *ERS Circular*. Washington, D.C.: Educational Research Service, American Association of School Administrators, 1972.

Amidon, E., and E. Hunter. *Improving Teaching: The Analysis of Classroom Verbal Interaction*. New York: Holt, Rinehart and Winston, 1966.

Berliner, D. C. *Microteaching and the Technical Skills Approach to Teacher Training*. Palo Alto: Stanford Center for Research and Development in Teaching, 1969.

Bogen, I. "Pupil-Teacher Rapport and the Teaching Awareness of Status Structures within the Group." *Journal of Educational Sociology* 28 (1964).

Cheong, G. W., and M. V. DeValut. "Pupil Perceptions of Teachers." *Journal of Educational Research* 59 (1966).

Coleman, P. "Organizational Effectiveness in Education: Its Measurement and Enhancement." *Interchange* 3, no. 1 (1972): 42–52.

Corwin, R. G. *Militant Professionalism: A Study of Organizational Conflict in High Schools*. New York: Appleton-Century-Crofts, 1970.

Etzioni, A. "Human Beings Are Not Very Easy to Change After All." *The Saturday Review*, 3 June 1972.

Flanders, N. A., and A. Simon. "Teacher Effectiveness." In R. L. Ebel, ed., *Encyclopedia of Educational Research*. 4th ed. New York: MacMillan, 1969.

Gage, N. L. *Teacher Effectiveness and Teacher Education: The Search for a Scientific Basis*. Palo Alto: Pacific Books, 1972.

Guthrie, J. W. "A Survey of School Effectiveness Studies." In *Do Teachers Make a Difference?* Washington, D.C.: Bureau of Educational Personnel Development, Office of Education, 1970.

Hanushek, E. "The Production of Education, Teacher Quality, and Efficiency." In *Do Teachers Make a Difference?* Washington, D.C.: Bureau of Educational Personnel Development, Office of Education, 1970.

Harvey, O. J., D. E. Hunt, and H. M. Schroeder. *Conceptual Systems and Personality Organization*. New York: Wiley, 1961.

Hunt, D. E. *Matching Models in Education*. Toronto: The Ontario Institute for Studies in Education, 1971.

Jackson, P. W. *Life in Classrooms*. New York: Holt, Rinehart and Winston, 1968.

Kahn, R. L., D. M. Wolfe, R. P. Quinn, J. D. Snock, and R. A. Rosenthal. *Organizational Stress: Studies in Role Conflict and Ambiguity*. New York: Wiley, 1964.

Klein, S. P. "The Uses and Limitations of Standardized Tests in Meeting the Demands for Accountability." *Evaluation Comment* **2**, no. 4 (1971): 1–7.

Levin, H. M. "A Cost-Effectiveness Analysis of Teacher Selection." *The Journal of Human Resources* **5**, no. 1 (1970): 24–33.

Moeller, G. H., and W. W. Charters. "Relation of Bureaucratization to Sense of Power among Teachers." *Administrative Science Quarterly* **10** (1966).

Mood, A. M. "Do Teachers Make a Difference?" In *Do Teachers Make a Difference?* Washington, D. C.: Bureau of Educational Personnel Development, Office of Education, 1970.

Morrison, A., and D. McIntyre. *Teachers and Teaching*. Baltimore: Penguin Books, 1969.

Rosenshine, B. "Enthusiastic Teaching: A Research Review." *School Review* **78**, no. 4 (1970): 499–512.

Ryans, D. G. *Characteristics of Teachers*. Washington, D.C.: American Council on Education, 1960.

Tannenbaum, A. S. "Control in Organizations: Individual Adjustment and Organizational Performance." *Administrative Science Quarterly* **7** (1962).

Thelen, H. A. *Classroom Grouping for Teachability*. New York: Wiley, 1967.

Tumin, M. M. "Evaluation of the Effectiveness of Education: Some Problems and Prospects." *Interchange* **1**, no. 3 (1970): 96–109.

Turner, R. L. "Task Performance and Teaching Skill in the Intermediate Grades." *Journal of Teacher Education* **14**, no. 3 (1963): 299–307.

Wagoner, R. L., and J. P. O'Hanlon. *Teacher Attitude Toward Evaluation,* n.d. (ED 013 236).

Wallin, H. A. *The Educational Employment Histories of the Professional Workforce in B. C. Schools, 1968–69*. Vancouver: Centre for the Study of Administration in Education, The University of British Columbia, 1971.

Yee, H. H. "Is the Minnesota Teacher Attitude Inventory Valid and Homogeneous?" *Journal of Educational Measurement* **4**, no. 3 (1967): 151–162.

STEPHEN P. KLEIN and
MARVIN C. ALKIN
University of California at Los Angeles

Evaluating Teachers for Outcome Accountability

The current emphasis on evaluation and accountability in education has resulted in a number of states passing laws to make them mandatory in one form or another. In California, for example, an accountability law was recently passed requiring the evaluation of teachers in terms of their students' performance. Although we support the rationale underlying such mandates, we often find it discouraging to see how they are worded or implemented. Frequently federal or state governments mandate laws prematurely and with insufficient lead time. Such action puts a severe burden on school personnel who may not be familiar with the issues and methods associated with developing effective evaluation systems. This, in turn, has led to professional evaluators being besieged with requests for advice on how to develop such systems so that they are professionally satisfactory and conform to both the letter and the spirit of the law. These requests usually take the form of questions such as "We have a Title III grant to improve student reading and attitudes: how should we evaluate this project?" or "We want to have a teacher-improvement and evaluation system; how should we set it up?"

This paper will focus on the kinds of general advice we would give to answer one facet of the latter question: How should a school set up a system to hold teachers accountable for student outcomes?

By selecting this topic for discussion, we are not addressing the question of whether or not such systems should be developed or, if they are, whether it is also imperative to develop principal, superintendent, and school board accountability systems along with the system for teachers. Those who wish to debate these issues may arm themselves with a paper by Alkin (1972). However, since teacher-evaluation systems are a reality, it is better to have good ones than poor ones. Furthermore, if a school uses a good teacher-accountability system, the quality of education being offered is likely to improve. The rationale to support this contention will be presented later, but first we will consider what a good system should look like.

From *Evaluation Comment* 3, no. 3 (1972): 5–11. Reprinted by permission.

REQUIREMENTS OF A GOOD TEACHER-EVALUATION SYSTEM

One way of describing what a good system should look like is to consider what it *should not* look like. First, it *should not* require *subjective* judgments by principals or panels on whether a teacher is performing competently. A good evaluation system should emphasize *objective* assessments of teacher performance. Thus, the common approach of having principals observe and rate teacher performance is not acceptable since it is too open to individual biases. Further, what one principal believes will constitute an effective teacher may not be too highly related to what another principal thinks nor is either of these two subjective judgments necessarily correlated with actual *student* performance. Because of this potential lack of a strong relationship between subjective assessments of teacher quality and demonstrated pupil performance, subjective judgments are likely to be a very poor basis for a good accountability system.

One of the first important features of a good teacher evaluation system, then, is that it be *objective*. Some school districts and state departments of education have sought to achieve such objectivity by relying on nationally-normed standardized tests of student ability and knowledge. The logic behind this approach is that if a teacher does his or her job well, then that teacher's students should learn more than the students of a teacher who is not effective. This seems reasonable, especially if one controls for important factors out of the teacher's control but which still might influence pupil scores. For example, it would be appropriate to compare teachers on the basis of their students' performance if one adjusted the measure of that performance for such factors as the students' previous skills and knowledge. Thus, with the proper controls on certain factors, evaluating teachers on the basis of their students' performance seems like a fair and objective approach.

Unfortunately, the practice of using nationally-normed standardized tests often violates the spirit of this logic. There are several reasons for this, but perhaps the most important is that such measures may be insensitive to the kinds of skills, knowledge, and attitudes that teachers are trying to transmit to their pupils. Nationally-normed tests provide only a single, global score on very general objectives that may have been combined in some very strange ways. These measures may also fail to assess certain objectives considered to be especially important in a given school and these objectives may be among those on which a teacher is devoting most of his class time (Klein, 1970, 1971). Therefore, the use of most nationally-normed standardized tests to assess a given teacher's performance would be analogous to using a bathroom scale to determine how many stamps to put on a letter. A teacher could be very effective and make an important impact on his or her students' performance, but that influence would not register on the measuring scale of nationally-normed tests because such instruments are simply not sensitive enough for the job.

So far we have disqualified one common base for a teacher-evaluation system—ratings from personal contact and observations—and have discussed the possible shortcomings of a second method—nationally-normed standardized measures. In discussing these two kinds of criteria we have mentioned some characteristics that should be considered for a good system. For example, the system should be objective and fair to all the teachers who are going to be evaluated by it. There must, therefore, be some means of adjusting for factors that may influence student performance but over which the teacher has no control. These factors range from prescribed instructional materials (and whether or not they arrive on time) to controlling for students with different kinds of ability, socio-economic backgrounds, and cultures. Alkin (1972) has elaborated such constraints on the teacher in the discussion of program accountability. Secondly, the basis for this system should be sensitive to the educational goals and objectives that the school is trying to achieve. It is senseless to say that one teacher is competent and another is not when the basis for this evaluation is how well each of them can teach students to do somehing which is irrelevant to the school's goals.

OBJECTIVES-BASED APPROACH TO OUTCOME ACCOUNTABILITY

One method of evaluating teachers for outcome accountability that meets the foregoing criteria involves the use of a set of tests or other devices to assess pupil performance on the *particular objectives* with which the school is most concerned. This approach is called "objectives-based evaluation." It usually takes the form of selecting a set of important objectives, constructing short tests to measure each of these objectives, and then administering the tests to all the pupils for whom the objectives are intended. The performance of teachers who are operating under the same conditions can then be compared. One never knows what a legislator is thinking when he drafts a bill, but it was probably the intent of the California legislators to use an objectives-based evaluation system when, in passing their teacher-evaluation law, they said:

> It is the intent of the Legislature to establish a uniform system of evaluation and assessment of the performance of certificated personnel within each school district of the state. The system shall involve the development and adoption by each school district of objective evaluation and assessment guidelines.[1]

This sounds good, but can it be implemented? First, one must determine what objectives are considered to be most important. To our knowledge, procedures for effectively and economically determining the most important objectives within each district have been developed and implemented statewide in at least one state (Klein, 1972). Thus, it is reasonable to assume that this might eventually be done in districts in other states which are adopting accountability procedures.

The second step in implementing an objectives-based accountability system

---

[1] Article 5.5, Section 13485. Evaluation and Assessment of Performance of Certificated Employees. California Legislature, 1972.

involves selecting and/or constructing measures to assess student performance on the important objectives. Selecting tests is, of course, a lot easier than constructing them; and books such as the CSE Pre-School/Kindergarten Test Evaluations (1971) and Elementary School Test Evaluations (1970) can be used to facilitate this process *if* there are existing published measures that overlap well with the district's objectives. The construction of measures to assess student performance, on the other hand, especially on objectives involving student attitudes, is a very costly undertaking and not likely to be supportable by each individual school district. It is also rather inefficient since many districts will have essentially the same objectives and, thus, there would be an unnecessary duplication of effort spent on test construction. A state department of education could, therefore, make an important contribution to setting up an accountability system by coordinating and/or supporting the development of the necessary objectives-based measures.

The third step in this process, the administration, scoring, and analysis of the data, could also be done much more efficiently if it were supervised by one central agency. To help ensure unbiased and confidential reports of results this agency might even be a private firm. Such an agency might also handle some of the inherent problems associated with objectives-based systems. One problem, for example, is the sheer number of objectives on which pupils might be assessed if a district wanted to evaluate every teacher's performance on all the objectives that were judged to be important for each teacher's pupils. This might require so much testing time that little would be left for instruction. Alternatively, to say in advance that only a certain group of important objectives will be assessed might encourage some teachers to ignore the other important objectives and thereby penalize those teachers who are conscientious about their profession and who treat all important objectives. In order to alleviate these problems, it has been suggested that when an objectives-based system is employed, it should also involve systematic sampling of students and objectives. This, in turn, will minimize testing time and costs.

PERFORMANCE TESTS

Another approach which has been suggested for establishing a fair and objective basis for a teacher-evaluation system is called "performance tests" (Popham, 1971a,b). This approach, analogous to the idea of a job sample, is designed to be more efficient than a total objectives-based system and involves selecting a few relevant objectives and constructing tests to measure student achievement of them. The objectives chosen for this purpose should deal with a relatively small but important unit of the curriculum in which the students have had *no previous instruction*. The next step is to assign students to teachers randomly or by means of fair matching techniques so that student characteristics and other factors beyond the teacher's control are counterbalanced among the teachers who are to be evaluated. The teachers are then given a fixed amount of time to teach these objectives and, at the end of that period, student performance is assessed. One assumption underlying this approach is that "teaching ability" is a general characteristic and not limited to just certain kinds of objectives. *Thus, how well a teacher's students do on a series of performance tests is presumed to correlate fairly well with how that teacher's students do on tests to measure end-of-year kinds of objectives.*

The use of performance tests in teacher accountability systems is quite new. There are not yet sufficient data to determine whether these job samples will really reflect teacher proficiency on more than just simple short-term objectives, but hopes are high that they will. One problem to be faced in the use of teacher proficiency tests is whether a test of teaching ability is a fair criterion or whether the more relevant dimension is teacher achievement. That is, one must view a teacher performance test as a kind of aptitude test rather than achievement test. This has led to the suggestion that teacher performance tests might be used in conjunction with objectives-based evaluation systems to obtain a less costly technique that is relatively easy to use. The procedure would require performing periodic statistical analyses demonstrating the relationships between scores on teacher performance tests and larger batteries of objectives-based measures. If the results were satisfactory, then teacher performance tests could be used as a reasonable proxy for end-of-year outcome measures. At this time, however, using teacher performance tests in this way is an unproven technique and caution is advised.

SETTING STANDARDS

No matter what method is chosen, if we are concerned about *judging* teacher performance, then standards must be set. This setting of standards illustrates how the term "evaluation" differs from "assessment" or "measurement" and it is important at this point to specify the nature of this difference. The term "assessment" is used to describe the collection and tabulation of such data as student scores on a test. The word "evaluation" includes assessment but goes beyond that to include a *judgment* of the quality of the obtained measurement. Thus, one could assess a teacher's performance in terms of his or her students' test scores; but to evaluate whether or not that performance is satisfactory one must also have a set of standards against which to judge the quality of that performance. One must ask the question, therefore, for an individual student, whether 75% is acceptable or is 99% needed? Obviously, a host of other kinds of standards or frames of reference might be employed. If one wishes to use the measurement of student performance as a means for judging the quality of teacher effectiveness, then one must set *some* standard against which to evaluate whether or not an individual teacher's performance is acceptable.

There are, of course, many different kinds of standards one might wish to employ. For example, one might set an arbitrary score for the class average. A different kind of standard would involve a comparison of a teacher's effectiveness in improving student performance relative to some norm group, such as students of other teachers. Another approach assumes that students should perform better if they are taught by a professional and qualified teacher rather than by someone who is not a credentialled teacher. Thus, a teacher's effectiveness might be judged in terms of whether his or her students' performance was more like the performance of students taught by a person with or without a credential. It should be noted, however, that Popham (1971b) investigated the utility of this approach and found the results somewhat disconcerting. The reason for his consternation was that he could find *no difference* in the performance of students who were taught by credentialled teachers versus those taught by people off the street. The students in both groups improved equally.[2] It appears, therefore, that if comparisons are to be made to some norm group rather than an absolute standard of performance, then this norm should probably be the performance of pupils of other teachers.

How one should make such comparisons fairly is also an important issue for an accountability system. For example, if one simply looks at the class average, then one ignores the possibility that a high or low average might have been due to just a few extreme cases. Lindman (1968) has suggested, therefore, a technique to see whether a teacher's class improves in performance uniformly or whether the observed end-of-year average score was a function of something happening (or not happening) to certain subgroups within the class (such as those with high, low, or medium ability).

A second problem in the use of a norm group against which to evaluate teacher performance is that pupils are not comparable across teachers. A teacher with bright students should obtain a higher level of performance from these students than that same teacher would with students who were less able. One way around this problem might be to construct different norms for different kinds of students such as those falling at different performance levels on a statewide or district-wide test and for groups using different sets of instructional materials. If other input variables, such as the students' socioeconomic status, were also to be considered, then one would need a very large number of categories and/or advanced statistical grouping techniques such as discriminant function analysis. In any event, the number of teachers in a given district with a sufficient number of pupils in even one category for a given grade (or age) level would probably be so small as to preclude any worthwhile analysis within that district. In short, the norm against which comparisons were to be made would be non-existent. This situation has led a number of researchers, such as Barro (1970), to suggest the use of a technique called regression analysis. The essential features of this approach as it might be applied to an accountability system for a single district are as follows:

---

[2] Similar results have been reported in connection with the Office of Economic Opportunity's study of performance contracting (OEO, 1972). In this experiment, the performance of pupils in regular classrooms with credentialled teachers was compared to that of comparable students receiving special instruction under diverse kinds of conditions. The instruction given to the experimental group ranged from the use of aides with only a few days training to master teachers employing incentives and the most advanced educational technology. OEO reported that there were no significant differences among these approaches! On the other hand, McNeil (1972) has found that students taught by more experienced teachers tend to do better than those taught by teacher trainees.

1. Administer a pretest to all the students within a given grade or age level. This test should assess each student's performance on all or a good sample of the relevant objectives for students at that level although it is not necessary to have separate scores for each objective. Thus, one might either use a nationally-normed standardized test if it matches the district's objectives, or construct a measure specifically for the objectives in question. Such a test should not take more than one or, at the most, two hours of testing time.

2. At the end of the year, administer a posttest covering the same objectives that were assessed with the pretest. It would probably be a good idea to use a different set of items for the two tests, however, so as to minimize potential biases.

3. Plot the two sets of scores (pretest and posttest) for each pupil within a given grade (or age) level. The pupil's teacher should also be identified in this process. The scores of five pupils in each of three classes have been plotted in Figure 1 to illustrate this procedure.

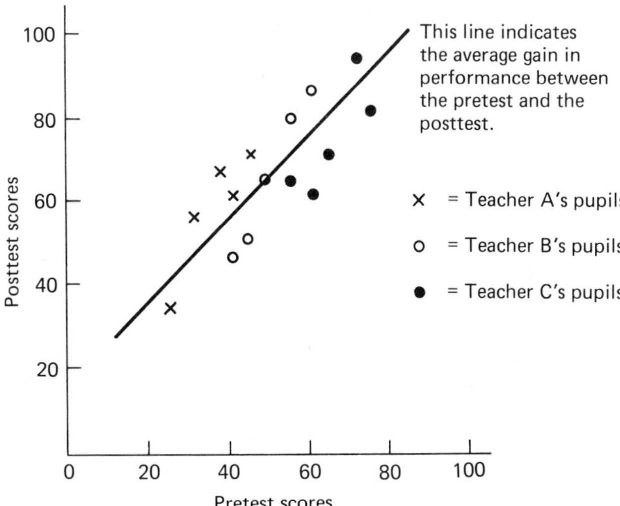

Figure 1

4. Fit a line among these points on the plot that would represent the average or typical relationship between pretest and posttest scores. The statistical procedure called regression analysis can be used for this purpose.

5. Inspect the results in terms of whether a teacher's class tends to fall above or below the line of expected performance as well as whether the average class performance tends to be above or below this line. Table 1 is an example of how these results might be summarized. An examination of this table reveals that although Teacher A's class had relatively poor pretest scores, they gained

more in relation to their starting position than did the students in either Teacher B's class or Teacher C's class. Five students per teacher is, of course, an insufficient number on which to base sound comparative judgments using this procedure and this number was used only for the purposes of illustration. One would need at least 20 or more students in order to get a stable estimate of how well a teacher's students did relative to the typical performance of students at the same grade (or age) level.

Table 1

	Teacher A	*Teacher B*	*Teacher C*
Average pretest score	35	50	65
Average posttest score	57	65	73
Expected posttest score	50	65	80
Difference between expected and actual posttest scores	7	0	7
Percent of pupils who are:			
Above expectancy	80%	40%	20%
At expectancy	0	10%	0
Below expectancy	20%	40%	80%

The major advantages of this procedure are that it takes into account the student's skills and knowledge before instruction begins, it is flexible enough (via a technique called multiple regression) to take into account several input factors (such as minority group membership and different instructional programs), and it examines more than just the class's average performance. Its major disadvantage, however, is that it requires that students be measured twice and, thus, might not be applicable for districts that have very high student mobility problems. It is also limited to comparing teachers only on a grade-by-grade basis in elementary school and on a subject-by-subject basis at higher levels.

It is apparent, therefore, that the setting of standards against which to evaluate teacher effectiveness can be a difficult job. To obtain adequate controls for potentially important input factors one must use a large sample of teachers and then wrestle with the question of what constitutes satisfactory performance. The problem is not one that will simply go away by itself. If educators fail to establish satisfactory standards, then alternate procedures will be employed. A school board member once suggested to the authors that the way to apportion teacher salaries is directly on the basis of student performance. This would mean that the highest paid teacher, regardless of experience or education (or students worked with) should be the one whose students are performing the best, and so on down the line until the salaries get so low that the "incompetents" seek employment elsewhere. It is apparent that most teachers would prefer some standard to aim for rather than be forced to comply with arbitrary schemes devised by others.

References

Alkin, M. C. "Accountability Defined." *Evaluation Comment* 3, no. 3 (1972): 1–5.

Barro, S. M. "An Approach to Developing Accountability Measures for the Public Schools." *Phi Delta Kappan* 52 (1970): 196–205.

Hoepfner, R., G. Strickland, G. Stangel, P. Jensen, and M. Patalino, eds. *CSE Elementary School Test Evaluations.* Los Angeles: Center for the Study of Evaluation, UCLA Graduate School of Education, 1970.

Hoepfner, R., C. Stern, and S. Nummedal, eds. *CSE-ECRC Preschool Kindergarten Test Evaluations.* Los Angeles: Center for the Study of Evaluation, UCLA Graduate School of Education, 1971.

Klein, S. P. "Evaluating Tests in Terms of the Information They Provide." *Evaluation Comment* 2, no. 2 (1970): 1–6.

Klein, S. P. "The Uses and Limitations of Standardized Tests in Meeting the Demands for Accountability." *Evaluation Comment* 2, no. 4 (1971): 1–7.

Klein, S. P. "An Evaluation of New Mexico's Educational Priorities." Paper presented at the Western Psychological Association Convention, Chicago, April 1972.

Lindman, E. *Net-Shift Analysis for Comparing Distributions of Test Scores* (Working Paper No. 5, 1968). Los Angeles: Center for the Study of Evaluation, University of California, 1968.

McNeil, J. *"Experienced Teachers versus Novices in Attaining Results with Young Learners."* Unpublished manuscript, University of California, Los Angeles, 1972.

Office of Economic Opportunity. "An Experiment in Performance Contracting: Summary of Preliminary Results." A press release from the Office of Economic Opportunity, Washington, D.C., 1 February 1972.

Popham, W. J. *Designing Teacher Evaluation Systems.* Los Angeles: Instructional Objectives Exchange, 1971a.

Popham, W. J. "Performance Tests of Teaching Proficiency: Rationale, Development, and Validation." *American Educational Research Journal* 8 (1971b): 105–117.

HENRY S. DYER
Educational Testing Service

Toward Objective Criteria of Professional Accountability in the Schools of New York City

THE CONCEPT OF PROFESSIONAL ACCOUNTABILITY

The concept of accountability can have many levels of meaning, depending upon where one focuses attention in the structure of the school system. Throughout this paper I shall be using the term in a restricted sense as it applies to the individual school as a unit. At this level I think of the concept as embracing three general principles:

1. The professional staff of a school is to be held collectively responsible for *knowing* as much as it can (a) about the intellectual and personal-social development of the pupils in its charge and (b) about the conditions and educational services that may be facilitating or impeding the pupils' development.

2. The professional staff of a school is to be held collectively responsible for *using* this knowledge as best it can to maximize the development of its pupils toward certain clearly defined and agreed-upon pupil performance objectives.

3. The board of education has a corresponding responsibility to provide the means and technical assistance whereby the staff of each school can acquire, interpret, and use the information necessary for carrying out the two foregoing functions.

CHARACTERISTICS OF AN EDUCATIONAL ACCOUNTING SYSTEM

Pupil-Change Model of a School

The theory behind the first of the three principles stated above is that if a school staff is to fulfill its professional obligations it must have extensive knowledge of the pupils it is expected to serve. This theory is based on the notion

From *Phi Delta Kappan* **51**, no. 4 (1970): 206–211. Reprinted by permission.

of a school as a social system that effects changes of various kinds in both the children who pass through it and in the professional personnel responsible for maintaining the school. The school as a social system becomes an educational system when its constituents are trying to ensure that all such changes shall be for the better. That is, the school as a *social* system becomes an *educational* system when its constituents—pupils, teachers, principal—are working toward some clearly defined pupil performance objectives.

There are four groups of variables in the school as a social system that must be recognized and measured if one is to develop acceptable criteria of staff accountability. These four groups of variables I call *input, educational process, surrounding conditions,* and *output.* Taken together, they form the pupil-change model of a school.

The *input* to any school at any given level consists of the characteristics of the pupils as they enter that level of their schooling: their health and physical condition, their skill in the three R's, their feelings about themselves and others, their aspirations, and so on.[1] The *output* of any school consists of the same characteristics of the pupils as they emerge from that particular phase of their schooling some years later.

According to this conception, the input to any school consists of the output from the next lower level. Thus, the output of an elementary school becomes the input for junior high, and the output of junior high becomes the input for senior high. It is important to note that the staff of an individual school which is not in a position to select the pupils who come to it has no control over the level or quality of its input. In such a case, the pupil input represents a *fixed condition* with which the school staff must cope. The pupil output, however, is a variable that depends to some extent on the quality of service the school provides.

The third group of variables in the pupil-change model consists of the *surrounding conditions* within which the school operates. These are the factors in the school environment that may influence for better or for worse how teachers teach and pupils learn. The surrounding conditions fall into three categories: home conditions, community conditions, and school conditions. Home conditions include such matters as the level of education of the pupils' parents, the level of family income, the family pressures, and the physical condition of the home. Community conditions include the density of population in the enrollment area, the ethnic character of the population, the number and quality of available social agencies, the degree of industrialization, and so on. School conditions include the quality of the school plant, pupil-teacher ratio, classroom and playground footage per pupil, the esprit de corps of the staff, and the like.

In respect to all three types of surrounding conditions, one can distinguish those that the staff of a school finds easy to change from those that it finds hard to change. For example, in respect to home conditions, the school staff is hardly in a position to change the socioeconomic level of pupils' parents, but it may

[1] Note the restriction of meaning of the term *input* as used here. It does *not* include such variables as per pupil expenditure, institutional effort, facilities, and the like.

well be in a position to change the parents' attitudes toward education through programs that involve them in the work of the school. Similarly, in respect to school conditions, it might not be able to effect much change in the classroom footage per pupil, but it could probably develop programs that might influence the esprit de corps of the staff through in-service training. The identification of hard-to-change as contrasted with easy-to-change surrounding conditions is of the utmost importance in working toward objective criteria of professional accountability, since the staff of a school can hardly be held accountable for changing those factors in its situation over which it has little or no control.

The final set of variables in the pupil-change model are those that make up the *educational process;* that is, all the activities in the school expressly designed to bring about changes for the better in pupils: lessons in arithmetic, recreational activities, consultation with parents, vocational counseling, etc. Three principal questions are to be asked about the educational processes in any school: (1) Are they adapted to the individual needs of the children in the school? (2) Do they work, that is, do they tend to change pupils, in *desirable* ways? and (3) What, if any, negative side effects may they be having on the growth of the children?

The four sets of variables just described—input, output, surrounding conditions, and educational process—interact with one another in complex ways. That is, the pupil output variables are affected by all the other variables. Similarly, the educational process variables are influenced by both the pupil input and the surrounding conditions. And certain of the surrounding conditions may be influenced by certain of the educational processes. This last could happen, for instance, if a school embarked on a cooperative work-study program with businesses in its enrollment area.

From the foregoing considerations, it is clear that if a school staff is to maximize pupil output in any particular way, it must be aware of the nature of the interactions among the variables in the system and be given sufficient information to cope with them in its work. This in turn means that, insofar as possible, all variables in the system must be measured and appropriately interrelated and combined to produce readily interpretable indices by which the staff can know how much its own efforts are producing hoped-for changes in pupils, after making due allowance for those variables over which it has little or no control. I call such indices *school effectiveness indices* (SEI's). They are the means whereby a school staff may be held responsible for *knowing* how well it is doing.

Nature of the SEI

The functioning of a school can be described by a profile of school effectiveness indices, so that each school staff can readily locate the points at which its educational program is strong or weak. Such a profile is fundamentally different from the traditional test-score profile, which is ordinarily generated from the grade equivalencies attached to the general run of standardized achievement tests. The underlying rationale of an SEI profile rejects grade equivalencies as essentially meaningless numbers that tend to be grossly misleading as indicators of a school's effectiveness. Appropriate indices in the SEI profile of any given school at any given level can be derived only through a procedure involving *all* the schools at the same level in the district. The procedure consists of a series of regression analyses which I shall touch upon presently.

Two features of an SEI profile differentiate it from the usual test-score profile. First, each index summarizes how effective the school has been in promoting one type of pupil development over a definite span of years; for example, the three years from the beginning of grade four to the end of grade six. Second, the profile has two dimensions: a pupil development dimension comprehending different areas of pupil growth (e.g., growth in self-esteem, growth in the basic skills, growth in social behavior) and a level-of-pupil-input dimension which might encompass three categories of children in accordance with their varying levels of development in any area at the time they entered grade four.

With this sort of profile it should be possible to discern in which areas of pupil development a school is more or less effective with different groups of pupils. Thus, an SEI profile for a grade four to six school should be capable of answering questions like the following: In its teaching of reading over the three-year period, has the school done a better or worse job with pupils who entered grade four with a low level of reading performance as compared with those who entered with a high level of reading performance? During the three-year period, has the school been more or less effective in developing children's number skills than in developing their sense of self-esteem, or their health habits?

The areas of pupil development to be incorporated in the educational accounting system for any district must grow out of an earnest effort to reach agreement among all the parties involved (teachers, administrators, board members, parents, pupils) concerning the pupil performance objectives that are to be sought. Such objectives will vary for schools encompassing different grade levels, and they will also vary, in accordance with local needs, among schools serving any given grade levels.

Securing agreement on the objectives is no mean enterprise, but it is obviously fundamental to a meaningful approach to the establishment of any basis for holding professional educators accountable for their own performance in the schools.

Derivation of the SEI

One important point to keep in mind about any school effectiveness index is that it is a measure that must be *derived* from a large number of more fundamental measures. These more fundamental measures consist of three of the sets of variables suggested earlier in the discussion of the pupil-change model of a school as a social system, namely, (1) the pupil input variables, (2) the *hard-to-change* surrounding conditions, and (3) the pupil output variables. Measures of *easy-to-change* surrounding condition variables and of the educational process variables do not enter into the derivation of SEI's. They become of central importance subsequently in identifying the specific actions a school staff should take to improve the effectiveness of its operations.

The fundamental measures from which the indices are to be derived can take many different forms: academic achievement tests; questionnaires to get at matters like pupil self-esteem; physical examinations to assess health and health habits; a wide range of sociological measures to assess community conditions; and measures of various aspects of the school plant, equipment, and personnel. Techniques for securing many of these measures are already available, but new and more refined ones will be required before a reasonably equitable educational accounting system can be fully operable.

Given the total array of measures required for the derivation of the SEI's, the first step in the derivation will be to apply such measures in all schools in the system at any given level—e.g., all the elementary schools, all the senior high schools—to secure the necessary information on pupil input and on the hard-to-change surrounding conditions.

The second step, to be taken perhaps two or three years later, will be to obtain output measures on the same pupils, i.e., those pupils who have remained in the same schools during the period in question.[2]

The third step will be to distribute the pupils within each school into three groups—high, middle, and low—on each of the input measures. Two points are to be especially noted about this step. First, the distribution of input measures must be "within school" distributions, with the consequence that the pupils constituting the "high" group in one school could conceivably be in the "low" group at another school where the input levels run higher with respect to any particular "area of development." Secondly, within any school, a pupil's input level could be high in one area of development (e.g., basic skills) and middle or low in another area of development (e.g., health).

The fourth step in deriving the SEI's is to compute, for each school, the averages of the hard-to-change condition variables that characterize the environment within which the school has had to operate.

The fifth step is to get, again for each school, the average values of all the output measures for each of the three groups of pupils as identified by the input measures.

When all these data are in hand it becomes possible, by means of a series of regression analyses, to compute the SEI's that form the profile of each school.

A rough impression of how this process works may be obtained from an examination of the chart in Figure 1, which was developed from reading test scores obtained on pupils in 91 schools.[3] The measures of input in reading

---

[2] The problem presented by the movement of pupils from school to school is one that can be handled in various ways at the district level, but not at the level of the individual school. Therefore, it will not be discussed here. Under the present conception of staff accountability, it appears reasonable to assume that the only *fair* index of school effectiveness is one that rests on input-output data obtained only on those pupils with whom the school staff has been in *continuous* contact over a specified period of months or years.

[3] It should be noted that this example does not include the important refinement that calls for assessing the school's effectiveness for each of three levels of pupil input in reading.

were taken at the beginning of grade four, and the measures of output at the end of grade six. The numbers along the horizontal axis of the chart summarize the level of grade four reading input and hard-to-change conditions with which each school has had to contend. This summarization is expressed in terms of the grade six predicted average reading levels as determined by the regression analysis.

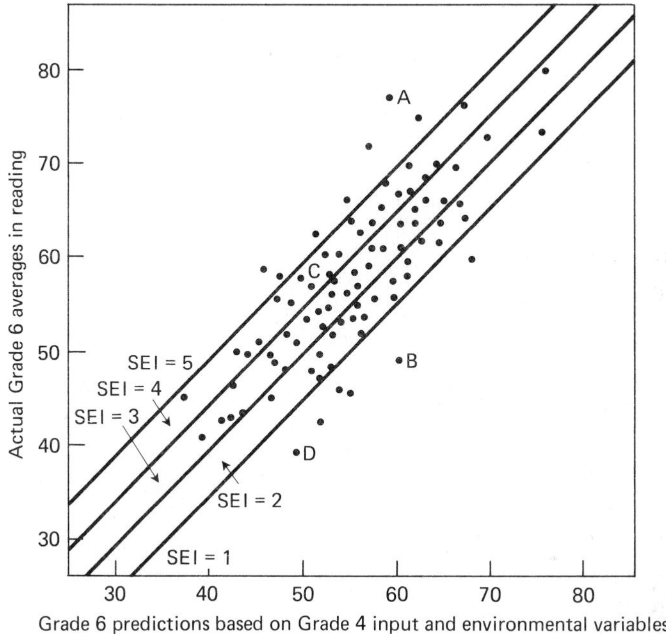

Fig. 1. Illustration of method of deriving school effectiveness indices in the teaching of reading.

The numbers along the vertical axis show the *actual* average reading levels for each school at the end of grade six. For each school, the discrepancy between its *predicted* grade six reading level and its *actual* grade six average reading level is used as the measure of the effectiveness with which it has been teaching reading over the three-year period. It is the discrepancy between predicted and actual level of performance that is used to determine the SEI in reading for any school. In this case the SEI's have been assigned arbitrary values ranging from a low of one to a high of five.

Consider the two schools A and B. They both have predicted grade six reading averages of about 60. This indicates that they can be deemed to have been operating in situations that are equivalent in respect to their levels of input at grade four and the hard-to-change conditions that have obtained over the three-year period during which their pupils have gone from grades four through six.

The actual reading output levels at grade six for schools A and B are considerably different. A's actual level is about 73; B's actual level is about 48. As a consequence, school A gets an effectiveness index for the teaching of reading of five, while school B gets an effectiveness index of only one.

Schools C and D present a similar picture, but at a lower level of pupil input and hard-to-change conditions. Both have predicted averages of about 50, but C's actual average is about 56, while D's is only 38. Therefore C gets an SEI of four, and D gets an SEI of only one.

From these two pairs of illustrations, it should be noted that the proposed method of computing school effectiveness indices *automatically* adjusts for the differing circumstances in which schools must operate. This feature of the index is a sine qua non of any system by which school staffs are to be held professionally accountable.

Uses of the SEI

It was suggested at the beginning of this paper that one of the general principles underlying the concept of professional accountability is that the staff of a school is to be held responsible for *using* its knowledge of where the school stands with respect to the intellectual and personal-social development of its pupils. This is to say that it is not sufficient for a school to "render an accounting" of its educational effectiveness. If the accounting is to have any educational payoff for the pupils whom the school is supposed to serve, the indices should point to some specific corrective actions designed to increase the school's effectiveness.

Many of such actions will perforce be outside the scope of the school itself, and responsibility for taking them must rest with the central administration. In most cases, however, a considerable number of such corrective actions should be well within the competence of the professional staff of the individual school. Responsibility for carrying them out can and should rest with that staff.

The function of school effectiveness indices in this connection is to indicate where a school staff might turn to find ways of improving its performance.

To illustrate how the SEI's might serve this purpose, let us speculate further about the relative positions of schools A and B in Figure 1. Since both schools show the same *predicted* output in reading for such pupils, it can be presumed that both schools are operating under equivalent advantages and handicaps in respect to the conditions that affect the reading ability of those pupils. Therefore, it is entirely legitimate to raise the questions: Why is school A doing so much better than school B in the teaching of reading? and What specifically is school A doing for its pupils that school B is not now doing, but presumably *could* be doing and *ought* to be doing to close the gap?

The reasons for the discrepancy between the two schools on this particular SEI are to be sought among the two sets of variables that did not enter into the derivation of the SEI's: namely, those variables that were designated "educational process" and those designated "easy-to-change surrounding conditions."

A systematic comparison of how the two schools stand with respect to these variables should provide the professional staff of school B with useful clues for actions that might be taken to increase its effectiveness in the teaching of reading.

The outcome of this exercise might turn up something like this:

1. School A conducts an intensive summer program in reading; school B does not.
2. School A has a tutorial program conducted by high school students for any pupil who wishes to improve his reading; school B has no such program.
3. School A conducts parent-teacher study groups to stimulate more reading in the home; school B has little contact of any kind with the parents of its pupils.

There is, of course, no absolute guarantee that if school B were to initiate such programs it would automatically raise its SEI in reading from one to five. The factors involved in the life and workings of a school are not all that certain and clear-cut. Nevertheless, there should be a plain obligation on the staff of school B to at least *try* the procedures that appear to be working for school A and to monitor such efforts over a sufficient period to see whether they are having the desired effects. This particularization of staff effort contains the essence of what must be involved in any attempt to guarantee the professional accountability of a school staff.

The approach to accountability through a system of SEI's, if it is well understood and accepted throughout the schools of the district, should provide a mechanism for stimulating directed professional efforts toward the continuous improvement of educational practice on many fronts in all the schools.

STEPHEN M. BARRO
Rand Corporation

An Approach to Developing Accountability Measures for the Public Schools

Progress in establishing accountability for results within school systems is likely to depend directly on success in developing two specific kinds of effectiveness information: (1) improved, more comprehensive pupil performance measurements; and (2) estimates of contributions to measured pupil performance by individual teachers, administrators, schools, and districts. As will be seen, the two have very different implications. The first calls primarily for expansion and refinement of what is now done in the measurement area. The second requires a kind of analysis that is both highly technical and new to school systems and poses a much greater challenge.

The need for more extensive pupil performance measurement is evident. If teachers, for example, are to be held responsible for what is learned by their pupils, then pupil performance must be measured at least yearly so that gains associated with each teacher can be identified. Also, if the overall effectiveness of educators and schools is to be assessed, measurement will have to be extended to many more dimensions of pupil performance than are covered by instruments in common use. This implies more comprehensive, more frequent testing than is standard practice in most school systems. In the longer run, it will probably require substantial efforts to develop and validate more powerful measurement instruments.

But no program of performance measurement alone, no matter how comprehensive or sophisticated, is sufficient to establish accountability. To do that, we must also be able to attribute results (performance gains) to sources. Only by knowing the contributions of individual professionals or schools would it be possible, for example, for a district to operate an incentive pay or promotion system; for community boards in a decentralized system to evaluate local schools and their staffs; or for parents, under a voucher system, to make informed

---

Excerpted from Stephen M. Barro, "An Approach to Developing Accountability Measures for the Public Schools," *Phi Delta Kappan* 52, no. 4 (1970): 196–205. Reprinted by permission.

decisions about schools for their children. To emphasize this point, from now on the term "accountability measures" will be used specifically to refer to estimates of contributions to pupil performance by individual agents in the educational process. These are described as "estimates" advisedly, because, unlike performance, which can be measured directly, *contributions* to performance cannot be measured directly but must be *inferred* from comparative analysis of different classrooms, schools, and districts. The analytical methods for determining individual contributions to pupil performance are the heart of the proposed accountability measurement system.

A PROPOSED APPROACH

In the following pages we describe a specific approach that could be followed by a school system interested in deriving accountability measures, as they have just been defined. First, a general rationale for the proposed approach is presented. Then the analytical methodology to be used is discussed in more detail.

For What Results Should Educators Be Held Responsible?

Ideally, a school system and its constituent parts, as appropriate, should be held responsible for performance in three areas: (1) selecting "correct" objectives and assigning them appropriate priorities, (2) achieving all the stated (or implicit) objectives, and (3) avoiding unintentional adverse effects on pupils. Realistically, much less can even be attempted. The first of the three areas falls entirely outside the realm of objective measurement and analysis, assessment of objectives being an intrinsically subjective, value-laden, and often highly political process. The other two areas can be dealt with in part, subject to the sometimes severe limitations to the current state of the art of educational measurement. The answer to the question posed above must inevitably be a compromise, and not necessarily a favorable one, between what is desirable and what can actually be done.

Any school system aims at affecting many dimensions of pupil performance. In principle, we would like to consider all of them—appropriately weighted—when we assess teacher, school, or district effectiveness. In practice, it is feasible to work with only a subset of educational outcomes, namely, those for which (a) objectives are well defined and (b) we have some ability to measure output. The dimensions of performance that meet these qualifications tend to fall into two groups: first, certain categories of cognitive skills, including reading and mathematics, for which standardized, validated tests are available; second, certain affective dimensions—socialization, attitudes toward the community, self-concept, and the like—for which we have such indicators or proxies as rates of absenteeism, dropout rates, and incidence of vandalism and delinquency. For practical purposes, these are the kinds of educational outcome measures that would be immediately available to a school system setting out today to develop an accountability system.

Because of the limited development of educational measurement, it seems more feasible to pursue this approach to accountability in the elementary grades than at higher levels, at least in the short run. Adequate instruments are available for the basic skill areas—especially reading—which are the targets of most efforts to improve educational quality at the elementary level. They are not generally available—and certainly not as widely used or accepted—for the subject areas taught in the secondary schools. Presumably, this is partly because measurement in those areas is inherently more difficult; it is partly, also, because there is much less agreement about the objectives of secondary education. Whatever the reason, establishing accountability for results at the secondary level is likely to be more difficult. Pending further progress in specifying objectives and measuring output, experiments with accountability measurement systems would probably be more fruitfully carried on in the elementary schools.

Fortunately, existing shortcomings in the measurement area can be overcome in time. Serious efforts to make accountability a reality should, themselves, spur progress in the measurement field. However, for the benefits of progress to be realized, the system must be "open"—not restricted to certain dimensions of performance. For this reason, the methodology described here has been designed to be in no way limiting with respect to the kinds of outcome measures that can be handled or the number of dimensions that can ultimately be included.

Who Should Be Accountable for What?

Once we have determined what kinds of pupil progress to measure, we can turn to the more difficult problem of determining how much teachers, principals, administrators, and others have contributed to the measured results. This is the key element in a methodology for accountability measurement.

The method proposed here rests on the following general principle: *Each participant in the educational process should be held responsible only for those educational outcomes that he can affect by his actions or decisions and only to the extent that he can affect them.* Teachers, for example, should not be deemed "ineffective" because of shortcomings in the curriculum or the way in which instruction is organized, assuming that those matters are determined at the school and district level and not by the individual teacher. The appropriate question is, "How well does the teacher perform, given the environment (possibly adverse) in which she must work and the constraints (possibly overly restrictive) imposed upon her?" Similarly, school principals and other administrators at the school level should be evaluated according to how well they perform within constraints established by the central administration.

The question then arises of how we know the extent to which teachers or administrators can affect outcomes by actions within their own spheres of responsibility. The answer is that we do not know *a priori;* we must find out from the performance data. This leads to a second principle: *The range over which a teacher, a school principal, or an administrator may be expected to affect outcomes is to be determined empirically from analysis of results obtained by all personnel working in comparable circumstances.* Several implications follow from this statement. First, it clearly establishes that the accountability measures will be relative, involving comparisons among educators at each level of the system. Second, it restricts the applicability of the methodology to systems large enough to have a wide range of professional competence at each level and enough observations to permit reliable estimation of the range of potential teacher and school effects.[1] Third, it foreshadows several characteristics of the statistical models needed to infer contributions to results. To bring out the meaning of these principles in more detail, we will explore them from the points of view of teachers, school administrators, and district administrators, respectively.

Classroom Teachers. We know that the educational results obtained in a particular classroom (e.g., pupils' scores on a standard reading test) are determined by many other things besides the skill and effort of the teacher. The analyses in the Coleman report (Coleman, 1966), other analyses of the Coleman survey data, and other statistical studies of the determinants of pupil achievement (Hanushek, 1968; Kiesling, 1969) show that a large fraction of variation in performance levels is accounted for by out-of-school variables, such as the pupils' socioeconomic status and home environment. Another large fraction is attributable to a so-called "peer group" effect; that is, it depends on characteristics of a pupil's classmates rather than on what takes place in the school. Of the fraction of the variation that *is* explained by school variables, only part can be attributed to teachers. Some portion must also be assigned to differences in resource availability at the classroom and school level and differences among schools in the quality of their management and support. Thus, the problem is to separate out the teacher effect from all the others.

To illustrate the implications for the design of an accountability system, consider the problem of comparing teachers who teach very different groups of children. For simplicity, suppose that there are two groups of pupils in a school system, each internally homogeneous, which we may call "middle-class white" and "poor minority." Assume that all nonteacher inputs associated with the schools are identical for the two groups. Then, based on general experience, we would probably expect the whole distribution of results to be higher for the former group than for the latter. In measuring gain in reading performance, we might well find, for example, that even the poorest teacher of middle-class white children obtains higher average gains in her class than the majority of teachers of poor minority children. Moreover, the ranges over which results vary in the two groups might be unequal.

If we have reason to believe that the teachers associated with the poor minority children are about as good, on the average, as those associated with the middle-class white children—that is, if they are drawn from the same manpower pool and assigned to schools and classrooms without bias—then it is apparent that both the difference in average performance of the two groups of pupils and

---

[1] This does not mean that accountability cannot be established in small school districts. It does mean that the analysis must take place in a broader context, such as a regional or statewide evaluation of performance, which may encompass many districts.

the difference in the range of performance must be taken into account in assessing each teacher's contribution. A teacher whose class registers gains, say, in the upper 10% of all poor minority classes should be considered as effective as one whose middle-class white group scores in the upper 10% for that category, even though the absolute performance gain in the latter case will probably be much greater.

This illustrates that accountability measures are relative in two senses. First, they are relative in that each teacher's contribution is evaluated by comparing it with the contributions made by other teachers in similar circumstances. In a large city or state school system, it can safely be assumed that the range of teacher capabilities covers the spectrum from poor to excellent. Therefore, the range of observed outcomes, after differences in circumstances have been allowed for, is likely to be representative of the range over which teacher quality can be expected to influence results, given the existing institutional framework. It may be objected that the range of outcomes presently observed understates the potential range of accomplishment because present classroom methods, curricula, teacher training programs, etc., are not optimal. This may be true and important, but it is not relevant in establishing teacher accountability because the authority to change those aspects of the system does not rest with the teacher.

Second, accountability measures are relative in that pupil characteristics and other nonteacher influences on pupil performance must be taken fully into account in measuring each teacher's contribution. Operationally, this means that statistical analyses will have to be conducted of the effects of such variables as ethnicity, socioeconomic status, and prior educational experience on a pupil's progress in a given classroom. Also, the effects of classroom or school variables other than teacher capabilities will have to be taken into account. Performance levels of the pupils assigned to different teachers can be compared only after measured performance has been adjusted for all of these variables. The statistical model for computing these adjustments is, therefore, the most important element in the accountability measurement system.

School Administrators. Parallel reasoning suggests that school administrators can be held accountable for relative levels of pupil performance in their schools to the extent that the outcomes are not attributable to pupil, teacher, or classroom characteristics or to school variables that they cannot control. The question is, having adjusted for differences in pupil and teacher inputs and having taken account of other characteristics of the schools, are there unexplained differences among schools that can be attributed to differences in the quality of school leadership and administration? Just as for teachers, accountability measures for school administrators are measures of relative pupil performance in a school after adjusting the data for differences in variables outside the administrators' control.

Consideration of the accountability problem at the school level draws attention to one difficulty with the concept of accountability measurement that may also, in some cases, be present at the classroom level. The difficulty is that although we would like to establish accountability for individual professionals, when two or more persons work together to perform an educational task there is no statistical way of separating their effects. This is easy to see at the school level. If a principal and two assistant principals administer a school, we may be able to evaluate their relative proficiency as a team, but since it is not likely that their respective administrative tasks would relate to different pupil performance measures there is no way of judging their individual contributions by analyzing educational outcomes. Similarly, if a classroom teacher works with a teaching assistant, there is no way, strictly speaking, to separate the contributions of the two. It is conventional in these situations to say that the senior person, who has supervisory authority, bears the responsibility for results. However, while this is administratively and perhaps even legally valid, it provides no solution to the problem of assessing the effort and skills of individuals. Therefore, there are definite limits, which must be kept in mind, to the capacity of a statistically based accountability system to aid in assessing individual proficiency.

District Administrators. Although the same approach applies, in principle, to comparisons among districts (or decentralized components of larger districts), there are problems that may limit its usefulness in establishing accountability at the district level. One, of course, is the problem that has just been alluded to. Even if it were possible to establish the existence of overall district effects, it would be impossible to isolate the contributions of the local district board, the district superintendent, and other members of the district staff. A second problem is that comparisons among districts can easily fail to take account of intangible community characteristics that may affect school performance. For example, such factors as community cohesion, political attitudes, and the existence of racial or other intergroup tensions could strongly influence the whole tone of education. It would be very difficult to separate effects of these factors from effects of direct, district-related variables in trying to assess overall district performance. Third, the concept of responsibility at the district level needs clarifying. In comparing schools, for example, it seems reasonable to adjust for differences in teacher characteristics on the grounds that school administrators should be evaluated according to how well they do, given the personnel assigned to them. However, at the district level, personnel selection itself is one of the functions for which administrators must be held accountable, as are resource allocation, program design, choice of curriculum, and other factors that appear as "givens" to the schools. In other words, in assessing comparative district performance, very little about districts can properly be considered as externally determined except, perhaps, the total level of available resources.[2] The appropriate policy, then, seems to be to include district identity as a variable in comparing schools and teachers so that net district effects, if any, will be taken into account. Districts themselves should be compared on a different basis, allowing only for differences in pupil characteristics, community variables, and overall constraints that are truly outside district control.

---

[2] In addition, of course, there are constraints imposed by state or federal authorities, but these are likely to be the same across districts.

A PROPOSED METHODOLOGY

The basic analytical problem in accountability measurement is to develop a technique for estimating the contributions to pupil performance of individual agents in the educational process. A statistical method that may be suitable for that purpose is described here. The basic technique is multiple regression analysis of the relationship between pupil performance and an array of pupil teacher, and school characteristics. However, the proposed method calls for two or three separate stages of analysis. The strategy is first to estimate the amount of performance variation that exists among classrooms after pupil characteristics have been taken into account, then, in subsequent stages, to attempt to attribute the interclassroom differences to teachers, other classroom variables, and school characteristics (See Hanushek, 1970). This methodology applies both to large school districts, within which it is suitable for estimating the relative effectiveness of individual teachers and schools in advancing pupil performance, and to state school systems, where it can be used, in addition, to obtain estimates of the relative effectiveness of districts. However, as noted above, there are problems that may limit its utility at the interdistrict level.

Pupil Performance Data

Since we are interested in estimating the contributions of individual teachers and schools, it is appropriate to use a "value-added" concept of output. That is, the appropriate pupil performance magnitudes to associate with a particular teacher are the *gains* in performance made by pupils while in her class. Ideally, the output data would be generated by a program of annual (or more frequent) performance measurement, which would automatically provide before and after measures for pupils at each grade level.

It is assumed that a number of dimensions of pupil performance will be measured, some by standardized tests and some by other indicators or proxy variables. Specific measurement instruments to be used and dimensions of performance to be measured would have to be determined by individual school systems in accordance with their educational objectives. No attempt will be made here to specify what items should be included.[3] The methodology is intended to apply to any dimension of performance that can be quantified at least on an ordinal scale. Therefore, within a very broad range, it is not affected by the choice of output measures by a potential user.

---

[3] Realistically, however, almost every school system will be likely to include reading achievement scores and other scores on standardized tests of cognitive skills among its output variables. Also, it will generally be desirable to include attendance or absenteeism as a variable, both because it may be a proxy for various attitudinal output variables and because it may be an important variable to use in explaining performance. Otherwise, there are innumerable possibilities for dealing with additional dimensions of cognitive and affective performance.

Data on Pupils, Teachers, Classrooms, and Schools

To conform with the model to be described below, the variables entering into the analysis are classified according to the following taxonomy:

1. Individual pupil characteristics (ethnicity, socioeconomic status, home, family, and neighborhood characteristics, age, prior performance, etc.).
2. Teacher and classroom characteristics.
   a. Group characteristics of the pupils (ethnic and socioeconomic composition, distribution of prior performance levels, etc., within the classroom).
   b. Teacher characteristics (age, training, experience, ability and personality measures if available, ethnic and socioeconomic background, etc.).
   c. Other classroom characteristics (measures of resource availability: class size, amount of instructional support, amount of materials, condition of physical facilities, etc.).
3. School characteristics.
   a. Group characteristics of the pupils (same as 2a, but based on the pupil population of the whole school).
   b. Staff characteristics (averages of characteristics in 2b for the school as a whole, turnover and transfer rates; characteristics of administrators—same as 2b).
   c. Other school characteristics (measures of resource availability: age and condition of building, availability of facilities, amount of administrative and support staff, etc.).

No attempt will be made to specify precisely what items should be collected under each of the above headings. Determination of the actual set of variables to be used in a school system would have to follow preliminary experimentation, examination of existing data, and an investigation of the feasibility, difficulty, and cost of obtaining various kinds of information.

Steps in the Analysis

The first step is to determine how different pupil performance in each classroom at a given grade level is from mean performance in all classrooms, *after* differences in individual pupil characteristics have been allowed for. The procedure consists of performing a multiple regression analysis with gain in pupil performance as the dependent variable. The independent variables would include (a) the individual pupil characteristics (category 1 of the taxonomy), and (b) a set of "dummy" variables, or identifiers, one for each classroom in the sample. The latter would permit direct estimation of the degree to which pupil performance in each classroom differs from pupil performance in the average classroom. Thus, the product of the first stage of the analysis would be a set of estimates of individual classroom effects, each of which represents the combined effect on pupil performance in a classroom of all the classroom and school variables included in categories 2 and 3 of the taxonomy. At the same time, the procedure would automatically provide measures of the accuracy with which each classroom effect has been estimated. Therefore, it would be possible to say whether average performance gains in a particular classroom are significantly higher or lower than would be expected in a "typical" classroom or not significantly different from the mean.

Heuristically, this procedure compares performance gains by pupils in a classroom with gains that comparable pupils would be likely to achieve in a hypothetical "average" classroom of the system. This can be thought of as comparison of class performance gains against a norm, except that there is, in effect, a particular norm for each classroom based on its unique set of pupil characteristics. It may also be feasible to carry out the same analysis for specific subgroups of pupils in each class so as to determine, for example, whether there are different classroom effects for children from different ethnic or socioeconomic groups.

Estimation of Teacher Contributions. The second stage of the analysis has two purposes: (1) to separate the effects of the teacher from effects of nonteacher factors that vary among classrooms; and (2) to determine the extent to which pupil performance can be related to specific, measurable teacher attributes. Again, the method to be used is regression analysis, but in this case with a sample of classroom observations rather than individual pupil observations. The dependent variable is now the classroom effect estimated in stage one. The independent variables are the teacher-classroom characteristics and "dummy" variables distinguishing the individual schools.

Two kinds of information can be obtained from the resulting equations. First, it is possible to find out what fraction of the variation in performance gains among classrooms is accounted for by nonteacher characteristics, including group characteristics of the pupils and measures of resource availability in the classroom. The remaining interclassroom differences provide upper-bound estimates of the effects that can be attributed to teachers. If there is sufficient confidence that the important nonteacher variables have been taken into account, then these estimates provide the best teacher accountability measures. They encompass the effects of both measured and unmeasured teacher characteristics on teacher performance. However, there is some danger that such measures also include effects of group and classroom characteristics that were inadvertently neglected in the analysis and that are not properly attributable to teachers. This problem is referred to again below.

Second, we can find out the extent to which differences among classrooms are explained by measured teacher characteristics. Ideally, of course, we would like to be able to attribute the whole "teacher portion" of performance variation to specific teacher attributes and, having done so, we would be much more confident about our overall estimates of teacher effectiveness. But experience to date with achievement determinant studies has shown that the more readily available teacher characteristics—age, training, experience, and the like—account for only a small fraction of the observed variance. It has been shown that more of the variation can be accounted for when a measure of teacher verbal ability is included (Hanushek, 1970). Still more, presumably, could be accounted for if a greater variety of teacher ability and personality measurements were available. At present, however, knowledge of what teacher characteristics influence pupil performance is incomplete and satisfactory instruments exist for measuring only a limited range of teacher-related variables. This means that with an accountability information system based on current knowledge, the excluded teacher characteristics could be at least as important as those included in determining teacher effectiveness. For the time being, then, the interclassroom variation in results that remains after nonteacher effects have been allowed for probably provides the most useful accountability measures, though the danger of bias due to failure to include all relevant nonteacher characteristics must be recognized.

The principal use of these estimates would be in assessing the relative effectiveness of individual teachers in contributing to gains in pupil performance. More precisely, it would be possible to determine whether each teacher's estimated contribution is significantly greater or significantly smaller than that of the average teacher. At least initially, until there is strong confirmation of the validity of the procedure, a rather stringent significance criterion should be used in making these judgments and no attempt should be made to use the results to develop finer gradations of teacher proficiency.

The analysis will also make it possible to determine the extent to which measured teacher characteristics are significantly correlated with teacher effectiveness. Potentially, such information could have important policy implications and impacts on school management, resource allocation, and personnel practices.

References

Center for the Study of Public Policy. *Education Vouchers: A Preliminary Report on Financing Education by Payments to Parents.* Cambridge, Mass.: Center for the Study of Public Policy, March 1970.

Coleman, J. S. *et al. Equality of Educational Opportunity.* Washington, D.C.: Office of Education, 1966.

Hanushek, E. A. "The Education of Negroes and Whites." Ph.D. dissertation, M.I.T., 1968.

Hanushek, E. A. *The Value of Teachers in Teaching.* Santa Monica: The Rand Corporation, 1970.

Kiesling, H. J. *The Relationship of School Inputs to Public School Performance in New York State.* Santa Monica: The Rand Corporation, 1969.

Chapter 9

Selected Readings: Using Appraisal Procedures and Techniques

Self-evaluative techniques, such as microteaching, cooperative goal setting, pupil evaluation of teaching, and judgment analysis, utilize to varying degrees the teacher's own expertise to determine appraisal criteria. By allowing teachers to actively participate in the appraisal system, these techniques make the data feedback process discussed in Chapter 4 less threatening and more meaningful to the teacher. This introduction describes several self-evaluative techniques often used to enhance other indices of teacher effectiveness, particularly pupil gain.

MICROTEACHING

Microteaching, as the term implies, is real teaching reduced in time and number of students. Developed in 1963 at Stanford University, the technique has five aims: (1) to provide a realistic teaching situation; (2) to minimize risks for both teachers and students; (3) to apply existing behavioral theories by providing, for example, numerous, distributed practice sessions, prompt feedback of results, and immediate opportunity to make corrections; (4) to present a wide range of teaching experiences; and (5) to save time and resources in teaching and appraising specific skills.

A typical microteaching sequence includes the following steps. A specific teaching skill, such as the ability to ask higher-order cognitive questions, is identified. The teacher then creates a short lesson of about five to twenty minutes in his or her area of specialization, with a very specific objective, and teaches it to a small number of pupils. The lesson is observed by a supervisor who may make a videotape recording to document the teacher's use of higher-order questioning—the focus skill of this particular session. Immediately after the lesson, the teacher and supervisor review the videotape together. The teacher then has an opportunity to reteach the lesson, followed by another meeting between teacher and supervisor.

Microteaching has become an important self-evaluative tool since the advent of the minicourse, a procedure that provides instruction in a specific teaching skill. The minicourse employs microteaching by showing instructional model films on a specific teaching skill, and then asking the teacher to microteach and reteach a lesson. This lesson is videotaped and played back to the teacher, who then evaluates his or her own performance and determines the degree to which the "taught" skill has been acquired. Minicourses have been used in the past to teach skills such as prompting, redirecting the same question to several pupils, framing questions that require the pupil to give longer responses or use higher cognitive processes, seeking further clarification or pupil insight, and reducing or eliminating undesirable teaching behaviors (Borg, 1972). With the development of related minicourses by the Far West Laboratory for Educational Research and Development, the microteaching-minicourse combination offers a particularly effective self-evaluative tool for the appraisal and improvement of teaching.

COOPERATIVE GOAL-SETTING

Cooperative goal-setting, another self-evaluative appraisal technique, assumes that the teaching task in any school is best defined in cooperation with the teacher. While some general aspects of the teaching task, such as broad goals and aims, can be established in group sessions, a basic understanding of the specific teaching assignment is best achieved through a conference between the teacher and the administrator to whom he or she is directly responsible. This conference, or goal-setting session, takes place before or at the beginning of an academic term. After pledging his or her support, the administrator joins the teacher in planning the acquisition of specific skills and behaviors. The administrator elicits the teacher's major goals for the year, summarizes them, and lists them on a goal-setting chart.

Opposite the listed goals and under the heading "Methods, Equipment, Facilities, and Special Assistance," the administrator enters those supportive elements the teacher believes will be necessary for the implementation of his or her goals. The teacher is asked to plan units of instruction covering at least two weeks' time, and is encouraged to view the teaching task as a whole rather than a day-to-day or week-to-week series of learning assignments. The teacher is assured that the appraisal of teaching performance will be made according to the successful acquisition of *his or her* goals over the entire year and that individual visits to the classroom will not be used as the basis of summative evaluations.

Throughout the term or year, evaluation conferences between teacher and administrator are periodically scheduled, and entries are made under the heading "Achieved and Unachieved Goals." Unachieved goals are either restated with the aim that continued effort will be made toward their realization, or, in some cases, deleted and replaced with more immediate, attainable goals. For example, some product (consequence) goals may be replaced with more attainable process goals, if the former have not been achieved. Each of these conferences helps the teacher and administrator plan for the next goal-setting period. Teaching methodology, classroom equipment, instructional materials, and a host of other factors can be discussed openly, and changes can be recommended. New objectives, and original objectives yet to be achieved, become the focus of the next appraisal period.

PUPIL APPRAISAL OF TEACHING

The third self-evaluative technique—pupil appraisal of teaching—is often maligned as a source of objective data concerning teacher effectiveness. Pupil perceptions of the teacher's success in the classroom, however, have proved to be reasonably stable and accurate. Though pupils cannot give credible information regarding issues with which they are unfamiliar or unconcerned, they can, and frequently do, provide accurate data in regard to the following categories (Dalton, 1971).

1. Teacher's general knowledge of subject matter.
2. Ability to explain clearly.
3. Fairness in dealing with students.
4. Ability to maintain good discipline.
5. Sympathetic understanding.
6. Amount students are learning.
7. Ability to make instruction lively and interesting.
8. Ability to get things done in an efficient and businesslike manner.
9. The importance of the pupils to the teacher.
10. Overall teaching ability.

JUDGMENT ANALYSIS

Judgment analysis (Houston and Boulding, 1974) is a relatively new technique, which has thus far been used in only a few settings. Its success, however, has been sufficient to warrant its discussion here. Judgment analysis allows the teacher to determine the criteria by which he or she will be appraised. Teachers within a school or school district rate a large number of hypothetical profiles containing various dimensions of teaching behavior. These profiles list behaviors chosen by the school district or the teachers themselves, perhaps in cooperative goal-setting sessions.

Each of the behavioral dimensions selected is randomly rated as outstanding (O), above average (A), satisfactory (S), or unsatisfactory (U), and then assigned to an individual profile. Teachers are asked to review and rank each of the profiles, thereby indicating the importance they ascribe to different dimensions of teacher behavior. These rankings are used to attain consensus across the school or school district in regard to the most desirable profiles. The top-ranked profiles represent "good teaching" while the bottom-ranked profiles exemplify "poor teaching." The accompanying configuration of profiles illustrates the procedure by which ratings and priorities are established.

Behaviors, skills, or competencies randomly rated	*Hypothetical teacher profiles to be ranked*									
	1	2	3	4	5	6	7	8	9	10 . . .
1	O	A	A	S	U	U	U	S	A	O
2	A	S	U	S	A	A	U	S	O	U
3	S	U	O	S	S	U	U	O	A	A
4	U	A	S	O	U	A	A	U	S	S
.										
.										
.										

SELF-EVALUATION IN RELATION TO PUPIL GAIN

The reader is asked to consider the four techniques described above in combination with indices of pupil gain. Cooperative goal-setting, judgment analysis, microteaching, pupil evaluation of teaching, and pupil achievement can function as interlocking elements within a single appraisal system. While cooperative goal setting and judgment analysis permit teachers to participate in selecting behaviors to be evaluated, microteaching helps them to learn these behaviors. In turn, student appraisals of teaching and pupil gain scores serve as indices of the effectiveness of these procedures.

The first reading in this chapter reviews eight commonly used appraisal techniques and procedures. The authors, McNeil and Popham, present evidence to establish the effectiveness of each of the procedures described. This evidence discourages the use of student, self-, and administrator and peer ratings, the first three procedures discussed by McNeil and Popham. Research shows little relationship between these criteria of effectiveness and pupil achievement, leading the authors to suggest that these rating schemes are often used more to communicate emotion than to describe teacher effectiveness. While general, diffuse feelings about the quality of instruction may be provided the teacher, these rating schemes are not likely to yield specific information about discrete teaching behaviors. The broad variables appearing on rating scales are *assumed* to enable the acquisition of immediate and intermediate process behaviors which, in turn, are *assumed* to relate to pupil outcome. McNeil and Popham point out that this lengthy and indirect sequence necessarily suffers from a lack of documentation.

It is important to note that while McNeil and Popham's discussion of rating procedures is somewhat pessimistic, their pessimism hinges on the use of these techniques as *sole* indicators of teaching effectiveness. These techniques, as well as the self-evaluative tools noted above, are most appropriately used to confirm and/or broaden the information obtained from other appraisal sources. Rating and self-evaluative schemes, then, may serve functions ignored by McNeil and Popham, who concentrate exclusively on finding a relationship between data from these devices and pupil achievement.

The second selection, by Merritt, introduces the concept of a teacher assessment center, a centrally located, performance-based laboratory where specific teaching skills could be observed and appraised for the purpose of certifying both preservice and inservice teachers within a region. These centers would, according to Merritt, (1) offer the preservice teacher specific behavioral experiences related to certification, (2) provide the inservice teacher opportunities to identify strengths and weaknesses, (3) undertake record preparation indicating individual prformance, and (4) act as an assessment service for both school districts and teachers.

Merritt's teaching-center concept has two general objectives: to implement certification procedures mandated by the adoption of performance-based criteria, and to plan and assess the inservice teacher's professional development program. Though such an assessment center might be unworkable for most inservice teachers, it would probably be appropriate for the evaluation of preservice and nontenured inservice teachers and, in this respect, offer a procedure far less subjective and arbitrary than that currently used by many teacher certification agencies.

In the third article, Berliner and Tikunoff describe the ethnographic approach to the observation of teaching. Ethnography is a process by which sensitive observers view and record the qualitative aspects of the classroom. This process has much in common with the humanistic, experiential, phenomenological, clinical, and case-study approaches often employed in other disciplines.

The heart of ethnography is an open-ended protocol which is completed by trained observers. This protocol is used to record the ongoing stream of interactive, behavioral events in the classroom. For example, a typical ethnographic protocol might contain the following episode within a much longer sequence of classroom events:

> As class started, John asked if he could read a story he had written the day before. Teacher gave him permission and he came to the front of the room. John began to read the story in a very low voice and when he had been reading for about thirty seconds, Sharon, who was sitting in a seat at the back of the room spoke up and asked John to read louder. At this point John tore up the pages he was reading and went back to his seat. Teacher seemed surprised but continued with class as usual.

Implicit in ethnographic records is the assumption that classroom behavior cannot be reduced to a single event since it is multivariate in nature, thus requiring continuous recording of the interaction between teacher and pupil.

The inclusion of the Berliner and Tikunoff selection in this volume serves two purposes. First, it presents the ethnographic procedure as an appraisal technique, which can be used alone or in conjunction with self-evaluative tools, systematic observations, or pupil indices of teacher effectiveness. Second, it describes the use of ethnography in identifying important qualitative variables that can eventually be quantified and related to pupil affective and cognitive outcomes. Berliner and Tikunoff identify sixty-one behavioral dimensions gleaned from ethnographic protocols in the California Beginning Teacher Evaluation Study—variables that may now be employed as quantitative indices of teacher process. They provide data indicating the degree to which these sixty-one variables have discriminated between teachers previously identified as "less effective" and "more effective." Ethnographic records uniquely capture the multivariate world of the classroom, thereby broadening the range of measures typically employed in appraisals of teaching.

The final three selections in this cnapter present technical discussions of two related procedures—multiple matrix sampling and domain-referenced testing —used to measure pupil gain in the product stage of appraisal. These concepts focus upon pupil achievement as an index of teacher effectiveness and, therefore, provide a set of procedures that differ from, but complement, the self-evaluative and ethnographic approaches described above. The following selections are arranged so that the reader is introduced first to the concept of multiple matrix sampling, then to domain-referenced testing, and finally to the application of both techniques in two Minnesota schools districts. Though these selections focus specifically on methods for measuring pupil outcome, the procedures described should be viewed in the larger context of the entire appraisal process, as two in a number of varied techniques for measuring teacher performance.

Multiple matrix sampling is based on the premise that effectiveness in teaching is best demonstrated by changes in the level of student achievement attributable to the teacher's performance. It is related to the measurement of consequence (pupil) competencies (Chapter 1), which occurs during the product stage of appraisal (Chapter 2). Multiple matrix sampling is also related to domain-referenced testing: the former refers to the process of dividing domains of behavior into a given number of subtests and assigning each subtest to a given number of students, with different students taking different subtests; the latter involves the process of generating test items according to rules that specify the common characteristics of items in given instructional domains.

When pupil achievement is used, either alone or in conjunction with other evaluative procedures, to appraise large numbers of teachers, multiple matrix sampling becomes particularly relevant. The concept rests in part on the assumption that, while it may be important to determine the performance of individual teachers, it is relatively *unimportant* to diagnose the achievement level of *each* student. Instead, different content items can be randomly arranged into different subtests and the subtests assigned to different groups of pupils.

Shoemaker illustrates this procedure, emphasizing its three main advantages: (1) it requires less testing time, since each student tested responds to only a portion of the items; (2) it provides a more comprehensive assessment of group performance by employing a large number of items; and (3) it yields estimates of pupil performance superior to those obtained through other testing procedures collecting the same amount of data.

The rules by which to construct test items prior to their assignment to individual subtests via multiple matrix sampling are discussed by Baker in the next selection. These rules insure that a large number of test items will be generated according to given specifications and randomly assigned to create comparable subtests representing a given domain. A domain consists of a subset of knowledge, skills, understandings, or attitudes, accompanied by a description of the content the pupil is expected to acquire and the way in which he or she is expected to demonstrate such acquisition. Domains focus on content to which the learner is to apply his or her skill. Thus, the central problem in specifying domains is defining rules or limits to insure that each test item generated represents the precise content area the teacher has presented to the learner.

In the final selection, Sension and Rabehl present practical applications of multiple matrix sampling and domain-referenced testing. Integrating the two techniques into a single procedure, they illustrate the functioning of these concepts in teacher appraisal at the school-district level. Their examples use multiple matrix sampling and domain-referenced testing to identify competencies of students across 134 domain skill areas. The authors illustrate how these data are then fed back to the school district to answer practical questions concerning curricular and training priorities.

References

Borg, W. R. "The Minicourse as a Vehicle for Changing Teacher Behavior: A Three-Year Follow-Up." *Journal of Educational Psychology* **63**, no. 6 (1972): 572–579.

Dalton, E. L. "Pupil Selection of Teachers." *Educational Leadership* **28**, no. 5 (1971): 476–479.

Houston, S. R., and J. R. Boulding, Jr. "Capturing Faculty Teaching Effectiveness Policies with Judgment Analysis." *California Journal of Educational Research* **25**, no. 3 (1974): 134–139.

JOHN D. McNEIL and
W. JAMES POPHAM
University of California at Los Angeles

Some Commonly Used Appraisal Techniques and Procedures

A caveat introduces this discussion. Any single criterion of effectiveness is confounded by a number of factors. One factor stems from who is doing the measuring; a second is the kind and quality of instrument used; a third is faithfulness in applying the instrument as its designer intended; and a fourth is the purpose for applying the criterion—how the data are to be used.

STUDENT RATINGS

The use of student ratings of instructors is growing, particularly at the college level. Increasingly colleges and universities are introducing policy requiring student evaluations of professors before they can be promoted. These evaluations, which may carry equal weight with faculty committee evaluations, range from formal written documents to conversations with department chairmen. The most common method employed in student ratings is the opinionnaire. Samples of these forms appear in publications such as those by Bannister, Sutherland, and Brown (1961), Fitch (1965), Orange Coast Junior College (1968), Overturf (1966), Rayder (1968), Schmidt (1968). Most forms ask the student simply to rate his instructor on various attributes. Open-ended questions and opportunity for making suggestions are sometimes provided.

The validity of student ratings is a problem. Considerable halo effect is found when students rate their teachers on several traits. As expressions of feeling, student ratings unquestionably have validity. They can be useful indicators that learners have or do not have favorable predispositions to teacher and the course. As one wag observed, "The purpose of teacher evaluations is not so much to give knowledge as to communicate emotion." In their classic review

Excerpted from John D. McNeil and W. James Popham, "The Assessment of Teacher Competence," in *Second Handbook of Research on Teaching,* ed. R. M. Travers (Chicago: Rand McNally, 1973), pp. 230–236. Reprinted by permission.

of quantitative studies of the effective instructor, Morsh and Wilder (1954) found evidence that if the instructor teaches for the bright students, he will be approved by them and there will be a positive correlation between ratings and grades; if he teaches for the weaker students, he will be disapproved by the bright students and a negative coefficient will be obtained. More recent research suggests that the student's sex, age and grade-point average, and the grade received from the instructor have little relationship to student ratings (Rayder, 1968). In an especially well-designed study, Davidoff provided strong evidence leading to the conclusion that student opinion of teacher behavior is very stable over time and that there is no consistent relationship between student opinion of teacher behavior and student gain (Davidoff, 1970). Contrary findings presented in a paper by Fortune (1966) are interpreted by Davidoff in terms of possible confounding of ratings by pupils with their perceptions of how well they achieved.

The many uses of student ratings—instructional improvement, teacher assessment, descriptions of teacher practice—make this measure a fruitful one. When one desires day-to-day observation of the teacher's behavior without the presence of outside observers, the use of student accomplices is an answer. Reliability of student observations can increase by having students focus on discrete observable behavior.

SELF-RATINGS

We would like teachers to be students of teaching, systematically assessing and revising their own teaching behavior. Theoretically, persons want to evaluate themselves in order to obtain an accurate picture of their own abilities (Festinger, 1954), but there are only a few studies indicating that some teachers are self-directing in their learning and expend effort in judging their behavior on the basis of the consequences of their teaching as revealed by the actions of pupils (Weiner & Kukla, 1970). Not having received training on how to focus on relevant aspects of their work, most teachers tend to criticize superficialities—personal mannerisms, appearance, voice and use of materials. Most teachers require orders "to keep them honest" and help them with their instructional problems. An interesting hypothesis is that teachers are not likely to change their performance unless they themselves see a discrepancy between what they want to achieve and what they are actually achieving. It has not been demonstrated, however, that the teacher can better his results with pupils by privately viewing himself via video-taped lessons. This is true even if these lessons are accompanied by data of pupil performance and guide sheets for self-appraisal (Allen, McDonald, & Orme, 1966, pp. 1–28; Orange Unified School District, 1968; Waimon & Ramseyer, 1970). A summary of results from studies of the effects of self-viewing, or video tape or film is reported in the work of Salomon and McDonald (1970). These authors also presented findings about the attitudinal changes and information selections of teachers when faced with their own recorded teaching performance. When no model of "good teaching" was presented, satisfaction with one's own performance determined what was noticed on the screen, how it was evaluated, and any attitudinal change. The investigators concluded that self-viewing will not produce any desirable attitudinal and behavioral changes unless it provides information about the amount of departure from a desired standard which has been accepted as a standard by the viewer.

There is a tendency for instructors to overrate themselves and there are negligible relationships of self-assessment with other criteria such as student ratings and measures of student gain.

ADMINISTRATOR AND PEER RATINGS

Principals and supervisors sometimes use rating scales as a tool for measuring teaching effectiveness. It is not uncommon to find such vaguely worded items on these scales as the following under the heading *teaching techniques:* planning and organizing appropriately, methods and instructional skills, classroom control, awareness of individual needs, concern for students and motivation. The compounding of instruction with political and other considerations is recognizable in instruments that call for evaluating the teacher on the basis of his staff relations, professional improvement, ethics, professional attitude, loyalty to the school, cooperation, enthusiasm for teaching, inservice activities, initiative and community activity.

Halo, lack of operational definitions, failure to control for sampling of teacher behavior, effect of observer on teacher performance—all such limitations make rating scales of doubtful worth in the hands of administrators, supervisors and peers.

CLASSROOM ENVIRONMENT

In their search for correlates of effective teaching, some investigators have turned to analyzing aspects of the classroom itself. They reason that environment is linked to pupil achievement since pupils interact with elements other than the teacher in the classroom, yet the teacher may manipulate many of these elements. Thus, it is argued, a fair and relevant criterion of teacher effectiveness is the manipulation of environmental elements in the classroom. By way of illustration, there is an investigation reported by Anthony (1968), who searched the literature to find pupil behavior considered relevant for academic achievement. She then tried to find classroom characteristics which might be capable of influencing these behaviors. Subsequently, Anthony collected data on environmental factors (including academic adornments and concrete objects used by teachers and pupils) in 21 fifth-grade classrooms and found an association between environment and classroom average achievement.

We cannot generalize much from this single study, especially since there were no demonstrated causal relations between classroom characteristics and achievement. One wonders, too, about which characteristics might be associated with particular outcomes and given learners. Nevertheless, Anthony has provided a more valid definition of classroom environment than is usually found on rating scales and check lists. At least there is a logical consistency between her environmental factors and achievement sought. Too typically, classroom environment is viewed as an end—teacher's awareness of physical environment, care of property, management of pupils, teaching techniques, and materials. The relation of the environment to more remote consequences is not questioned.

SYSTEMATIC OBSERVATIONS

Systematic observations are most beneficial for recording and analyzing the teaching act—not judging it. Data from systematic observations are necessary for designing alternative teaching tactics and for suggesting instructional objectives previously overlooked. Effective teaching cannot be proven by the presence or absence of any instructional variable—even those with high probabilities for effecting change, such as the teacher's provision of opportunities for learners to practice the desired behavior, giving knowledge of results to pupils, using reinforcers in accordance with a theory for shaping behavior and presenting information in a logical sequence. Warranted judgment of teaching competence rests upon information about how pupils are different as a result of instruction.

PERSONAL ATTRIBUTES

It appears that lack of success in predicting teacher effectiveness is due to the fact that decision-makers have tried to predict an unstable criterion variable from an illogical predictor. Without agreement on the specific outcomes for learners it is difficult to see how personality factors, course work and letters of recommendation could be expected to predict a teacher's success with pupils. Grooming, emotional stability, health, use of English, punctuality, humor, tact, poise, friendliness, vitality, and acceptance of criticism are largely in the eyes of the beholder and, therefore, may predict retention in a teaching position (as contrasted with instructional effectiveness) if the one making the prediction is the same as the one who will later assess the teacher for retention purposes. Perhaps it is true that assessment of a teacher by predictive criteria tells more about the assessor than the teacher.

Further items often used to assess personal characteristics are seldom adequately defined and at times are not consistent with each other. Dress has been and increasingly is a matter of personal preference; except for extreme cases, emotional stability is something even psychologists have difficulty agreeing on; the factor of initiative seems to contradict the predisposition to accept regulations. Although ratings of personal attributes are not sufficient for evaluative purposes, they are popular. In a recent description of the nature of teacher evaluation throughout the nation, Ingils analyzed samples of teacher evaluation programs from 70 school districts in 38 states (Ingils, 1970). His analysis revealed a commonality of procedure and purpose. The common purposes were:

1) to improve the quality of instruction, 2) to assist the teacher in identifying areas that need improvement, and 3) to protect the competent teacher and eliminate the incompetent. Procedures for achieving these purposes were chiefly through ratings of teachers in the general categories of professional attitudes, teaching techniques and personal characteristics.

CONTRACT PLANS USING STUDENT GAIN

A recently employed alternative for assessing teacher competence involves the use of contract plans which are based on student gain. One recommended contract plan rests on the premise that the ends of instruction must be agreed upon before teacher competency can be assessed. The essence of this technique involves the development of a carefully selected set of objectives for the pupil. Supervisors and teachers agree in advance what they will accept as evidence that the teacher has been successful in changing the skills, competencies or attitudes of his students. An agreement is drawn up before the teacher instructs and is designed to counter the prevailing practice of trying to make an ex post facto judgment about the desirability of ends. Subsequently, evidence is collected to see how well the learners achieved the stated objectives as well as whether unintended outcomes have emerged. The plan need not exclude the use of analytical schemes in the observation of instruction but does relegate their use as aids in guiding one while making a descriptive record of the teaching act and in suggesting alternative teaching procedures. An excellent source of ways in which teachers and others can participate in the analysis of instruction is *Clinical Supervision* by Goldhammer (1969). On the recommended contract plan, teacher competency is judged in terms of the results the teacher gets with learners, not by the procedures he is following in the classroom. Only those methods which are found to be directly related to the attainment of desired outcomes are judged effective. Promising findings from research can, of course, be considered by the teacher in generating alternative teaching tactics. Contracts are prepared for varying periods of time—a single day's lesson, a semester plan, a year of instruction. This contract system demands that data by which to judge more clearly what the instruction has done to those who have been subjected to it be supplied, and, when coupled with instructional analyses, ought to enable a teacher to revise and better in some respect the procedures employed in previous work.

One district plan, for example, has teachers setting objectives for end-of-quarter instruction, objectives for which the teacher is held accountable. Results are reported to the administrator as a factor to be weighted in evaluating the teacher. Simultaneously during the quarter the teacher sets objectives for single lessons which are observed by peers who make systematic observations and help the teacher devise alternative teaching tactics when the results signal instructional deficiencies. The results from these short-term contracts with peers are not reported to the administration because the emphasis is on instructional improvement, not accountability. Personnel in the district believe that when the purpose is improvement a teacher should be encouraged to reveal his weaknesses—to try to reach objectives about which he is most doubtful. An underlying assumption is that participation in improvement sessions focuses upon producing changes in learners which will increase the probability of the teacher having success in reaching the longer-term objectives for which he is accountable.

Options in the system are many. Peers can report to the administrator the number of times teachers succeed or fail with certain learners when teaching to specific kinds of objectives, thereby shifting the emphasis from improvement to accountability. Also the system permits collecting evidence for (a) unplanned effects of instruction as well as planned, and (b) holding the teacher accountable for some objectives, but not for those of a high risk nature, that is, those which are desirable but likely to be unattainable.

Detailed descriptions of the previously mentioned contract system appear in a number of sources (Cohen, 1967; McNeil, 1971). The effects upon teachers and pupils of using the system with both student teachers and experienced teachers have been reported (McNeil, 1967; Moffett, 1967; Nwana, 1968; Smithman, 1970).

The strength of this particular contract plan is that it allows the individual teacher to establish outcomes and standards that are deemed most appropriate for a particular teaching situation. Prior learning of pupils, intelligence, dynamics of the classroom, etc., can be taken into account in setting expectations for which one is to be accountable. Instead of comparing teachers on the basis of normative criteria, for example, standardized tests, this contract plan permits the teacher to serve as his own control, similar to the practice of Bloom who used different but parallel achievement tests for his classes—tests that matched the objectives of the course—and was able to produce yearly gains (practical differences) in the number of students achieving mastery (Bloom, 1968). Information indicating that a teacher is increasing the achievement of his pupils year after year should be of value to the administrator who must make decisions about that teacher. This is the case at least when achievement is measured by pupil performance on instruments that indeed sample the behavior called for in the objective, e.g., ability to apply a concept in new situations, rather than by pupil response to test items that have been presented in rote drill.

Other kinds of plans have been presented to achieve teacher accountability —payment by results, merit plans, performance contracting, voucher systems and the like. Historical analyses of these varied manifestations show a) that there is no single way to make one accountable in teaching and b) that particular plans may be identified with failure without destroying the concept of accountability. Rusk, in his *History of Infant Education*, for instance, documented that in the last half of the nineteenth century British educational commissioners made it possible for managers of schools to claim a fixed amount of money for certain pupils who attended regularly but one-third of the sum thus claimable was forfeited if the scholar failed to satisfy an inspection in reading, one-third if he failed in writing, and one-third if he failed in arithmetic (Rusk, 1933). An adverse side effect of this plan was that teachers tended to concentrate on the pupils whose grant earnings depended on passing the examinations. Treating "scientific management" in American schools from 1910 to

1930, Callahan also described administrative practices by which the quality of instructional effectiveness was indicated by a variety of measures, including pupil performance on a number of specific tasks, e.g., the ability to add at a speed of 65 combinations per minute with an accuracy of 94 percent (Callahan, 1962). Negative consequences associated with many of the accountability plans of this period were said to be increased lay influence on the curriculum, more limited freedom of the teacher, exposure of educators' lack of talent and funds necessary for developing effective teaching, and a disproportionate share of educators' time spent on accounting. Most criticism of early accountability plans has been linked with criticisms of the achievement-testing movement as it was known at the beginning of this century. That is, measures did not cover all outcomes desired in the educational program; many of the sweeping conclusions drawn from test data were fallible; there was too much concentration upon static educational objectives; and teacher and pupils concentrated their efforts upon those aspects that were to be tested—testing itself tending to enforce conformity. Such criticisms have had considerable influence in shaping the changes in newer accountability plans although there is current evidence, as seen in a special issue of the *Phi Delta Kappan,* that many of the difficulties in implementing accountability programs have not been overcome (Lieberman, 1970).

PERFORMANCE TESTS

It is invalid to rank a teacher as effective when the teacher has not been confronted with a comparable set of teaching conditions as have other teachers. Yet at times it is necessary to differentiate among teachers—to identify who excels or falls below his peers. The problem, then, is to design tests of teaching power by which teachers have an equal chance to succeed or fail. Performance tests or teaching power tests are responses to the problem (Popham, 1967, 1968, 1971). A number of teachers are given one or more identical objectives and a sample of the measures based on the objective(s) to be administered to pupils following instruction. The objectives may be cognitive, affective or psychomotor in nature. The teachers may also be given resource materials from which to plan a lesson designed to accomplish the objectives. The instructional tactics to be employed are left entirely to the teacher. In other words, only the ends are given, the means are up to the instructor. Often the objective is novel, both to pupils and teacher, thereby eliminating major "contamination" due to the learner's previous exposure to the subject. The teachers are allowed a specific period of time for planning the lesson and for teaching it. Groups of learners, perhaps only a few students per group, are assigned to the teacher as pupils. These learners are drawn from a common population of pupils and randomly assigned to a group. If prerequisite skills are required on the part of pupils, this stipulation is acted upon in making up the population from which the learners are drawn. Following the teacher's instruction a test is administered to measure pupil attainment of the objectives. Although the nature of the test may be inferred by the teacher from the objective, the actual test is not available to the teacher and, indeed, is usually administered by someone other than the teacher. The mean posttest score becomes the criterion of effectiveness. In some instances test scores may be adjusted for the initial abilities of the pupils. If relatively large learner groups are employed, the randomization of assignment is to be preferred. Noninstructional control groups may also be used to further substantiate the amount of learning that occurred as a result of instruction.

The reliability with which one can determine teaching competencies through the use of these performance tests can be increased by using a number of lessons and different kinds of objectives—different subject matter, different levels of expected behavior, etc. Also, the total number of pupils can be shared in the small groups so that no teacher teaches the same group of pupils more than one lesson and no group receives a particular lesson more than once.

Retention tests can also be given to learners, thereby adding another dimension to the teacher's ability to accomplish prespecified objectives. The utility of performance tests as measures of teaching effectiveness has been demonstrated in the work of Borgerding (1970), Justiz (1969), Morsh, Burgess, and Smith (1955), Popham (1967, 1971), and Taneman (1970). These studies suggest the conclusion that when there is reasonable control for extraneous factors (teacher familiarity with content and pupil populations) some teachers are consistently more successful than others in getting desired results. There is, however, need for verifying that teachers who can produce desired effects under conditions of teaching performance tests maintain their effect over time and in the presence of a greater range of conditions such as exist in conventional classrooms.

References

Allen, D. W., F. J. McDonald, and M. E. J. Orme. *Experiment II: Effects of Feedback and Practice Conditions on the Acquisition of a Teaching Strategy.* Stanford, Calif.: Stanford University, 1966.

Anthony, B. M. "A New Approach to Merit Rating of Teachers." *Administrator's Notebook* **17**, no. 1 (1968): 1–4.

Bannister, J., J. Sutherland, and J. W. Brown. "Evaluating College Teaching." *Curriculum Reporter Supplement No. 1,* December 1961.

Bloom, B. S. "Learning for Mastery." *Evaluation Comment* **1**, no. 2 (1968): 1–12.

Borgerding, J. C. "Practice versus Practice and Reflection in the Improvement of Instruction." Master's thesis, University of California, Los Angeles, 1970.

Callahan, R. E. *Education and the Cult of Efficiency.* Chicago: The University of Chicago Press, 1962.

Cohen, A. M. "Defining Instructional Objectives." *Systems Approaches to Curriculum and Instruction in the Open-Door College* (Junior College Leadership Program Occasional Report No. 9). Los Angeles: University of California, School of Education, 1967.

Davidoff, S. H. *The Development of an Instrument Designed to Secure Student Assessment of Teaching Behaviors that Correlate with Objective Measures of Student Achievement.* The School District of Philadelphia, Office of Research and Evaluation, March 1970.

Festinger, L. A. "A Theory of Social Comparison Process." *Human Relations* 7 (1954): 117–140.

Fitch, N. *Evaluation of Instructors in California Junior Colleges.* Berkeley: University of California, 1965.

Fortune, J. C. *The Generality of Presenting Behaviors in Teaching Pre-School Children.* Memphis, Tenn.: Memphis State University, 1966.

Goldhammer, R. *Clinical Supervision.* New York: Holt, Rinehart and Winston, 1969.

Ingils, C. R. "Let's Do Away with Teacher Evaluation." *The Clearing House* 44 (1970): 451–456.

Justiz, T. B. "A Reliable Measure of Teacher Effectiveness." *Educational Leadership Research Supplement* 3, no. 1 (1969): 49–55.

Lieberman, M., ed. "Eight Articles on Accountability." *Phi Delta Kappan* 52 (1970): 194–239.

McNeil, J. D. "Concomitants of Using Behavioral Objectives in the Assessment of Teacher Effectiveness." *The Journal of Experimental Education* 36, no. 1 (1967): 69–74.

McNeil, J. D. *Toward Accountable Teachers: Their Appraisal and Improvement.* New York. Holt, Rinehart and Winston, 1971.

Moffett, G. M. "Use of Instructional Objectives in the Supervision of Student Teachers." Ph.D. dissertation, University of California, Los Angeles, 1967. *Dissertation Abstracts International* 27 (1967) 2430A, University Microfilms No. 67, 466.

Morsh, J. E., G. G. Burgess, and P. N. Smith. *Student Achievement as a Measure of Instructor Effectiveness* (Project No. 7950, Task No. 77243). Lackland Air Force Base, Texas: Air Force Personnel and Training Center, 1955.

Morsh, J. E., and E. W. Wilder. *Identifying the Effective Instructor: A Review of the Quantitative Studies. 1900–1952* (Project No. 7714, Task No. 77243). Chanute Air Force Base, Ill.: Air Force Personnel and Training Research Center, 1954.

Nwana, E. M. "An Investigation into an Objective Way of Examining Student Teachers in Practical Teaching in West Cameroon Teacher Training Institutions." Ph.D. dissertation, University of California, Los Angeles, 1968. *Dissertation Abstracts International* 29 (1968), 1809A. University Microfilms No. 68–16, 566.

Orange Coast Junior College. *Instructor Rating Scale Study, Orange Coast College, Fall Semester, 1968.* Costa Mesa, Calif.: Orange Coast Junior College, 1968.

Orange Unified School District. "Teacher Self-Appraisal In-Service Program." *Educational Resources Information Center (ERIC) Abstract* 4 (1968).

Overturf, C. L. *Student Rating of Faculty at St. Johns River Junior College, with Addendum for Albany Junior College.* Palatka, Fla.: St. Johns River Junior College, 1966.

Popham, W. J. *Development of a Performance Test of Teaching Proficiency* (USOE, Final Report, Contract No. OE-6-10-254). Los Angeles: University of California, 1967.

Popham, W. J. "The Performance Test: A New Approach to the Assessment of Teaching Proficiency." *Journal of Teacher Education* 19 (1968): 216–222.

Popham, W. J. "Performance Tests of Teaching Proficiency: Rationale, Development, and Validation." *American Educational Research Journal* 8 (1971): 105–117.

Rayder, N. F. *College Student Ratings of Instructors.* Lansing, Mich.: Michigan State University, Office of Educational Services, 1968.

Rusk, R. R. *A History of Infant Education.* London: University of London Press, 1933.

Salomon, G., and F. J. McDonald. "Pretest and Posttest Reactions to Self-Viewing One's Teaching Performance on Video Tape." *Journal of Educational Psychology* **61** (1970): 280–286.

Schmidt, R., ed. *Insight: A View of the Faculty Through the Eyes of Their Students.* San Marcos, Calif.: Palomar College, 1968.

Smithman, H. H. "Student Achievement as a Measure of Teacher Performance." Ph.D. dissertation, University of California, Los Angeles, 1970.

Taneman, I. "A Teaching Power Test: A Method of Using Pupil Gain as a Criterion in Teacher Education." Ph.D. dissertation, University of California, Los Angeles, 1970.

Waimon, M. D., and G. C., Ramseyer. "Effects of Video Feedback on the Ability to Evaluate Teaching." *The Journal of Teacher Education* **21** (1970): 92–95.

Weiner, B., and A. Kukla. "An Attributional Analysis of Achievement Motivation." *Journal of Personality and Social Psychology* **15** (1970): 1–20.

DANIEL L. MERRITT
University of Toledo

The Teacher Assessment Center: A Concept

Historically, many educators persist that competent teaching cannot be defined. Such a philosophy has hindered attempts to account for the products of teacher education and frustrated the establishment of systematic procedures to evaluate teacher performance in the classroom.

Currently, however, states such as Florida and New York are moving toward the adoption of performance-based certification programs to help evaluate preservice teacher behavior. Educators subscribing to such programs are faced with the problem of defining, in measurable terms, those behaviors that a competent, certified teacher should exhibit. Problems of organizing and using the clusters of performance behaviors in study programs are also present.

Such efforts would be aided by the organization and implementation of an effective evaluative agency. I suggest that performance-based certification programs would be greatly facilitated by the establishment of teacher assessment centers (TAC). These centers would offer the following services:

1. Specific behavioral experiences related to certification for the preservice teacher
2. Opportunities for the experienced teacher to identify areas of strengths as well as any behaviors which need modification
3. Record preparation indicating individual performance
4. Assessment service for either employers or employees

These services have two general thrusts: one in the direction of certification that is mandated by the adoption of performance criteria; the other in the direction of teacher renewal, commonly called continuing education.

ORGANIZATION

The concept of an assessment center for organization personnel is not new. Industrial personnel have had the opportunity to benefit from such a facility for some time. Private corporations have established their own centers in order to assess the performances of new personnel and reassess experienced company personnel. The concept is valid for educational enterprises as well. Centers may be established as a necessary first step toward implementation of performance-based certification plans.

Personnel

Initially, the center would probably have to function only during peak graduation or employment months. A small cadre of permanent staff to monitor general administrative operations of the center might be composed of state education department personnel. Personnel who are selected to serve as performance assessors should be drawn from university, public school, and educationally related groups. The assessors should serve on a full-time basis and be assigned by an appropriate state education official to observe, interpret, and record performance. The terms of appointment for assessors should be staggered and limited. This would allow for some team proficiency to be maintained and establish the equality of team member influence.

Facilities

Centers might be located in university or public school settings to minimize cost and speed implementation of the program. They should not be permanently maintained in university settings however, for this might involve a conflict of interests. Therefore, the use of a university setting should be considered as a temporary phase. Eventually the centers should be established in separate facilities maintained by agents of the state education department. Where possible, regional offices of state education departments may house center activities. As performance criteria are developed or modified, university and public school officials may have disagreements about content that could be eliminated or reduced by the influence of a third interested party: the state education department. Certification activities for new teachers are viewed as a major part of center activities in the beginning, but certification activities for experienced teachers or administrators may assume the greater role as the centers develop.

Funding

Teacher assessment centers may be funded by state or federal agencies during the initial implementation phase. Since university or public school sites might house the centers initially, the state or federal funds needed would be minimized. It is hoped that as the centers develop the certification services they render might generate a "pay as you go" operation.

Fees for performance certification of new teachers would provide the major portion of income. As certification programs develop the income base should shift to performance certification activities for experienced teachers and other school personnel.

Sample Programs

Activities undertaken in a TAC may focus on a number of performance-based situations. Experiences for the preservice teacher who desires initial certification will probably have to be conducted over a number of days. The program will be more compact for the experienced teacher. An outline of possible activities for a two-day preservice teacher session is listed below:

First Day

Morning:	General orientation Task: Demonstrate ability to *plan* and *organize* classwork Task: Demonstrate ability to *manage* classroom
Afternoon:	Task: Demonstrate ability to motivate and *create a learning environment.* Task: Demonstrate *interpersonal behavior toward pupils*
Evening:	Interview involving *Educational Attitudes*

Second Day

Morning:	Task: Demonstrate ability to *instruct* pupils
Afternoon:	Task: Demonstrate ability to *evaluate* pupils
Evening:	Feedback session on teacher performance

In the various demonstrations of teacher competency, we suggest that a video tape recorder be used to provide members of the TAC and the candidate with information to study and restudy in determining performance levels attained.

SERVICE ACTIVITIES

Preservice Teacher Certification

State teacher assessment centers may be located in regional offices to serve a geographic area. The center may be used by preservice teachers graduating from institutions in that area, teachers desiring employment in that area, or educators already serving in that geographic region. The center would provide a series of situations for the preservice teacher to react to. The certification activities might also be organized so an individual could reach a given performance criteria by alternate routes. It is assumed that university and public school representatives will influence the establishment of a state-approved set of performance certification objectives. Members of the TAC would certify whether or not the candidate completed the performance mandated. The center would also be responsible for preparing a performance record for each participant which would indicate the level of performance reached in each area monitored. Appropriate checks and balances might be contained in the recording system so that an objective team report would be produced. This certification service would be rendered for an appropriate fee that would be paid by the person wishing to gain teacher certification.

Experienced Teacher Certification

The behavioral experiences developed for certification purposes may also be used by experienced teachers. Local school districts may, for example, arrange to have selected teachers periodically participate in the TAC experiences to identify needed areas of in-service training. Groups or individuals may also elect to participate in the experiences in order to obtain certification of their current teaching performance levels. Such certification may be recognized for pay purposes.

Special programs in local school districts may require teachers with special skill strengths. The certification experience of the TAC may help identify the teachers with the necessary skills. Indeed local in-service programs may be keyed to local TAC. The various competencies related to differentiated staffing may be identified in the TAC performance program. Profiles of performance may then be established for each role on the differentiated staff. Teachers may then participate in activities designed to help select members of a differentiated team. TAC functions as an aid in identifying experienced teacher talents that may be used and also points out deficiencies that should be strengthened for more effective use by the employing school system.

Paraprofessional Certification

Paraprofessionals are used extensively in educational programs, especially in elementary schools. New programs for preparing young men and women to enter these educationally related positions are part of the near future. The TAC is a ready tool which could be used to help certify candidates for these positions or other educational positions as the criteria develop.

SUMMARY

The Teacher Assessment Center is a conceptual alternative to the process of certifying teacher ability that is being used at present. The TAC offers the opportunity to certify the skills that teachers exhibit and the opportunity to shape the future of education by identifying those skills. The center concept also recognizes that only persons seriously interested in teaching would seek certification.

The center concept also provides the opportunity to prescribe profiles of teaching performance and to test the performance of present and future teachers. This concept seems to be a realistic and fair way of resolving some teacher certification, evaluation, and reward problems.

DAVID C. BERLINER and WILLIAM TIKUNOFF
Far West Laboratory for Educational Research
and Development

Ethnography in the Classroom[1]

The Far West Laboratory for Educational Research and Development has been conducting research on teacher effectiveness. Under contract to the California Commission for Teacher Preparation and Licensing, with funding provided by the National Institute of Education, the Laboratory is studying teachers in second- and fifth-grade classes in order to identify teacher behavior and classroom qualities that are related to reading and mathematics.

The California Commission is the agency charged with certifying the appropriateness of teacher training programs throughout the state. To carry out its duties, the Commission needs information about what teacher behaviors are related to student outcomes. This information will then be used jointly by the Commission and the State institutions that it certifies in order to better insure that beginning teachers receive training in areas that have been empirically demonstrated to affect student learning.

To obtain the information they need, the Commission has undertaken a multi-year research effort entitled *Beginning Teacher Evaluation Study* (*BTES*). During 1974–1975, as part of this study, the Laboratory did work on five major tasks. One of these was to inquire whether ethnographic approaches to the study of teaching could yield new insights into the teaching-learning process.

Our goal was to obtain protocols of classrooms written by sensitive observers who were unaware of the measured effectiveness of the teachers they observed. The BTES staff believed that "single-act" psychology and hypothesis testing psychology had yielded little of value for studying the complex world of the classroom. Thus we turned elsewhere for a way of viewing classroom phenomena.

This paper was presented at the Conference on Research on Teacher Effects: An Examination by Policy-Makers and Researchers, The University of Texas at Austin, November 3–5, 1975. Used with permission of the authors.

[1] The research to be described was directed by Dr. William Tikunoff. A complete report of these activities is given in W. Tikunoff, D. C. Berliner, and R. C. Rist, "An Ethnographic Study of the Forty Classrooms of the Beginning Teacher Evaluation Study Known Sample," Technical Report No. 75-10-5 (San Francisco, Calif.: Far West Laboratory for Educational Research and Development, October, 1975).

Recently, our own feelings of uneasiness with traditional psychological approaches have been echoed by others. Lutz and Ramsey (1974) have been concerned that the teaching acts and learning outcomes that have been studied to date are those that, for the most part, can be subjected to measurement by paper and pencil tests and/or by the development of behaviorally defined coding systems. Descriptions of the activity in a classroom, therefore, have been limited by the "screens" through which events have been recorded—those "screens" being soundly based from a psychometric quantitative point of view, but lacking in terms of qualitative information surrounding the reality of what actually occurred. They say:

> Variables are operationalized because there is some available printed test with some kind of statistical reliability and validity measure, and after data are collected, it can be submitted to a computer for an analysis usually much too esoteric and powerful for the nature of the hypothesis. In such a case, the hypothesis is not grounded, the variables may not be recurring or important, the operational measures may have little relationship to operational reality, and the number in the sample makes test of it much more powerful than the hypothesis is compelling (Lutz and Ramsey, 1974, p. 5).

The result of the shortcomings from research on teaching, and the uneasiness shared by many with the intellectual style of psychological research has established an introspective stance by some educational researchers toward their accomplishments to date (Campbell, 1974; Cronbach, 1975; Glass, 1972). Such reflection has led to an intensive questioning of the research questions which are asked, and therefore, the research methodology being employed to answer them. It is out of that questioning that the impetus has grown to look beyond the methodologies of experimental psychology to other disciplines of the social sciences for the purpose of studying teaching. Particularly important is anthropology or social anthropology and their observational techniques. The use of the direct observer, fully imbedded in the on-going process of the classroom, seems to be an emerging tool for use in some current evaluations of NIE-funded projects (Campbell, 1974), and the use of such anthropological field methodology over a longer period of time should result in accumulation of more qualitative data of, potentially, great utility (Lutz and Ramsey, 1974). Our goal must be to gather more *qualitative* information along with the *quantitative* information we usually collect. Campbell (1974) characterizes the contrast between these two approaches:

> For *quantitative* read also scientific, scientistic and naturwissenschaftlich. For *qualitative* read also humanistic, humanitistic, geisteswissenschaftlich, experiential, phenomenological, clinical, case study, field work, participant observations, process evaluation, and common-sense knowing.

The gathering of such qualitative evidence, suggests Cronbach, involves intensive local observation that goes beyond disciplines to an open-eyed, open-minded appreciation of the surprises nature deposits in the investigative act

(Cronbach, 1975). It necessitates the "direct observation of human activity and interaction in an ongoing, naturalistic fashion" (Rist, 1973). It allows the researcher to:

> File descriptive information . . . instead of reporting only those selected differences and correlations that are nominally "greater than chance." (Cronbach, 1975).

It was because of these concerns and beliefs that an ethnographic study was designed and conducted.

RECRUITMENT OF ETHNOGRAPHERS

The first task was the recruitment of sensitive observers to send to the specially selected classrooms to obtain the qualitative information that was desired. Most were doctoral candidates, in anthropology or sociology, and most had served as nonparticipant or participant observers previously.

Training of these ethnographers consisted of (1) reading educational ethnographies, including those of Jules Henry and others; (2) practice in classrooms; and (3) observing films of classrooms. Protocols produced during training were read and critiqued by the Laboratory staff. Three weeks of effort was directed into getting the ethnographers ready to focus on reading and mathematics lessons in natural classrooms. A sample protocol is given as Figure 1 and should be read carefully to give you a feel for the kind of data we collected and worked with. This particular sample is a training protocol which was read and critiqued by the Laboratory staff during the time the ethnographers were being trained.

Although we were interested in obtaining qualitative information, we did not ignore the chance to "calibrate" our data collectors. An expert ethnographer was used as criterion during some training exercises. From a film clip of a classroom discussion he picked nine events that were salient to him. The ethnographers saw the same film clip and wrote protocols on what they observed. The information on percent agreement with the expert is to be interpreted as a form of a validity check. The information on percent agreement among the raters is to be interpreted as a form of a reliability check. All disagreements were used for discussions about recording observations. When reliability and validity were judged high enough, these observers were sent out into the field.

DATA BASE

The ethnographers were trained to provide:

1. A reading protocol, each day, if reading was taught;
2. A mathematics protocol, each day, if mathematics was taught;
3. Three to five informal protocols based on observations during recess, talks with principals, conversations in the teachers' lounge, etc.;

Protocol Number: 06
Name of Researcher: Gail
Date of Observation:
Subject of Observation: 2nd Grade Class, Open Classroom, with two team teacher and two other adults, this is a joint observation with Elizabeth. I will be observing two reading groups today, simultaneously, including 9 children. Out of the nine children, 2 are girls, 7 are boys.

8:30 Noise level 2 At 8:30 the noise level is 2. The children have just been let into the classroom, taking their coats off and wandering around the room. Several boys are in the corner fighting, and some girls are sitting on the floor playing a puzzle. The teacher is walking back and forth in the back of the classroom not attending the children. The noise continues and the children are running around. There is much confusion in the room. Two teachers
8:35 stand at the desk talking to one another. At 8:35, Mrs. Tyler leaves the room. The team teacher stays seated behind the classroom at her desk. At 8:40 Mrs. Tyler comes back into the room. She walks to the desk at the far left hand side of the classroom, which is a round table, and sits on the edge. She says "Blue Group, get your folders and go up in the front. Green Group, come here." Noise level drops to 1, and the children begin to follow her orders. She says, "Anybody loose a quarter." No one responds, and she repeats the question again with irritation in her voice. She says I know someone found, someone lost a quarter because it was found in the coat room. Look in your pockets and see." No one says anything. She now stands up and pulls a pile of workbooks from across the table over to her. They are the ________ reading workbooks. She opens one of them on the top and says, "Ah Daniel!" She says this with a loud sharp voice. She continues, "Your work yesterday was not too bad but you need some work. Evidently there are still some words you don't understand." She thumbs through the rest of his lesson. Danny is standing at the outside of the circle around her, not listening to what she is saying. Mrs. Tyler now stands and gives instructions to the Green Group. She tells them to go through 8 through 13, reading the two stories between those pages and to go over the work in the workbooks that she is about to give back. She tells them that they may seat any place but not together and she says, "And I don't want any funny business." She now opens the next workbook which is Nicole's. She tells Nicole that she is having the same problem that Danny is having without specifying further. Nicole looks up at her with an expectant look on her face. She then looks at a third book and says Michelle you're having the same problem. She says, "Snatch means to grab. Beach, what does it mean?" Michelle doesn't answer. She has her finger in her mouth and looks anxious. The teacher closes the workbook and pushes it to Michelle. Michelle takes it and walks away, with Nicole. Teacher then opens the next workbook and says, Mike, I don't appreciate all these circles.

Fig. 1. A sample protocol.

4. A summary protocol emphasizing important anthropological concepts useful for studying education. These concepts include competitiveness, work ethic, patriotism, play ethic, etc.

Thus the data set, with one ethnographer observing for one week in each classroom, includes five reading protocols, five mathematics protocols, at least three informal protocols, and one summary protocol done after observation was completed. Four weeks were required to collect data from all the teachers in the study. All data were collected blind. The ethnographers had, typically, two more effective and two less effective teachers to work with and worked only at one grade level. Classroom notes were read into a cassette recorder each day and sent to the Laboratory for immediate transcription. Teams of typists helped to turn out thousands of pages describing classrooms of these teachers who were known to vary in measured effectiveness.

At this point you now have knowledge of how this particular sample of teachers was chosen, what the goal of the study was, what the training of the ethnographers was like, and a description of the data sets obtained in each of forty classrooms.

GENERATING DIMENSIONS

Six raters were brought together for two weeks to read a pair of protocols a day. One protocol described a more effective classroom and one protocol described a less effective classroom. These raters included one expert in classroom observation instrumentation, a classroom teacher, a curriculum coordinator, one graduate student in educational psychology, and two ethnographers who were thought to write very sensitive descriptive protocols. The raters were asked to describe as many ways as possible that the two classrooms differed. They were free to use any terminology they wanted. They were aware that they had a more effective and a less effective classroom paired together, but they did not know which classroom was which. The hope was to keep this task relatively hypothesis free and at a common sense level. To help them in their task the raters used cards like those presented in Figure 2. This task was, essentially, a concept-definition task. At the end of each day, the raters came together and shared their concepts. Each rater helped other raters define the concepts and each provided exemplars and non-exemplars of the concepts from their own protocols. The list generated by these raters contained 211 concepts.

Remember, that each of these sometimes exotic variables, dimensions, or concepts was linguistically defined in a rather precise manner. Thus concepts like "psychotic autism," or a view that "children are evil," were concepts that we had no preconceived desire to work with. But they were chosen as concepts that differentiated between more and less effective classrooms by at least one of the raters and the concepts were agreed to, refined, and defined, by the other raters. We purposefully did not place any limits on the type of concepts that could be generated. To this list eight additional concepts were added. These included five concepts from Kounin's (1970) work (withitness, smoothness, transition, etc.), and three variables that were experimentally manipulated in a study conducted at the Stanford Research and Development Center. It was thought that an independent correlational check of those variables could be made in this study.

We are looking for THINGS THAT DISCRIMINATE BETWEEN CLASSROOMS. When you find one DESCRIBE IT:

A. What it is and/or looks like (descriptors, characteristics, connotations, synonyms)

B. What it is not (antonyms, descriptors, characteristics, non-examples)

GIVE EXAMPLES:

1.

2.

3.

LABEL IT: ______________________

Fig. 2. Teacher, student, or instructional characteristics card for generating dimension.

The list of 211 dimensions was much too big to work with and contained a good deal of overlapping concepts. The dimensions were combined into 61 variables which were thought to capture most of what the "dimension pickers" had chosen. Variables were also chosen on the basis of whether or not they appeared frequently in the protocols. The final list of 61 dimensions, and brief definitions, is given as Table 1. A "T" or "S" denotes the variables as related to the teacher or the student as the focus of observation. These 61 variables were next used to do more extensive analysis of the protocols.

Table 1. Sixty-one dimensions for comparing known sample classrooms.

1. *abruptness (T):* unanticipated "switching" by teacher, e.g., from instruction to classroom management, to behavior management, to instruction, to behavior management.
2. *accepting (T):* teacher reacts constructively (overt, verbal, non-verbal) to students' feelings and attitudes.
3. *adult involvement (C):* adults other than the teacher are allowed to instruct.
4. *attending (T):* teacher actively listens to what a student is saying, reading, reciting.

5. *awareness of developmental levels (T):* teacher is aware of a student's emotional, social educational needs and therefore assigns tasks appropriate for these.
6. *being liked (T):* teacher seeks approval from students in an ingratiating manner, often at expense of instruction.
7. *belittling (T):* teacher berates child in front of others.
8. *competing (T):* competition, outdoing others is emphasized by the teacher.
9. *complimenting (control) (T):* teacher's action reinforces student(s) whose behavior is in the right direction.
10. *consistency of message (control) (T):* teacher gives a direction or a threat and follows through with it.
11. *conviviality (C):* warmth, family-like quality to classroom interaction; good feelings between teacher-students, students-students.
12. *cooperation (S):* students cooperate with other students, teacher; willingness on part of students to help each other.
13. *defending (T):* teacher defends a student from verbal or physical assault by another.
14. *defiance (S):* a student's open resistance to teacher direction; refuses to comply.
15. *democracy (T):* teacher provides opportunities to involve students in decision-making re class standards, instruction, procedures, etc.
16. *distrust (T):* teacher expresses doubt for validity of student's work or behavior.
17. *drilling (T):* teacher emphasizes regularization, rote memory, retrieval of facts on part of student learning.
18. *encouraging (T):* teacher admonishes student effort in order to motivate them.
19. *engagement (S):* students express eagerness to participate, appear actively, productively involved in learning activities.
20. *equity (T):* teacher appears to divide her time, attention equally among all students.
21. *ethnicity (T):* teacher expresses positive, informative comments about racial, class, ethnic contributions; encourages class discussion about cultural contributions.
22. *excluding (T):* teacher banishes student from class activity—to corner, cloakroom, out of room, etc.
23. *expectation (T):* teacher attributes scholastic problems or predicts success for student on basis of past information or student's "background."
24. *filling time (T):* teacher fills "empty" time periods with "busy work".
25. *flexibility (T):* teacher adjusts instruction easily to accommodate change in plans, time schedule, absenteeism, or change of students' behavior.
26. *gendering (T):* teacher assigns roles on basis of male or female (boy-girl) and reinforces these.
27. *harassing (T):* teacher taunts, pesters, nags, hazes, "puts down," or physically hits a student.
28. *ignoring (T):* teacher appears to deliberately "not hear" or "not see" so as to treat a student as being invisible.
29. *illogical statements (T):* teacher makes a statement whose consequences would be ridiculous if carried out.
30. *individualizing (T):* teacher assigns to each student learning tasks designed to match his/her individual abilities and interests.
31. *job satisfaction (T):* teacher seems to enjoy teaching.
32. *knowledge of subject (T):* teacher seems confident in teaching a given subject, and demonstrates a grasp of it.
33. *manipulation (S):* student is able to get on demand a desired response from the teacher.
34. *mobility (S):* students move freely and purposefully around the room; teacher allows students to work at places other than at their assigned seats.
35. *mobility (T):* teacher moves spontaneously about the room.
36. *modeling/imitation (S):* students copy teacher's behavior, and are encouraged to do so by teacher.
37. *monitoring learning (T):* teacher checks in on student's progress regularly and adjusts instruction accordingly.

38. *moralizing (T):* teacher emphasizes goodness vs. badness, verbally expresses ideal behavior model.
39. *oneness (T):* teacher treats whole group as a "one" often in order to maintain peer control.
40. *openness (T):* teacher verbally acknowledges to students feelings of anger or frustration, admits mistakes, expresses need for self-improvement.
41. *open questioning (T):* teacher asks questions which call for interpretive responses and are open-ended.
42. *optimism (T):* teacher expresses positive, pleasant, optimistic attitudes and feelings.
43. *pacing (T):* teacher appears to perceive learning rate of students and adjusts teaching pace accordingly.
44. *peer teaching (S):* students help other students instructionally and are encouraged to do so, whether "olders" with "youngers" or students of same age group.
45. *personalizing (T):* teacher calls on students by name.
46. *policing (T):* undue emphasis on quietness, orderliness, good behavior, and teacher spends disproportionate time with monitoring student behavior and controlling for discipline.
47. *politeness (T):* teacher requests rather than commands, uses "please" and "thank you", encourages same in student-student interaction.
48. *praising (T):* teacher verbally rewards student.
49. *promoting self-sufficiency (T):* teacher encourages students to take responsibility for their own classwork.
50. *recognition-seeking (T):* teacher calls attention to self for no apparent instructional purpose.
51. *rushing (T):* teacher does not give students adequate response time, or answers for them; is tied to a pre-set time limit, and hurries students to finish work.
52. *sarcasm (T):* teacher responds in a demeaning manner, uses destructive/cutting remarks.
53. *shaming (T):* teacher instills guilt in students for their behavior in order to establish control.
54. *signaling (control) (T):* teacher uses body language, non-verbal signals to change students' behavior.
55. *spontaneity (T):* teacher capitalizes instructionally on unexpected incidents that arise during class time.
56. *stereotyping (T):* teacher labels and judges students by socio-economic, ethnic, or racial characteristics.
57. *structuring (T):* teacher prepares students for lesson by reviewing, outlining, explaining objectives, summarizing.
58. *teacher made materials (T):* teacher provides instructional materials other than textbooks, and arranges for their use by students.
59. *time fixedness (T):* teacher emphasizes promptness, begins and ends activities by clock rather than by student interest.
60. *waiting (T):* after asking a question, teacher waits in silence for student responses or waits in silence after student response before reacting.
61. *warmth (T):* teacher seeks contact with students, talks with them, shows affection toward them.

Twenty raters from all walks of life were brought together to rate pairs of protocols for the presence or absence, or the occurrence of more or less of the variables. They received training in the use of a specially constructed rating form and in understanding the definitions for variables. In the rating forms used in conjunction with the manual defining each of the 61 dimensions, each variable is clearly defined and examples of each variable are taken directly from the protocols that describe natural classroom behavior.

Table 2. Paired comparisons for sixty-one dimensions

Dimension	Second-grade mathematics			Second-grade reading			Fifth-grade mathematics			Fifth-grade reading			
	More effective teachers*	Less effective teachers*	p	More effective teachers*	Less effective teachers*	p	More effective teachers*	Less effective teachers*	p	More effective teachers*	Less effective teachers*	p	% Rater agreement
(−) 1. abruptness (T)	13	23	.0475	9	27	.0013	11	25	.0099	10	26	.0035	.81
(+) 2. accepting (T)	26	10	.0035	25	11	.0099	24	12	.0228	26	10	.0035	1.00
(+) 3. adult involvement (C)	28	8	.0003	23	13	.0475	23	13	.0475	23	13	.0475	.75
(+) 4. attending (T)	26	10	.0035	30	6	.00003	25	11	.0099	25	11	.0099	.81
(+) 5. awareness of developmental levels (T)	23	13	.0475	29	7	.0002	22	14	.0918	26	10	.0035	.88
(−) 6. being liked (T)	11	25	.0099	15	21	.1587	9	27	.0013	14	22	.0918	.69
(−) 7. belittling (T)	11	25	.0099	12	24	.0228	12	24	.0228	12	24	.0228	.81
(+) 8. competing (T)	19	17	.7414	12	24	.0456	14	22	.1836	14	22	.1836	.81
(+) 9. complementing (control) (T)	20	16	.2514	26	10	.0035	23	13	.0475	19	17	.3707	.75
(+) 10. consistency of message (control) (T)	26	10	.0035	24	12	.0228	28	8	.0003	27	9	.0013	.69
(+) 11. conviviality (C)	25	11	.0035	30	6	.00003	23	13	.0475	27	9	.0013	.75
(+) 12. cooperation (S)	26	10	.0035	29	7	.0002	24	12	.0228	27	9	.0013	.81
(+) 13. defending (T)	19	17	.3707	21	15	.1587	17	19	.3707	23	13	.0475	.63
(−) 14. defiance (S)	11	25	.0099	4	32	.000003	13	23	.0475	7	29	.0002	.81
(+) 15. democracy (T)	25	11	.0099	23	13	.0475	22	14	.0918	26	10	.0035	.75
(−) 16. distrust (T)	10	26	.0035	12	24	.0228	14	22	.0918	17	19	.3707	.88
(+) 17. drilling (T)	14	22	.1836	13	23	.0950	19	17	.7414	12	24	.0456	.69
(+) 18. encouraging (T)	28	8	.0003	30	6	.00003	21	15	.1587	25	11	.0099	.75
(+) 19. engagement (S)	27	9	.0013	28	8	.0003	23	13	.0475	30	6	.00003	.88
(+) 20. equity (T)	23	13	.0475	27	9	.0013	22	14	.0918	26	10	.0035	.94
(+) 21. ethnicity (T)	22	14	.0918	26	10	.0035	18	18	.5000	25	11	.0099	.69
(−) 22. excluding (T)	11	25	.0099	16	20	.2514	13	23	.0475	13	23	.0475	.75
(−) 23. expectation (T)	11	25	.0099	13	23	.0475	14	22	.0918	14	22	.0918	.75
(−) 24. filling time (T)	11	25	.0099	9	27	.0013	10	26	.0035	9	27	.0013	.81
(+) 25. flexibility (T)	27	9	.0013	27	9	.0013	22	14	.0918	23	13	.0475	.88
(+) 26. gendering (T)	17	19	.7414	11	25	.0198	16	20	.5028	16	20	.5028	.63

(−) 27. harrassing (T)	12	24	.0228	8	28	.0003	14	22	.0918	10	26	.0035	.75
(−) 28. ignoring (T)	10	26	.0035	7	29	.0002	16	20	.2514	9	27	.0013	.75
(−) 29. illogical statements (T)	13	23	.0475	8	28	.0003	12	24	.0228	11	25	.0099	.50
(+) 30. individualizing (T)	26	10	.0035	28	8	.0003	20	16	.2514	23	13	.0475	.94
(+) 31. job satisfaction (T)	29	7	.0002	29	7	.0002	22	14	.0918	28	8	.0003	.75
(+) 32. knowledge of subject (T)	27	9	.0013	29	7	.0002	25	11	.0099	28	8	.0003	.88
(−) 33. manipulation (S)	17	19	.3707	6	30	.00003	9	27	.0013	8	28	.0003	.69
(+) 34. mobility (S)	27	9	.0013	27	9	.0013	22	14	.0918	21	15	.0158	.69
(+) 35. mobility (T)	26	10	.0035	28	8	.0003	19	17	.3707	17	19	.3707	.69
(+) 36. modeling/imitation (S)	22	14	.0918	23	13	.0475	19	17	.3707	21	15	.1587	.63
(+) 37. monitoring learning (T)	29	7	.0002	29	7	.0002	23	13	.0475	24	12	.0228	.88
(−) 38. moralizing (T)	7	29	.0002	8	28	.0003	20	16	.2514	21	15	.1587	.63
(−) 39. oneness (T)	11	25	.0099	12	24	.0228	12	24	.0228	11	25	.0099	.63
(+) 40. openness (T)	20	16	.2514	26	10	.0035	22	14	.0918	21	15	.1587	.56
(+) 41. open questioning (T)	24	12	.0456	27	9	.0026	26	10	.0070	19	17	.7414	.63
(+) 42. optimism (T)	28	8	.0003	29	7	.0002	23	13	.0475	27	9	.0013	.88
(+) 43. pacing (T)	27	9	.0013	26	10	.0035	23	13	.0475	25	11	.0099	.69
(+) 44. peer teaching (S)	26	10	.0035	19	17	.3707	18	18	.5000	24	12	.0228	.94
(+) 45. personalizing (T)	24	12	.0228	25	11	.0099	23	13	.0475	22	14	.0918	.56
(−) 46. policing (T)	7	29	.0002	9	27	.0013	14	22	.0918	14	22	.0918	.81
(+) 47. politeness (T)	23	13	.0475	26	10	.0035	25	11	.0099	21	15	.1587	.88
(+) 48. praising (T)	29	7	.0002	29	7	.0002	21	15	.1587	23	13	.0475	.81
(+) 49. promoting self-sufficiency (T)	25	11	.0099	30	6	.00003	23	13	.0475	24	12	.0228	.44
(−) 50. recognition seeking (T)	10	26	.0035	11	25	.0099	12	24	.0228	12	24	.0228	.69
(−) 51. rushing (T)	10	26	.0035	12	24	.0228	16	20	.2514	18	18	.5000	.75
(−) 52. sarcasm (T)	10	26	.0035	12	24	.0228	11	25	.0099	18	18	.5000	.75
(−) 53. shaming (T)	13	23	.0475	8	28	.0003	12	24	.0228	14	22	.0918	.63
(+) 54. signaling (control) (T)	17	19	.7414	15	21	.3174	8	28	.0006	8	28	.0006	.69
(+) 55. spontaneity (T)	26	10	.0035	28	8	.0003	25	11	.0099	23	13	.0475	.81
(−) 56. stereotyping (T)	16	20	.2514	11	25	.0099	14	22	.0918	16	20	.2514	.69
(+) 57. structuring (T)	24	12	.0228	28	8	.0003	26	10	.0035	25	11	.0099	.75
(+) 58. teacher made materials (T)	21	15	.1587	29	7	.0002	21	15	.1587	19	17	.3707	.75
(−) 59. time fixedness (T)	11	25	.0099	10	26	.0035	18	18	.5000	18	18	.5000	.81
(+) 60. waiting (T)	26	10	.0035	27	9	.0013	22	14	.0918	23	13	.0475	.75
(+) 61. warmth (T)	27	9	.0013	26	10	.0035	22	14	.0918	24	12	.0228	.81

* Number of times in 36 paired comparisons the more effective/less effective teacher's protocol was rated as evidencing more of the dimension.

Ten raters worked on second grade reading protocols and then were switched to work on fifth grade mathematics protocols. Ten other raters worked with fifth grade reading protocols and then were switched to second grade mathematics protocols. Each of the ten more effective teachers were treated as an interchangeable set and each of the ten less effective teachers were viewed as an interchangeable set. Pairs of classes were randomly picked for raters to examine. Out of the total 100 pairs possible, 32 pairs were rated by one rater, and four additional pairs were rated independently by two raters. When this process was repeated for each category (reading and mathematics, second and fifth grade) we had sixteen reliability checks nested within the actual ratings. Within each grade and subject matter area 36 pairs of classrooms were compared. Each more effective classroom was compared three or four times with a less effective classroom.

FINDINGS

Table 2 provides the summary data from this study. The simple binomial test was used to examine the ratings. Thirty-six opportunities for rating occurred, thus a split of eighteen and eighteen would have meant that the dimension, say "abruptness," was found eighteen times to be rated as occurring more often in the less effective classrooms and eighteen times to have occurred more often in the more effective classrooms. A split by the raters of twenty-two and fourteen has a probability of occurrence of .09 and a split of twenty-three and thirteen has a probability of occurrence of .05.

This Table reveals that there are twenty-one variables that were generic. That is, these variables discriminated between more and less effective teachers in second grade reading, second grade mathematics, fifth grade reading, and fifth grade mathematics. Variables such as "teacher monitors learning (No. 37)," and "students are engaged (No. 19)," were consistently associated with the more effective teachers. A variable such as "teacher belittles students (No. 7)" was consistently found in the less effective teachers' classrooms, regardless of the subject matter taught or the grade level examined.

Other variables were significantly associated with the more or less effective teachers within a single grade of a single subject matter area. And some variables were associated with effectiveness only in a particular grade x subject matter context. *All* 61 variables were significantly associated with the measured effectiveness of the teachers at least once when the various combinations of curriculum area and grade level were examined.

CONCLUSION

As our work continues each of these variables will be given closer examination in partial replications. In that way increased assurance about the validity of these variables for differentiating more and less effective teachers will be obtained. For now, this work meets the project goal which was to generate variables of promise in the study of teacher effectiveness. Both the methodology used and the results of this study are, in the opinion of the BTES staff, worth further investigation.

References

Campbell, D. T. "Qualitative Knowing in Action Research." Paper presented at the meeting of the American Psychological Association, New Orleans, Louisiana, September, 1974.

Cronbach, L. J. "Beyond the Two Disciplines of Scientific Psychology." *American Psychologist* **30** (1975): 116–127.

Glass, G. V. "The Wisdom of Scientific Inquiry on Education." *Journal of Research in Science Teaching* **9** (1972): 3–18.

Kounin, J. S. *Discipline and Group Management in Classrooms.* New York: Holt, Rinehart and Winston, 1970.

Lutz, F. W., and M. A. Ramsey. "The Use of Anthropological Field Methods in Education." *Educational Researcher* **11** (1974): 5–9.

DAVID M. SHOEMAKER
Southwest Regional Laboratory for Educational Research and Development

The Contribution of Multiple Matrix Sampling to Evaluating Teacher Effectiveness

The procedure for evaluating teacher effectiveness given here makes use of two recent improvements in our ability to measure student achievement associated with an instructional program: the implementation of the item universe concept, and multiple matrix sampling. Although evaluating teacher effectiveness is a complex process, the position taken here is that effectiveness in teaching is best demonstrated by changes in the level of student achievement attributable to the teacher's performance. When one adopts this point of view, it is easy to see how improvements in measuring student achievement in the classroom go hand-in-hand with improvements in evaluating teacher effectiveness.

Our discussion begins with some introductory comments on the relationship between an instructional program and all achievement tests associated with that program. Next, multiple matrix sampling is described in some detail and illustrated with a few simple computations. Finally, how one uses multiple matrix sampling for the appraisal of teaching is discussed.

FRAMEWORK FOR ACHIEVEMENT TESTING

Whenever a test is administered in a classroom, a particular framework for achievement testing is being implemented at that point in time. It is natural, therefore, for the reader to wonder what particular framework for achievement testing is being implemented when one uses multiple matrix sampling. The framework used by the author is summarized here, while a more detailed discussion is given in the *Review of Educational Research* (Shoemaker, 1975).

This article was specially prepared for this volume. Research on this topic was pursuant to contract NE-C-00-0064 with the National Institute of Education. The opinions expressed herein are those of the author and do not necessarily represent the position of the Southwest Regional Laboratory for Educational Research and Development.

The Basic Rationale

For every instructional program there exists one and only one item universe that is inseparable conceptually from it. The program and the item universe are analogous to two sides of the same coin. The instructional program is the vehicle for providing students with the necessary knowledge and skills to answer correctly all items in the item universe. When viewed from this perspective, the item universe limits and defines the instructional program which itself is defined operationally by the item universe. This relationship between item universe and instructional program has been alluded to previously. Dyer (1967), for example, commented that

> . . . in the last analysis, an educational goal is defined only in terms of the agreed-upon procedures and instruments by which its attainment is to be measured. It is to say that the development of educational goals is practically identical with the process by which we develop educational tests. It is to imply what in some quarters might be regarded as the ultimate in educational heresy: teaching should be pointed very specifically at the tests the student will take as a measure of output; otherwise, neither the students nor the teachers are ever likely to discover where they are going or whether they are getting anywhere at all.

The implications of this relationship between item universe and instructional program are important. Those particularly relevant for evaluating teacher effectiveness are:

1. Teaching specifically to the item universe should be the one and only goal of the teacher (and of the instructional program as well).
2. The only relevant metric for assessing student achievement is student performance on the item universe associated with the instructional program.
3. Standardized achievement tests as currently constructed will be of minimum usefulness in assessing student achievement associated with an instructional program.

Coming to Grips with Item Universes

The argument up to this point has been very straight-forward: the instructional program is defined operationally by the item universe which in turn is the logical bailiwick from which any achievement tests associated with the program should be constructed. Here, there are direct and clearly definable links among the instructional program, teacher, item universe, and achievement tests. Obviously, the only way this framework is made useful is if the item universe associated with the instructional program can be defined and the items within it enumerated. For some instructional programs, the associated item universe will be well-defined and easily manageable. For others, the item universe may be either extremely large (and unmanageable) or ambiguous. In this latter case, an approximation called a workable item universe or *item domain* is used. An item domain is a clearly definable and enumerable subuniverse of items extracted through expert selection from the larger item universe. The item domain—which, in most cases, will be a large collection of items—is constructed such that, for all practical purposes and to the best of our knowledge, student achievement as measured by the item domain is equivalent to that defined by the item universe.

Why Bother with Multiple Matrix Sampling?

Multiple matrix sampling will be described in detail in the next section. However, as a brief overview let it be said that, in multiple matrix sampling, an item domain is divided through random sampling of items into a given number of subtests. Each subtest is assigned subsequently to a given number of students, with different students taking different subtests. At the end, it is possible to estimate the results which would have been obtained had all students been administered all items in the item domain.

We bother with multiple matrix sampling because it permits us to assess the performance of a group of students over any item domain. This is a very important point because almost any item domain will be too large to be administered in its entirety to any individual student.

THE MULTIPLE MATRIX SAMPLING MODEL

Multiple matrix sampling is explained easily through an example. Consider the hypothetical matrix of scores given in Fig. 1 obtained by administering to each of 15 students the same nine-item test. This is one example of a *matrix* (a rectangular array of numbers) to which the term multiple matrix sampling refers and shows exactly how all students answered all items. The rows indicate students and the columns indicate items. Using the scoring system (1 = correct, 0 = incorrect) we see, for example, that the first student (Number 1) answered correctly items 2, 3, 4, and 8 and answered incorrectly items 1, 5, 6, 7, and 9. Now, the goal of multiple matrix sampling is to estimate the characteristics of this complete matrix (one important characteristic would be, for example, the average test score) through only collecting (or, *sampling*) part of the item scores. In practice, we "sample" item scores from this complete matrix by administering initially only certain items to certain students.

To estimate the characteristics of a matrix through multiple matrix sampling, the general procedure is:

Step 1: Through random sampling without replacement, divide the items into multiple subtests. (When items are sampled randomly and "without replacement" for each subtest, the items selected from the item domain for one subtest are *not* returned to the item domain before selecting the items for the next subtest.)

Step 2: Administer each subtest to a subgroup of students selected randomly and without replacement from the total group.

Students	Items 1	2	3	4	5	6	7	8	9	Total test score	
1	0	1	1	1	0	0	0	1	0	4	
2	1	0	0	0	1	1	1	1	1	6	
3	1	0	1	1	1	1	0	1	1	7	
4	0	1	0	1	0	1	1	1	0	5	
5	1	1	1	1	1	1	1	1	1	9	
6	1	1	1	1	1	0	1	0	0	6	
7	1	1	1	1	1	1	1	1	0	8	Average
8	1	1	1	1	1	1	1	0	1	8	test score
9	1	1	1	1	1	1	0	1	1	8	is 5.93
10	0	0	0	0	0	0	0	0	0	0	
11	1	0	0	0	0	0	1	0	0	2	
12	1	1	1	1	0	1	1	1	0	7	
13	1	1	1	1	1	1	1	1	1	9	
14	1	1	0	0	0	0	1	0	0	3	
15	1	1	1	1	1	0	0	1	1	7	

Fig. 1. Example of a student-by-item score matrix.

If the characteristics of the matrix given in Fig. 1 were to be estimated through multiple matrix sampling, one method (of several) for doing this would be to (a) construct three 3-item subtests, and (b) administer each subtest to five students randomly selected from the total group. In both cases, items and students are selected randomly and without replacement. Suppose that we do this and obtain the results given in Fig. 2. Looking back at Fig. 1, we see that the scores in Fig. 2 are a part of the matrix given in Fig. 1. Because items have been selected randomly for subtests and students selected randomly for subgroups, the results in Fig. 2 constitute three random samples from Fig. 1. In practice, the results in Fig. 1 are unknown to us and the results we obtain through multiple matrix sampling are like those given in Fig. 2.

Students	Items 1	2	3	4	5	6	7	8	9
1							0	1	0
2							1	1	1
3							0	1	1
4							1	1	0
5							1	1	1
6	1	1	1						
7	1	1	1						
8	1	1	1						
9	1	1	1						
10	0	0	0						
11				0	0	0			
12				1	0	1			
13				1	1	1			
14				0	0	0			
15				1	1	0			

Fig. 2. Example of results obtained from multiple matrix sampling.

Before proceeding further, it is important to make three points clear: (a) Although in Fig. 1 items have been scored dichotomously (1 = correct, 0 = incorrect), an example could have been used just as easily where items had been scored polychotomously using, for example, the scale 1, 2, 3, 4, and 5; (b) It is *not* necessary that all students be included in some subgroup or all items included in some subtest; (c) An important assumption in multiple matrix sample is that both items and students are selected randomly.

An Example

An example of multiple matrix sampling is given here and our goal will be to estimate the average test score for the fifteen students on the nine-item test given given in Fig. 1. Although we know in advance that the average test score is 5.93, we will estimate this value using the data given in Fig. 2.

In Fig. 2, we have the results from three subtests; those for the first subtest are:

		Items			
		7	8	9	Total subtest score
Students	1	0	1	0	1
	2	1	1	1	3
	3	0	1	1	2
	4	1	1	0	2
	5	1	1	1	3

where the average total subtest score is 2.20. Because the three items in the subtest were selected randomly from the nine-item test, we expect that the performance of the first subgroup on the remaining six items would be about the same as that demonstrated on their three-item subtest—or, that they would receive the same average subtest score (2.20) on the other two subtests. Reasoning this way, their estimated average score on the nine-item test would be $(2.20 + 2.20 + 2.20) = 6.60$. Using the results for subtests 2 and 3, we obtain 7.20 and 4.20 as estimates of the average score on the nine-item test for subgroups 2 and 3. Because subgroups have been sampled randomly, all three estimates (6.60, 7.20, and 4.20) of the average test score are equally good and our single best estimate is found by taking the average of these three estimates. The result here is $6.00 = (6.60 + 7.20 + 4.20)/3$, which is our final estimate of the average test score. It should be noted that, had the number of students per subgroup and items per subtest not been constant, a weighting procedure would have been used in combining these individual estimates of the average test score.

We know that 6.00 is an *estimate* of the true average test score and, to acknowledge this fact, we cite a range within which the true average test score is expected to fall with a given probability. (We probably would have obtained a different estimate if, for example, different subgroups had been assigned different subtests, different items were in different subtests, or different students in different subgroups.) This is comparable to saying that the true average test score is "6.0, give or take a little." In multiple matrix sampling, the amount which we should "give or take a little" may be estimated statistically and, in our case, was computed to be .67. Our best estimate of the true average test score then is a value between 5.33 and 6.67. Although in this example we have focused solely on estimating the average test score, procedures for estimating additional characteristics (e.g., the variance of test scores, the reliability of the total test score) of the data base are available and given by Shoemaker (1973).

MULTIPLE MATRIX SAMPLING CONTRASTED WITH TRADITIONAL ASSESSMENT PROCEDURES

Traditional approaches to assessing student achievement may be classified as *census testing, item sampling, examinee sampling,* or *item-examinee sampling.* All are illustrated in Fig. 3 and serve to accent more clearly the uniqueness of multiple matrix sampling. In Fig. 3, the cross-hatched areas indicate students tested.

In census testing, all students are administered all items—there is no sampling involved. In item sampling, a random sample of items is administered to all students. In examinee sampling, all test items are administered to a random sample of students. And, in item-examinee sampling, a random sample of items is administered to a random sample of examinees. Within this framework, multiple matrix sampling is equal to "multiple item-examinee sampling."

WHY USE MULTIPLE SAMPLING?

Although multiple matrix sampling is *not* the answer to all testing problems, it is a good solution to a large class of problems we encounter frequently in education. That class of problems is labeled "group assessment" and assessing the effectiveness of teachers is only one example of group assessment. To make clear the distinction between *group assessment* and *individual assessment,* consider, for example a school district which has initiated a new teacher appraisal program and which, at the end of the school year, wants to know which teachers have been most effective in improving the level of reading achievement for second grade students. If achievement in reading were being measured by a 300-item reading test, the school district would be primarily interested in determining the average reading test score for the group of students (group assessment) and not the individual test score for each student (individual assessment). The reason here is that, when assessing teacher effectiveness, it is relatively unimportant to diagnose the achievement level of each individual student.

Specific Advantages in Using Multiple Matrix Sampling

There are several advantages in using multiple matrix sampling for group assessment and those listed below are the most important:

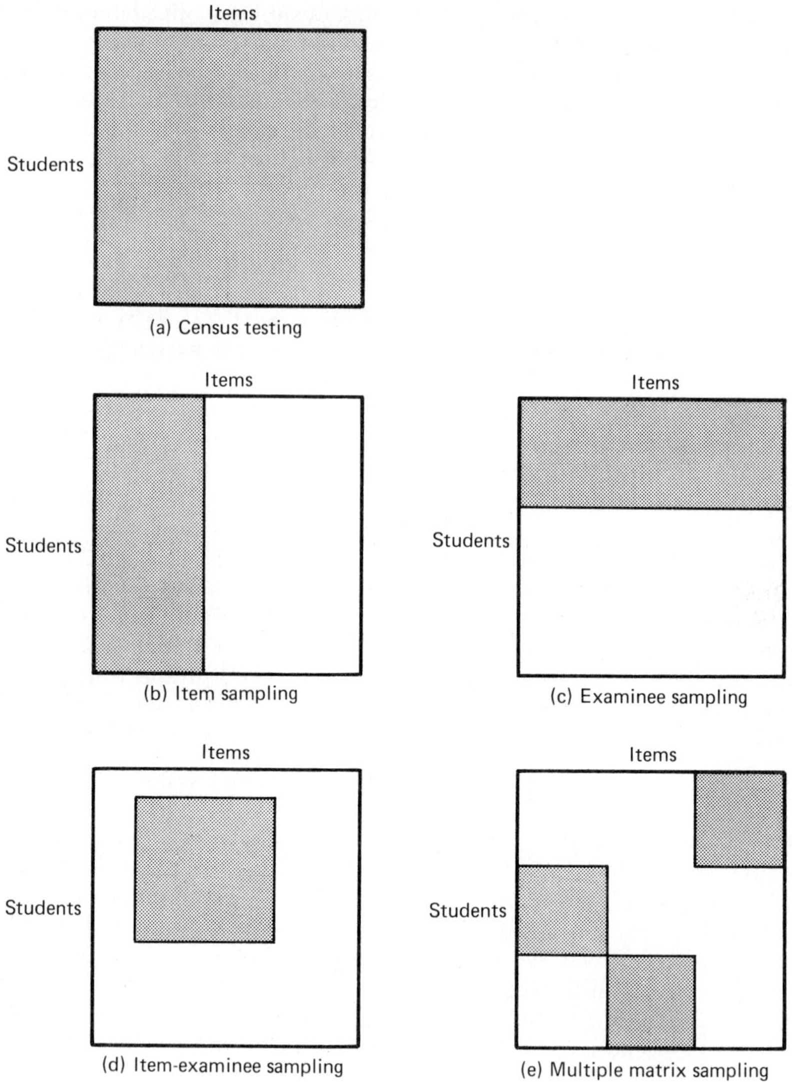

Fig. 3. Traditional approaches to assessment (a-d) contrasted with multiple matrix sampling (e).

1. Multiple matrix sampling requires *less testing time* for each student selected for testing. In multiple matrix sampling, each student tested responds to only a portion of the complete set of test items. Two important points here are (a) a school district may participate more willingly in a teacher appraisal program which does not require much testing time, and (b) the normal classroom routine will be disrupted less and more time may be spent on instruction.

2. With multiple matrix sampling, it is possible to obtain a *more comprehensive assessment of group performance*. Frequently and understandably, test constructors have limited the items in a particular test to a number not too tiring for any one student. Now, with multiple matrix sampling, we can assess group performance on a broader spectrum of items because the testing time per student is a function of the subtest length, not the total test length. Because more items are involved in the appraisal (and the testing time per student tested is still within reasonable limits), we gain more useful information about the effect of a teacher upon student achievement.

3. A major advantage (which we will discuss here but not prove) in using multiple matrix sampling for group assessment is that *estimates of group performance are superior to those obtained from any other testing procedure collecting the same number of observations,* where one observation is defined as the score obtained by one student on one item. To see what is meant here, look at Fig. 1 where the nine item scores are given for each of fifteen students. Here, there are $135 = (9)(15)$ observations. In Fig. 2, only $45 = (3)(5) + (3)(5) + (3)(5)$ observations were collected. Looking at Fig. 1, we see that we could have collected 45 observations through examinee sampling by testing only five students on all nine items or, through item sampling, by testing all fifteen students on only three items or, through item-examinee sampling, by testing nine students on five items. The point here is that, for a given number of observations, estimates of group performance obtained through multiple matrix sampling will be closer on the average to the true level of group performance than those obtained through item sampling, examinee sampling, or item-examinee sampling. A more formal way of saying this is that the standard error of estimate will be less using multiple matrix sampling.

ASSESSING TEACHER EFFECTIVENESS

The first step in evaluating the effectiveness of a teacher or group of teachers involves evaluating student achievement in the instructional program on the relevant item domain (and not just a part of it.) Lest the reader think that an item domain consists of only "paper-and-pencil" items, let it be said here that such is not the case. If one considers an item to be a stimulus for eliciting a response, "paper-and-pencil" items are merely one class of stimuli. Other classes of stimuli, frequently of interest, are those whose items deal with student affect and with psychomotor skills.

An Example

As an example of how multiple matrix sampling might be used to evaluate teacher effectiveness, consider a grade-two reading program for which, say, a 300-item domain has been constructed. Assume that the 300-item domain consists of six separate content subdomains and that our goal is to estimate the achievement of thirty students (one class, one teacher) on each subdomain. One procedure for doing this would be to construct ten 30-item subtests, with the

30 items in each subtest selected by randomly sampling five items (without replacement) from within each item subdomain. Each of the ten subtests would be randomly assigned to three students within the class. The same set of subtests, once constructed, could be used for both pretesting and posttesting—the only precaution being that an individual student not be administered the same subtest on both occasions.

The Necessary Second Step

So far, we have been talking about the *first* step in evaluating teacher effectiveness. In the necessary *second* step, the estimated student achievement on the item subdomains for each teacher must be compared to (a) the results obtained by other teachers using the same instructional program, or (b) results obtained by the same teacher over past times in which the same instructional program has been used. This second step is necessary because, after we have estimated student achievement, we cannot tell if that achievement is generally the result of the instructional program or the result of the individual teacher. Assuming that students within classes are approximately homogeneous at the start of instruction, it is only by making such comparisons that we are able to separate the two effects.

References

Dyer, H. S. "The Discovery and Development of Educational Goals." In J. C. Stanley, ed., *Proceedings of the 1966 Invitational Conference on Testing Problems*. Princeton, N.J.: Educational Testing Service, 1967.

Shoemaker, D. M. *Principles and Procedures of Multiple Matrix Sampling*. Cambridge, Mass.: Ballinger, 1973.

Shoemaker, D. M. "Toward a Framework for Achievement Testing." *Review of Educational Research* 45 (1975): 127–147.

EVA L. BAKER
University of California at Los Angeles

Contribution of Domain-Referenced Tests to Evaluating Teacher Effectiveness

What options are available to an evaluator who is charged with the responsibility of providing data to facilitate instructional improvement? Domain-referenced testing can supply both the data needed for assessment of instructional programs and information suitable for feedback to teachers to facilitate planning.

DOMAINS AND TRANSFERABLE SKILLS

A domain consists of a subset of knowledge, skills, understandings or attitudes where the essential attributes of the content which the student is expected to acquire and the behavior through which he or she is expected to demonstrate such acquisition are carefully described. Rather than measuring a single point within the vast universe of knowledge, e.g., "To list four causes of the formation of the Confederate States of America," or a general, but unmanageably broad area, e.g., "To write an essay on civil strife," domains for teaching and testing represent an attempt to find a reasonable compromise between vagueness and over-precision. Domains should function so that a large number of test items could be generated according to given rules and randomly sampled to constitute comparable tests.

The problem of specifying domains for testing can be compared to a more familiar problem in the field of educational psychology: the definition and promotion of transfer skills. Educational goals or objectives seldom should be articulated for the mastery of single items. For instance, an objective where the learner is required to write the analysis of Antony's speech in Shakespeare's *Julius Caesar* cannot in itself be justified. One expects that, if the learner is able

Excerpted from Eva L. Baker, "Beyond Objectives: Domain-Referenced Tests for Evaluation and Instructional Improvement," in *Domain-Referenced Testing*, ed. W. Hively (Englewood Cliffs, N.J.: Educational Technology Publications, 1974), pp. 16–30. Reprinted by permission.

to write such an analysis, the ability will transfer to other instances of literature, encountered both within and outside of formal schooling. The danger in specifying an objective similar to the one presented above is that it may be taught in a manner which is likely to result in minimum generalization. Teachers may focus on Antony's speech *qua* Antony's speech; they may frequently ignore, in this situation, pointing up the salient aspects included in his oratory and demonstrating their application in other persuasive writing. The main idea behind transfer of training, the provision of multiple examples, is missing from objectives that focus on a single instance of content. Antony's speech, *David Copperfield, Silas Marner,* among numerous other literary classics, were made forgettable for most of us by low-generality teaching of this type.

Domains require the objective-maker to focus on the range of eligible content to which the learner's skill is to apply. Rather than formulate the above objective in terms of Antony's rhetoric, one would instead describe the class of rhetoric his speech represented and attempt to generate rules by which other speeches could be judged as similarly appropriate representatives of the class of rhetoric.

Thus, central to the problem of specifying domains is the definition of content rules or limits. Such rules specify the common characteristics of eligible examples, problems, or more generally, *stimuli* which will be presented to the learner in the testing and teaching situations. The designation of content rules represents the most significant departure of domain-referenced testing from the more common objectives-based evaluation. Thus, the use of domains in the design of instruction and in the design of tests, in effect, prohibits the production of trivial objectives. The force of domain preparation is to influence the writer in the direction of significant, generalizable skills. The ability to list three causes for the depression could only be a suitable objective if, in domain context, it were modified to concern the generalizable causes of economic decline, of which the 1929 depression was only one example.

Content limits may be simple or complex. Examples of simple limits may be derived from the field of mathematics, where it is relatively easy to specify what the replacement set for content is, e.g., "two digit numbers," "fractions where the numerator is one and the denominator less than 100." On the other hand, domains specified for disciplines such as history, e.g., "to analyze in writing a totalitarian government," require a complex set of rules for selection of content, e.g., examples of totalitarian governments might include those drawn from any geographical area, where absolute power was aggregated to a small number of individuals, where individual rights, as exemplified in the U.S. Constitution and amendments, were abrogated without recourse, etc.

The force of such content limits, *under theoretical circumstances,* is not only to provide clear guidance for what is a suitable stimulus for presentation during teaching or testing; one would also expect that performance on content sampled from the domain would be homogeneous. Students should not have any more difficulty in dealing with totalitarianism in 17th century China or 20th century Spain. Even if homogeneity of student response could not be demonstrated, the result of domain specification at minimum is to emphasize the generalizable attributes of the subject matter and to increase the probability of transfer.

GUIDELINES FOR PREPARING DOMAINS

If domain-referenced tests are theoretically important, how can those charged with evaluation responsibility learn to prepare such instruments? A simplified version of the production of domain-referenced tests will be presented below. The procedure emphasizes certain aspects of the domains assumed to require most attention. Let us take as a point of departure the rules or guidelines usually prescribed for the production of criterion-referenced tests. Criterion-referenced, or objectives-based, tests ordinarily focus on the following attributes of instructional design:

Objectives-Based Tests

1. Objectives are operationally (behaviorally) stated.
2. Criteria for scoring are provided.
3. Conditions for the administration of the test are described.
4. A sample test item may be given.

These guidelines were assembled from books such as Mager's (1962) and materials designed to assist schools with evaluation such as the *Collections* of objectives and measures distributed by the Instructional Objectives Exchange at UCLA.

CLARIFYING SUBSTANCE

Domain specifications include attributes very similar to those listed for objectives-referenced test design. However, domain specifications require attention to dimensions beyond those normally considered by criterion-referenced design.

Elements of Domain Specifications

1. Domain Description
2. Content Limits
3a. Criteria, or
3b. Distractor Domains
4. Format
5. Directions
6. Sample Item

Let us proceed sequentially. Domain descriptions obviously correspond to what are usually termed behavioral objectives.

Domain Description: A general, but operational statement of the behavior and content upon which the test focuses.

The *domain description* term is preferred because the word *objectives* implies *intent.* Tests may also be written to measure in a systematic way performance other than that encompassed in the goals of an instructional program. For instance, an instructional program on transformational grammar could also be evaluated by sampling a domain involving principles of structural grammar as well, to determine the extent of overlap. In most situations, however, the terms "objective" and "domain description" may be interchanged.

The statement of the domain description or objective serves to delimit the general area of concern for the producer of the domain specifications. If the objective calls for the student to "write essays on post-impressionist artists," we know that the area of interest is art rather than mathematics, post-impressionists rather than expressionists and that an essay will be the form in which the response is to be generated. Thus, from the infinite range of content and behavior available to people, the use of an objective or domain description has significantly focused our attention.

The critical and unique aspects of the domain specifications are contained in the next two sections. The first, *content limits,* provides a set of rules to describe what content is appropriate to include or to sample in the text or instructional examples. The content limits describe the range of content to which the learner is expected to respond.

Content Limits: A set of rules (or a list) of content eligible for inclusion in the test items or in instruction.

There is no component in the objectives-referenced test guidelines which corresponds to the notion of content limits. In effect, the test designer is fencing off the area of content which is considered to be essential in the mastery of the more general domain description or objective. For instance, if the domain description called for the student to diagram standard English sentences, then the content limits for such an objective might contain the following:

Content Limits

I. Sentences in the structural patterns:

Noun$_1$-verb-noun$_2$	*Example:*	I like you.
Noun$_1$-linking verb-noun$_1$	*Example:*	Mary is a doctor.
Noun-linking verb-adjective	*Example:*	John has been unhappy.
Noun-verb	*Example:*	The crowd roared.

II. Any tense or number may be used.

III. Patterns may be modified by single or series of adjectives or adverbs.

These content limits delineate more precisely sentences which are eligible contenders for correct answers. The teacher or designer, when made aware of such limits, has the following information available:

1. Students are expected to generalize their skills to four basic declarative sentence patterns. They are not expected to be competent with less familiar structures. (N_1-V-N_2-A: The girls thought him rude.)
2. They should be able to discern appropriate sentence structures regardless of the tense of the sentence or whether the number is singular or plural.
3. They will not be given complex sentences as stimuli. A modified sentence such as this example would be acceptable: *Quickly and efficiently, the agile forward rebounded the ball.* The next sentence would not: *With grace and cunning, the runner sidestepped his opponent, and in a split second, carried the ball over the goal line.*

Precision about the class of sentences which should be emphasized can enormously assist the planner of instructional sequences, for the relevant content areas are limited. Instructional time need not be spent parsing complex sentences. It should be devoted to providing a range of relevant models for the learner to confront. Thus, in an instructional improvement situation, where a set of learners has not performed to specified standards, the teacher is much advantaged by having a copy of the rules by which content was selected for inclusion on the instrument. Access to rules is a far different and infinitely more appropriate condition than providing teachers with copies of the test to be used. If content limits are defined and disseminated, the teacher has a clear idea of the type of sentence which should appear on the examination, but not the exact set of sentences which *will* appear. Thus, the teacher must teach toward the skill at the transfer or generalization level rather than a rote skill to be drummed methodically into the minds of students.

The set of content limits in the example provided still allows a wide range. Certain aspects of sentence formation were left to vary freely, such as complexity of vocabulary and familiarity of topic. If desirable for a given instructional program, these aspects could be specified as well. The amount of information the instructional planner has available as a consequence of reasonable content limits is significantly improved from that which is included in the usual instructional objective.

A third critical component of a domain specifications approach to the generation of teaching and testing domains is the statement of criteria for constructed responses.

> **Criteria for Constructed Responses:** Rules by which the adequacy of response to the item can be judged.

A criterion statement has been ordinarily considered as the part of the objective which clarifies what serves as an adequate response. For instance, in an objective where an essay on economic systems is desired, a statement of criteria might describe what points the learner should make in order to be considered correct. For example, the learner might be asked to include political, social and educational consequences of a set of described economic systems. In addition to substantive points, the learner might also be required to provide his or her answers in a particular format, providing references for any statement in standard bibliographic style. Criteria for constructed response, in this way, further specify what is to be taught. For instance, if an important criterion for the above objective relates to the relationship of economic systems to other institutions, then the teacher should include in the instructional program some place for the learner to gain access to needed principles. If bibliographic style were a serious criterion, then instruction relevant to citations, footnotes, etc., would be requisite. The actual implementation of criteria, however, often involves applying standards in evaluating a learner's product beyond what has been taught during the instructional program. Teachers have been known to use talent dimensions such as originality as a basis for evaluating student responses. If such a criterion is included in a statement of a domain, some attempt to operationalize it must be made. The thrust of the domain specifications is to describe clearly what relevant attributes a response should encompass. Where these cannot be well explained, then one might argue that such a dimension is inappropriate for inclusion in teacher evaluation designs, for the chance a teacher has to improve performance is low.

Another problem is posed when the learner is expected to select the correct response from among alternatives. A critical error in the design of tests is often made when the distractors, the presented but incorrect choices, are generated on an unplanned basis. Wrong answers can be described in more detail than "they are not the right ones." In many cases, critical discriminations are important to learning. One does not wish the learner to choose correct answers when presented with *any* set of distractors. One may wish to discern that the learner can choose correctly when presented with the most confusable alternative set. For instance, that a child can choose a "d" from a random selection of other letters may be adequate; however, to test his or her skill at a more sensitive level, one might wish to limit the distractors to those composed of lines and curves (p, r, b) rather than certain readily identifiable letters like x, s, and i.

For selected responses:
Distractor Domain: specifies the rules for inclusion of wrong-answer alternatives.

Imagine that you are a teacher whose students have been given an achievement test in the area of chemistry. Suppose you wish to re-teach or remediate students' performances that fall below a certain criterion level. If you understood the multiple-choice test to be developed according to traditional procedures, you could not plan specifically to provide the students with relevant selection practice, for wrong answers might be drawn from the entire range of beginning chemistry. If, on the other hand, you were presented with the rules by which wrong answers were selected, such as equations were imbalanced, -ites and -ates were interchanged, etc., you should be able to see that you would be in a decidedly stronger position. You could not only teach students what the right answers would be but you could also teach them about errors they might be likely to make.

To prepare a section in the domain specifications on distractor domains, the same procedure as for content limits is involved. The rules are specified to delimit the range of wrong answers. The test designer need only to generate an appropriate population of wrong answers and to sample from among them.

CLARIFYING FORM

In each of the preceding topics, the primary concern was the further clarification of the substantive portion of the objective. One was encouraged to describe rules for the generation of appropriate content; to identify suitable scoring criteria when the task is a constructed one; to define the limits of distractor domains when the response format requires the learner to select responses.

So far, our domain specifications look like this:

Partial Domain Specifications

1. Domain description (objective):
2. Content limits:

3a. Criteria (for constructed responses): or

3b. Distractor domains (for selected responses):

Two additional components to the domain specifications are required to clarify fully the design for the set of items. These concerns are more similar to typical concerns in test design, and thus will be only briefly treated.

A further clarification of the format of the item, beyond that stated in the Response Description, may be required. If the objective calls for the learner to select from alternatives the correct sum of an addition problem, the form in which the item is presented to the student can seriously influence his or her achievement on it. For instance, if an addition problem is displayed horizontally, $34 + 45 = \ldots$, the learner may not do as well if his or her previous experience consisted of problems arrayed vertically: $\begin{array}{r} 34 \\ \underline{+45} \end{array}$

One might argue that the ability to solve addition problems should not be contingent upon their spatial orientation, and I would agree. However, the testing situation is not the time to spring previously unencountered displays on a child. If a range of positions were to be included on the test, these should be specified in the format section of the domain specifications, precisely so that teachers could provide suitable practice situations for their students.

Format: A description of the form in which the items will be presented to students.

A common type of objective calls for the learner to identify an example of concept when presented with a series of distractors, for instance,

Which of the following is a correct octal number?

a. 16

b. 18

c. 94

The problem becomes more complex, of course, as the number of alternatives increases, for chance correct answering is reduced, reading time expanded, and the individual comparisons the learner must make are increased. The instructional planner should be told whether items are to consist of three, four or five alternatives. She can gear instruction to provide practice in exactly the formats to be tested. Thus, the format statement provides a physical description of the item: how long it will be, how many distractors, what additional cues (such as graphs or displays) the learner may have available and (if significant, as in addition) how the items will be arrayed on the page. The purpose of format statements, beyond providing guidance in instruction, is to constrain item writers to adhere to a specified set of rules in order to avoid the introduction of error into the test by varying the properties of the item inadvertently. A second feature of the specifications which serves to control a formal rather than substantive concern is the description of test directions:

Directions: Facsimile of directions provided the learner in the test situation.

Unfortunately, the provision of carefully planned directions is often overlooked in locally prepared tests. The wording of the directions must be in language that the student can comprehend. The directions should be checked to determine that they do not require the learner to make responses different from those anticipated in the response description.

SYNTHESIS

The last element of the domain specifications is the inclusion of an item sampled from within the content limits and intended as a representative of the class of response desired. The item should adhere to all rules (content limits, distractor domains, format statement) included in the domain specifications. It merely serves to clarify, by example, what was meant in the various sections. The sample item is not sufficient in itself to serve the clarifying function, for unless augmented by the verbal description of each of the item form elements, the evaluator is forced to again infer, with attending errors, the relevant attributes the item exemplifies.

A total plan for domain test specifications is as follows:

Work Sheet for Domain Specifications

Domain description:
(objective)

Content limits:

Criteria for constructed responses

or

Distractor domains for selected responses

Format statement

Directions

Sample item

Most decisions regarding content limits, criteria or distractor domains, formats, etc., are arbitrary, as are most curriculum decisions. The use of domain-referenced tests will have power when decisions regarding goals and content are made according to justifiable rather than incidental bases.

It is suggested that you take an important objective in your own field, and attempt to prepare domain specifications for it. Only when you begin to interact with the problem can you appreciate some of its difficulty. For this reason, domain specifications are not suggested for across-the-board preparation. Only goals of significance are worthy of the design effort. As a corollary, only goals worthy of adequate test design should actually be measured. The use of domain specifications should be highly selective. If the procedure operates as I think it should, it will reduce the number of specific goals which are formally evaluated and focus on a relatively few but important outcomes. Thus, the drive for evaluating every classroom activity—every instructional encounter—would be reduced and evaluation efforts would assume their proper functions: contributors to the design of effective, significant instruction.

References

Bloom, B. S., M. D. Engelhart, E. J. Furst, W. H. Hill, and D. R. Krathwohl. *Taxonomy of Educational Objectives, Handbook I: Cognitive Domain*. New York: McKay, 1956.

Mager, R. F. *Preparing Instructional Objectives*. Palo Alto, California: Fearon, 1962.

Scriven, M. "The Methodology of Evaluation." *Perspectives of Curriculum Evaluation* (AERA Monograph Series on Curriculum Evaluation, No. 1). Chicago: Rand McNally, 1967.

DONALD B. SENSION
Hopkins, Minnesota Public Schools
and
GEORGE J. RABEHL
Osseo, Minnesota Public Schools

Applications of Multiple-Matrix Sampling and Domain-Referenced Testing in Two School Systems

Domain-referenced tests are currently being used in the implementation of accountability procedures at Hopkins, Minnesota and Osseo, Minnesota. In the 1972–1973 school year, the testing programs in these two systems served over 300 teachers and 15,000 students in the subject matter areas of mathematics, science, reading, social studies, language arts, speech and music.

Efforts to develop and implement domain-referenced achievement testing systems were stimulated by ESEA Title III grants in both school districts. Hopkins worked through its "Demonstration Evaluation Center" and "Comprehensive Achievement Monitoring" (CAM) projects. The Osseo work has been done largely through a project to develop and implement "An Accountability Model for Local Education Agencies" (Independent School District No. 279, 1972 and 1973).

USEFUL TEST DESIGNS

Individual Data

A number of distinct basic test designs have been used with success in the two school systems. The first involves the administration of a test to an individual student based on one objective. Typically, 10 items are sampled at random from a single domain and administered to obtain an estimate of a student's competence on that particular objective. This approach is useful with carefully defined programs of instruction in which mastery levels of performance are specified for each stage in a sequence. Failure of a student to meet the criterion may result in more instruction, perhaps of an alternative form, followed by

Excerpted from D. B. Sension and G. J. Rabehl, "Test-Item Domains and Instructional Accountability," in *Domain-Referenced Testing*, ed. W. Hively (Englewood Cliffs, N.J.: Educational Technology Publications, 1974), pp. 45–62. Reprinted by permission.

retesting on another random sample of items from the same domain. This general approach is used in the Articulation Program in Osseo. An additional feature involves the administration of items from a terminal domain at the end of each major step in the sequence of instruction. The results, graphed as in Figure 1, help to meet a motivational need of the student and provide excellent documentation of achievement to be used in evaluating the program as a whole.

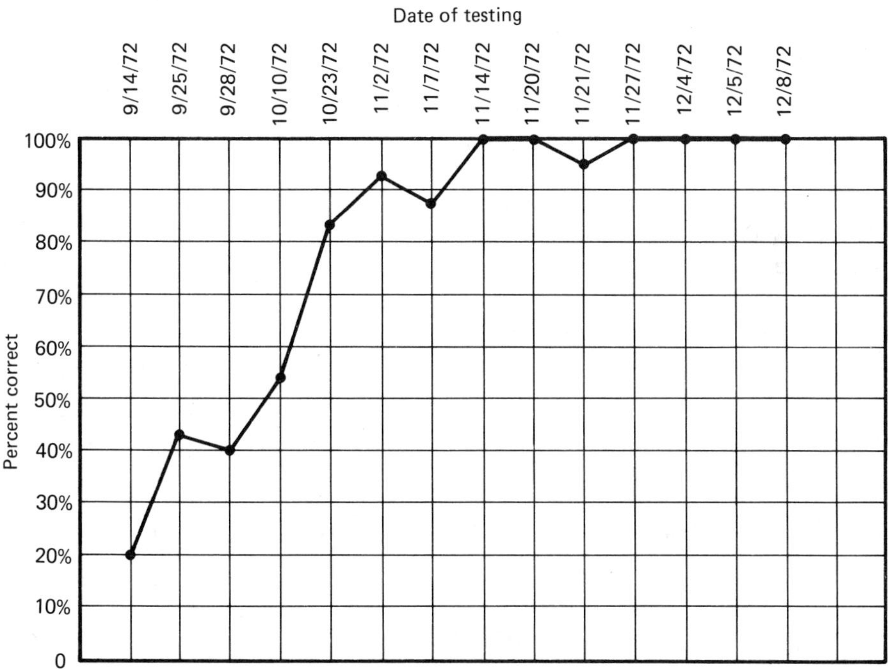

Fig. 1. Individual performance record on a terminal objective of the Osseo Articulation Program.

The Hopkins system has utilized the Comprehensive Achievement Monitoring (CAM) program extensively in implementing domain-referenced achievement testing on an individual basis in the regular classroom. The CAM system facilitates the collection, summarization and dissemination of pre-, post-, and retention test data. Feedback of information to teachers and students often takes the form of cumulative records similar to the one shown in Figure 2. Domain code numbers appear at the left and testing dates are across the top. An index to the code numbers is kept by the teacher and made available to students.

Students insert pluses and minuses in the record which indicate correct and incorrect responses, respectively. A blank shows that an item from that objective

Objective	Sept. 15	Oct. 1	Oct. 15	Nov. 1	Nov. 15	Dec. 1	Dec. 15	Jan. 15	Feb. 1	Feb. 15	Mar. 1	.	.	.	.
101	+	+	+					+	.	.	.	.	.	.	.
102	−	+			−	+			.	.	.	.	.	.	.
103		−	−	+	+		+		.	.	.	.	.	.	.
201	−		−	−	+	−	+	+	.	.	.	.	.	.	.
202	+	+	+	+	+		+		.	.	.	.	.	.	.
203	−	−	−	−	−	−	−	−	.	.	.	.	.	.	.
205	−	−	−	−	−	−	−	−	.	.	.	.	.	.	.
310	+	.	+	+	+	+	+		.	.	.	.	.	.	.
315	+	+	+	−	+			+	.	.	.	.	.	.	.
320			−	−	+	+	−	+	.	.	.	.	.	.	.
.	.	.	.	.	.	.	.	.	.	.	.	.	.	.	.
.	.	.	.	.	.	.	.	.	.	.	.	.	.	.	.
.	.	.	.	.	.	.	.	.	.	.	.	.	.	.	.
TOTAL															

KEY + = correct response
− = incorrect response
Blank = objective not tested

Fig. 2. Student response grid.

was not given on the occasion indicated. In consultation with his teacher, the student can use his cumulative record to decide what to review and what to tackle next. This type of data analysis obtains its power from its longitudinal nature. Normally, only one item is sampled from a domain class. Reliability of an objective score at any one testing depends to a certain degree on the homogeneity of the particular domain used. Confidence in results is thus confirmed on several testings.

Group Data

Useful data from domain-referenced achievement tests have also been collected and summarized on a group basis. At Osseo, for example, random samples of items from each of the 134 computation domains were given to students from each grade in elementary schools. Matrix sampling plans were used, in which not every student had the same items. This made it difficult to compare students, but the larger samples obtained from each domain made it possible to obtain fairly accurate estimates of group performance on each objective.

Figure 3 shows the proportion of children in each grade who were able to do particular kinds of arithmetic problems at one school in November. Line No. 1 shows composite scores on four kinds of basic facts; line No. 2 shows the results on items involving the subtraction of a one-place subtrahend from a three-place minuend with repeated regrouping; line No. 3 shows the scores on items involving long division of a three-place dividend by a two-place divisor with remainder possible.

The approach has been to pinpoint the competencies of students in each grade across the 134 domain skill areas and then ask the following questions:

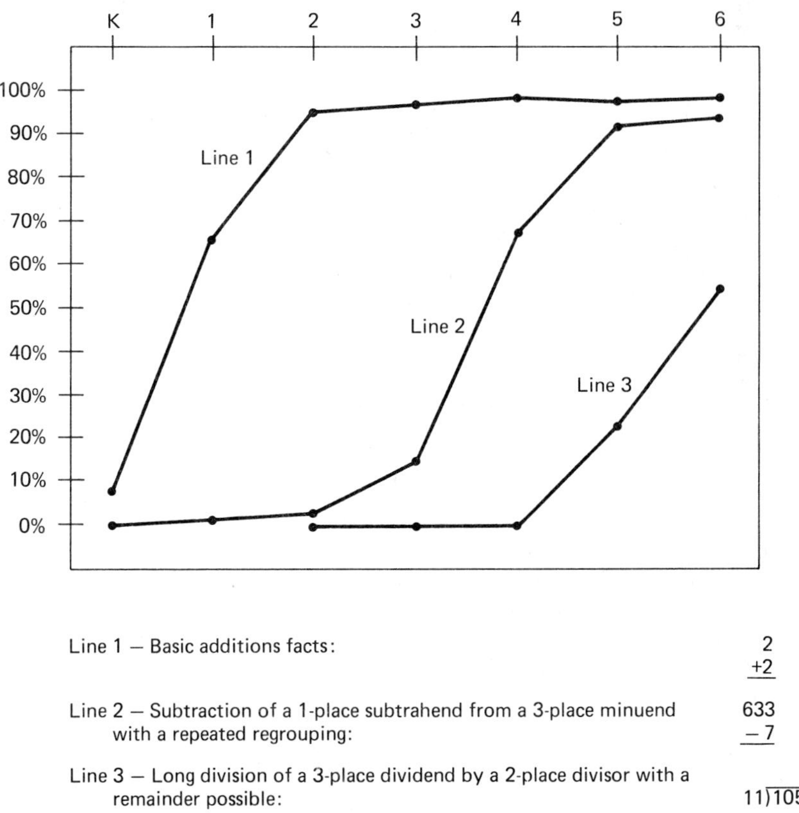

Fig. 3. Proportion of students in each grade at Crestview Elementary School (Osseo) who could do problems of certain kinds in November, 1972.

1. Are all entering competencies as low as expected, i.e., is it necessary to include the skill in the curriculum of a certain grade level?
2. Are all terminal competencies (sixth grade) as high as desired?
3. Are the skills being learned in the proper order?
4. What particular skills should receive priority given limited resources for program revision and curriculum change?

Profiles No. 1 and No. 2 show rather complete group mastery in two respective areas of addition and subtraction with differences due apparently to the time that the two skills were introduced and practiced. Instruction in long division of the type shown here occurs primarily in the fifth and sixth grades. Failure of scores to increase substantially could indicate a need for increased emphasis on that part of the program.

Domain-referenced testing of this type has given teachers highly specific information about the achievement of their students as a group. It helps a school faculty to evaluate priorities and plan program revisions when combined with other information about student needs.

DOMAIN DEVELOPMENT AND STORAGE

Item forms are being used in domain development and storage, particularly at Osseo. A useful approach in both systems has been to type generated or composed items onto file cards, which are coded and stored in central item banks within sections devoted to course related or subject matter related topics. See Figure 4.

A teacher or other staff person may call for a test having certain kinds of items. A clerk goes to the file (or item form), assembles the test and sends one

Which of the following facts is most relevant to this situation? "John J. Jones is now unemployed, and has been on relief for 2 years, even though he is actively seeking work."

A. Unemployment is a big problem in the trucking industry.
B. John Jones has been fired for drinking on the job by six different employers.
C. John Jones has a high school education.
D. Federal government relief programs have risen by 50 percent over the past five years.

612 0002-1 B

Fig. 4. Sample item card.

or more copies to the requester. The test may be saved and duplicated for others who have the same needs or new ones may be developed as the situation requires. None of this, of course, precludes the maintenance of test-item domains by individual teachers.

Domains have been developed largely by committees of teachers and resource persons in target subject matter areas with the technical assistance of evaluators in each school system, who drew heavily on techniques developed by Hively and his associates at the University of Minnesota School Mathematics and Science Teaching Project. (See Hively, Maxwell, Rabehl, Sension, and Lundin, 1973; Rabehl, 1971; Rabehl, 1972a; Rabehl, 1972b.)

References

Hively, W., M. G. Maxwell, G. J. Rabehl, D. B. Sension, and S. Lundin. *Domain-Referenced Curriculum Evaluation: A Technical Handbook and a Case Study* (CSE Monograph Series in Evaluation). Los Angeles: Center for the Study of Evaluation, 1973.

Rabehl, G. J. "The Experimental Analysis of Educational Objectives." Ph.D. dissertation, University of Minnesota, 1971.

Rabehl, G. J. *An Item Form System.* Unpublished manuscript, Osseo, Minnesota Public Schools, 1972a.

Rabehl, G. J. *Developing a Domain.* Unpublished manuscript, Osseo, Minnesota Public Schools, 1972b.

Chapter 10

Selected Readings: Developing a Valid Appraisal System

This final chapter contains three readings that pose, and to some extent answer, one of the most critical questions raised about the teacher appraisal process: "How reliable and valid are the methods we use to determine teacher effectiveness?" Though at first glance the following selections may appear a pessimistic assessment of current efforts to evaluate teacher performance, they are included here on the optimistic assumption that they will alert appraisers to the need for reliable and valid measures of teacher effectiveness and to methods for attaining them.

These readings discuss the same general issue addressed in Chapter 5: the validity of appraisal. However, while Chapter 5 described steps taken *prior to* appraisal to insure a valid plan, this chapter examines procedures taken *during* appraisal to insure valid measurement. Thus, the introductory chapter concentrated on the *design* of appraisal systems, while the corresponding readings address their *implementation*.

This change of focus involves a shift from a relatively general to a highly specific and technical level of discussion. Though *designing* a valid appraisal system requires consideration of a number of important factors, it does not demand the sophisticated statistical procedures entailed in valid measurement. Several of these statistical procedures are described on the following pages because, though they are often complex, their explication is essential to a discussion of the reliability and validity of our measures of teacher effectiveness.

Before proceeding, it is important to note four distinct requirements for accurate measurement of teacher effectiveness: (1) consistency of observations between those judging the behavior; (2) stability of the behavior measured across pupils, content, and time; (3) convergence of the behavior assessed across similar measures of teaching effectiveness; and (4) divergence of the behavior assessed across dissimilar measures of teacher effectiveness. Since a reliable index of teacher effectiveness is not necessarily valid, and a valid index must always be reliable, we will discuss the contribution of reliability to the appraisal of teaching before turning to the more encompassing topic of validity.

Interjudge reliability, as noted in our discussion of observation systems employed in the immediate stage of appraisal (Chapter 2), is the consistency or agreement between two or more independently derived observations, recorded on the same coding instrument. Interjudge reliability is essential, but not sufficient, for the attainment of other types of reliability and, ultimately, validity. Unfortunately, interjudge reliability is often the only index employed in determining the usefulness of teacher performance measures. Consequently, the selections which follow have been chosen to introduce the concept of *stability* of teacher behavior across pupils, content, and time.

The results of any appraisal system used to make diagnostic, formative, or summative decisions about particular teachers must be reasonably stable when the same teacher teaches different pupils and different content. If a teacher's performance varies widely across these conditions, a separate index of teacher effectiveness must be constructed for each instructional condition. To circumvent this problem, it is often assumed (1) that teacher behavior can be reliably observed by different raters who are similarly trained and who use the same observational format, and (2) that a teacher's effectiveness remains reasonably stable across separate but homogeneous classes of pupils, different subject-matter areas, and different occasions, if no intervening training has occurred.

The following selections show mixed results in regard to the stability of teaching behavior. While teacher effects appear moderately consistent over brief instructional units and across pupils, they are less stable over long periods of time and across different content.

This instability may be explained in two ways. The most pessimistic stance assumes that teacher behavior of almost any type *is* basically unstable. That is, teachers do not perform consistently from day to day or from class to class. While this pessimistic explanation may eventually prove correct, it lacks convincing support at this time.

An alternative explanation, which appears somewhat more tenable on the face of research evidence, is that our measures of teacher behavior are inadequate and, therefore, do not allow us to record the consistency that may, in fact, characterize teacher behavior. This explanation contains two corollary assumptions: (1) at least some of our instruments for appraising teacher effectiveness are not tapping those specific behaviors that are relatively stable across subject matter and time; and (2) the constructs currently used as indices of teacher effectiveness are measured so poorly by existing instruments that stable teacher behaviors are almost impossible to record. These two assumptions are related to the concepts of validity and reliability, respectively.

Validity may be defined as the extent to which an instrument measures the teacher or pupil behaviors it purports to measure. While the validity of an index of teacher effectiveness can be improved only through a reconceptualization of the construct being measured (a considerable investment in time and effort), reliability can be improved either by increasing the number of occasions on which the behavior is rated or observed *or* by increasing the number of individuals doing the rating or observation—or both.* The reliability estimates obtained for a particular behavior, of course, may not apply when the instrument is used in other contexts or when different content and different pupils are involved.

A lack of validity, as noted above, is more complex than a lack of reliability. The former leaves us little alternative but to reconceptualize the operational definition of the behavior of interest and to create a new instrument to measure it.

The validity issue can be conveniently divided into two areas of interest: convergent validity and discriminant validity. Convergent validity, the confirmation of a behavior by independent measuring methods, requires significant correlation between two methods measuring the same behavior. Discriminant validity, which is slightly more complex, requires that the correlation between different instruments measuring the same behavior exceed (1) the correlations obtained between that behavior and any other behavior not having method in common, and (2) the correlations between different behaviors that happen to employ the same method. By determining intercorrelations among behaviors in a method-by-behavior matrix, one can identify indices of teaching effectiveness which pass specified tests of convergent and discriminant validity.

The premises underlying convergent and discriminant validation are: (1) the correlation between the same behavior measured by the same method (reliability) should be higher than (2) the correlation between the same behavior measured by two different methods—which, in turn, should be higher than (3) the correlation between two different behaviors measured by the same method—which, in turn, should be higher than (4) the correlation between two different behaviors measured by two different methods. A simple method-by-behavior design for determining the convergent and discriminant validity of two separate teacher behaviors, each measured by different instruments would be as follows:

		Methods			
		A behaviors		*B* behaviors	
		Accepts 1	Questions 2	Values 1	Delves 2
A	1	(.86)			
	2	.36	(.70)		
B	1	.43	.31	(.58)	
	2	−.12	−.01	−.14	(.84)

* Of course, it is entirely possible that for some indices of teacher behavior, the number of occasions and raters needed to reach an acceptable level of reliability would outstrip one's resources. In this case, it must be assumed that the behavior of interest is logically unstable—the pessimistic alternative.

For illustrative purposes, let us assume that (1) *A* and *B* are two different classroom observation systems purporting to measure the same teacher behaviors and that (2) the operational definition of teacher *accepts* pupil response on instrument *A*, is similar to that of teacher *values* pupil response on instrument *B*. Likewise, the behaviors *questions* and *delves* are similarly defined across the two instruments. By referring to the premises underlying convergent and discriminant validity, we can determine that relatively good convergent and discriminant validity is indicated for the behavior *accepts,* but poor convergent and discriminant validity is indicated for the behavior *questions.* Whether the behavior *questions* or the behavior *delves* is invalid or whether, in fact, both fail to measure the construct they purport to measure cannot be known. However, given such evidence, it would be foolhardy to use either instrument for measuring the desired behavior.

While the above paradigm is rarely employed by teacher behaviorists, it provides an example of the type of reconceptualization which should be undertaken when the instability of teacher behavior is due to the invalidity of the instrument rather than the unreliability of the measure. If lack of validity stems solely from a failure to consistently measure the behavior, we need only find the optimal number of occasions and observers needed to increase reliability to an acceptable level and thereby increase our validity. If, however, reliability is not at issue, then we must redefine and remeasure the construct.

The above issues and assumptions are prerequisite to a full understanding of the readings in this chapter. These issues are by no means simple, and as we have seen, they impinge upon the very definition of teaching effectiveness. If teacher behavior is to be measured reliably and validly, we must discover which indices of teacher effectiveness are the most reliable and valid.

In the first article, Glass reviews three methods for determining teacher effectiveness: (1) pupil gains on standardized tests of achievement; (2) teacher performance tests; and (3) observations, ratings, and student evaluations of teacher behavior. Interestingly, Glass suggests that process rather than product measures are the most stable index of teacher effectiveness.

Glass bases his opposition to the use of pupil outcome on *statistical* grounds. Examining twenty-one short-term studies, including those reviewed by Rosenshine in the second selection in this chapter, Glass points out that confidence intervals for only four out of twenty-one stability coefficients failed to span zero. Glass effectively demonstrates that even when teachers are shown to be relatively consistent over content and pupils, the stability coefficients themselves may not be accurate estimates of the consistency of teacher performance—though product measures of teaching effectiveness often assume such consistency.

These findings lead Glass to argue against the use of either standardized achievement tests or performance tests of teaching effectiveness (which compare different teachers by requiring them to teach a specified topic to a randomly formed group of pupils for one class period, after which the pupils are tested for mastery of the material taught). He suggests, instead, that process evaluations of the teacher, made by trained observers or students, are the most stable indices of teacher effectiveness. Such evaluations, he proposes, should perhaps focus on the eleven teacher variables identified by Rosenshine (1971) as "promising." Glass qualifies his endorsement of these variables, however, by specifying that no characteristic of teaching should be incorporated into rating scales until research has established that it can be reliably observed and that it significantly relates to desired pupil outcomes.

Finally, Glass takes pains to distinguish his observational process evaluations from the "principal or supervisor judgment system," commonly plagued with methodological problems and personal biases, by indicating that past failures to reliably rate teacher behavior stemmed from poor rater training and vague, general definitions of the behaviors to be rated. The reader may be challenged to dispute Glass's conclusions with data presented in Chapter 9 by McNeil and Popham, who favor contract plans and performance tests of teaching effectiveness over rating systems.

The second selection, by Rosenshine, reviews nine studies concerned with the stability of teacher effects across content, time, and pupils. While nine studies are too few to support any global conclusions, especially when study designs were not equally rigorous, Rosenshine does call attention to the existing research (as of 1970) and to the problems in interpreting results concerned with the stability of teacher effects. This latter concern, the reader will note, is precisely what Glass found most disturbing about existing methods that claim to produce consistent indices of teaching effectiveness.

Rosenshine's small but exhaustive review classifies existing research on stability of teacher effects into three categories: (1) same material taught to different students; (2) different material taught to same students; and (3) different material taught to different students.

Rosenshine points out that results from the category "teaching same material to different students" should be most useful in developing indices of teaching effectiveness since this context closely parallels the natural teaching environment. It is within this category that Rosenshine finds the most consistent teacher effects upon pupil achievement. Five long-term and three short-term studies in which teachers taught the same material to different students provided Rosenshine's most positive findings. Short-term studies in which different material was taught to the same students or different material to different students revealed less consistent teacher effects and proved the least desirable contexts in which to appraise teacher performance.

Since Rosenshine's review, two additional studies of teacher stability have been undertaken to update his findings.

The first of these studies (Brophy, 1973) reports stability data for the Brophy-Evertson research included in Chapter 6. Recall that Brophy and Evertson chose teachers for their study on the basis of each teacher's consistency over a four-year period. Pupils' scores on a given subtest of the Metropolitan Achievement Test were collected, and the mean scores for each teacher's pupils were judged for the presence of a linear pattern. Overall, 28 percent of these judgments indicated linear constancy, 13 percent linear improvement, 11 percent linear decline, and forty-nine percent nonlinearity; thus, about half of the assigned judgments indicated some form of consistency in the ways various teachers engender pupil achievement. When considered in conjunction with the findings of Rosenshine, the results suggest that at least some teachers behave consistently over a long (four-year) period of time.

Shavelson and Atwood (1975), in a precursor to the final selection in this chapter, review all available long-term and short-term studies of teacher stability *since* the 1970 Rosenshine review. Their findings, when integrated with those of Rosenshine, in some cases confirm earlier beliefs about the stability of teaching effectiveness and in other cases expand and clarify earlier findings. Reviewing Rosenshine's five long-term studies of teacher effectiveness as well as three additional studies (Brophy, 1973; Creemers, 1974; Veldman and Brophy, 1974), Shavelson and Atwood conclude, like Rosenshine, that teachers teaching the same material to different students are moderately consistent. More recent data uncovered by Shavelson and Atwood (Connor, 1969; Millman, 1973) also support this conclusion as well as Rosenshine's contention that the magnitude of stability coefficients for teachers teaching different content to the same students varies greatly. The range of stability coefficients, however, is even greater than Rosenshine reported.

It should be noted that the Rosenshine, Brophy, and Shavelson and Atwood reviews all indicate a fairly high degree of consistency among teachers in generating pupil gain, at least when the same content is taught to different (although similar) students. This context, as Rosenshine points out, is most like natural, day-to-day teaching circumstances *and* the appraisal situation. However, these findings must be interpreted cautiously in light of the criticism of Glass. In turn, Glass's endorsement of process behaviors as the most stable index of teacher effectiveness must be qualified by more recent (1976) findings of Shavelson and Atwood, which are presented in the final selection.

Shavelson and Atwood, in an extensive review of the generalizability of measures of teacher effectiveness, give *qualified* support to Glass's promotion of teacher process variables. Reviewing teacher process behaviors, identified as important in thir own right or linked in previous studies to desirable pupil outcomes, Shavelson and Atwood conclude that the stability of teacher behavior depends on teaching conditions, or "facets" (i.e., grade level, subject matter, and type of students). While the variables "teacher presentation," "positive and neutral feedback," "probing," and "direct teacher control" were relatively stable across facets, the consistency of six additional variables was unclear. In other words, some process variables are stable and some unstable.

The Shavelson and Atwood discussion assumes importance when considered in conjunction with the preceding selections. Most of these studies have assumed that pupil achievement is caused by teacher behavior; that is, if pupil gain was inconsistent, it was assumed that teacher behavior was unstable. Of course, it is possible for pupil performance to be unstable, *regardless* of teacher behavior. Or it can be stable *in spite of* teacher behavior. It should be clear, then, that we must first determine the stability of teacher process variables in order to make inferences about teacher behavior from pupil achievement. Though we would like to believe that stable teacher behavior leads to stable pupil achievement and that unstable teacher behavior leads to unstable pupil achievement, research indicates that we cannot make such assumptions. We must instead study teacher behavior separately and then relate our findings to pupil achievement, thereby including both process and product measures in our assessment.

The following three readings are perhaps the most technical in this volume, and the issues they raise are the most critical. These studies provide a path toward the eventual success of teacher appraisal by indicating the directions in which our measurement efforts must go if they are to provide reliable and valid estimates of teacher performance.

References

Brophy, J. E. "Stability of Teacher Effectiveness." *American Educational Research Journal* **10**, no. 3 (1973): 245–252.

Connor, A. *Cross-Validating Two Performance Tests of Instructional Proficiency.* UCLA. U.S.D.E. Project No. 8-1-174, 1969.

Creemers, B. *Evaluation of Styles of Teaching Initial Reading: An Educational Investigation into the Relationship between Teachers' Use of a Specific Method and Pupil Achievement* (with summary in English). Utrecht: Drukkerij Elinkwijk B. V., 1974.

Millman, J. "Psychometric Characteristics of Performance Tests of Teaching Effectiveness." Paper presented at the meeting of the American Educational Research Association, Chicago, Illinois, 1973.

Shavelson, R. J., and N. K. Atwood. *Generalizability of Measures of Teacher Effectiveness and Teaching Process* (Tech. Report No. 75-4-2), Beginning Teacher Evaluation Study. Far West Laboratory for Educational Research and Development, San Francisco, California, 1975.

Veldman, D. J., and J. E. Brophy. "Measuring Teacher Effects on Pupil Achievement." *Journal of Educational Psychology* **66**, no. 3 (1974): 319–324.

GENE V. GLASS
University of Colorado

A Review of Three Methods of Determining Teacher Effectiveness

Three separate means for evaluating teacher effectiveness are discussed here, each for a different reason: the first—standardized testing—because its use for teacher evaluation would be an egregious error; the second—controlled simulated assessment of teachers impact on pupil performance—because it has been vigorously urged on schoolmen; and the third—observation and rating of teacher behavior and students' evaluation of teacher performance—because it is the method of choice under current circumstances.

PUPIL GAINS

Although few evaluation experts would defend the practice, there is still danger that some school districts might use pupil gains on standardized achievement tests to evaluate teachers. The danger is sufficiently real that such attempts at evaluation deserve attention here. Evaluating teachers by measuring their pupils' gains from September to June on commercially available standardized tests is patently invalid and unfair. Standardized tests will uncover gross educational deficiencies in basic skills, but such instruments are not designed to reveal the variety of ways in which teaching and learning can be creative, favorably opportunistic, and uniquely meaningful to students. The inadequacy of standardized tests for evaluating school learning has become a favorite theme of several contemporary educational researchers (Stake, 1971; Bormuth, 1970; Anderson, 1972).

Aside from the irrelevance of much of the content of standardized achievement tests, their use in evaluating teachers is unjust. Nonrandomly constituted classes give teachers of brighter pupils an unfair advantage. This remains true whether the statistician calculates simple gains, residual gains, true gains, true

From H. J. Walberg, ed., *Evaluating Educational Performance* (Berkeley, California: McCutchan, 1974), pp. 11–32. Reprinted by permission.

residual gains, or covariance adjustments. Nothing short of random assignment of pupils to teachers as an ironclad administrative necessity would ensure that the teachers were in a fair race to produce pupil gains.

Even if the validity and fairness objections to using standardized tests could be met, available evidence indicates that teachers' effects on pupils' gains in knowledge across one year are not reliably measured by such tests. Assume that teachers' true ability to teach traditional subject matter is a stable trait which fluctuates little from year to year. We shall measure this ability by administering a standardized test to many teachers' pupils and correcting for the initial status of the class by partialing out that portion of the end-of-year mean score which is linearly predictable from the beginning-of-year mean score (a procedure which has everything in its favor except logical good sense; see Cronbach and Furby, 1970). How stable from one year to the next will this "residualized" measure of the teacher's effect be? How subject is it to the vagaries of the shifting composition of the class across years, the fallibility of the test scores on individual pupils, and the compounding of measurement errors in the calculation of "gain scores?" In Table 1, I have integrated the findings from three unpublished studies which provide some answers to these questions. In each study the investigator calculated residual gain scores across September to May for two successive years of each teacher's class. The correlations of these gains across two years are "stability-reliability coefficients." They tell us the reliability with which we can measure what we assume to be teachers' true ability to teach their pupils what standardized tests measure. The low reliability of such measures should eliminate any temptation to evaluate teachers with standardized tests.

If the reader is still unconvinced of the inadvisability of attempting to evaluate teachers by means of pupil gains on standardized tests, he need only consider some predictable results of such a policy. Teachers would teach the "safe" topics, possibly at the expense of the elusive but important ones. Teachers would not be permitted to administer their own standardized tests; an expensive external proctoring system would be required, and its cost in terms of trust might even exceed its cost in dollars.

THE POPHAM-McNEIL-MILLMAN METHOD

W. James Popham and John D. McNeil pioneered in the study of teacher effectiveness by means of the direct measurement of teacher impact on pupil behavior (knowledge, skills and attitudes). Recently they have been joined in these endeavors by Jason Millman, who has teamed with Popham to offer school districts in California and across the nation their techniques for evaluating teachers.

With the Popham-McNeil-Millman method of assessing teacher effectiveness (the PMM method), a group of teachers is given advance notice of a few hours or a day or more that they are to teach a particular topic to an unfamiliar group of pupils. The teachers are often prepared by being allowed to study reference materials, instructional objectives, and even test items comparable

Table 1. Summary of one-year stability coefficients of teacher effects (residual mean gain-scores) on standardized test performance.

Nature of Subtest	Average r for the row	*Bennet (1971) Grade level: 1 Test: Metro Ach. Covariate: Metro. Readiness*	*Harris (1966) Grade level: 1 Test: Stanford Ach. Covariate: Stanford Ach.*	*Harris (1966) Grade level: 2 Test: Metro Ach. Covariate: Metro. Ach.*	*Brophy (1972) Grade level: 2 Test: Metro Ach.*				*Brophy (1972) Grade level: 3 Test: Metro. Ach.*			
		No. of teachers: n=34	*No. of teachers: n=30*	*No. of teachers: n=24*	*Title I Schools*		*Non-Title I Schools*		*Title I Schools*		*Non-Title I Schools*	
		r's	*r's*	*r's*	*n=26*	*n=22*	*n=42*	*n=36*	*n=24*	*n=20*	*n=44*	*n=42*
Reading	.23	.05[b]	.32	−.08	.31	.00	.40*	.42*	.54*	.39	.26	−.07
Arithmetic	.30	−.01[b]			.24	−.12	.35[a]	.39[a]	.34[a]	.42[a]	.51[a]	.56[a]
Spelling	.49	.73*	.52*	.21								
Word knowledge	.38	.23	.53* (Word reading) −.01 (Vocabulary)	.19	.49*	.18	.41*	.42*	.52*	.78*	.39*	.45*
Word discrimi-nation	.36	.69*		.26	.26	.28	.63*	.42*	.28	.19	.30	.26

* Significantly different from zero at the .05 level (two-tailed test).

[a] Average of stability coefficients for arithmetic computation and arithmetic reasoning.

[b] An "outlying" case more than four standard deviations below the mean was removed before calculation of the correlation.

to those which will be used as posttests. Frequently, the topic to be taught is one with which the teachers have had little prior experience. Ad hoc groups of six to thirty or more pupils are randomly formed from a large pool of pupils available for the assessment. The pupil group is taught for a period of thirty minutes to an hour. Because of the random assignment of pupils from the large pool, all teachers begin the instructional period with pupil groups randomly equated with respect to knowledge of the topic, ability, motivation, etc. Hence, the posttest pupil performance is an unconfounded measure of the teacher effect; "simple gain," "residual gain," "percent gain," and gain scores are unnecessary. Teacher effects can be further studied by randomly reconstituting the ad hoc pupil groups, by changing the topic of instruction, etc.

Logical Arguments Advanced for the PMM Method

This basic technique underlies the system of measuring and evaluating teacher effectiveness which Popham has advanced as the preferred technique of teacher evaluation. As he wrote in *Designing Teacher Evaluation Systems,* "Another possible valuable augmentation of our appraisal techniques is the use of a teaching performance test or, as it is sometimes called, an instructional mini-lesson." (Popham, 1971, p. 36).

The major logical arguments advanced by Popham and Millman for the superiority of their conception of teacher evaluation are 1) that the PMM method of appraising teachers is "objective," whereas other methods (notably rating scales and observations schedules) are "subjective," and 2) that the changes in pupil behavior like those which teachers produce during the simulated instructional periods are "the real thing" about schooling.

The hobgoblin of "subjectivity" can still be invoked to threaten the lay audience, even though it has been a dead issue in the philosophy of science for decades.

> All measurement yields, not a property, intrinsic to the object being measured taken in isolation, but a relation between that object and the others serving as standards of measurement. When the relation is to other human beings, or even to the observer himself, it is not therefore a subjective one. As always, everything hinges on the controls which can be instituted, and on the sensitivity and reliability with which the discriminating judgments are being made. (Kaplan, 1964, p. 212).

Every act of measurement, experimental design, hypothesis formulation, or data interpretation in scientific inquiry involves human judgment; indeed they may even involve aesthetic and, particularly, value judgments. In this sense, all science is subjective. The only "subjectivity" one need fear—both in science and in educational evaluation—is capricious and unsubstantiated opining. In this pejorative sense, the PMM method in its selection of instructional topics, statement of objectives, and selection of test items could be used as "subjectively" as the worst rating scales and observation schedules.

Second, is the teacher's ability to produce behavioral changes in pupils "the real thing" about schooling? Hardly. Education is many "real things." Changing children's behavior is just one of them. Permitting children to grow in supportive and interesting environments is another. Simple custodial care is a third "real thing" about schools that sounds trivial until one begins to contemplate the economic and social consequences of deschooling society.

Changing pupil behavior is one of the teacher's many responsibilities. However, we can currently conceive of and recognize in particular instances many more types of behavioral change than modern techniques can reliably measure. In spite of their commendable success in measuring even complex cognitive processes, measurement specialists have ample cause for humility. So far, practical measurement of many affective behaviors and personality characteristics is more hope than reality. Measurement of an educational goal as basic as creative (or at least "original") writing skill is still enormously complex and expensive. Teachers affect children's assessments of personal worth which are closely linked to the children's feeling of satisfaction and dissatisfaction with themselves. Yet few children trust the adults they deal with in school enough that they will disclose their true feelings about themselves.

Empirical Evaluation of the PMM Method

The testimonies for the empirical validity of the PMM method have been imprudent and immodest. Justiz (1969, p. viii) claimed no less for his study than that it had produced "... the first reliable measure of general teaching ability." Connor (1969, p. 16) wrote that his study not only "validated" the teacher performance assessment technique but also verified "the construct of instructional proficiency as a measurable variable." Popham (1971, p. 116) cited Justiz and Connor as having "recently reported high positive correlation between teachers' achievements on two different short-term performance tests. . . ." McNeil (1972, p. 622) considered such performance tests to be an "answer to the problem of identifying the effective instructor."

In the face of this partisan enthusiasm for the PMM technique, I wish to examine the following anti-thesis: The technique has not been shown to possess reliability adequate for measuring individual differences among teachers. The very data which are said to establish the reliability of the PMM method are consistent with the claim that the method has near zero reliability for generalizing across factors for which it must show stable measurements. A careful examination of the data obtained by Connor, Justiz, Popham, McNeil, and others will reveal no evidence to disprove the assertion that the teacher's effect on pupil performance is measured with near zero reliability across both topics taught and different groups of pupils by the PMM techniques. In short, I shall argue that the PMM technique has yet to pass the minimum requirement for measurement utility.

To be useful in teacher evaluation, the PMM method must show substantial reliability across different topics and different groups of pupils. The construct "good teaching" forces the issue of "topics" generalizability. "Good teaching" means more than the ability to teach isolated curiosities of the curriculum. If "good teaching" is not evident in the same teacher's consistent impact across a reasonably broad range of topics (even within a domain itself as narrow as secondary school social studies, for example), then "good teaching" is not actually being measured. For practical reasons, the PMM method must yield stable measures across different (possibly randomly constituted) groups of pupils. If teachers produce highly unstable effects when teaching the same topic to several different pupil groups, then fair comparisons among teachers can be bought only under two conditions, the first fatuous, the second cumbersome and impractical: 1) all teachers in a group (a school district, perhaps) about whom decisions are to be made must teach the same standard groups of pupils or, 2) each teacher's effect must be measured by averaging his or her effects across many randomly different groups of pupils. The PMM method either shows reliability across topics and pupil groups or else it remains a laboratory technique, useful for teacher training and research, perhaps, but not up to standards of utility, economy, and fidelity required of a teacher evaluation technique for individual diagnosis or determination of merit.

CRITIQUE OF RELATED RESEARCH

The Rosenshine Review

Rosenshine (1970) compiled the results of several studies of the short-term stability of teacher effect on change in pupil behavior which used methods like those of the PMM technique. Twenty stability coefficients from five separate studies were reported by Rosenshine (1970). The twenty correlation coefficients, correlating the teacher effect on two separate (but closely related) topics on two distinct (but randomly equivalent) pupil groups, range from a low of .45 to a high of .87; only two of the coefficients are statistically significantly different from zero at the .05 level (two-tailed test). Rosenshine (1970, p. 660) concluded that "when teachers taught different topics to different students, the direction of the correlations were [sic] . . . erratic, and few correlations were significant."

The Justiz Studies

Justiz (1969) conducted two studies in two different high schools. In School A, ten student-teachers each taught a group of about twenty pupils a half-hour lesson on "news story structure"; the pupils taught by each student teacher were randomly drawn from a pool of available pupils in the school. (The only compromise with complete randomization was that no teacher was assigned one of his own pupils.) After the lesson, the pupils were given a fifteen-minute test on the content of the instruction. The pupil groups were reconstituted, again nearly at random, and the student teachers instructed their new pupils on "concepts of the computer punch card." A fifteen-minute posttest was given, as before. The study was completed within two hours.

Justiz reported a Spearman rank-order correlation of .64 for his data, which I have confirmed. A Pearson's r seems equally appropriate, or even more so; its value for the data is 0.58, which is just barely statistically significant (alpha = .05, two-tailed test). But the 95 percent confidence interval for $r = 0.58$ with $n = 9$ better reflects how accurately the teacher-effect stability coefficient has been determined in this study; the interval extends from .08 to .89, an extraordinarily broad range. Thus we learn that the teacher effect is somewhere between nearly completely unstable and perfectly stable across two topics.

One of the ten student teachers was dropped before the end of the study. The reason given was that this student teacher "... refused to teach the Punched-Card Computer Concepts subject for lack of preparation" (Justiz, 1969, p. 47). Presumably if the teacher had been required to participate in the study then we could have expected some discrepancy in the performance of his pupils between the "news story" lesson, for which he felt prepared, and the "punch card" lesson, which he refused to teach. To assess the potential influence on the stability coefficient of having dropped this teacher, I assumed that his pupils would have achieved an average score on the "news story" lesson and the poorest score on the "punch card" lesson. The value of Spearman's rank-order correlation coefficient for this plausible set of complete data is 0.47, which is nonsignificant even for $\alpha = .10$, two-tailed test. One missing case can have a marked effect in such a small sample.

In the second high school, School B, Justiz repeated essentially the same procedures with the same topics, one exception being that the seven teachers in this sample instructed the same group of pupils on the two topics. Two of the student teachers were dropped before completion of the study because of irregularities in posttesting. Justiz reported a Spearman rank-order correlation of .90, "significant at the .05 level of confidence." The calculations and conclusion deserve closer scrutiny. For $n = 5$, an $r_s = .90$ is significant at only the alpha = .10 level for a two-tailed test; the two-tailed test is justified in this instance in view of the frequency of negative stability coefficients in similar studies (Rosenshine, 1970).

But a more fundamental problem exists here (if the reader is unimpressed with quibbles over .05 versus .10 levels of significance). Justiz broke a tie on one variable between two teachers in favor of a higher correlation. If the tie is broken in the other direction, the value of r_s is .80, which with $n = 5$ is nonsignificant at any reasonable alpha-level. The best resolution of the tie is to assign a rank of 4.5 to both student teachers, which yields a third nonsignificant r_s of 0.87.

Conclusion: disappearing subjects, miniscule sample sizes, errant correlation coefficients, and nonsignificant statistics hardly add up to "... the first reliable measure of general teaching ability" (Justiz, 1969, p. viii).

The McNeil Study

McNeil (1972) reported data which bear on the question of reliability of the PMM method. Teachers were randomly paired with groups of three elementary school pupils. A topic such as code breaking was taught, the pupils were excused for a short recess, and a second group of three pupils randomly constituted for the second instructional period. In some cases the instructional topic changed between the two instructional periods, and in some cases it did not.

McNeil's (1972, p. 626) results section was brief and is reproduced below.

McNeil refers to the correlations which he has computed as being "positive." The one instance which he reports in detail (between Tests 3 and 4 with ten weeks intervening) produced an r of .39 ($n = 30$); the 95 percent confidence interval is .03 to .62. Unfortunately, we don't know whether the one instance reported was the most favorable finding among the "positive" correlations McNeil calculated, or whether it is genuinely representative of all the coefficients.

McNeil's table (Table 2), reproduced below, first appears to be based on the r of .39 to which he referred in the text of his paper. However, the situation is unclear, principally because the original sample contained thirty teachers, and the table, which is said to contain half of the teachers ("top 25 percent and bottom 25 percent") is based on twenty-six and thirty-two teachers instead of fifteen. We must presume that Table 2 contains data from studies independent of the study which yielded the r of .39.

Table 2. Chi squares for high and low teacher performance on tests of ability to teach two different tasks of reading.

		Task 4		
		High	Low	
Task 3	High	9	4	$\chi^2 = 4.54$
	Low	4	9	

		Task 4		
		High	Low	
Task 3	High	12	4	$\chi^2 = 4.40$
	Low	6	10	

Both contingency tables in McNeil's table are said to yield statistically significant associations (chi-square test, alpha = .05) between high and low teacher effectiveness across the two topics. My calculations show otherwise. I obtain a χ_1^2 of 3.85 without the continuity correction—a figure which should have corresponded exactly to McNeil's 4.54—and a χ_1^2 of 2.46 with the correction. The continuity correction is clearly in order due to the small sample size; the χ_1^2 of 2.46 is nonsignificant even at alpha = .10. (Fisher's exact test similarly failed to reject with alpha = .10.) For the lower half of McNeil's Table 1, the value of χ_1^2 corrected for discontinuity is 3.17, nonsignificant with alpha = .05. (However, Fisher's exact test yields a probability of .04 of a more extreme occurrence under the null hypothesis of no association.)

The import of McNeil's data is uncertain. The confidence intervals are broad, the nonsignificant findings also need to be reported, and some of the results reported as statistically stable appear not to be. . . . Correlations between teachers' performances on the different tests given ten weeks apart with different kinds of pupils were positive. For instance, thirty teachers took Test 3 at the end of their methods course and completed Test 4 ten weeks later after a student teaching assignment. Their scores showed a Pearsonian r of .388 ($p < .05$). As indicated in Table 1 . . . one could have made a probable prediction about the likelihood of high achieving teachers (top 25 percent and bottom 25 percent) making a similar showing on a second test weeks later.

The Connor Study

Connor (1969) arranged for seventeen experienced male teachers to instruct subgroups of seventy-seven high school pupils in the topics "propaganda techniques" and "chance (probability)." A systematic, but probably nearly random, method of assigning five pupils to each teacher was employed, with the condition that no teacher was assigned to a pupil with whom he was acquainted.

Pupils in each teacher's "class" were tested on "propaganda techniques" before a fifty-minute instructional period. A comparable posttest followed instruction. Later in the day, the pupils were reassigned to teachers and the new ad hoc classes were taught "chance" for fifty minutes; pretests and posttests were again administered. A pretest-to-posttest gain score was calculated by subtracting the pretest number of items correct (times the number of pupils) from the posttest number of items correct (times the number of pupils) and dividing by the difference between the highest possible score and the pretest score. Thus, "gain as a percent of possible gain" was used as the measure of each teacher's effect on pupil performance.

Connor did not report either the value of r or r_s, Spearman's rank-order coefficient. However, I have calculated both using his raw data (Connor, 1969, p. 14). They are small ($r_{xy} = .26$ and $r_s = .35$) and statistically nonsignificant. Clearly, Connor's data give no evidence of nonzero stability across topics. Instead of reporting either of the above two coefficients, Connor reported a coefficient "corrected for attenuation," r'_{xy}, of .72. He applied an inappropriate significance test to this value, testing it as one would test a typical Pearson's r on seventeen cases. Appropriate inferential tests (Rogers, 1971; Forsyth and Feldt, 1969) reveal that even Connor's corrected coefficient is statistically nonsignificant at any reasonable alpha level.

Moreover, the correction for attenuation procedure was inappropriate. Test reliabilities were estimated from internal consistency coefficients and do not embody a meaningful definition of measurement error for the purposes of the correction. More important, although correlations corrected for attenuation may have conceptual meaning, they are seldom useful in practice. There is small comfort in the fact that true scores on X and Y are highly correlated if one is considering making decisions about individuals with the only available data, namely the fallible observed scores.

The Belgard, Rosenshine, and Gage Study

Forty-three teachers taught two fifteen-minute lessons on the economic, political, and social conditions of Yugoslavia and Thailand to their regular classes on successive days. Class sizes varied from ten to thirty-one students. One week before the study, each teacher received copies of the instructional materials and half of the items from the posttests to be administered to pupils after each lesson.

To equate the abilities of the nonrandomly constituted classes, Belgard, Rosenshine, and Gage (1971) administered a tape-recorded lesson on Israel to all classes on the third day. Pupil's performance on a subsequent posttest was then used as a controlling variable for equating the forty-three classes. Essentially, residual "gain scores"—the difference between the class mean on the Yugoslavia test, for example, and the regression estimate of this class mean from the Israel class mean—were computed and correlated across the two topics to measure the reliability of the teacher effect. At this point, two fundamental questions can be raised. Pupils were not randomly assigned to teachers; instead, an ex post facto attempt was made to control statistically for pupil differences. The equivalence sought may not have been achieved. The classes may still have differed to a nonrandom degree on variables (e.g., some aspect of learning ability or motivation) not controlled statistically. Also, observation of the control variable (the Israel test) was made after the two instructional periods. The possibility exists that the statistical equating removed stable variance in the teacher effect present in the variance of the Israel class means because of positive transfer effects, motivation carry-over effects, etc., from the previous lessons. It would have been preferable to observe the control variable (Israel test) before the teacher-directed instructional periods. The first influence (lack of complete equating of classes) may have spuriously inflated the stability coefficient: the latter influence may have deflated it.

Belgard, Rosenshine, and Gage reported a correlation of the Yugoslavia and Thailand residual class means of .47 ($t = 3.37$ with $df = 40$; $p < .01$). The investigators recognized that this coefficient was based on different topics taught to the same pupils. To correct for this condition, the investigators divided the data in each class in half by designating even- and odd-numbered pupils. The correlation of Thailand residual means for the even-numbered pupils with Yugoslavia residual means for the odd-numbered pupils (or vice versa) is then a measure of teacher stability across both topics and pupil groups. The authors report the following two stability coefficients:

Yugoslavia residual means for odd-numbered pupils with Thailand residual means for even-numbered pupils: $r = .16$ ($p < .01$)

Thailand residual means for odd-numbered pupils with Yugoslavia residual means for even-numbered pupils: $r = .38$ ($p < .01$)

The authors then applied the Spearman-Brown formula to estimate the size of these two coefficients for classes twice as large as the "half-classes" on which they were derived. The resulting stability coefficients equalled .28 and .55—a very large discrepancy. The investigators averaged the two figures and settled on a stability coefficient of .41.

Belgard, Rosenshine, and Gage's (1971, p. 185) conclusion seems most appropriate: "The correlations were not high enough to indicate that the effectiveness of individual teachers can be measured with adequate reliability with only two lessons, ten-item tests, and classes of about twenty-one students. For such reliability, higher than about .40, additional lessons, longer tests, and larger classes would be needed."

The Popham Studies

Although Popham's (1971b) comparisons of the effects of experienced and inexperienced teachers on pupil performance were not addressed directly to the question of the reliability of the measurement techniques, they provide collateral evidence on the question.

Popham arranged for groups of experienced teachers, college students, and laymen to teach various topics to groups of high school and junior college students. A variation of "randomized blocking" insured equivalence of the student groups taught by the teacher and nonteacher groups. Popham (Table 3) presented three comparisons of teacher and nonteacher performance in terms of the average "percent items correct" earned by the students.

Table 3

Topic	*Comparison groups*	*No. of instructors*	*Average percent items correct*
Social science research methods	a) Experienced teachers	13	67%
	b) College students	13	65%
Auto mechanics (carburetion)	a) Experienced teachers	28	49%
	b) Garage mechanics	28	47%
Electronics (basic power supplies)	a) Experienced teachers	16	52%
	b) TV repairmen and electronics workers	16	50%

Popham (1971b, p. 601) wrote that "there appear to be no readily available (methodological) loopholes by which we can explain away the nonsignificant outcomes. A more straightforward explanation is available. *Experienced teachers are not particularly skilled at bringing about specified behavior changes in learners.*"

However, there does exist an alternative explanation which is both consistent with the available data concerning the reliability of the PMM method and more generous in its assessment of teachers. Zero reliability measurement techniques can not show statistically significant discriminations among any groups; at least such differences will not be found at a rate greater than the size, alpha, of the significance test. Nonzero measurement reliability is a necessary condition for discriminating among groups on a measure. A test of "heads flipping ability" in which one's score is the number of heads tossed in one hundred flips of a fair coin—a test with zero reliability in the stability sense—will not show consistent, significant differences among streetcar conductors, waitresses, bank cashiers, or men-on-the-street.

CONCLUDING ASSESSMENT OF PMM STUDIES

The PMM group may have stacked the cards against demonstrating reliability for their technique. In most cases, the teachers taught new material, such as the computer punch card or news story structure, so that no teacher "had an advantage" over the other teachers because of familiarity with the material. In fact, the use of novel materials may have taken away from teachers the very "advantage" which makes one teacher better—and consistently better—than another. Teachers' knowledge of their materials is certainly a stable characteristic and may, particularly at higher grade levels, play a part in determining their effectiveness. Perhaps PMM and others (Fortune—see Rosenshine, 1970; Belgard *et al.,* 1971) systematically eliminated from their studies an important stable variable related to teacher effectiveness. On the other hand, a few studies (McNeil, 1972, for example) used material more familiar to the teachers (e.g., teaching multiplication of two-digit numbers or pronouncing initial vowels in words with a silent final "c") and failed to produce convincing evidence of stability of teacher effects.

But fine points about naive versus knowledgeable teachers can do little to brighten the dismal composite picture presented in Figure 1 of the results of the available short-term stability studies. Presented in Figure 1 are the 95 percent confidence intervals on the twenty-one relevant coefficients that can be found in the published literature (principally the 1970 Rosenshine review and the studies reviewed here). Only four of the intervals fail to span zero. All but one span .15.

In theory, low reliability problems are among the simplest measurement problems to solve. Given that in its present form a measurement procedure has nonzero reliability, no matter how low its reliability may be, it can be made more reliable by lengthening it, that is, by duplicating and averaging repeated measurements from the procedure. Assume that from the dismal picture of the reliability (across topics and pupil groups) of the PMM technique, one draws the most generous possible conclusion, namely that the technique has a reliability in the region $\rho_{XX} = .20$ to .30. These estimates are based on the conditions which obtained in the studies reviewed above, the most important condition for our present purpose being that the entire procedure per teacher measurement involved at least one hour of about a dozen pupils' time, at least three or four hours time per teacher, and several hours of professional time for development and administration per episode. If the PMM method actually has initial reliability .30, it would have to be lengthened by ten times to achieve a composite reliability of .81 according to the Spearman-Brown formula for the reliability of a lengthened test. In other words, the simple methods typical of the studies reviewed above would have to be repeated across ten different instruc-

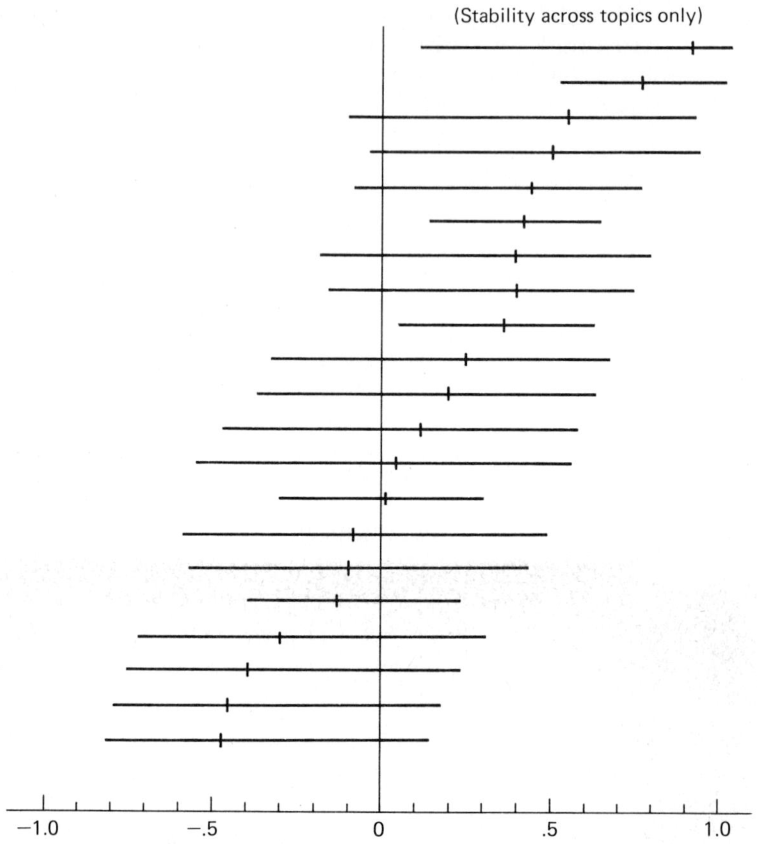

Fig. 1. Summary of estimations (95 percent confidence intervals) of the stability of the teacher effect across instructional topics and pupil groups.

tional topics with ten different pupil groups before the average score for a single teacher attained a reliability above .80. Net costs of reliable PMM testing? Staggering, if we even bothered to pause and calculate them. Add to this gloomy picture the developmental costs of devising new topics and tests each year (obviously the topics are "consumable" year in and year out), the administrative costs of shuffling pupils around (the procedure is unfair unless the pupil groups are randomly equivalent across *all* teachers about whom differential decisions are to be made from the measurements), and we behold an enormously expensive evaluation system.

In a 1929 study of teaching behaviors, A. S. Barr concluded that instability of teachers' behavior from one lesson to another is the dominant source of unreliability in the effect of teachers' actions on student learning. The contemporary studies reviewed above prove Barr's conclusion beyond reasonable doubt.

No conclusion is more fitting for this section than a quotation of Popham's own prudent remarks:

> "It now appears, in light of the grossness of the measurement devices likely to be available in the near future, that we shall be pleased even if the performance tests are suitable for use only with groups. In other words, it will be a sufficient advance to develop a reliable *group* criterion measure which could be used in myriad educational situations such as to assess the efficiency of teacher education programs." (Popham, 1971b, p. 116) (Italics added.)

AN OBSERVATIONAL-JUDGMENTAL SYSTEM

The observational-judgmental system envisioned has three principal elements: (1) trained observers' ratings of teachers' specific classroom behaviors; (2) students' evaluation of teachers; and (3) collateral data.

Observation of Teachers' Classroom Behaviors

The word "specific" distinguishes the first component of this observational-judgmental system from our pathetic history of attempting to rate teachers' "openness," "professional manner," or "sensitivity." Past failures to rate teacher behavior reliably stemmed largely from vague, general definitions of the behaviors to be rated and lack of rater training. When these two defects are remedied, ratings reach surprisingly high levels of consistency and long-term stability (Medley and Mitzel, 1963). I would propose that no characteristic of teaching be incorporated into the rating scales until research has established both that it can be reliably observed and that it bears some significant relationship to desired pupil cognitive and affective states. Research evidence (Rosenshine, 1971) currently justifies observing and judging the following teacher behaviors: clarity of presentations and explanations, enthusiasm, variety in use of instructional materials and techniques, task orientation and "businesslike" behavior, and provision of ample learning opportunities. This same research suggests observation of many other potentially important teacher behaviors: teacher use of students' ideas, use of multiple levels of discourse, absence of negative criticism, and "probing." Each characteristic can be precisely defined and can be reliably measured by trained observers.

Pupils' Evaluation of Their Teachers

The second element of the observational-judgmental system involves the collection of pupils' evaluations of their teachers. The data collected from students may be of several types; at the least, it should include information to corroborate outside observers' ratings of teacher behaviors.

Second, the system could include students' judgments of the learning environment, as defined and studied by Walberg and Anderson (1968); Walberg

(1969), for example. Walberg and Anderson's work on the "Learning Environment Inventory" seems particularly promising and immediately useful. Their inventory, to be filled out by the students, gives class mean scores on fourteen factor-analytically derived dimensions of learning environment, each score being derived from individual pupil responses to seven items. The names of some of the dimensions and their internal consistency are: Intimacy (.78); Friction (.78); Satisfaction (.80); Difficulty (.66); and Apathy (.83).

Third, pupils' contributions to the observational-judgmental system could include their reports on the state of basic human decency that prevails in the classroom. McClellan (1971) reminds us that all teaching is simultaneously a "saying, doing, and making." We must judge what teachers "do" to children as well as what they "make" of them. Even if their actions had no visible residual effects on the pupils' adult behavior, teachers' rudeness, bad manners, and ill-tempered repression would be contemptible in themselves.

In proposing teacher evaluation based in part on pupil and outside-observer judgment, I am not recommending a ragtag system of uncritically collected data of dubious validity. The properties of the data should be studied periodically by means of the various statistical tools available for examining the reliability and validity of measurements. If two independent observers looking at adequate samples of teachers' performance can't agree on their judgments of teachers' "use of appropriate illustrations," then work needs to be done with the judges, the rating scales, the methods of sampling teacher behavior, or all three. Finding that principals' ratings of teacher rapport with pupils do not correlate with pupils' expressions of rapport with the teachers casts doubt on the principals' ratings, the pupils' ratings, or both—and something must be done about the situation.

Collateral Data

I have omitted from this teacher evaluation system any data of the type upon which teaching credentials are typically awarded, namely preservice credit hours, degrees, grade-point averages, inservice credit hours, etc. The omission is intentional and is based on the judgment that such factors are not valid indicators of teacher effectiveness. (Gutherie's 1970 review revealed weak, but consistent, correlations of "credential-type" variables and student outcomes; but the relationships may be due to uncontrolled variables such as socioeconomic status.) The lack of validity of "credentials" data stems from two sources: 1) nearly all teachers have been selected on such variables, hence in the selected group the restricted ranges of the variables work against their showing any correlation with effectiveness (e.g., intelligence and income are virtually uncorrelated among the alumni of the Harvard Graduate School of Business, though they are not uncorrelated in the general population); 2) many such "credentialling" factors have no direct effect on teaching effectiveness. Rosenbloom et al. (1966, p. 108) concluded from a study of high school mathematics teachers that

> The effectiveness of teachers using the SMSG materials and measured by student learning is not influenced to any significant degree by the length

of the teachers' experience in teaching mathematics, his undergraduate and graduate courses and grades, and his participation in professional mathematics organizations. Apparently, if a teacher meets acceptable qualifications in these respects, higher qualifications do not make a difference.

One exception to the ban on "credentialling" data seems justified. It seems obvious—particularly at the high school level—that there are minimum levels of subject matter knowledge below which teachers are incompetent to teach. There may be arguments for the instructional value of having ignorant teachers, but even when such arguments can be made to stick, it's hard to justify paying high wages to ignorant teachers. Infrequently, a teacher's own grasp of the subject he is teaching drops below one of these minimum levels, as in the case of the football coach covering Algebra II who can't graph a linear equation, or the choral music teacher who can't read music. Such instances are, no doubt, so rare that correlational studies of teacher knowledge and student learning continue to show zero relationships. Nonetheless, they are present in the personal experience of each of us, and are sufficiently repugnant that they deserve attention in a teacher evaluation system, provided the costs are reasonable. Costs for this kind of evaluation can be held to a reasonable level by centralizing the knowledge testing of high school teachers, perhaps in the state education agency. Such an exam could be administered every other year or less, instead of only once at entrance into the profession. Thus some control would be exercised over shifting teaching assignments that make for administrative convenience but for no academic sense. Once again, the purpose of the testing would be to detect the one in a thousand egregiously indefensible teaching assignments, not to grade or rank teachers on their subject matter knowledge. The program would have a very modest goal; if its costs per teacher per year exceeded ten cents, it probably wouldn't be worth maintaining .

References

Anderson, R. C. "How to Construct Achievement Tests to Assess Comprehension." *Review of Educational Research* 42 (1972): 145–170.

Belgard, M., B. Rosenshine, and N. L. Gage. "Exploration of the Teacher's Effectiveness in Learning." In I. Westbury and A. A. Bellack, eds., *Research into Classroom Processes: Recent Developments and Next Steps.* New York: Teachers College Press, 1971.

Bormuth, J. *On the Theory of Achievement Test Items.* Chicago: University of Chicago Press, 1970.

Connor, A. *"Cross-Validating Two Performance Tests of Instructional Proficiency"* (U.S. Office of Education Project No. 8-I-174). Mimeographed. Los Angeles: University of California, 1969.

Cronbach, L. J., and L. Furby. "How Should We Measure Change—Or Should We?" *Psychological Bulletin* 74 (1970): 68–80.

Forsyth, R. A., and L. A. Feldt. "An Investigation of Empirical Sampling Distributions of Correlation Coefficients Corrected for Attenuation." *Educational and Psychological Measurement* 29 (1969): 61–71.

Gutherie, J. W. "Survey of School Effectiveness Studies." In A. M. Mood, ed., *Do Teachers Make a Difference?* Washington, D.C.: U.S. Government Printing Office, 1970.

Justiz, T. B. "A Method of Identifying the Effective Teacher." Ph.D. dissertation, University of California, Los Angeles, 1969. (University Microfilms No. 29-3022-A)

Kaplan, A. *The Conduct of Inquiry.* San Francisco: Chandler, 1964.

McClellan, J. "Classroom-Teaching Research: A Philosophical Critique." In I. Westbury and A. A. Bellak, eds., *Research into Classroom Processes: Recent Developments and Next Steps.* New York: Teachers College Press, 1971.

McNeil, J. D. "Performance Tests: Assessing Teachers of Reading." *The Reading Teacher* **25** (1972): 622–627.

Medley, D. M., and H. E. Mitzel. "Measuring Classroom Behavior by Systematic Observation." In N. L. Gage, ed., *Handbook of Research on Teaching.* Chicago: Rand McNally, 1963.

Popham, W. J. *Designing Teacher Evaluation Systems: A Series of Suggestions for Establishing Teacher Assessment Procedures as Required by the Stull Bill (AB 293), 1971 California Legislature.* Los Angeles: The Instructional Objectives Exchange, 1971a.

Popham, W. J. "Performance Tests of Teaching Proficiency: Rationale, Development, and Validation." *American Educational Research Journal* **8** (1971b): 105–117.

Rogers, W. T. "Jackknifing Disattenuated Correlations." Ph.D. dissertation, University of Colorado, Boulder, 1971.

Rosenbloom, P. E. *et al. Characteristics of Mathematics Teachers that Affect Students' Learning* (Cooperative Research Report). Minneapolis, Minn.: University of Minnesota, 1966. (ERIC Document Reproduction Service No. 021 707)

Rosenshine, B. "The Stability of Teacher Effects upon Student Achievement." *Review of Educational Research* **40** (1970): 647–662.

Rosenshine, B. "Teaching Behaviors Related to Pupil Achievement: A Review of Research." In I. Westbury and A. A. Bellack, eds., *Research into Classroom Processes: Recent Developments and Next Steps.* New York: Teachers College Press, 1971.

Stake, R. E. "Testing Hazards in Performance Contracting." *Phi Delta Kappan* **52** (1971): 583–588.

Walberg, H. J. "Predicting Class Learning: An Approach to the Class as a Social System." *American Educational Research Journal* **6** (1969): 529–542.

Walberg, H. J., and G. J. Anderson. "Classroom Climate and Individual Learning." *Journal of Educational Psychology* **59** (1968): 414–419.

BARAK ROSENSHINE
University of Illinois

The Stability of Teacher Effects upon Student Achievement

This review focuses on the stability, or consistency, of teacher effectiveness. In the review the term "teacher effects" refers to residual class mean achievement scores in which a measure of prior achievement or student aptitude is used to adjust posttest scores by regression. Although there have been numerous studies seeking to determine the correlates of teacher effects within a given time period, much less effort has been devoted to assessing the consistency of teacher effects across two intervals (e.g., two lessons or two years). This paper reviews and discusses nine studies concerned with the generality of teacher effects across two instructional periods. Nine studies are too few to support any conclusions, especially when the designs of the studies were not equally rigorous. Therefore, one of the purposes of writing the review is to call attention to the existing research in this area, and to the problems in interpreting the results. It is hoped that future studies will be conducted to replicate the existing studies and to help resolve some of the issues which they raise.

The stability of teacher effects might be measured in three situations. The most common situation is one in which a teacher teaches the same material to different students. The different students could be taught concurrently (as in high-school physics classes) or across successive school years (as in fifth-grade, self-contained classes). The two other situations would be those in which the teacher taught different material to the same students (e.g., two units on American history to the same class) or taught different material to different students (e.g., two units on American history to different classes).

In all three situations the research question is whether a teacher who is effective or ineffective once is equally effective or ineffective a second time. Currently the most interesting question is the stability of teacher effects when they use the same material but instruct different students, because this question has the greatest generalizability to the effectiveness of teachers in specific instruc-

Excerpted from "The Stability of Teacher Effects upon Student Achievement." *Review of Educational Research* **40**, no. 5 (1970): 647–662. Reprinted by permission.

tional programs. The results of such studies are also easiest to interpret because the same instructional materials and tests are used twice; in the other two situations, different tests and different instructional materials are used, and such differences confound the measurement.

The studies of the stability of teacher effects might also be divided into "long-term" studies in which the period of instruction lasts for a month or a school year, and "short-term," studies in which the period of instruction is 30 minutes or less. Although it is possible to conduct three types of long-term and three types of short-term studies, I was able to locate only four types of studies: (*a*) long-term studies in which teachers taught the same material to different students, (*b*) short-term studies in which teachers taught the same material to different students, (*c*) short-term studies in which teachers taught different material to the same students, and (*d*) short-term studies in which teachers taught different material to different students.

LONG-TERM STUDIES OF TEACHER CONSISTENCY

Long-term studies are presented first and given the greatest importance because the teaching situation is most generalizable to "natural teaching" as currently practiced. Specific results were obtained in four long-term studies (Morsh, Burgess & Smith, 1955; Harris *et al.,* 1st grade, 1968; Harris *et al.,* 2nd grade, 1968; Soar, 1966), and descriptive statements were obtained in the fifth study (Torrance & Parent 1965) (see Table 1). In all studies but one (Morsh *et al.,* 1955), the period of instruction was a school year. In all studies, research on the stability of teacher effects was a minor aspect of the research project; no long-term study was found which focused specifically on this question.

These five studies were the only long-term studies on the stability of teacher effects that I was able to locate. Five studies hardly form a sufficient basis for generalization, even though the studies were widely discrepant in settings, subject areas, and students. In these studies the setting diminishes generalizability to public school instruction. Morsh *et al.* studied Air Force instruction in hydraulics, and Harris *et al.* conducted experimental studies of four methods of teaching reading. Although Harris *et al.* did not find significant differences in student achievement across methods, the fact that the teachers were using new, specific reading instruction procedures confounds the interpretation and generality of their two studies as examples of teacher consistency.

In general, the term "effective teacher" has been taken to mean that a teacher remains effective across a number of years. Yet, on the basis of these studies, evidence on the consistency of teacher effects is weak because correlations as high as .5 were obtained in only one study (Harris *et al.,* 1st grade 1968) and all other correlations were about .35 or much lower. There is a need for further research to establish whether terms such as "effective teaching" or "ineffective teaching" have any stable meaning.

Questions of teacher consistency might also cause one to reconsider the results of studies relating teacher behaviors to student achievement; there is a need for a comprehensive review of the consistency of teacher *behaviors* across

Table 1. Stability coefficients for four long-term studies.

Investigator, sample, and length of instruction	*Criterion tests*	*Stability coefficients* Test	*r*
Morsh *et al.*, 1955; 106 Air Force instructors; eight one-hour periods.	Airplane hydraulics	Written test	.34§
		Performance test	.32§
		Combined written and performance test	.38§
Harris *et al.*, 1968; 30 1st-grade teachers; one school year.	Reading (Stanford Achievement Tests, Primary I)	Vocabulary	−.01
		Word reading	.53‡
		Paragraph meaning	.32*
		Spelling	.52‡
		Word study skills	.36†
Harris *et al.*, 1968; 24 2nd-grade teachers; one school year.	Reading (Metropolitan Achievement Tests, Advanced Primary, Form C)	Word knowledge	.19
		Word discrimination	.26
		Reading	.08
		Spelling	.21
Soar, 1966; 55 teachers, 3rd through 6th grade; one school year.	Reading and arithmetic (Iowa Tests of Basic Skills)	(Vocabulary, Reading, Arithmetic Concepts Arithmetic Problems)	
		Stability of factor labeled "Achievement Gain"	.09
Torrance and Parent, 1966; 63 teachers, 7th through 12th grade; one school year.	Math (Sequential Tests of Educational Progress)	—	—

* $p < .10$
† $p < .05$
‡ $p < .01$
§ $p < .001$

time. Present reviews suggest that some aspects of teacher classroom behavior are relatively stable, even across successive *years* (Soar, 1965). If teachers are consistent in their behavior, but inconsistent in their effects, it is no wonder that research in this area has proved to be so difficult to pursue and so bewildering in its findings. Finally, the lack of high stability coefficients in teacher effects may explain why studies of teacher characteristics have proven so futile. Teacher characteristics such as aptitude, attitudes, marital status, years of education, and number of courses in a given field are relatively stable. If these stable characteristics are correlated with unstable residual gain measures, we should expect "correlations that are nonsignificant, inconsistent from one study to the next, and usually lacking in psychological and educational meaning [Gage, 1963, p. 118]."

SHORT-TERM STUDIES OF TEACHER CONSISTENCY

In short-term studies the total period of instruction is reduced, and in the studies presented below, no teacher taught longer than 30 minutes. A major advantage of these studies is that they can be designed to control for the threats to internal validity discussed above. In practice, each investigator controlled only for certain aspects of design, but as a group these studies contain a variety of ideas which might be incorporated into future studies.

The studies by Fortune are particularly important because the design, procedures for selecting students, and methods for adjusting posttest scores were the same in all three situations; any differences among the stability coefficients across these situations cannot be easily dismissed. In these studies each teacher taught Topic A to Group 1 and again to Group 2. Each teacher also taught Topic B to Group 1 and Topic C to Group 2. Although each teacher taught only four lessons, the design allowed for the calculation of six correlation coefficients, each indicative of one of three forms of teacher consistency (see Figure 1).

	Topic A to Group 2	Topic B to Group 1	Topic C to Group 2
Topic A to Group 1	a	b	c
Topic A to Group 2		c	b
Topic B to Group 1			c
Topic C to Group 2			

a = the same material to different groups
b = different material to the same group
c = different material to different groups

Fig. 1. Teaching situations for measuring three types of teacher consistency in short-term studies.

Same Topics to Different Students

Of the three designs for measuring teacher consistency, the one requiring teachers to teach the same topic to different students appears most similar to the five long-term studies reported above (see Table 1). In the three studies designed by Fortune, there was one instance in which teachers taught the same materials to different students. In two of the studies (Fortune, 1966, 1967), the students were random halves of the same class, and in the third study the students were stratified by grade level and then randomly assigned to classes. The stability coefficients (see Table 2) were quite consistent. In five of the six samples, the correlations ranged from .45 to .70, and four correlations were significant at the .05 level or better.

Table 2. Consistency of results in short-term studies when teachers taught the same topic to different groups of students.

Investigator	*Grades*	*Subject*	*N*	*r*
Fortune (1966)	Headstart	Social studies	15	.45*
	Headstart	Social studies	15	.22
Fortune (1967)	4–6	Social studies	13	.70‡
	4–6	English	15	.57†
	4–6	Math	14	.68‡
Fortune *et al.* (1966)	7–9	Social studies	40	.51§

* $p < .10$
† $p < .05$
‡ $p < .01$
§ $p < .001$

In the long-term studies (see Table 1) in which teachers also taught the same topics to different students, only 2 of the 12 correlations (see Harris *et al.*, grade 1, 1968) were above .40. The discrepancy between the stability coefficients obtained in the long-term studies and those obtained in these short-term studies is striking.

Different Topics to the Same Students

Research in this area focuses on teacher consistency when the topics are changed, but the students remain the same across two occasions. For example, social studies teacher-trainees were asked to teach different topics in their subject areas to the same group of students. The measure of teacher consistency across these topics is analogous to measures of teacher consistency across different parts of a year-long curriculum.

The three studies by Fortune and his associates were designed so that each teacher had two opportunities to teach different material to the same students (see Figure 1). One "class" was taught Topics A and B, and the second "class" was taught Topics A and C. This procedure yielded two stability coefficients for each sample of teachers (see Table 3).

In the fourth short-term study (Belgard *et al.*, 1968), experienced 12th-grade social studies teachers taught two 15-minute lessons on successive days to their regular classes. Random assignment of students to classes was impossible; the 43 participating teachers and their classes were located in schools dispersed throughout the San Francisco Bay area. On the third day, all students heard an identi-

Table 3. Consistency of results in short-term studies when teachers taught different topics to the same group of students.

Investigator	*Grades*	*Subject*	*N*	*r's*	
Fortune (1966)	Headstart	Social Studies	15	−.27	.12
	Headstart	Social Studies	15	.49 *	.40
Fortune (1967)	4–6	Social Studies	13	−.14	−.43
	4–6	English	15	−.27	.12
	4–6	Math	14	−.17	.04
Fortune *et al.* (1965)	7–9	Social Studies	40	.03	.13
Belgard et al. (1968)	12	Social Studies	43	.47 †	

* $p < .10$
† $p < .001$

cal audiotape lecture on a third topic, and class mean scores on the test following this lecture were used to adjust posttest scores on the other two lectures for differences in the ability of the classes to learn from lectures. The lecture material and criterion tests were selected from the same materials which had been used in the study by Fortune *et al.* (1966), and teachers were provided with 5 of the 10 criterion questions.

The stability coefficients for seven samples of teachers in the four studies are presented on Table 3. Compared to the consistent and usually significant correlations obtained when teachers taught the same material to different classes (see Table 2), the correlations in Table 3 are quite different. One would expect that, when different topics are taught to the same students, the correlations would be lower than when the same topics are taught to different students since the instructional materials and posttests would be different and the teachers could be using different teaching methods in the two situations. The correlation coefficients *were* lower in almost all cases, although I was not prepared for the negative correlations reported by Fortune (1967). The exception on Table 3 is the moderately high correlation ($r = .47$, $p < .001$) obtained when experienced teachers lectured on different topics to their regular classes (Belgard *et al.*, 1963). The sample studied by Belgard *et al.* consisted of experienced teachers who volunteered for the study and were restricted to lecturing during both lessons. Unfortunately, no comparable data on experienced teachers are available in the other short-term situations. There is a need for further studies employing experienced teachers and restricted teaching methods.

Different Topics to Different Students

In the studies by Fortune and his associates, the design permitted three correlation coefficients to be computed for each sample of teachers when they taught different topics to different groups of students (see Figure 1). The three correlation coefficients for each of the six samples of teachers are presented in Table 4. These correlations are the most perplexing of all; they tend to be higher *in both directions* than those presented on the other tables. In comparison to the correlations on the other tables, one would expect those on Table 4 to be consistently lowest because in this situation both the instructional materials, posttests, and students are different, and the teacher might use different methods in the two situations. Yet, such confounding cannot easily explain correlations of −.45, −.42, and .42 within the same sample of teacher-trainees.

Table 4. Consistency of results in short-term studies when teachers taught different topics to different groups of students.

Investigator	*Grades*	*Subject*	*N*		*r*'s	
Fortune (1966)	Headstart	Social studies	15	.21	.42	.45
	Headstart	Social studies	15	−.08	.13	.25
Fortune (1967)[a]	4–6	Social studies	13	−.45	−.42	.42
	4–6	English	15	−.35	−.07	.53
	4–6	Math	14	−.29	.05	.82
Fortune *et al.* (1966)	7–9	Social studies	40	−.10	.01	.43
Justiz (1969)	Senior High School	Varied	10		.63[a]	(.05)
	Senior High School	Varied	7		.90[a]	(.01)

[a] Rank order correlation using posttest scores only. All other correlations are product-moment using adjusted posttest scores.

In contrast to the studies by Fortune, the results obtained by Justiz (1969) across two samples showed amazing consistency and statistical significance. Each of the student-teachers taught two 30-minute lessons on subjects not currently taught in senior-high schools. Students were randomly assigned to newly constituted classes (12 to 18 students in a class), teachers were randomly assigned to classes, and each teacher taught the two lessons to different classes. Class mean posttest scores for each teacher were used to compute the Spearman rank order correlations. Separate coefficients were reported for each of the two schools used in the study.

SUMMARY AND SUGGESTIONS FOR FUTURE RESEARCH

The available studies of teacher consistency can be classified into four types: (*a*) long-term studies in which teachers taught the same material to different students, (*b*) short-term studies in which teachers taught the same material to different students, (*c*) short-term studies in which teachers taught different material to the same students, and (*d*) short-term studies in which teachers taught different material to different students. Positive and consistent correlations were obtained in both (*a*) and (*b*), but the size of the correlations and the percentage of significant results were highest in (*b*).

The consistent results in (*b*) must be considered carefully because all these studies were conducted by Fortune *et al.*, and the same materials, criterion tests, students, and methods of adjusting posttest scores which were used in (*b*) were also used in deriving the stability coefficients in the other two short-term settings —(*c*) and (*d*); yet the results were quite different. When teachers taught the same topic to different students, the stability coefficients were all positive (r's = .22 to .70), and four of the six correlations were significant. When teachers taught different topics to the same students, the direction of the correlations was erratic (r's = −.43 to .49), and none was significant. When teachers taught different topics to different students, the direction of the correlations was again erratic (r's = −.45 to .82), and few correlations were significant.

The overall conclusion from the three studies by Fortune is that there was reasonable stability of teacher effects in only one of the three situations: when the teacher-trainees taught the same material to different students. The variable which appears to distinguish this situation from those in the other two short-term situations is control over variation in teacher behavior. Although Fortune did not present data on the stability of teacher *behavior* in the various situations, it is possible that the least amount of variation occurred when teachers taught the same topic twice. In the other situations, the teacher-trainees taught different topics, and because they were allowed to instruct in any manner they wished, there may have been greater variation of behavior in those situations. Similar control over variation in teacher behavior was maintained in the study by Belgard *et al.*, in which the experienced teachers were limited to lecturing, even though they taught two different topics. In this study, the stability coefficient was relatively high ($r = .47$).

It is difficult to estimate the extent to which instructional materials that are related to the posttest contribute to the consistency of teacher effectiveness. This variable appears to distinguish the short-term studies in which teachers taught the same materials to different students from the long-term studies of similar design. However, instructional materials related to the posttests were also used in the other short-term studies, and the results were erratic in those other two situations. Unfortunately, only teacher-trainees were used as subjects in almost all of the short-term studies, and we cannot predict the results which might have been obtained on this variable had experienced teachers served as subjects across all three situations.

Even if there is congruity between the materials and the items on the posttest, there may be significant differences across teachers in the *relevance* of their instruction to the posttest. In future studies the relevance of the instruction to the posttest might be increased by providing teachers with some of the posttest questions (Fortune *et al.*, 1967; Belgard *et al.*, 1968). The relevance might be measured by asking students whether they had an opportunity to learn each of the items on the posttest (see Husén, 1967), or by coding transcripts of the lesson for the relevance of the content to each posttest item (see Rosenshine, 1968; Shutes, 1969). A measure of the content relevance of the lesson might be used as a covariate or as a stratifying variable, or it could be used to deselect from the sample those teachers whose teaching was not equally relevant across two occasions.

The current long-term studies show that one cannot use the residual achievement gain scores in one year to predict the gain scores in a successive year with any confidence. But only a few such studies exist, and not all of these have equal generalizability to natural classroom teaching. On the basis of the short-term studies, one might suggest that stability coefficients can be increased if there is greater congruence between the events in the classroom and the items on the posttests, and less variation in the behavior of the teacher across successive instructional occasions. One area for future research might be to determine whether attention to these variables will yield reasonable stability coefficients in long-term studies.

References

Belgard, M., G. Rosenshine, and N. L. Gage. "The Teacher's Effectiveness in Explaining: Evidence on Its Generality and Correlations with Pupils' Ratings and Attention Scores." In N. L. Gage *et al.*, *Explorations of the Teacher's Effectiveness in Explaining* (Tech. Rep. 4). Stanford, Calif.: Stanford Center for Research and Development in Teaching, Stanford University, 1968. (ERIC Document Reproduction Service No. 208 147)

Fortune, J. C. *A Study of the Generality of Presenting Behavior in Teaching Preschool Children.* Memphis, Tenn.: Memphis State University, 1966.

Fortune, J. C. *A Study of the Generality of Presenting Behavior in Teaching* (U.S. Office of Education Project No. 6-8464). Memphis, Tenn.: Memphis State University, 1967. (ERIC Document Reproduction Service No. 016 285)

Fortune, J. C., N. L. Gage, and R. E. Shutes. "The Generality of the Ability to Explain." Paper presented at the meeting of the American Educational Research Association, Chicago, February 1966.

Gage, N. L. "Paradigms for Research on Teaching." In N. L. Gage, ed., *Handbook of Research on Teaching.* Chicago: Rand McNally, 1963.

Harris, A. J., *et al. A Continuation of the CRAFT Project: Comparing Reading Approaches with Disadvantaged Urban Negro Children in Primary Grades* (Cooperative Research Project No. 5-0570-2-12-1). New York: Division of Teacher Education, City University of New York, 1968. (ERIC Document Reproduction Service No. 010 297)

Husén, T., ed. *International Study of Achievement in Mathematics: A Comparison of Twelve Countries.* Vol. 2. New York: Wiley, 1967.

Justiz, T. B. "A Reliable Measure of Teacher Effectiveness." *Educational Leadership, Research Supplement* 3 (1969): 49–55.

Morsh, J. E., G. G. Burgess, and P. N. Smith. *Student Achievement as a Measure of Instructor Effectiveness* (Project No. 7950, Task No. 77243). San Antonio, Texas: Air Force Personnel and Training Research Center, Lackland Air Force Base, 1955.

Rosenshine, B. *Objectively Measured Behavioral Predictors of Effectiveness in Explaining* (Tech. Rep. 4). Stanford, Calif.: Stanford Center for Research and Development in Teaching, Stanford University, 1968. (ERIC Document Reproduction Service No. 028 147)

Shutes, R. E. "Verbal Behaviors and Instructional Effectiveness." Ph.D. dissertation, Stanford University, 1969.

Soar, R. S. *An Integrative Approach to Classroom Learning.* Public Health Service Grant No. 5-R11-MH 01096 and National Institute of Mental Health Grant No. 7-R11-MH 02045). Philadelphia, Penn.: Temple University, 1966. (ERIC Document Reproduction Service No. 033 749)

Torrance, E. P., and E. Parent. *Characteristics of Mathematics Teachers that Affect Students' Learning* (Cooperative Research Project No. 1020). Minneapolis, Minn.: Minnesota School Mathematics and Science Center, Institute of Technology, University of Minnesota, 1966. (ERIC Document Reproduction Service No. 010 378)

RICHARD SHAVELSON and NANCY ATWOOD
University of California at Los Angeles

Generalizability of Measures of Teaching Process

The teaching process paradigm focuses on teacher and student behaviors identified as important in their own right or linked to desirable student outcomes in previous studies. A wide variety of teacher behavior has been investigated using numerous observation instruments. When measures of teacher behavior are examined over more than one point in time, they have not been particularly stable. It may be that certain characteristics of the teaching situation affect the stability of particular teaching acts over time. For example, if a teacher is observed teaching high ability students at two different points in time, the frequency of, say, higher order questions may be fairly stable over occasions. However, if this teacher is observed teaching high ability students at one point in time and low ability students at another point in time, the frequency of higher-order questions for that teacher may be very unstable over observation occasions.

Rosenshine and Furst (1973) defined the stability problem as one of "representativeness" or determining whether a sample of observed classroom transactions is a trustworthy representative sample of total behavior. Armstrong, DeVault, and Larson (1967) attempted to address this problem by determining the amount of observation time necessary to adequately sample a teacher's verbal communication using the Wisconsin Teacher Education Research Project (TERP) observation system and the Flanders system. They concluded that when sampling a teacher's behavior during reading instruction one should observe for approximately 150 minutes in order to obtain an adequate sample of teaching behavior in a one-week period. If the observations occur during arithmetic or social studies instruction, they concluded that the teacher's be-

This article was specially prepared for this volume. The work described herein was completed pursuant to Contract #400-75-0001 between the Department of Health, Education and Welfare, National Institute of Education and the California Commission for Teacher Preparation and Licensing. The Far West Laboratory for Educational Research and Development, San Francisco, California, is the primary contractor of the California Commission.

havior should be sampled for approximately 120 minutes. Unfortunately, due to problems of sampling and design, the results and conclusions from this study are open to several possible interpretations. However, this study does illustrate an important problem for future research on teaching.

Data on the stability of measures of teacher behavior, reviewed below, are examined to determine the extent to which they generalize over different teaching situations. As with the studies of teacher effectiveness, situational and observational facets have not been systematically varied in the literature to test the effect of a particular facet on stability. Therefore, conclusions about stability for a particular facet are confounded by unsystematic variation of other facets. However, results can be examined for patterns which suggest consistency or inconsistency.

Studies which present data on the stability of measures of teacher behavior are summarized in Table 1 (see Appendix). The rows of the table identify the studies. The columns provide information about them, including various situational and observational facets.

The entries in the table provide critical information about each study. Entries under the student, content, teacher, and dependent-variable categories may be interpreted as follows. The column labeled *assignment* identifies how students were assigned to teachers; randomly, quasi-randomly (students *within* an intact classroom were randomly assigned to one of two teachers; more than two teachers or classrooms were used in the study), or nonrandomly. The *similarity* facet identifies the similarity of students taught across observation occasions: same (exactly the same students at two or more occasions), similar (students drawn from the same population as in the first observation), or different (students from different populations at different occasions). The grade level and type of student facets are self-explanatory.

Two content facets were identified. The *type* facet refers to the specific subject matter taught during the study period. The *similarity* facet refers to the correspondence of curricula from one observation to the next: same (exactly the same topics or curricula), similar (same general content area but perhaps differing in specific topics, curricula, or in an unspecified way), or different (topics or curricula differing in content and perhaps in other unspecified ways).

Teachers in each study are identified as practicing (P) if they were employed as a regular teacher in a school, trainee (T) if they were enrolled in a teacher training program, or undergraduate (U) if they were students enrolled in a school of education but not necessarily pursuing a teaching credential at the time of the investigation.

Finally, important facets of the dependent variable are identified. Number of observation occasions is self-explanatory. The *type of measure* facet refers to whether the measure of teacher behavior is a frequency count of specific, denotable behaviors such as frequency of verbal reinforcements, a factor score representing a cluster of teacher behaviors, or a more general rating of such variables as clarity or enthusiasm which requires the observer to process many cues before making a decision. Finally, the behavior observed and corresponding stability coefficients are reported for each study. The primary measure of stability of teacher behavior in these studies consisted of correlations between measures of teacher behavior obtained at two or more points in time.

In the Hiller, Fisher, and Kaess (1969) study, videotapes from the Belgard, et al. (1968) study were examined for significant verbal characteristics of the experienced teachers' lecture performance. The teachers delivered two different 15-minute lessons about the economic, social, and political conditions of Yugoslavia and Thailand to their twelfth-grade classes on successive days. Hiller, et al. used a computer program to identify the frequency of 35 categories of verbal responses (words, phrases) found in the Hiller Explanation Dictionary. The 35 categories dealing roughly with teachers' explanations were consolidated into a set of five factors based on the experimenters' *a priori* theoretical expectations for an optimal grouping of the categories. Correlations of these factors across observation occasions were reported. The two factors exhibiting greatest stability were verbal fluency (0.76) and vagueness (0.84). The other factors showed only moderate stability: optimal information amount (0.37), knowledge structure cues (0.29), and interest (0.20).

The high stability coefficients for verbal fluency and vagueness are difficult to interpret. The authors noted that vagueness arises as a speaker commits himself to deliver information he can't remember or never really knew. Therefore, it may be that the high stability of vagueness in this study is accounted for by the fact that the subject matter of these lessons was unfamiliar to the teachers. The authors also suggested that the verbal fluency factor may be a correlate of vagueness. That is, low verbal fluency, marked by hesitations in speech, may be correlated with vagueness. Therefore, the high stability of this factor may also be due to the unfamiliarity of the content being taught. However, this explanation is not confirmed by the data. The correlation between fluency and vagueness was −0.08 in the Yugoslavia lesson and −0.24 in the Thailand lesson.

In the Emmer and Peck (1973) study, videotapes of 28 fifth- and eighth-grade teachers were taken on five occasions. Each fifth-grade class was observed during mathematics, social studies, and science lessons. Eighth-grade classes included approximately equal numbers of mathematics, social studies, English, and science classes. Five systems were used to code the observations: Observation Schedule and Record (OScAR 5), Fuller Affective Interaction Records (FAIR), Cognitive Components System (CCS), Brophy-Good Dyadic Interaction System, and the Coping Analysis Schedule for Educational Settings (CASES). (Only the first four observation systems are considered here since the fifth system dealt exclusively with student behavior.) Data from each of the different systems were factor analyzed. (Eight to ten factors were identified for each of the four observation systems.) Intraclass correlations over one and five observation periods were computed for each factor in each observation system.

In order to examine the pattern of stability, we classified factors from each system into one of the following categories of variables: cognitive, affective, style, classroom management, and interpersonal. These categories of factors and their corresponding stability coefficients are presented in Table 1 (see Appendix). The first category, cognitive variables, includes factors heavily loaded on behaviors relating to academic activities and the content being taught. For example, the problem-solving factor reflects teacher behaviors which initiate and structure problems for the class to consider. The stability coefficients for all but one of these cognitive dimensions are very low, ranging from below 0.10 to 0.18. (Emmer and Peck did not report intraclass correlations below 0.10 for factors in their table; hence, we say below or <0.10.) The problem-solving factor showed slightly more stability (0.27).

The affective category refers to factors which are heavily loaded on the teacher's expression of feelings to students and teacher responsiveness to student feelings. For example, the positive affect dimension includes the teacher's praise or encouragement of pupils. The stability coefficients for these factors are also generally low (0.11 to 0.19).

The style category refers to factors which reflect a preferred orientation or mode of instruction on the part of the teacher. Three styles were identified. The first set of four factors reflected an orientation to student ideas rather than teacher ideas. The stability coefficients for these factors ranged from <0.10 to 0.22. A second set of factors was concerned with teachers' use of convergent questions versus divergent questions. They seemed to reflect an underlying dimension representing a focus upon single, correct answers rather than divergent discussion. The stability coefficients for these two factors were 0.36 and 0.14. The last set of style factors reflected teacher lecturing and indicated activities in which the teachers' presentation of content is the overriding concern. These factors showed the highest stability of all factors (0.28 to 0.51).

The next category of variables relate to classroom management. Two factors, procedural interaction and controlling, are heavily loaded on teacher behaviors which are procedural and nonsubstantive in nature. These factors show low stability (0.11 to 0.13). The other two factors in this category, desist statements and criticizing and asking for a behavior change, involve teacher requests for students to stop doing something. These factors were somewhat more stable (0.34 to 0.39).

The last category of factors concerns interpersonal variables relating to specific kinds of teacher-pupil interactions. The stability for these factors was also rather low (<0.10 to 0.29).

In general, the factors isolated by Emmer and Peck range from unstable to moderately stable. The set of factors appearing to be most stable were those relating to teacher lecture. As Emmer and Peck pointed out, the class conditions in which observations were made were not homogeneous over time. Many facets, such as *grade level, type of content,* and *similarity of content,* varied from observation occasion to observation occasion. For example, in the fifth-grade classes, type of subject matter (e.g., mathematics, science) varied from occasion to occasion while in the eighth-grade classes the type of subject matter remained the same with individual topics differing. Furthermore, data from both grade levels were combined in the factor analyses. It may be that the unsystematic variation of these facets over observation occasions accounts for the low stability observed and that teacher lecture is less affected by the variation of these situational facets than the other behavior observed.

In both the Hiller et al. (1969) and Emmer and Peck (1973) studies, frequency count variables were clustered either conceptually (Hiller et al.) or empirically (Emmer and Peck). Questions about the consistency and replicability of the clusters aside, problems of interpretation arise. Unlike high inference variables, such as ratings of warmth where specific definitions for rating exist, clear definitions of clusters of variables do not exist. How are the variables within a cluster to be put together by the teacher into smooth teaching performance? How should a teacher be trained to perform the teaching represented by clusters? How should he or she be evaluated? While parsimony is welcome, especially with respect to observation systems of teaching, the techniques used in these two studies may achieve this goal at too great a cost. The teaching process which was the original focus of the studies may be masked by conceptual or statistical factor analysis. Statistical techniques from information theory or from statistical theories of runs or stochastic processes might be better suited to identifying patterns of teaching acts without compromising the process itself.

Moon (1969, 1971) observed the verbal behavior of 32 primary-grade teachers during science lessons. Half of the teachers had participated in Science Curriculum Improvement Study (SCIS) workshop which emphasized manipulation of materials and child-to-child communication as an integral aspect of science lessons. The teachers using SCIS materials were observed on five occasions while the teachers teaching conventional science were observed on two occasions. The Flanders' instrument was used to collect interaction data and stability coefficients were calculated for two interaction ratios and five categories of questions for each group of teachers.

The I/D ratio is defined as the amount of indirect teacher influence in verbal classroom behavior divided by the amount of direct teacher influence. Teacher talk refers to the percentage of time teachers spent talking during science activities. The stability coefficients were fairly high for the teachers teaching conventional science (0.64 for I/D ratio and 0.76 for teacher talk) but very low for the teachers teaching SCIS science (0.18 for I/D ratio and 0.12 for teacher talk).

The following types of questions, categorized by Moon as lower-order, showed virtually no stability with the SCIS teachers: questions which ask students to recall facts (0.12) and questions which ask students to see relationships (0.05). These questions showed moderate stability with the conventional science teachers: 0.42 for recall questions and 0.43 for relationship questions. Two types of questions, categorized by Moon as higher-order, also showed essentially zero stability for both groups: questions which require observations (0.05 for SCIS teachers and 0.17 for conventional teachers) and questions which require testing hypotheses (0.00 for both samples). One type of higher-order question, questions which require generating hypotheses, showed somewhat more stability with both samples (0.19 for the SCIS sample and 0.17 for the conventional sample). It should be noted that questions calling for seeing relationships, hypothesizing and testing hypotheses are extremely infrequent events. Means for the frequency of occurrence of each of these question types ranged from 0.00 to 1.40 on any given occasion. The low correlations for these behaviors may reflect this restriction of range. The higher stability of the control teachers on some behaviors may reflect the fact that these teachers were teaching a familiar curriculum in their customary way, while the SCIS teachers were teaching an unfamiliar curriculum using somewhat new techniques for the first time.

Campbell (1972) observed five junior high school science teachers near the end of the spring semester and midway through the fall semester of the following academic year. Only teachers teaching students in the low achievement tract were studied. Three interaction ratios were calculated for each teacher on both observation occasions from data obtained with Flanders' system. From these data we calculated Spearman rank-order correlations for each interaction ratio.

Two interaction ratios involving indirect and direct teacher behavior were calculated by Campbell. The I/D ratio included the following indirect (I) teaching acts: teacher accepts student feelings and student ideas, teacher praises, and teacher questions. Direct (D) teaching acts were: teacher gives directions, teacher criticizes, and teacher lectures or gives own opinion. The stability coefficient for this ratio (I/D) was 0.10. The revised i/d ratio did not include teacher questioning or lecturing behavior and is considered to be more sensitive to the affective areas of a teacher's behavior. The stability coefficient for this ratio (i/d) was −0.90!

The third interaction ratio was the ratio of student talk to teacher talk (S/T). This ratio (S/T) showed the greatest stability over time (0.80). In all cases, these ratios were extremely low, indicating that the teachers dominated the verbal behavior of their classes. The high stability coefficient indicates that this pattern was consistent over time. This finding is substantiated by Bellack et al. (1966) who found that 80% of all classroom time is spent in teacher talk.

The pattern of stability coefficients for the interaction ratios of indirect to direct teacher behavior is difficult to interpret. The first observation of teachers occurred during the final teaching weeks of the spring semester, and the second observation was recorded midway through the fall of the following academic year. As Campbell pointed out, the spring observations may reflect the cumulative fatigue of nine months of teaching, while the fall observations show a more normal pattern of interaction. Therefore, the instability of the I/D ratio and the i/d ratio may be due, at least in part, to the timing of the observations.

In the Friedman (1973) study, 18 teachers of grades one, three, five, or seven were observed on four separate occasions over a six-month period. The Observation Schedule and Record (OScAR) was used to record pupil-initiated interchanges and teacher reinforcement of spontaneous student behavior. Only those interactions pertaining directly to classroom content (substantive interchanges) were recorded. The "exit" from an interchange occurred when the teacher either evaluated the child's verbalization or continued without evaluating it. Observation records were screened for six types of teacher exits to an interchange. Stability coefficients were calculated for each of the six exits. The "acknowledged" exit (the teacher responds to what the child has said but does not indicate whether it is correct or not) and the "not evaluated" exit (the teacher makes no response to a child's verbalization) are the most stable (0.61, 0.58). The "approved" exit (the teacher indicates that what the child has said is acceptable but no enthusiasm or praise is given) and the "neutrally rejected" exit (the teacher indicates that what the child has said is unacceptable but no disapproval is expressed) are moderately stable (0.49, 0.48). The least stable exits were the "supported" exit (the teacher enthusiastically indicates that what the child has said is correct or acceptable) and the "criticized" exit (the teacher clearly indicates with disapproval that what the child has said is incorrect or unacceptable) (0.37, 0.26).

In order to analyze variations in teacher reinforcement of interchanges, a set of five orthogonal reinforcement categories was derived from the six original OScAR exits. These statistically orthogonal categories were scored as combinations of the original six exits. For example, the following weighting of the original six variables comprised the transformed variable, feedback: supported (½), approved (½), acknowledged (−1), not evaluated (−1), neutrally rejected (½) and criticized (½). In general, the stability coefficients were higher for the transformed exits than the original exits (see Table 1). Encouragement 1 and encouragement 2 showed the highest stability (0.70, 0.73) with the feedback and positivity categories showing somewhat less stability (0.63, 0.61). The lowest stability was found for the enthusiasm exit (0.53).

Trinchero (1974a, 1975) examined the stability of teacher trainees' use of positive reinforcement, higher-order questions, and probing questions over a nine-month period. Observations occurred after technical skills training in August and at the end of student teaching in May. Teacher trainees were randomly assigned to teach a 40-minute English or social studies lesson to student volunteers from secondary schools in the Palo Alto, California, area. Students were randomly assigned to groups of approximately 22 each. The English lessons focused on some aspects of semantics, while the social studies topics dealt with economics. Each teacher was given an outline of the topic content, a list of topic objectives, and a copy of the topic test beforehand. Videotapes of these teaching sessions were rated for teacher acts reflecting use of reinforcement to increase student participatory behavior (positive reinforcement), teachers' use of questions which call for inferential responses (higher-order questions) and teachers' use of questions which require the student to go beyond his first response (probing). Stability coefficients were calculated for these teaching acts.

The stability coefficient for total reinforcement, the summation of frequency scores for all reinforcement categories, was 0.64. However, since there was a significant difference between the means of the English and social studies teachers on this variable, we calculated Spearman rank-order correlations separately for each subsample. These coefficients were 0.47 for the English teachers and 0.63 for the social studies teachers.

Stability coefficients were also calculated with frequency scores and proportions for each of five categories of reinforcement (see Table 1). Positive nonverbal reinforcement was most stable (0.74). Separate calculations for each subsample yielded coefficients of 0.57 for English teachers and 0.64 for social studies teachers. Moderate stability coefficients were obtained for positive verbal reinforcement (0.44) and qualified verbal reinforcement, i.e., statements containing both positive and negative elements (0.48). However, when stability coefficients are calculated separately for positive verbal reinforcement for each subsample of teachers, an extremely low coefficient was found for English teachers (0.04), while a much higher one was found for the social studies teachers (0.57). The least stability was found for negative verbal reinforcement (0.13) and negative nonverbal reinforcement (−0.15). Stability coefficients for proportion scores were similar to coefficients for frequency scores (see Table 1).

Stability coefficients were also reported for frequency scores and proportions of higher-order questions. Very low stability (0.16 to 0.17) was observed for frequency of teacher-initiated questions, lower-order questions, and higher-order questions. Coefficients for proportion scores were much higher but in opposite directions (−0.52 for proportion of lower-order questions and +0.54 for proportion of higher-order questions). No explanation of these data is given by Trinchero; we are just as perplexed by them.

Stability coefficients for frequencies and proportions of probing are also shown in Table 1. The frequency of pupil-initiated talk seems to be much less stable (0.04) than the frequency of opportunities to probe (0.24). The frequency of total probes and individual probes are moderately stable (0.40, 0.31), although the proportion scores for these variables are somewhat less stable (0.35 for total probes, 0.20 for individual probes).

Three specific types of probing are reasonably stable over time: individual redirects (0.54), group redirects (0.43), and clarifying and prompting questions (0.62). However, virtually no stability over time was shown for questions involving repeating, rephrasing, and refocusing (−0.09) or critical awareness (−0.05). Similarly, stability coefficients for proportion scores for all five types of probing questions were low (−0.29 to 0.14).

Borg (1972) observed 38 teachers immediately after completion of a minicourse designed to develop discussion skills and again four months later. Each teacher was instructed to prepare a 20-minute class discussion lesson based on content from current class work. Lessons were videotaped and later analyzed to determine the teacher's use of skills taught in the minicourse. We computed stability coefficients for these behaviors (see Table 1).

Two behaviors relating to general questioning showed low to moderate stability: teacher questions (0.14) and average length of pause (0.27). Two measures of questioning, "words in pupil response to information level questions," which was interpreted as indicating teacher's asking for sets of related facts and proportion of higher-order to fact questions showed virtually no stability (0.01; 0.07). Three types of probing questions showed moderate stability: redirection (0.40), prompting (0.30), and clarification (0.55).

Three skills considered undesirable in discussion showed low to moderately high stability: repeating own question (0.23), repeating pupil answer (0.22), and answering own question (0.10). Percentage of teacher talk as measured by the Flanders system was also moderately stable (0.38).

In the Ehman (1972) study, 84 preservice secondary teachers (undergraduates) taught seven microteaching lessons to groups of four to six ninth-grade students as part of a social studies methods course. The first lesson, taught only to peers, was aimed at familiarizing students with the methods and mechanics of microteaching and was not included in the present analysis. The remaining six lessons were taught in pairs at about three-week intervals through the semester. In the first pair of lessons, the preservice teacher invented a lesson in which one or more historical or social science concepts were taught. Two days later, the same lesson was retaught under similar conditions to a new group of students. The second pair of lessons involved eliciting student hypotheses in response to a problem while the third set concerned the analysis of a value proposition or controversial issue. Audiotapes of each lesson were coded using a modified version of the Flanders system, and stability coefficients were computed for each set of lessons (see Table 1).

The praises/encourages category showed moderate stability (0.41 to 0.47), while the accepts/uses student ideas category was less stable (0.08 to 0.47). Two questioning categories were fairly stable: overall questioning (0.33 to 0.52) and cognitive-memory questions (0.47 to 0.52) with one exception (−0.01). The other question types showed less stability (−0.01 to 0.35). Closed teacher questions or the ratio of cognitive-memory and convergent questions to total questions also showed low stability (0.07 to 0.26).

The lecturing category was fairly stable (0.58 to 0.60) while the gives directions category was less consistent (0.15 to 0.44). Stability coefficients for teacher criticism were low (−0.04 to 0.25). Productive silence or confusion was moderately stable (0.49 to 0.55), while unproductive silence or confusion was much less consistent (0.14 to 0.36). Stability coefficients for the I/D ratio were quite high (0.57 to 0.66).

Ehman also computed stability coefficients between adjacent occasions for data from the Bellack et al. (1966) study in which 15 high school teachers were observed on four occasions. Teachers were given a pamphlet and teachers' guide on international economic problems and were asked to base their four lessons on this material. Typescripts were prepared from audiotapes of these lessons which were then analyzed using the Bellack system.

The ratio of teacher talk to student talk showed moderate to high stability over the four experimental sessions (0.41 to 0.84). Structuring moves by the teacher which set the context for subsequent behavior were also highly stable (0.72 to 0.76). Soliciting moves which include questions, commands, and requests showed high stability in two instances (0.61, 0.74) but not in the third (−0.09). Coefficients for teacher responding which involves a response to a soliciting move and teacher reacting which serves to modify or evaluate previous statements were less consistent (0.22 to 0.66).

Marzano (1973) randomly selected 27 teachers from a group of 50 first-grade teachers attending a two-day orientation workshop in which the teachers were trained to use the *Distar Language 1* program. The Distar programs are designed to teach basic concepts at a fast pace so that children who start out behind average youngsters have the opportunity to catch up. The program is unique in that the teacher's behavior is programmed. The teacher's role is one of teaching a particular format to mastery by saying and doing exactly what the materials prescribe.

Each teacher was audiotaped while teaching one lesson during each of five one-week segments. The five taping segments were equally spaced throughout a six-month period (October to March) so that lessons taught from Books A, B, and C of the *Distar Language 1* program were observed. The variable observed was the degree to which the teacher followed the Distar format in group activities and individual activities.

Analysis of variance procedures (teachers × occasions × books) were carried out for each type of activity. Unbiased estimators of each of the components of variance were calculated and then used to construct estimates of the generalizability coefficients. The values of this coefficient were 0.52 and 0.54 for group and individual activities respectively. Even though, in computing these coefficients, Marzano omitted the variance component due to the occasion by book interaction in his definition of observed score variance, this did not affect the stability estimate since the interaction variance equalled zero. When teacher scores are averaged over the three books and five occasions, the coefficients are 0.92 for group activities and 0.92 for individual activities.

Wallen (1969) observed 33 teachers teaching "academic" lessons on ten occasions using the STEP Observation Schedule which includes ratings taken after every five minutes of observation and global ratings taken after the entire observation period (20–35 minutes). Five observations were obtained in the fall and five in the spring. Mean scores across each set of five observations were obtained for each teacher and correlation coefficients were calculated between the fall and spring mean scores (see Table 1).

The stability coefficients for the global ratings were very high, ranging from 0.71 to 0.92 with one exception (0.03). In general, the five-minute ratings were much less stable. For example, teacher methods for focusing pupil's attention on the learning activity and allowing them to respond overtly were generally unstable (−0.02 to 0.21) with three exceptions (0.38, 0.42, 0.67). Clear instances of teacher individualization based on diagnosis of student needs were stable (0.62, 0.87) while other individualization variables were not (−0.09 to 0.21). Two feedback variables, feedback from teacher and no provision, were moderately stable (0.34 to 0.43) while the others were not (−0.22 to 0.00).

Direct controlling responses or ignoring of irrelevant behavior were also stable (0.61 to 0.77) while direct controlling responses to disruptive behavior and indirect controlling responses to both irrelevant and disruptive behavior were less stable (−0.13 to 0.42).

Two studies (Brophy and Evertson, 1974a,b; Sandoval, 1974) were located which are potential sources of data on stability of teacher behavior; however, no conclusions can be drawn at this point. Brophy and Evertson studied the teaching behavior of second- and third-grade teachers from both high SES and low SES schools selected because they had previously shown relatively high consistency in the amount of student learning gain that they produced on standardized achievement tests. The teachers were observed on 18 occasions over a two-year period using a variety of high-inference and low-inference measures. Pearson correlations between these process measures and student outcome measures as well as multiple regression analyses designed to indicate nonlinear relationships between these measures were done. Unfortunately, correlations were not reported for the measures of teacher behavior over observation occasions. However, with the variety of teacher behavior measures used and the large number of observation occasions, this project is a rich source of data for examining the stability of teacher behavior measures over time. Furthermore, the effect of two systematically varying facets, *type of measure* and *time of day* (morning, afternoon, or reading group), could be examined with four populations of teachers (second and third grade; Title 1 and non-Title 1 schools).

In the Sandoval (1974) study, 12 teachers were videotaped during both reading and mathematics on four occasions during the school year. Lessons taught on the second, third, and fourth observation occasions were coded using the Teacher Instruction Lexicon, Teacher Feedback Lexicon, and the Observation Classroom Summary Record from the APPLE system and a videotape rating of teacher behaviors and characteristics. Lessons from the second and third observation occasions were also coded using interaction analysis. Lessons from occasions one through three were coded with a videotape rating of teaching style as well. (Data from the first observation occasion was discarded for use with the other observation systems because of the poor quality of the videotape.)

The data from these observations were analyzed with an analysis of variance nested design (teachers nested within observers). However, this design does not permit an examination of the stability of teacher behaviors over time. The main effect for teachers and the interaction of teachers and observation occasions is confounded by the effect of raters.

SUMMARY: STUDIES OF TEACHER BEHAVIOR

In order to determine the effects of various situational and observational facets on the generalizability of measures of teacher behavior, teaching acts which were defined similarly were examined as a group (see Appendix, Table 2). If two or more variables from one study fell into a cluster, correlational evidence, if available, was examined to verify the clustering. For example the cluster, teacher presentation, contained three variables (teaching acts) from the Emmer and Peck (EP) study; these three variables were highly correlated with each other. In addition, the cluster included lecturing (Wallen; Ehman), teacher talk (Moon; Borg), student/teacher talk ratio (Campbell; Bellack), and three I/D ratios (M, C, E).

In clustering these teaching acts, an already apparent problem became critical. It was impossible to verify that measures of the same variable, observed by two different investigators using the same instrument on questionably similar populations of teachers, were actually measuring the same thing. More commonly, the same or slightly different variable was measured by two different instruments in two different studies. The validity of interpretations of such measurements is suspect, at best. This is an issue of the validity of construct interpretations of these measures (Borich and Malitz, 1975). In addition, standardization[1] of measurements, or the lack thereof, has played a major part in

[1] "A standardized test is one in which the procedure, apparatus, and scoring have been fixed so that precisely the same testing procedures can be followed at different times and places" (Cronbach, 1970, p. 27).

inhibiting the advance of knowledge about teaching. The lack of evidence on construct validity and standardization makes the validity of our interpretations of teacher variables and so our clustering quite tentative.

In drawing together evidence on the generalizability of various measures of teacher behavior, a distinction between global ratings and other types of measures will be maintained. Only Wallen's (1969) study reported the stability of global ratings. The stability of these ratings stands in striking contrast to the stability of most other measures, as will be seen. Whether the stability is in the teachers observed or is in the beholder's (observer's) eye, cannot be untangled in this review.

The frequency count, factor score, and short-term rating measures were clustered into 12 categories: teacher presentation, presentation of content, teacher questions, teacher feedback, teacher motivational skills, expressive teaching style, student-centered teaching style, interpersonal behavior, affective style, teacher following procedures, teacher's classroom management, and teacher individualization.

Teacher Presentation

Twelve variables were grouped into the *teacher presentation* cluster (see Table 2). In most cases, measures of teacher presentation are reasonably stable. Since the SCIS teachers in the Moon study received training which encouraged student inquiry rather than teacher lecture, instability in measures of their presentation, compared to conventional teaching, might be expected. The low coefficients from Wallen and Campbell, then, need some explanation—possibly in terms of differences in facets from the other studies. Students in the Wallen study were from the inner-city and students in the Campbell study were low achievers. Information about students in the other studies is not given. One might speculate that the type of student population in the Wallen and Campbell studies did not allow stable lecturing behavior. That is, lecturing may be difficult or inappropriate with low achieving or poorly motivated students. However, this represents conjecture, at best. Furthermore, the Campbell coefficient is based on only five teachers.

Presentation of Content

The second cluster, *presentation of content,* might be considered a further delineation of the teacher presentation cluster—various types of presentations fall into this cluster. Of the 13 variables in the cluster, three are related to explaining in general, four to higher-order cognitive processing (as opposed to factual recall), one to lower-order cognitive processing, and one to structuring of the lesson. Finally, four variables are related to the teacher's speaking style (see Table 2). While teacher presentation seems to be somewhat stable, the stability coefficients of variables further delineating teacher presentation—presentation of content—appear to be quite low, with the exception of the structuring and speaking style variables. The low stability coefficients in this cluster came predominantly from the Emmer and Peck study. The major difference in facets between this study and the other three studies (H, E, Be) was the type of subject matter (EP = mathematics, social studies, English, science; H, E, Be = social studies). Perhaps the subject matter in the Hiller et al., Ehman and Bellack studies permitted consistency of presentation and speaking style that would not have been found with Emmer and Peck's different subject matters all combined. Or perhaps the difference lies in the qualitatively different variables examined by Emmer and Peck in contrast to the structuring and speaking style variables in the other studies.

Teacher Questions

The third cluster, *teacher questions*, contains 24 variables. Five related to frequency of questions, 11 referred to particular types of questions, and eight related to clusters representing patterns of questioning (see Table 2).

The data from these seven studies indicate that teacher questioning behavior is unstable. The exceptions for overall frequency of questions are: Ehman ($r = 0.33, 0.34, 0.52$) and Bellack ($r = -0.09, 0.61, 0.74$). The exceptions for particular types of questions are Moon's conventional teachers asking what he termed lower-order questions (0.42, 0.43) and Bellack's teachers asking cognitive-memory questions (−0.01, 0.47, 0.52).

Examination of the facets of studies showing stability (E, Be) and instability (T, W, B) in overall questioning shows that stable questioning behavior resulted when the same or similar topics from a particular subject matter, social studies, were taught. Instability occurred when subject matters were combined and different topics taught (T = English, social studies; W = "academic" lessons; Borg = unknown). A similar pattern occurred when lower-order questioning was examined. Stability in lower-order questions occurred when one subject matter (M = science; B = social studies) with the same or similar topics was taught. Instability occurred when subject matters were combined and different topics taught (T = English, social studies; EP = mathematics, social studies, English, science; B = unknown).

A conjecture about differences in stability between Moon's SCIS and conventional teachers is also possible. Since Moon's SCIS teachers received training which encouraged asking higher-order questions, the training may have interfered with their normal lower-order question asking. If training were less than successful, this might account for the instability in higher-order questions.

Teacher Feedback

Another cluster of variables deals with the teacher's use of *feedback* (reinforcement) in the classroom. Of the 23 variables relating to feedback, five referred to total reinforcement, seven dealt with positive feedback, four related to neutral feedback, and seven variables were related to criticism or negative feedback (see Table 2). A consistent pattern of stability coefficients emerges from the six studies examining teacher feedback. Teachers' use of positive and neutral feedback appears to be moderately stable. Teachers' use of criticism or negative feedback appears to be unstable. This pattern seems to be stable over variations in such facets as grade level, similarity of students, and differences in subject matter similarity, at least to the limited extent such a generalization is warranted.

Motivational Skills

The cluster, *teacher motivational skills,* contains four variables (see Table 2). It should be noted that selling is a very infrequent event. Therefore, the low stability coefficient for this variable may reflect this restriction of range. The variables fit quite loosely in the cluster, come from only two studies, and thus do not deserve further comment.

The five clusters just discussed—teacher presentation, presentation of content, questions, feedback, and motivation—might be thought of as relating to quality of interactive instruction. The next four clusters—expressive teaching style, student-centered style, interpersonal behavior, and affective teaching style—reflect a personal style in teacher-student interactions.

Expressive Teaching Style

Five variables comprise the *expressive teaching style* cluster (see Appendix, Table 2). Since the Friedman variables are orthogonal and the two Emmer and Peck variables share only a small portion of variance, these variables represent different aspects of expressive style. All variables represent combinations of low inference variables, and the pattern of coefficients reflect the general magnitude of coefficients reported in the two studies. Differences and similarities in facets do not seem to account for differences in the magnitudes.

Student-Centered Teaching Style

The cluster, *student-centered teaching style,* contains six variables. Five of them reflect a student-centered orientation, and the last variable represents the opposite of a student-centered orientation (see Table 2). Student-centered teaching style, based on data from three studies, appears to be relatively unstable with the exception of one coefficient in the Ehman study (0.47). This coefficient is not unexpected since it occurred in a lesson involving an analysis of values which easily lends itself to accepting and using student ideas. The last variable representing teacher control of interaction suggests that teachers might be stable in their control of interaction and somewhat unsystematic in allowing students to control the interaction. But this interpretation hinges on one coefficient and represents speculation, at best.

Interpersonal Behavior

The cluster, *interpersonal behavior,* contains 26 variables (see Table 2). The first four are from EP, and the next seven relate to teacher provisions for overt pupil responses. Nine variables are from Trinchero's probing category. Two reflect classroom opportunities for probing, and the others reflect the teacher's response to a student response. Another three variables are from Borg and are similar to Trinchero's probes. The last three variables are also from Borg and represent teacher responses during discussion. While these variables fit loosely into this cluster, the variables from the EP and W studies seem unrelated to those from the T and B studies. This lack of overlap, along with a lack in consistency in the magnitude of coefficients, makes these findings difficult to interpret. The probing variables, however, in both the T and B studies appear to be moderately stable. Since these variables come from only two studies, no statement about the generalizability over facets can be made.

Affective Style

The last cluster in the style series—affective style—contains three variables (see Table 2). The coefficients from EP are quite low; the coefficient from C is based on only five teachers. Affective variables in these studies, then, appear to be unstable over time.

The last three clusters are administrative in nature (see Table 2).

Following Procedures

One cluster refers to *teachers following procedures*. The differences between the results of Marzano and Wallen are probably due to the differences in the nature of the variables. Marzano's teachers were given a Distar curriculum which prescribed each teacher task. The Wallen variables come from less controlled teacher-student interaction.

Classroom Management

The next cluster, *classroom management,* includes administrative variables and classroom control variables. Of the 19 variables in the cluster, two related to classroom administration, seven variables related to direct controlling responses to undesirable student behavior, and ten variables related to indirect controlling responses to undesirable student behavior.

The administrative variables were moderately stable in one study (E) but not in the other (EP). However, the data come from only two studies, and it is unclear whether this difference resulted from differences in facets or in the nature of the variables. In general, direct controlling responses of the teacher to undesirable student behavior appear to be moderately stable. Indirect controlling responses appear to be unstable with two exceptions: praising desired behavior (0.42) and ignoring (0.66) in response to irrelevant student behavior. However, the other indirect controlling behaviors were extremely infrequent. Therefore, the low coefficients for these behaviors may reflect this restriction of range.

Teacher Individualization

The last cluster, *teacher individualization,* relates to teacher provision for individual differences among students and includes seven variables, all from the Wallen study. The only variables in this cluster which appeared to be stable were instances of individualization and ability grouping which were rated as showing clear indication of teacher diagnosis of student needs. It is unclear whether this stability indicates consistency of teacher diagnosis or consistency of observer perception.

Global Ratings

Wallen (1969) was the only study to report stability of global ratings. Stability coefficients ranged from 0.92 for the variable, warm-friendly, to 0.03 for the variable, control of academic behavior. Instability in the latter rating might be expected since this variable related to the extent to which a teacher's lessons are highly structured and controlled and both subject matter and topics varied from observation to observation. The global ratings reported by Wallen are substantially more stable than the other types of measures in general and higher than those variables in clusters which consistently showed stable behavior (viz. teacher presentation, positive and neutral feedback). As noted above, we cannot determine whether this stability represents an attribute of the teachers observed or of the observers' perceptions.

In summary, global ratings appear to be the most stable of all measures examined. In addition, four clusters of variables appeared moderately stable over variations in facets: teacher presentation, positive and neutral feedback, probing, and direct teacher control (classroom management).

The stability of six clusters was unclear; that is, some variables within the cluster were stable while others were not. These clusters were: presentation of content, teacher motivational skills, expressive teaching style, teachers following procedures, classroom administration, and teacher individualization. The reason for these differences in stability, however, is unclear. For example, any of the following explanations for these inconsistencies are possible: (1) lack of standardization of measures, (2) qualitative differences between variables within the cluster, or (3) variations in one or a combination of facets between studies.

The remaining clusters appeared unstable: teacher questioning, negative feedback, student-centered teaching style, interpersonal behavior, affective style, and indirect teacher control (classroom management). However, since facets were not systematically varied within studies, the limits of generalizability over particular facets are unclear.

CONCLUSIONS

A careful examination of the stability of measures of teaching process suggests that generalizability may be extremely limited in an educational context. The lack of systematic variation in situational and observational facets and lack of standardization of measurements, however, makes our conclusions tentative, at best. With this in mind, the following conclusions are in order.

1. Of all the measures of teacher behavior examined, global ratings appear to be the most stable. It is unclear whether this consistency represents an attribute

of the teachers observed or of the observers' perceptions. Frequency counts tended to have the lowest bound stability coefficients. In some cases these low coefficients could be explained by restricted range due to the low frequency of occurrence of certain teacher behaviors (e.g., variables in the indirect teacher control cluster.)

2. Four clusters of teacher behavior variables based on other measures appeared moderately stable over variations in facets: teacher presentation, positive and neutral feedback, probing, and direct teacher control (classroom management).

3. The stability of the variables in six of the clusters was unclear; that is, some variables were stable and some were unstable within the cluster: presentation of content, teacher motivational skills, expressive teaching style, teachers following procedures, classroom administration, and teacher individualization. Any of the following explanations for this inconsistency are plausible: (a) lack of standardization of measures, (b) qualitative differences between variables within the cluster, or (c) variations in one or a combination of facets between studies.

4. Variables in six of the clusters appeared unstable: teacher questioning, negative feedback, student-centered teaching style, interpersonal behavior, affective style, and indirect teacher control (classroom management). Systematic variation of facets is required in order to explain this apparent instability.

APPENDIX

Table 1. Studies of teacher behavior.

	STUDENTS				CONTENT		TEACHER		DEPENDENT VARIABLE			
Study	*Assignment to teacher*	*Grade level*	*Similarity*	*Type of population*	*Type*	*Similarity*	*N*	*Level of experience*	*No. of observation occasions*	*Type of measure(s)*	*Behavior observed*	*Stability coefficients*
Hiller et al. (1969)	non-random	12th	same	—	Social studies (economic, social, political conditions of Yugoslavia and Thailand)	different	23	P	2	factor score	verbal fluency	0.76
											optimal information amount	0.37
											knowledge structure cues	0.29
											interest	0.20
											vagueness	0.84
Emmer and Peck (1973)	non-random	5th, 8th	same	—	math, social studies, science, English	different	28	P	5[a]	factor score	*Cognitive:*	
											problem-solving	0.27
											conceptual	<0.10
											descriptive vs. inferential	<0.10
											explanation	0.16
											association, drill	<0.10
											higher cognitive level student behavior	<0.10

descriptive interchange	0.18
Affective:	
positive teacher affect	0.11
teacher candor	0.19
teacher support	0.15
Style:	
student ideas vs. teacher ideas	0.16
student presents vs. teacher questions	0.16
expansive teacher behavior	0.22
students discussion	<0.10
convergent vs. divergent teacher behavior	0.36
convergent questions	0.14
teacher informing vs. student statements	0.28
teacher lecture	0.51
teacher presents (i.e., lecture)	0.45

Table 1. Studies of teacher behavior (*continued*).

	STUDENTS				*CONTENT*		*TEACHER*		*DEPENDENT VARIABLE*			
Study	*Assignment to teacher*	*Grade level*	*Similarity*	*Type of population*	*Type*	*Similarity*	*N*	*Level of experience*	*No. of observation occasions*	*Type of measure(s)*	*Behavior observed*	*Stability coefficients*
Emmer and Peck (1973) cont.	non-random	5th, 8th	same	—	math, social studies, science, English	different	28	P	5[a]	factor score	*Classroom Management:*	
											procedural interaction	0.13
											desist statements	0.39
											controlling	0.11
											criticizing, asking for behavior change	0.34
											Interpersonal:	
											private pupil-teacher contacts	0.29
											teacher behavior when no pupil response	0.18
											teacher behavior when incorrect pupil response	0.18
											criticizing wrong answer	0.16
											teacher seeking correct answer	0.26
											criticizing pupil work	<0.10

											asking opinion question	0.14
											asking open question—correct answer given	0.23
											asking self reference question—teacher negates answer	0.13
Campbell (1972)	non-random	junior high	similar	low achievers	science	similar	5	P	2	frequency count	I/D ratio	0.10[b]
											i/d ratio	−0.90[b]
											S/T ratio	0.80[b]
Friedman (1973)	non-random	1st, 3rd 5th, 7th	same	—	—	—	72	P (female)	4	frequency count	*Teacher Original Exits:*	
											supported	0.37
											approved	0.49
											acknowledged	0.61
											not evaluated	0.58
											neutrally rejected	0.48
											criticized	0.26
										transformed scores	*Transformed Exits:*	
											feedback	0.63
											positivity	0.61
											enthusiasm	0.53
											encouragement 1	0.70
											encouragement 2	0.73

Table 1. Studies of teacher behavior (*continued*).

	STUDENTS				CONTENT		TEACHER		DEPENDENT VARIABLE				
Study	*Assignment to teacher*	*Grade level*	*Similarity*	*Type of population*	*Type*	*Similarity*	*N*	*Level of experience*	*No. of observation occasions*	*Type of measure(s)*	*Behavior observed*	*Stability coefficients* Teachers SCIS	*Stability coefficients* Conventional teachers
Moon (1969, 1971)	non-random	primary	same	—	science	similar	32	P	5(SCIS teachers) 2(Control teachers)	frequency count)	ID ratio	0.18	0.64
											teacher talk	0.12^{c}	0.76
											Teacher Questions:		
											fact or recall	-0.12^{c}	0.42
											relationships	0.05^{c}	0.43
											observations	0.05^{c}	−0.17
											hypothesizing	0.19^{c}	0.17
											testing hypothesis	0.00^{c}	0.00
Trinchero (1974, 1975)	random	9th, 10th	similar	—	social studies, English	different	20	T	2	frequency count	*Reinforcement:*		
											Total [d]		0.64
											English teachers		0.47^{b}
											social studies teachers		0.63^{b}
											positive verbal		0.44
											English teachers		0.04^{b}

social studies teachers	0.57[b]
positive verbal / total verbal	0.53
negative verbal	0.13
negative verbal / total verbal	0.05
qualified verbal	0.48
qualified verbal / total verbal	0.42
positive nonverbal	0.74
English teachers	0.57[b]
social studies teachers	0.64[b]
positive nonverbal / total nonverbal	0.67
negative nonverbal	−0.15
negative nonverbal / total nonverbal	−0.09
Higher-order Questions:	
teacher-initiated	0.16
lower-order	0.17
lower order / teacher initiated	−0.52
higher-order	0.17
higher order / teacher initiated	0.54
Probing:	
pupil-initiated talk	0.04
opportunities to probe	0.24
total probes	0.40

Table 1. Studies of teacher behavior (*continued*).

	STUDENTS				CONTENT		TEACHER		DEPENDENT VARIABLE			
Study	*Assignment to teacher*	*Grade level*	*Similarity*	*Type of population*	*Type*	*Similarity*	*N*	*Level of experience*	*No. of observation occasions*	*Type of measure(s)*	*Behavior observed*	*Stability coefficients*
Trinchero (1974, 1975) cont.	random	9th, 10th	similar	—	social studies, English	different	20	T	2	frequency count	total probes / opportunities to probe	0.35
											individual probes	0.31
											individual probes / total probes	0.20
											individual redirects	0.54
											individual redirects / total probes	−0.09
											group redirects	0.43
											group redirects / total probes	−0.11
											total repeating, rephrasing, refocusing	−0.09
											repeating, rephrasing, refocusing / total probes	−0.29
											total clarifying, prompting	0.62
											clarifying, prompting / total probes	0.03
											total critical awareness	−0.05
											critical awareness / total probes	0.14

	STUDENTS				CONTENT		TEACHER		DEPENDENT VARIABLE					
Study	*Assignment to teacher*	*Grade level*	*Similarity*	*Type of population*	*Type*	*Similarity*	*N*	*Level of experience*	*No. of observation occasions*	*Type of measure(s)*	*Behavior observed*	*Stability coefficients*		
Ehman (1972)	—	9th	similar	—	social studies (historical/social science concepts, eliciting student hypotheses in response, analysis of value proposition or controversial issue)	same	84	U	2	frequency count		*Concept lesson*	*Hypothesis lesson*	*Value lesson*
											praises, encourages	0.41	0.47	0.42
											accepts, uses student ideas	0.20	0.08	0.47
											asks questions: overall	0.34	0.52	0.33
											cognitive-memory	−0.01	0.52	0.47
											convergent	0.12	0.13	0.01
											divergent	0.35	0.18	−0.01
											evaluative	0.32	0.21	0.23
											closed	0.26	0.07	0.26
											lectures	0.59	0.55	0.60
											gives directions	0.44	0.15	0.38
											criticizes	−0.08	0.25	−0.04
											productive silence/confusion	0.55	0.53	0.49
											unproductive silence/confusion	0.36	0.33	0.14
											I/D ratio	0.57	0.66	0.57
Bellack (1966) (Ehman reanalysis)	nonrandom	10th, 12th	same	urban and suburban, mean verbal IQ = 70th percentile	social studies (economics)	similar	15	P	4	frequency count		*Sessions I–II*	*II–III*	*III–IV*
											teacher talk/student talk	0.84	0.78	0.41
											structuring	0.72	0.72	0.76
											soliciting	0.74	0.61	−0.09
											responding	0.66	0.32	0.22
											reacting	0.37	0.54	0.29

Table 1. Studies of teacher behavior (*continued*).

	STUDENTS				*CONTENT*		*TEACHER*		*DEPENDENT VARIABLE*			
Study	*Assignment to teacher*	*Grade level*	*Similarity*	*Type of population*	*Type*	*Similarity*	*N*	*Level of experience*	*No. of observation occasions*	*Type of measure(s)*	*Behavior observed*	*Stability coefficients*
Borg (1972)	non-random	—	same	—	varied	—	38	P	2	frequency count	teacher questions	0.14
											total zeros	0.18
											average length of pause	0.27
											words in pupil response to information-level question	0.01
											higher order / fact	0.07
											redirection	0.40
											prompting	0.30
											clarification	0.55
											repeating own question	0.23
											repeating pupil answer	0.22
											answering own question	0.19
											% of teacher talk	0.38

Marzano (1973)	non-random	1st grade	same	—	language	different	27	P	5	ratings after every activity	*Following the format:*	*Group activities*	*Individual activities*
											$\hat{\rho}^2_{teachers}$	0.52	0.54
Wallen (1969)	—	—	same	—	—	—	33	—	10	global ratings	praise encouragement		0.79
											warm, friendly		0.92
											control of personal behavior		0.72
											positive regarding children		0.83
											adaptable		0.71
											confident		0.91
											committed		0.86
											appropriate communication		0.81
											control of academic behavior		0.03
											personal enthusiasm		0.79
											sensitivity		0.83
										ratings every 5 minutes	Attention:		
											procedures		0.01
											selling		−0.02
											compulsion		0.42
											questioning		0.19
											lecturing		0.19
											no attempt		0.67

Table 1. Studies of teacher behavior (*continued*).

	STUDENTS				CONTENT		TEACHER		DEPENDENT VARIABLE			
Study	*Assignment to teacher*	*Grade level*	*Similarity*	*Type of population*	*Type*	*Similarity*	*N*	*Level of experience*	*No. of observation occasions*	*Type of measure(s)*	*Behavior observed*	*Stability coefficients*
Wallen (1969) cont.	—	—	same	—	—	—	33	—	10	ratings every 5 minutes	Teacher provisions for pupil response:	
											opportunities—	
											few	0.09
											many	0.24
											encouragement	0.20
											compulsion—	
											few	0.19
											many	0.12
											precludes—	
											few	0.38
											many	0.24
Wallen (1969)	non-random	—	same	inner-city	—	—	33	P	10	ratings every 5 minutes	Individualization:	
											diagnosed	0.87
											unclear	−0.09
											not diagnosed	0.19
											no provision	0.14
											Grouping:	
											ability	0.62
											unclear	0.21
											not diagnosed	−0.04
											Feedback:	
										ratings every 5 minutes	from children	−0.22
											from procedures	0.00

	from teachers	0.43
	no provision	0.34
ratings every 5 minutes	*Classroom Management:* Response to irrelevant behavior:	
	hostility, reprimand	0.77
	direct control	0.61
	praise desired behavior	0.42
	humor, distraction	—0.13
	changing-activity	—0.07
	empathy	0.09
	ignores	0.66
ratings every 5 minutes	*Classroom Management:* Response to disruptive behavior:	
	hostility, reprimand	0.14
	direct control	0.30
	praise of desired behavior	0.00
	humor, distraction	—0.01
	changing activity	0.00
	empathy	0.10
	ignores	0.25

[a] One class observed only three times.
[b] Spearman rank-order correlations. All others are Pearson product-moment correlations.
[c] Based on Fisher's z-transformations.
[d] Refers to sum of all reinforcement categories.

Table 2. Clusters of teacher behavior variables.

Teacher presentation		*Presentation of content*		*Teacher questions*		*Teacher feedback*	
Variables (study[e])	*Stability coefficients*	*Variables (study[e])*	*Stability coefficients*	*Variables (study[e])*	*Stability coefficients*	*Variables (study[e])*	*Stability coefficients*
teacher lecture (EP)	0.51	explanation (EP)	0.16	teacher-initiated questions (T)	0.16	feedback (W)	0.43
teacher presents (EP)	0.45	descriptive interchange (EP)	0.18	questioning (W)	0.19	feedback (F)	0.63
teacher informing vs. student statements (EP)	0.28	optimum information amount (H)	0.37	teacher questions (B)	0.14	total reinforcement (T)	0.64
lectures (E)	0.55 to 0.60	higher cognitive level of student behavior (EP)	<0.10	overall questions (E)	0.33 to 0.52	provision for feedback (W)	0.34
lecturing (W)	0.19	conceptual (EP)	<0.10	soliciting (Be)	−0.19 to 0.74	reacting (Be)	0.29 to 0.54
teacher talk (M)	0.12 (SCIS) 0.76 (conventional)	problem-solving	0.27	factual (M)	−0.12 (SCIS) 0.42 (conventional)	support (F)	0.37
teacher talk (B)	0.38	knowledge structure cues (H)	0.29	lower-order (T)	0.17	approval (F)	0.49
S/T ratio (C)	0.80	association/drill (EP)	<0.10	cognitive-memory (E)	−0.01 to 0.52	acknowledged (F)	0.61
S/T ratio (Be)	0.41 to 0.84	structuring (Be)	0.72 to 0.76	length of pupil response to information level questions (B)	0.01	positivity (F)	0.61
I/D ratio (M)	0.18 (SCIS) 0.64 (conventional)	verbal fluency (H)	0.76	relations (M)	0.05 (SCIS) 0.43 (conventional)	positive verbal reinforcement (T)	0.44
I/D ratio (C)	0.10	vagueness (H)	0.84	descriptive vs. inferential (EP)	<0.10	English teachers	0.04
I/D ratio (E)	0.57 to 0.66	productive silence or confusion (E)	0.49 to 0.55	observations (M)	0.05 (SCIS) −0.17 (conventional)	social studies teachers	0.57
		unproductive silence or confusion (E)	0.14 to 0.36	hypotheses (M)	0.19 (SCIS) 0.17 (conventional)	positive nonverbal reinforcement (T)	0.74
				testing hypothesis (M)	0.00 (SCIS) 0.00 (conventional)	praises, encourages (E)	0.41 to 0.47
						not evaluative (F)	0.58
						neutrally reject (F)	0.48
						qualified verbal reinforcement (T)	0.48
						responding (Be)	0.22 to 0.66
						criticism (F)	0.28
						critical of pupil work (EP)	<0.10
						critical of wrong answers (EP)	0.16

[e] Studies are identified as follows:

H = Hiller, et al. (1969)
EP = Emmer and Peck (1973)
C = Campbell (1972)
F = Friedman (1973)
M = Moon (1969, 1971)
T = Trinchero (1974)
E = Ehman (1972)
Be = Bellack (1966)
B = Borg (1972)
Mz = Marzano (1973)
W = Wallen (1969)

higher-order (T)	0.17	self-reference question with negative answer (EP)	0.13
higher-order/fact (B)	0.07	negative verbal reinforcement (T)	0.13
convergent (EP)	0.14	negative nonverbal reinforcement (T)	−0.15
convergent (E)	0.01 to 0.13	criticizes (E)	−0.04 to 0.25
divergent (E)	0.01 to 0.35		
opinion (EP)	0.14		
evaluative (E)	0.21 to 0.32		
open (EP)	0.23		
closed (E)	0.07 to 0.26		
average length of pause (B)	0.27		

Motivational skills		*Expressive teaching style*		*Student-centered teaching style*		*Interpersonal behavior*	
Variables (study[e])	*Stability coefficients*	*Variables (study[e])*	*Stability coefficients*	*Variables (study[e])*	*Stability coefficients*	*Variables (study[e])*	*Stability coefficients*
interest (H)	0.20	expansive teaching behavior (EP)	0.22	feedback from students (W)	−0.22	student-teacher contacts (EP)	0.29
selling (W)	−0.20	enthusiasm (F)	0.53	student-discussion (EP)	<0.10	teacher seeks correct answer (EP)	0.26
compulsion (W)	0.42	encouragement I (F)	0.70	student vs. teacher ideas (EP)	−0.16	teacher behavior and no student response (EP)	0.18
no attempt (W)	0.67	encouragement II (F)	0.73	student-presents vs. teacher questions (EP)	0.16	teacher behavior and incorrect student response (EP)	0.18
		teacher support (EP)	0.15	accepts, uses student ideas (E)	0.08, 0.20, 0.47	opportunity for few (W)	0.09
				convergent vs. divergent teacher behavior (EP)	0.36	opportunity for many (W)	0.24
						encouragement (W)	0.20
						compulsion for few (W)	0.19
						compulsion for many (W)	0.12
						precludes for few (W)	0.38
						precludes for many (W)	0.24
						pupil-initiated talk (T)	0.04

Table 2. Clusters of teacher behavior variables (*continued*).

Motivational skills		*Expressive teaching style*		*Student-centered teaching style*		*Interpersonal behavior*	
Variables (study[e])	*Stability coefficients*	*Variables (study[e])*	*Stability coefficients*	*Variables (study[e])*	*Stability coefficients*	*Variables (study[e])*	*Stability coefficients*
						opportunities to probe (T)	0.24
						total probes (T)	0.40
						individual probes (T)	0.31
						individual redirect (T)	0.54
						group redirect (T)	0.43
						total redirections (T)	−0.09
						total clarifying probes (T)	0.62
						total critical awareness (T)	−0.05
						redirection (B)	0.40
						prompting (B)	0.30
						clarification (B)	0.55
						repeating own question (B)	0.23
						repeating pupil answer (B)	0.22
						answering own question (B)	0.19

Affective style		Following procedures		Classroom management		Individualization		Global ratings	
Variables (study[e])	Stability coeffi-cients	Variables (study[e])	Stability coeffi-cients	Variables (study[e])	Stability coeffi-cients	Variables (study[e])	Stability coeffi-cients	Variables (study[e])	Stability coeffi-cients
teacher affect (EP)	0.11	following format (Mz)		procedural (EP)	0.13	individualization (W):		praise, encouragement (W)	0.79
candor (EP)	0.19	individual activities	0.52	gives directions (E)	0.15, 0.38, 0.44	diagnosed	0.87	warm, friendly (W)	0.92
i/d ratio (C)	−0.90	group activities	0.54	controlling (EP	0.11	unclear	−0.09	control of personal behavior (W)	0.72
		attention-getting procedures (W)	0.01	desist statements (EP)	0.39	not diagnosed	0.19	positive regarding children (W)	0.83
		feedback procedures (W)	0.00	criticizing, asking for behavior change (EP)	0.34	ability grouping (W):		adaptable (W)	0.71
				direct control (W):		diagnosed	0.62	confident (W)	0.91
				irrelevant behavior	0.61	unclear	0.21	committed (W)	0.86
				disruptive behavior	0.30	not diagnosed	−0.04	appropriate communication (W)	0.81
				hostility, reprimand (W):		no provision for individualization (W)	0.14	control of academic behavior (W)	0.03
				irrelevant behavior	0.77			personal enthusiasm (W)	0.79
				disruptive behavior	0.17			sensitivity (W)	0.83
				praising desired behavior (W):					
				irrelevant behavior	0.42				
				disruptive behavior	0.00				
				humor distraction (W):					
				irrelevant behavior	−0.13				
				disruptive behavior	−0.01				
				empathy (W):					
				irrelevant behavior	0.09				
				disruptive behavior	0.10				
				changing activity (W):					
				irrelevant behavior	−0.07				
				disruptive behavior	0.00				
				ignoring (W):					
				irrelevant behavior	0.66				
				disruptive behavior	0.25				

References

Armstrong, J. R., M. V. DeVault, and E. Larson. "Consistency of Teacher Communication: A Sampling Problem in Interaction Analysis. *Psychology in the Schools* 4, no. 1 (1967): 74–76.

Belgard, M., B. Rosenshine, and N. L. Gage. "The Teacher's Effectiveness in Explaining: Evidence on Its Generality and Correlation with Pupils' Ratings and Attention Scores." In N. L. Gage, ed., *Explorations of the Teacher's Effectiveness in Explaining* (Tech. Rep. 4). Stanford, Calif.: Stanford Center for Research and Development in Teaching, Stanford University, 1968.

Bellack, A. A., M. Kliebard, R. T. Hyman, and F. L. Smith. *The Language of the Classroom.* New York: Teachers College Press, 1966.

Borg, W. R. "The Minicourse as a Vehicle for Changing Teacher Behavior: A Three-Year Follow-Up. *Journal of Educational Psychology* **63**, no. 6 (1972): 572–579.

Borich, G. D., and D. Malitz. "Convergent and Discriminant Validation of Three Classroom Observation Systems." *Journal of Educational Psychology* **67**, no. 3 (1975): 426–430.

Brophy, J. E., and C. M. Evertson. *Process-Product Correlations in the Texas Teacher Effectiveness Study: Final Report* (Report No. 74–4). Austin, Texas: Research and Development Center for Teacher Education, The University of Texas, 1974a.

Brophy, J. E., and C. M. Evertson. *The Texas Teacher Effectiveness Project: Presentation of Non-Linear Relations and Summary Discussion* (Report No. 74–6). Austin, Texas: Research and Development Center for Teacher Education, The University of Texas, 1974b.

Campbell, J. R. "A Longitudinal Study in the Stability of Teachers' Verbal Behavior." *Science Education* **56**, no. 1 (1972): 89–96.

Cronbach, L. J. *Essentials of Psychological Testing.* 3rd ed. New York: Harper & Row, 1970.

Ehman, L. H. "Stability of Social Studies Classroom Verbal Interaction Patterns across Repeated Micro-Teaching Performances." Paper presented at the National Council for the Social Studies, Boston, Mass., 1972.

Emmer, E. T., and R. F. Peck. "Dimensions of Classroom Behavior." *Journal of Educational Psychology* **64**, no. 2 (1973): 223–240.

Friedman, P. "Relationship of Teacher Reinforcement to Spontaneous Student Verbalization within the Classroom." *Journal of Educational Psychology* **65**, no. 1 (1973): 59–64.

Hiller, J. H., G. A. Fisher, and W. Kaess. "A Computer Investigation of Verbal Characteristics of Effective Classroom Lecturing." *American Educational Research Journal* **6**, no. 4 (1969): 661–675.

Marzano, W. A. "Determining the Reliability of the Distar Instructional System Observation Instrument." Thesis, University of Illinois, 1973.

Moon, T. C. "A Study of Verbal Behavior Patterns in Primary Grade Classrooms during Science Activities." Ph.D. dissertation, Michigan State University, 1969.

Moon, T. C. "A Study of Verbal Behavior Patterns in Primary Grade Classrooms during Science Activities. *Journal of Research in Science Teaching* **8**, no. 2 (1971): 171–177.

Rosenshine, B., and N. Furst. "The Use of Direct Observation to Study Teaching." In R. Travers, ed., *Second Handbook of Research on Teaching*. Chicago: Rand McNally, 1973.

Sandoval, J. *Beginning Teacher Evaluation Study Completion Report, Task K: Sub-Study of Consistency of Teacher Behavior*. Princeton, N. J.: Educational Testing Service, 1974.

Trinchero, R. L. "The Longitudinal Measurement of Teacher Effectiveness." *California Journal of Educational Research* 25, no. 3 (1974): 121–127.

Trinchero, R. L. *Three Technical Skills of Teaching: Their Stability and Effect on Pupil Attitudes and Achievement*. Ph.D. dissertation, Stanford University, 1975.

Wallen, N. E. *Sausalito Teacher Education Project: Annual Report*. San Francisco State College, San Francisco, California, 1969.

Index

Subject Index